The Second Happiest Day

The
Second Happiest Day

John Phillips

HARPER & BROTHERS, PUBLISHERS

New York

To the memory of C. S. P.

B O O K I

Serenade at the Water Club

Chapter One

As friends go, George Marsh and I were the best and loyalest. Loyalty meant the world to George Marsh. That is one explanation, among many, of why his story and mine were so inextricably bound. Indeed, as it progresses, his story becomes more properly mine than his own.

People think how tragic we are friends no longer. And yet I know that we couldn't have ended any other way. We never did have very much in common, although, when stated, that strikes me as the most gigantic paradox. For we shared everything, or at least George shared everything, and I and everybody else complied. He could never face the fact that I betrayed him, and perhaps he yet believes that all will be patched up somehow, that God will get back in His Heaven, and I will rejoin the Marsh galère. This is to state that I could not, even did I wish to.

Nor do I consider anything I did a triumph, or a cruel deed. I suppose that I think unduly often about George Marsh, but never with a feeling of smugness, or of guilt. I think first of George Marsh as a name, then of George Marsh as a man about twenty-eight years old. Next I think of Loyalty, not the quality of loyalty, but the seven-letter word which is still stenciled across my mind like a title on a theater marquee, because George used it so much. And then inevitably, not without some trace of boyish marvel still, I begin to think about his life.

Upon his father's death, when he was in the Fourth Class at Emmanuel Academy, George Marsh inherited from his grandfather's estate. The original George Warwick Marsh, after whom son and grandson were named, had held several directorships, the most significant of which was that of Consolidated Imperial Carton and Can. Though there had been inroads made by the Treasurer of the United States and by George Warwick Marsh, Jr., who had been responsible for a series of unmonitored investments over the years the estate had been in his name, the trustees had competently preserved the remainder, so that it yielded a total of forty-eight or fifty thousand dollars a year after taxes. This, as the trust lawyers told George Marsh, was not all the money in the world. But, they emphasized, it was money. And at the time he was told this George Marsh was not yet sixteen years old.

Before I met him, George Marsh had been tutored by men and women of European nationalities and he had spent three years in the early thirties attending Le Rosey, a school in Switzerland. While I was his classmate at Emmanuel Academy in East Northrup, Massachusetts, he was twice elected captain of football. At Emmanuel he had had the best-known nickname, Gopher Marsh, and he was called it by boys and masters alike. Once, in an offhand way, he had been called it by Bishop Wash, the President of the Trustees, when Bishop Wash had publicly awarded him a certificate naming him a Trustees' Scholar, on Trustees' Sunday in the Trustees' parlor on the ground floor of Phelps House.

George Marsh was president of the Mission Society, Custodian of the Flag, treasurer of the Ciceronian Debaters, vice-president of the Sophoclean League, a member of the Glee Club, of the Skeet Shooters, and chairman of the Ithacan Athletic Society. His was the sort of record that pleased the Dean of Admissions; Bishop Wash and the Trustees, were equally pleased. And so was Dr. Kew, Emmanuel's new Headmaster who had replaced old Dr. Trimble several years previous, following the latter's conversion to Buchmanism.

On Awards Day, June 5, 1941, not only a Diploma in Merit, but three coveted prizes, including the Geoffrey Murdock Medal for the boy who most successfully combines conscience, diligence, and integrity in his contribution to the Academy, were won by George Warwick Marsh III.

George Marsh did well enough at Harvard too, though from the very start his achievements were less golden there. During the entire time he was at college, he roomed with two of his oldest friends from Emmanuel, Walter Baxter Eaton and myself, Augustus Taylor.

When war came he responded instinctively—not without a feel-

4

ing of release. He ended the war as an artillery officer, with a shrapnel wound on his right thigh, a Silver Star, a Croix de Guerre replete with palm, an E.T.O. ribbon with four battle stars. He never wore a one of these except, at the insistence of his fiancée, Lila Norris, when he posed for a Bachrach photograph.

Probably the most perceptive commentary on the world into which George Marsh was born, and on its tinseled security, was the glimpse his great-uncle, Marcus Marsh, caught in the home of George's parents the night George was brought into the world and of which he told me once:

Family sentiment ran stronger in Marcus Marsh than it ran in his elder brother, George Warwick Marsh, Sr., who, in 1923, still had six years to live. Marcus Marsh had felt himself called upon to represent the older generation at the unique ceremony his nephew, George Junior, and George Junior's recent wife, Barbara, had arranged for the birth of their first and only child. When the elder Marsh learned that his daughter-in-law's accouchement was to be an occasion of hilarity and debauch, he had been shocked. He interpreted it as his son's ultimate rejection of the basic tenets of taste and dignity.

So, Marcus Marsh had gone in his brother's place. The younger Marshes had welcomed him warmly, more warmly, he could not help feeling, than they would have welcomed his brother George. No sooner had he entered the apartment than young George, his nephew, had set him at his ease. He had done this with a lively speech for the benefit of the guests assembled, to the effect that Uncle Mark, as the young couple respectfully called him, was far and away the most red-blooded member of the family. What was more, his nephew had concluded, as his new niece winked playfully from the chaise longue, Uncle Mark was the least frightened of the facts of life. And that was a lucky thing; tonight the facts of life were staring them in the face.

They were an engaging couple, the young George Marshes; both were fair-haired and wreathed in smiles and surrounded by friends. At least a dozen of these friends were present tonight at the duplex apartment on Sixty-fourth Street. They were an attractive crowd, though giddy, and they called one another by unconventional names. His nephew and his nephew's wife, for example, were known as Andy and as Baby Marsh, names which would not have been used in the bosom of the family but which seemed happily appropriate to the vibrant atmosphere of the Marsh apartment that November evening in 1923.

Only that morning Andy—once started on his third sloe gin fizz, Marcus Marsh thought it only natural to think of his niece and nephew by their nicknames—had informed each guest on the telephone that this was to be the night. Andy Marsh had said that Baby was fine and had her heart set on making her contribution to the evening exactly according to schedule. As added assurance Dr. Gumdrop McClough, who as Gummering McClough had been Andy's roommate at Harvard and Baby's beau before Andy stole her, had examined her only an hour before. Gumdrop had made a clandestine trip up from Roosevelt Hospital, at some personal risk since he was in residence at the hospital and the freshest addition to the obstetrical staff. He had given his solemn word that as nearly as could be predicted the infant would be born sometime between nine o'clock and midnight.

The party had got under way more rapidly, if that were possible, than Baby and Andy had planned. The three maids, one of them a loan from the Marsh house in Great Neck, and Pitney, Marcus Marsh's butler, showed early signs of disgruntlement. To make matters worse, the canapés and the Stilton cheese, on which the hostess had relied as a base for the gin and applejack, had given out. By eight Nosey Gluyas, the architect of the crowd, had vomited in the hall coat closet which he had mistaken for the lavatory.

Meanwhile Gumdrop McClough had accompanied Baby on the piano while she sang "Drink to Me Only with Thine Eyes" from the chaise longue, haltingly and with a forced smile. In the dining room, they had scarcely finished the soup when the pains were coming too quickly for her to remain at table—even under the hypodermic that Dr. McClough had administered in the bedroom. Baby had been sitting in the wheelchair Andy had thought to rent for the occasion, and when the nurse started to wheel her back to the bedroom, Gumdrop McClough had risen from his chair and toasted her, breaking his champagne glass, then hurried after her amid a burst of applause. The last the guests saw of Baby Marsh that evening was the top of her bobbed blond head as it lolled uneasily against the back of the wheelchair.

6

If things had gone exactly according to plan, George Marsh would have been born within the next two hours. If things had gone according to plan and if Dr. McClough had permitted, George Marsh would have been held groggily in his mother's arms while he was toasted in his birth chamber by the assembled gathering and while a particularly good friend, Whitey Emmons, who could work wonders with a camera, recorded the scene by time exposure. But, as Dr. McClough had warned the Marshes from the first, one shouldn't predict these things.

Two of the guests were Princeton graduates, and as the champagne supply dwindled, more abruptly than Andy Marsh had dreamed it would, they and their wives had fallen to arguing with the Harvard faction over the then sensitive question of sportsmanship on the gridiron. In the living room afterward a wholly conjectural discussion of the private life of President and Mrs. Harding had given way to a more thoroughly researched analysis of the Eighteenth Amendment. In turn this had led to a comparison of speakeasy cards pulled from eight ready wallets. By midnight, the power of suggestion being what it was at this hour, stronger certainly than the power of family sentiment, nearly everyone had left to visit the establishment in Greenwich Village that Bette Gluyas had been taken to by Nosey Gluyas the night he proposed.

When George Marsh achieved his delayed entrance into the world, at twenty minutes past two in the morning, his father had retired to the upstairs guest room. Baby's maid of honor, Midge Ferris, who after words with her husband had decided to remain the night, was sleeping in a wrinkled dress on the davenport. Marcus Marsh was himself dozing on the chaise longue, but he had awakened with a smile with Gumdrop McClough's shouted announcement of the infant's arrival. He followed the doctor to the bedroom and there had the honor, an honor he was to boast of frequently, of being the first male Marsh to view the newcomer before noon of the day he was born. Marcus Marsh phrased it thus because he intended it as a jocular reproof of the baby's father who had not awakened till noon. Though Marcus Marsh was to recount incalculably often the story of young George's birth, and in such a way as to convince George that it had been the greatest anticlimax since the false armistice, he had truthfully been shown no more than a glimpse of the world into which his great-nephew

7

had been born. But it had been a good glimpse of the life that Baby and Andy Marsh led in the eight years that they were married; and Marcus Marsh, who admired Dickens, remembered it all his years quite as sentimentally as the birth of Oliver Twist.

"People aren't born like that every day. I guess I was one of the last," George Marsh said once. He was one of the last, in this and many another way. But it was not apparent to us then, when he had said it, in November of 1946 shortly after he had moved into the apartment on East Seventy-first Street.

The apartment faced on a courtyard on the side of the building that was farthest from the Third Avenue El, thus keeping the noise at a minimum. It had six rooms—a living room, and a study, two bedrooms, a dining room and kitchen, and after his fashion Manuelo cleaned all of them. He also cooked, shined our shoes, and attended to our laundry and dry cleaning. George had engaged Manuelo, the Filipino valet his father had had in the bachelor days that followed his divorce. There was something ceremonial about Manuelo. He was not the young man he had been when he took care of Mr. Marsh, Jr., but he was proud, he would say, to be young enough to be taking care of Mr. Marsh number three. He took care of Mr. Marsh number three in every way possible, ordering theater tickets, arranging train and airplane reservations, tossing the medicine ball with him in the mornings, and polishing the silverware that George Marsh had inherited from his father. The silverware and the portrait that hung in the dining room were more sacrosanct than anything else that George Marsh kept at East Seventy-first Street.

It was an oil portrait, which the artist had copied in bright, sure colors from a photograph of Andy Marsh as he had posed in skeet-shooting attire in the back meadow at Marshmain, his father's home in Great Neck, Long Island. The figure in the portrait wore deep gray plus-fours, a tannish tweed jacket, belted in back, and a visor cap to match. His blue shirt was unbuttoned about the neck. One arm hung at his side and the other cradled a splendid Greener shotgun which was open at the breech. The face looked directly out onto the room with green-blue eyes, a short, quite stubby nose, and a thin half smile. The hair that protruded in a shock from beneath the brim of the cap and along the temples was a darkish blond. Anyone who had known him never failed to say that that was certainly Andy Marsh, the image of Andy Marsh.

George Marsh, the same people said, was his father's son, but he was bigger, heavier, and his hair was darker. Young George had really brown hair. But they said he dressed as well as his father had and he moved the same way. Especially with his hands, when he moved them to his face when he was unsure of something. The likeness seemed eerie to some observers. Though Andy Marsh had been dead eight years, they hadn't forgotten him.

I grew accustomed to the apartment when I had lived in it a year, after I had accepted the idea of living with the shade of Andy Marsh. I went there to live when I began Columbia Law School. Eventually Harry Tilton moved in too. We paid George a shamefully low rent in view of all the luxuries. He hadn't minded, ever. It had been a comfortable arrangement, mainly because it was on the cuff. George Marsh had wanted it that way, and he could afford it. He wanted people about him, people to talk to. And we knew that it was only a temporary setup. Tilton and I had been ready to move out when George asked us. We knew, everybody knew, that he would marry Lila Norris when the time came and that would be the end of the Great Free Load. He wanted to get married and that was all he had ever wanted, George used to say.

The engagement was announced in April, 1948. It was a very long engagement, which does something to explain the fact that George Marsh, when last I heard, was a bachelor. There were many many causes and theories conjectured. I considered I was the greatest single cause, though of course he would not admit that that was so.

At any rate, I had to get out of that apartment.

And George Marsh never understood why. He had asked me, in a voice of bewilderment, "What I want to know is—Sport-o, where do we go from here on in?"

Chapter Two

His best qualities are a stupendous sense of noblesse oblige, and an inexorable loyalty toward friends. He considered Harry Tilton one of his closest friends. So when Harry Tilton eventually married Doris Slater, it was not surprising that George Marsh was included among the ushers. I had moved from Seventy-first Street months before; so I missed seeing George receive the invitation but I re-created the scene in my mind as it must have been—George pacing the living room, halting by the fireplace and turning to pace back again across the hallway, the thick fingers rubbing nervously against his cheek, the quizzical half smile, and finally the uplifted eyebrows and the grayish eyes shining. "Look, you don't have to ask me. I don't want you to feel any obligation." Obligation, insofar as George Marsh was concerned, was not to be felt by anyone other than himself.

In the scene I re-created Harry would have been polishing his shoes in the bathroom adjoining, or adjusting his bow tie in the bathroom mirror, or slicking his dark hair into the proper waves that would bulge boyishly over his forehead and fall in immaculate shiny licks just in back of his ears. Whatever Harry was doing at this idle moment was apt to be some form of self-adornment. During his freshman year at Yale Harry had overheard a Long Island matron's chance remark that he was "the most striking-looking boy" she had seen about New York in ages.

"Leave us not be an imbecile," Harry would have said, going on to emphasize his point wholeheartedly so that George believed him. "I said I wanted you in my wedding. It's not every day a man takes the plunge, and I want you right there beside me when I do. I would have wanted you for best man, but I might have hurt somebody else's feelings. I don't like to hurt feelings so don't you

10

hurt mine. It wouldn't be the same without you. It wouldn't be genial."

It couldn't have been more than a week afterward that Doris Slater received her first wedding present, a pair of Georgian candlesticks with the identical inscription on the base of each, "To two of the best friends and the finest people, with wishes for all luck and happiness—G.W.M. III."

Harry Tilton and I were friendly, in the way that two people can be friendly when they have never got along, but there had never been the question of my being an usher at Harry Tilton's wedding. For a time I had thought seriously of not going to the wedding at all.

Chee Wee Gibbons took it upon herself to persuade me otherwise. She pressured me into appearing, by way of compromise, at the reception which followed the ceremony. My absence there would be conspicuous and bound to cause comment. The only solution, she concluded, was for me to take her to the reception.

Though Chee Wee had been known to appear at parties by herself, she preferred on the whole to come escorted. During the infrequent intervals when she was not romantically involved, she was discriminating in her choice of an escort. She evaluated him either according to his personal connections or his physical appearance, and was sometimes able to secure in the one man a combination of both these attributes. When she was not that lucky, she compensated for the dearth of one with the abundance of the other. It was clear that in choosing me to escort her to Harry Tilton's wedding reception, Chee Wee was deviating from her pattern. I was a mere apprentice in a law office, just one of Chee Wee's "old, old friends."

"You could be so attractive, Gussy, if you would stand up straight. And if you wouldn't sound so baleful when you talk to people. You could be a good piano player, too, if you only put your mind to it."

Chee Wee had often spoken like this, but never as forcefully as on the morning of Harry Tilton's wedding day when she called me on the office telephone. She wanted me to lunch with her at Giovanni's, in order to brief me for the afternoon. When I told her that I was not entitled to a lunch hour long enough for a conversation with her, let alone long enough to travel all the way up to

11

Fifty-fifth Street, she was good-natured about it. Chee Wee had a self-conscious and undisciplined laugh. It started on a falsetto note and descended in range to a tremolo and there it would end abruptly with a sort of wheeze and a sharp intake of breath. This laugh came to me distinctly and in all its phases through the ear-piece.

"Gussy, why do I laugh at you? Are you a funny man?"

"No," I said. "Just wise to you, dear heart." But she won out in the end. I agreed to pick her up at four o'clock.

I hung up hastily so as to avoid prolonged conversation. I knew I was disturbing Macy, my dour, birdlike companion in that corner of the office allotted to recent law-school graduates. Macy was the most intense and dedicated young member of the staff at Swain, Seidel, and Lawler; he was overcome with queasiness each time the telephone rang. Mrs. O'Mara, who had handled the firm's incoming and outgoing calls for seventeen years, had a knack of joggling the switch on a connection she judged had been busy long enough.

Chee Wee had spoken to me for five minutes, but I had not heard that reproachful joggle of the switch, and so I felt, as everyone in the office had felt at one time or another, that Mrs. O'Mara had made herself a third party to our conversation. I wanted nothing—and particularly nothing Chee Wee Gibbons had to say—filtered through Mrs. O'Mara's earphones for dissemination among the clerical staff.

There was, for that matter, no part of the conversation that I wanted Macy to hear. Of late Macy had been exhibiting a marked curiosity about my private life, and I scarcely knew him from Adam.

"I am sorry," I told him when I had hung up. "I didn't mean to talk that long, Mace."

Macy gazed at me over an open volume. "Oh, no bother," he said. He was chewing on an unlit pipe. "Well. Nothing like someone to talk to, I always say. Huh?"

"Right, Mace. It was just an old friend."

"I'd like it better if you called me Hal."

"Hal," I said, "will you hold the fort? I have to go to a wedding this afternoon."

"Yuh?"

"It's all right. I'll clear it with Seidel. He knows all about this wedding."

"I'll hold the fort. Sure."

"Some Friday if you're going home for the weekend, why don't you knock off early? I'll look out for things, Hal."

"I don't go home too much," Macy said thoughtfully. "You go ahead, Taylor. You have a good time, you hear?"

Chee Wee and I drove to the Water Club, where the Tiltons' wedding reception was, in a convertible Buick. It was a lime color, and it had white-walled tires and a radio with such impressively modulated tones that the most sickening commercial sounded imperative and consequential. Chee Wee wanted the top down and she wanted me to drive. She was firm about these details and I wondered why until presently I realized that they had been prearranged as part of the setting Chee Wee intended for that afternoon.

We paused for a traffic light on the corner of Fifty-seventh and Second Avenue and Chee Wee turned to me. "Put your coat collar down, Gussy. And please, oh please stand up straight—and don't look baleful. Are you depressed, darling?"

"I didn't want to go," I said. "Don't forget you're dragging me there."

"Oh, Gussy. You're going to be foul and critical. I can see it now."

"Sweets, you don't have to worry about me. I can handle myself. And I promise to do it in such a way as to reflect no discredit on you."

"You're sweet, Gussy, and you could be so attractive. You've got splendid white teeth and a good chin and nice eyes and nice black hair. You could be so divine, but you can be so difficult." She was smiling now, and she tossed her head backward in a theatrical gesture. A streak of peroxide ran back from her temple and through her hair, which was jet black in the sun and glossy. "I can see how hard it must have been for Lila," she said. "When are you going to talk about Lila?"

"Not today," I said. "Some other day."

"Darling, at least try to smile."

It was, of course, important to Chee Wee that I stand up straight

13

that afternoon and that I drive her to the Water Club in a car that was a lime color and that the top be down. Appearances were supremely important. The effect she sought depended to as great an extent upon my affability and decorum as upon the costume she had chosen. She wore a dress of light gray foulard with a yellow pattern that would have been more appropriate to a necktie. It was a dress suited to Chee Wee's figure; it distended nicely about the pleasant bosom and concealed the unremarkable hips and legs with an ample swirl of skirt. The dress did justice to the dark lashes, the green eyes and the skin, which in the second week of June, was already a healthy tan. It was as genuine a manifestation of Chee Wee as the heady perfume she wore or the festoons of bracelets that jingled like miniature cowbells with each motion of her wrist.

"What are you staring at?" Chee Wee wanted to know.

"You. You're dressed up."

"Certainly. We're going to the Water Club. . . . And wouldn't I love to know how I'm going to pay for this outfit?"

"Wear it once or twice and take it back. Tell them you don't like it. What's returned merchandise to Bonwit Teller? Even slightly soiled."

"That's it. Be horrid," she said. "You know the kind of girl that would do that."

"I'm kidding you," I said and reached across to pat her knee. "You're a nice kind of girl. You pay promptly for your clothes and you work for a living."

"And you work for a living and I love you madly. Dear old Gussy."

We turned down Fifty-seventh and rode the block in silence. The light switched against us unexpectedly at First Avenue, causing me to press too hard upon the unfamiliar brake. We came sharply to a stop. Chee Wee was thrown slightly forward and the engine stalled. I had trouble finding the starter, which turned out to be on the accelerator, and trouble shifting the gears which weren't there at all because of Dynaflow.

"Drive much?" Chee Wee asked.

"Why don't you drive? This isn't my kind of car."

"No, I'm the passenger. I want to be driven for once."

"Whose car is it?"

14

"It belongs to Telemachus," she said. "He's in Europe for the summer. He's let me have the car, and the cottage in Montauk."

"Telemachus thinks highly of you."

"Only in a professional way." She tilted her head back and rushed through her unusual laugh. "Telemachus isn't too interested in girls."

Telemachus, the photographer, had been Chee Wee's mentor for almost four years. It was he who had encouraged her to quit *Blythe* Magazine and to enter the realm of fashion photography on her own. Chee Wee had not done badly with her little studio, though she was swimming in debt. Scuffing about the car floor with your foot, you touched begrimed, unopened envelopes from the credit managers of Bonwit's or Bendel's.

"He sailed in May," Chee Wee said. "I've had the car simonized and lacquered. Have you noticed the Bermuda bell?"

We were moving again, rolling south on First Avenue, hearing the boat whistles from the river over the radio music. A bit of soot lodged briefly in the corner of my eye.

"I can use the car as a prop," Chee Wee said, "for some color stuff I'm planning."

"Sensational," I said.

I knew what she meant. Long and sleek and like an enormous lime lozenge, this car was the ideal vehicle around which to display smiling, paper-thin girls with plucked eyebrows and high cheekbones in gaily colored summer costumes waving milky arms from the red leather upholstery. It was an integral part, this car, of Chee Wee's vision, a part of the elegant, expensive myth to which she was dedicated. It was symbolic of her privately cherished ideal. She loved it as she loved all things that identify her with the image of that munificent and graciously endowed woman who is the by-product of her husband's position, the mannequin of his wealth. "Wallis Warfield Simpson," Chee Wee had said. "Now there's a woman who went about things the right way." Chee Wee's was the oddly tenable proposition that if all that glitters is not gold there is a fair chance of its being uranium. She was deeply proud of her former association with *Blythe* and of the fact that she was a pet of Ava Norris, who was *Blythe's* editor-in-chief and also the mother of her great and dear friend, Lila.

I reached for the radio switch.

"Leave it," Chee Wee said. "It's WQXR. Chamber music, pretty violin music, Gussy."

"I'm listening to the boat whistles," I told her. "And they're prettier."

"We'll be right in the river with them in a minute, if you don't watch where you're going."

"Let's skip the Water Club. What do you say we go to Jones Beach and take a swim?"

"You're being difficult, Gussy. I should think you'd want to go. Everyone will be there."

"Not me. I'm a recluse."

"Bat shingles to you, Gus Taylor. You can sit in a corner and brood. . . . You are so silly. How long have you been out of circulation?"

I thought for a second. "Since February ninth. Exactly forty-eight hours after George had the ushers' dinner," I said.

"You don't want to see George Marsh even?"

"No, I don't frankly."

"You were a lot of things but you never were cold-blooded," she said. "I don't understand. You'll be seeing Fuzzy Eaton again, and Ava Norris— Don't make that face at me, Gussy. Oh, try and sit up straight and *look* as if I didn't bore you to death."

"But do I have to see Ava Norris?"

"I don't see how you can avoid her. Honestly, Ava is mad for you! What *is* it, Gussy? I never saw you like this."

"I'm fine," I said. "I promise to make a splendid impression on everyone."

"I'm worried, and I know Ava is worried. Did you ever think what it does to Liles to have you act like this?"

"Liles is in California. Thousands of miles away."

"She knows, she knows," Chee Wee said in a quiet voice. "I can tell it from her letters. . . . Darling, you are in love with Liles?" She glanced at me, and when she was satisfied with my expression she turned the radio up a little. "I couldn't bear it. All she ever writes about is you. Why don't you run out there and marry her before you lose her? You are in love with her. It's obvious."

"Sweets, just once, just this one time, why not mind your own business?"

"Ouch," said Chee Wee. "Or was I supposed to laugh?"

"That wasn't meant for you," I said, "especially."

"For Ava?"

"I told Ava I planned to lead my own life. That was five months ago. Maybe she's softened up since. She wasn't very graceful about it."

"What did you expect when you were so rude? Lila loves you. She wants you two to get married."

"On the contrary I was composed and polite, and I held onto my temper."

"Oh you," Chee Wee said. "You should be pounding your head against a wall. Oh you. When I think what Ava Norris could have done for you."

"You're talking like Ava," I said. I could not suppress a kind of laugh, and Chee Wee looked over hopefully.

The chamber music stopped momentarily. We listened to another snob value commercial. This was for an invisible hearing aid that cost only a few cents more per week than the inferior brands. *Is there someone, someone in your family circle, who is hard of hearing but too proud to seek help?*

"All right," Chee Wee said. "If it will make you happy."

With a fairy jingle of bracelets she turned off the switch.

"Poor Gussy," she said, making the most of her opportunity. "I know it's dreadful, but try. Try and I promise it won't be so bad. Just persevere for Lila's sake. In three months she'll be home and it will all be over. It will just seem like a bad dream, Gussy."

"I'll persevere," I said.

"I'm counting on you too, remember. There will be people who don't think much of me either."

"Then why don't we go to Jones Beach?"

"Don't, Gus Taylor, don't try to break me down. This is an important do. I'll look out for you and you'll look out for me. Is that a bargain?"

"Of course."

"It might be fun," Chee Wee said hopefully. "We can help each other out for a change instead of baiting each other. We're in the same boat really. You because of George and Liles, and me—well, because of me. I don't think you really know me, darling. I know you."

"I read you like a book," I said, smiling.

"Bat shingles. You just know what Liles told you. I bet she lied her head off."

"No, I really know you, sweet. For instance your first name is Frances. How many people know that?"

"Please, none of that corny stuff about me being an arty climber and why am I named after a cocktail appetizer? That's so *old*, Gussy."

But Lila Norris had never lied and she had known Frances Gibbons very well. She had been the first to know her.

As a child in a small Rhode Island town, Frances' dreams had been nebulous and fanciful, conditioned chiefly by magazines like *Blythe* which she read in the beauty parlor while her mother enjoyed her semiannual permanent wave. Frances immersed herself in a wonderland of fashions and faces and names. She clipped, hating to defile those impeccable glossy pages, photographs of groomed women and enchanting photographic accounts of the lives some people were leading on the Riviera. These she treasured in scrapbooks, and they grew into a formidable dossier on the life she had staked out for herself. Through the charity of a great-aunt, Frances was able to leave high school after her freshman year and board in the house of her aunt in Providence, where she was entered as a day student at Miss Eustis' School. Girls came to Miss Eustis' from giddy and unconventional homes in Washington and New York, in Detroit and Baltimore, and spoke of their fathers as playful big brothers and their mothers as gay, predatory creatures, really just little girls themselves. Frances Gibbons' mother belonged to the Parent-Teacher Association in her town, and Frances' father was a real-estate agent, and they had remained married and reasonably happy for more than twenty years. These humble, healthy details presented a shabby contrast to the aura of the wealthy broken home. The bland normality of her past was a humiliation to Frances.

Lila Norris was an old girl at Miss Eustis' the year Frances Gibbons came. In keeping with the school tradition that each new girl be "sponsored" by a classmate, Lila first cultivated the friendship. Lila could never put her finger on the precise moment she became aware of a flamboyant quality emerging from Frances Gibbons' docile veneer. But, as nearly as Lila could tell, it reached full blossom during the Christmas holiday of their next to last year at school, when Lila invited her friend to visit the Norris winter house at Palm Beach, less than three weeks after Pearl Harbor.

It was by no means Frances' first visit with the Norris family (she had visited the Norrises monotonously often in New York since meeting Lila). But this time, the girls met a full-grown man in Palm Beach, a sun-tanned lieutenant in the Coast Guard. He took them dancing in West Palm Beach night clubs, where the girls chain smoked and drank lime cokes which the lieutenant laced with rum. And the lieutenant had a jeep in which he took them for drives by the ocean. Lila knew that Frances would never forget the rides in the open little car with its preposterous roaring engine. How luxuriously the night air swept her cheeks, bringing tears to her eyes, as the jeep's sealed headlights gave off their minute reflections against the white sandy bunkers of the golf course and the blacked-out windows of the Coral Beach Club. And how Frances had wanted to call over the noise of the engine that they shouldn't go so fast, that the ride should last and last, because when it was over she would be simply herself again, in a borrowed evening dress and a wilted magnolia in her hair. But the visit wasn't entirely like that. After one of those rides, when he had walked them to the front door, the lieutenant had stooped and ceremoniously kissed them on the lips, first Frances and then Lila. Once inside the house, the girls had burst into shrieks of laughter. And next day by the pool, when the lieutenant said something about Frances' two-piece bathing suit being a cute fit, Frances had given him a disdainful look, and later remarked to Lila that the lieutenant was definitely cornball.

When she returned, sunburned and enlightened, to Miss Eustis', girls began to show interest in Frances Gibbons. With amazement and the very faintest ill will they watched her strut through the chaste mahogany corridors, dark hair draped provocatively over her shoulders and with the suggestion of a sway to her hips. They overheard her singing a ballad familiar to many a ripening maiden:

> Oh, violate me in the violet time,
> In the vilest way that you know. . . .

And other indications were forthcoming: The clandestine application of lipstick in the locker room after basketball practice. The slightly inappropriate bloomers worn in Creative Dancing Class. The suggestion of red polish on fingernails tapping in synco-

19

pation to the school hymn at Monday morning assembly. Finally the studied laugh that began in a girlish peal and broke at the end into something like a wheeze.

Even before the year ended, when old Miss Eustis in a flowered hat tearfully awarded the diplomas, the girls were recognizing a formidable contemporary. For from the drab chrysalis Chee Wee Gibbons had emerged. Lila Norris did not know who was responsible for the nickname. Nicknames flowered and died at Miss Eustis' like leaves with the season, but this one had stuck.

Chee Wee's history was similar to mine, though neither of us acknowledged it. Each of us belonged on the outside of a world we never hoped to achieve, admiring and wondering at the life within. We had been content to scrabble about on the periphery, talking brightly, smiling, and shaking hands with all comers, one a little jealous of the other at times, but always careful not to crowd him off the edge.

Here we were, all grown up, on our way to Harry Tilton's big party. Chee Wee was drawn to such gatherings as a moth to a porch light, but it would have been unkind to tell her so. At the reception, as Chee Wee had just now suggested, we were to be partners. We must each stand by the other. I must not let Chee Wee suppose that I had lost interest in her world, that I had left her standing alone on the periphery or that I no longer cared about making an impression. My support was as valuable to her as the lime-colored convertible or as the dress she wore. Like Alice, Chee Wee needed a particle of courage and a step cushion before passing through the looking glass. She had chosen me to boost her through.

"You don't really want to go to Jones Beach?" Chee Wee said as we turned into the last block. "You're not really going to be difficult?"

"I promise I'll behave. I won't insult anybody."

"You can talk to your friends," she said nervously.

A uniformed attendant was waving us to a line of cars waiting to enter an empty lot where two men in shirt sleeves were busy with the parking.

"You can play the piano or something like that," she said.

"I have news for you. I've about given up the piano."

"What *is* it, Gussy? Why didn't you want to come?"

20

"If you have to know," I said, meaning to state this flatly but gently, "you and I don't belong on this merry-go-round. You want to hang on and I want to keep off. That's the difference between us."

"Gussy, don't be so melodramatic. Don't you even want to say hello to George Marsh? . . . Oh, do please turn your coat collar down and try to smile."

Chapter Three

The reception was held in the Water Club's Main Room, which was also known as the Ballroom and which adjoined the terrace that faced onto the East River. Guests were received in the ballroom from a line that stretched deep into the front hall. The line was at its longest when Chee Wee and I arrived; so that it was a full fifteen minutes before we reached the entrance of the Ballroom. We fell in at the end of the line and stood by the lobby wall until we were moved forward imperceptibly as more people filled in behind and we found ourselves by the cloakroom. A hat-check girl wearing a parlor maid's uniform was working a crossword puzzle there. Before her on a card table was a dish scattered with twenty-five-cent pieces intended to decoy similar sums from guests. I laid my hat on the counter and the girl handed me a yellow ticket.

"You should get yourself a coconut straw," Chee Wee said, "with an India-print hatband. Men look well in coconut straw."

When we reached the doorway to the ballroom we craned our necks to see past the people and past the women's large hats for a glimpse of Harry and Doris receiving their guests.

"Look at Harry," Chee Wee said. "Look at him shaking hands."

"He's got a barrelful of personality," I said, and I remembered right away that I was not meant to be critical like that. "What I don't understand," I said, "is why the wedding was in New York. Why couldn't they get married at Hartford, at the home of the bride?"

"Who wants to be married in Hartford?"

"Maybe Doris. Her family wanted it maybe."

"Harry wants her to have her roots in New York. She's smart enough to see that. She *asked* to be married here!"

"I'm sure Harry had nothing to do with the wedding plans," I said. "He just sat idly by."

22

"You leave Harry alone. He loves his Doris."

"Does he?" I said.

"Let's not start predicting about how long the marriage will last," she said, lowering her voice. "That's all you ever hear at weddings. I don't think it's nice."

"I hope it lasts a thousand years," I said. "I was only wondering why he married her."

"You don't understand people, darling. Harry may not seem it to you but he's quite insecure. Harry needs a girl to utterly love and admire him. He wouldn't pick a glamour puss. Handsome men never do. . . . Of course he wouldn't pick a girl who was *penniless*."

"Heaven forbid," I said.

"If you're starting in on Harry again, I'm going to talk to somebody else."

"Don't go, sweetie pie. Don't leave me yet."

"You better make up to me, Gus Taylor," she said. "And you be nice to Harry too."

Waiters were circulating with trays of champagne and on a table on the far side of the room a heavily confectioned wedding cake waited to be cut. Before it, on a lace tablecloth, was a silver tea service that Chee Wee said was too ugly to be the property of the Water Club. She decided that it had been brought down from Hartford by Doris' mother. As they left the receiving line, people would look hastily about the room and make directly for the French doors which opened onto the terrace. It was hot and humid in the ballroom and the windows were closed so as to keep out the soot.

Behind the open doors a small group of musicians were playing. They wore white flannel trousers and double-breasted jackets of a powder-blue color and were perspiring freely. Between numbers the pianist mopped his forehead with a red pocket handkerchief and then replaced it, with a fastidious three-point fold, in his breast pocket. In addition to the piano there was a set of traps, a violin, an accordion, a trumpet, and a saxophone, all playing a medley of sentimental tunes as we waited in the line. Chee Wee said they were a part of an orchestra that played at the Fence Club proms in New Haven, not a very good orchestra but all devoted to Harry Tilton, and they had gone to a great deal of trouble to be at the wedding. The leader was the tall, red-headed fellow playing the saxophone. He could play nearly any instrument and was espe-

23

cially good with the trombone. He was a great friend of Harry's. They were playing:

A hundred and one—pounds of fun,
That's my little honey bun—

"There's a cute tune," Chee Wee said. "It's Harry's favorite." In a minute they swung into "The Most Beautiful Girl in the World" and Chee Wee hummed along with the music. "That's a beautiful song," she said. "It's Harry's and Doris' theme song."

I started to answer her, but before I could, we were shaking hands, first with Mr. Slater of Hartford, Connecticut, Doris' father, who was apparently unaware that it was not his role to greet the guests, then with Harry Tilton's mother, whose name was Mrs. Webb, and then with Doris Slater's mother, who also came from Hartford, Connecticut, and whose name, by what seemed almost a coincidence at a Water Club wedding reception, was the same as that of her daughter's father.

"Well it's Gus Taylor," Harry Tilton was saying. His hand gripped tight on my shoulder. "Glad to have you aboard, Gus-bo. Step up and buss the blushing bride. One kiss and it's rationed, not too long and not too wet. . . ."

"For Christ's sake, Harry," I started to say.

". . . because that's mine all mine from now on in. . . ."

"Oh darling," his bride said.

Harry Tilton laughed. "If you won't kiss my wife, at least you can tell her something nice. Tell her she's looking like the breath of spring."

"Oh Harry," Doris said.

I kissed Doris on the cheek briefly. Her nose had begun to shine and her cheek and neck were moist from contact with the lace veil. Though many girls manage to smell quite delicious with the heat, Doris was not one of them and she had omitted to wear perfume. There clung to her an acrid odor of sulphur soap, heightened in the humid air, a sharp, medicinal aura. Sulphur soap was a sensible soap and it did a thorough job of cleaning the pores.

"You must be very happy, Doris," I said.

"Yes, Gus, and have you ever seen Harry looking happier?"

"I don't suppose I ever have," I said and we turned for that moment to look at Harry. He was in the arms of a rotund woman

24

with a feather hat, slapping fondly upon her broad back. She embraced him like a mother bear, disarranging the immaculate wave of his hair and rumpling the front of his starched shirt, with her immense bosom heaving and her fleshy elbow and dimpled arms squeezing.

"That's Mrs. Burke," Doris said. "She was Harry's Scotch nanny."

We were silent for another moment, both absorbed by the exuberant bellowing of Harry in the embrace of his nanny. Doris smiled a seraphic smile, "They're devoted to each other. Nanny Burke wants to help out when we move into the apartment. She's been such a sweetheart with me too."

I walked by the bridesmaids, seven girls of assorted shapes dressed in organdy gowns the shade of well-creamed coffee. They wore floppy straw hats with red ribbons falling down their backs. Four of them had long hair that hung about their shoulders anachronistically, in contrast to the fashionably cropped heads of the New York girls. Two or three had pudgy and shining faces. They were healthy girls and they smiled modestly—a little nucleus from out of town, firmly united, loyal to Doris Slater and determined to see her through. It was their first and likely their last visit to the Water Club but there was something refreshing and encouraging about their being there at all.

I walked out onto the terrace, alone. Chee Wee had already dropped behind to fend for herself among the guests. Charley Lewis was there, and his wife, and Amor Parish with his girl and Rudy Johnson with a girl who shared an apartment with Parish's girl, and a married couple who lived on George Marsh's floor at Seventy-first Street. Segregated from us, on that side of the terrace that lay in the shade of the building, were the parents, relatives, and family friends. The men seemed uncomfortably aware of their seniority. They cast smiling glances toward us, squinting a little as they faced into the sun.

"Hey, Tommy."

"H'lo, Mr. Evans."

"How about dropping out to see us? We've moved back out now for the summer. Back out to Syosset."

"I'd be happy to do that, Mr. Evans."

"We'll play some golf."

"Sure thing, Mr. Evans."

25

There was something plaintive in the voice. We had the impression, at times, that the Old Man was frightened of us. He was constrained and apologetic, effusive, and for the most part generous. Particularly since the war, he had been showing off his sons and his sons' friends with an inordinate pride and devotion. He would speak of his boys in delighted and expansive tones, automatically accepting you on equal terms because you were his boy's friend and that made you a hero by proxy. When he spoke to you like this, you were privileged and important. He was good to you and kind and you felt thankful for that, though you wondered why he went to all the trouble. It was ridiculous, you couldn't help feeling, that he should struggle to come to terms with us. We had so very little in common, we and he and these fat, tired old men.

Yet there were many things we could thank him for, and the wisest among us acknowledged our appreciation tacitly without ever bending over backward and being always careful not to let him feel that they held us in obligation. We worked in his firm. In college we were sponsored for his club. We were flirted with and fussed over by his wife. We made love to his daughter and frequently married her after. We accepted the Old Man's favors and his patronage and some would inherit money from him, and some few like George Marsh in considerable amounts. But we had never quite known what to make of him.

We spoke unkindly of the Old Man at times when we were resentful, and we ridiculed him. But it was not rebellious ridicule. It was not revolt. Revolt requires a form of opposition, a restriction, and we felt nothing like that. There had been no regimentation, no enforced set of standards for us to counteract. The Old Man had taken pains not to burden us with anything so rigid, for, he had said to us so often, it was important that we grow up to be individuals, to think and to choose for ourselves. He had wanted us to learn, to learn early, the things that had taken him years to learn. Just what these things were he had never specifically told us. We gathered that he and his contemporaries had been forced into patterns, and before he had properly broken away he had had to cope with his war. The war was something of which the Old Man and his contemporaries were very proud indeed. The war they had in mind, like so many of the other things that had hap-

26

pened to them, was clearly something we would never understand, though not through their failure to speak of it.

Then abruptly the war had been over and they had had a wonderful time. Some of them had traveled in Europe and had visited the battlefields and the trenches where someone, most frequently an older brother or an older friend, had fought or died. They had solemnly done these things, and afterward they had sailed home on floating palaces the likes of which we could never hope to see and they had gone on having a wonderful time, dancing to tunes the likes of which we could never hope to hear, and meeting all species of incredible people.

And while they were about it, they had met and married the women who became our aunts and mothers and stepmothers and had begotten us and our brothers and sisters and half-brothers and sisters and stepbrothers and sisters at a furious though birth-controlled pace. Often these marriages had not worked the way the Old Man and his contemporaries had hoped that they would work, for they had been young people then and very impressionable. But they had been crazy about one another at the time.

To think back on it now, after all the interim of mistakes and good and bad times, made him uncomfortable and a little sad. It sometimes left him wishing that he could go through those days again. Perhaps if he could he would get more out of them and he might behave differently, a little more grown-up.

To think of living them over again was obviously ridiculous. A man only lived once, unless he was a Hindu. None of the people the Old Man knew were Hindus. They had been young just that once and had made the most of it, stretching the years as long and as thin as possible. They had been told, though they hadn't really believed it themselves, that those years would not last forever. They had worked hard at being gay, because, as the Old Man might say, gaiety had been a serious business in those days. And since the old man was a romanticist at heart—and who on earth was not?—and since he was not averse to quoting poetry, he quoted from Edna St. Vincent Millay.

> My candle burns at both ends;
> It will not last the night,
> But, ah, my foes, and, oh, my friends—
> It gives a lovely light.

Here was a philosophy that did not apply to Hindus.

The Old Man worried about our opinion. Somehow he felt it mattered more than God's. Somewhere out of everything we had heard, out of the recollections of pleasures denied us, out of all his justifications and explanations, we had got the idea that the Old Man expected us to judge him. He held to this with a quiet desperation, which was all the more sad, since we had no wish to judge. You were grateful to the Old Man for having conceived you, loved you, fed you, clothed you, and you wanted him to know it and drop the matter there. But he would persist. It was embarrassing, his dogged struggle to ingratiate himself. Much as you might have wished otherwise, you knew your life was not to be the by-product of his. And if the Old Man convinced you that he had made a sort of anarchy of his life, you might envy him that privilege but you certainly did not blame him for it. Your life would be pretty different from his. You took heart from the algebraic consolation that two minuses must make a plus.

They stood in the shadowed part of the terrace. They talked among themselves and some were strutting wearily like old roosters, bewildered by the bejeweled flock of wives and ex-wives who babbled and plucked insistently at their sleeves. Lila Norris' old man was among them. He wore Peale shoes and gold cufflinks and a regimental striped tie. He looked thinner and happier and more relaxed than he had last winter. It was because he had been on the wagon since April and because now that summer was beginning again nothing was as bad as it had seemed, and he was still Hadley Norris, one of the sharpest investors in the East, they still said, and he had just bought nicely into the Texas Company. And he was among friends: Old Man Crane wearing white flannels, Old Man Hallman limping on his fractured kneecap, a hunting accident, and Old Man Pritchard, still agile and a pretty fair squash player, demonstratively refusing a cigar.

(If he were alive, George Marsh's old man would certainly have been there with them. Andy Marsh, laughing and telling stories and kissing ladies—the most personable of all.)

They were all there, the survivors of their line, the Mohicans of Aiken and Tuxedo Park. Why did they call out to us? Why did they wave?

Separately, and across from their progenitors, the young were assembled in the center of the terrace. It was pleasant there where the sun was shining and I stood among them, lifting a fresh glass of champagne from a silver tray in the hands of a bustling waiter. It was early in the party, much too soon to break the spell of self-enchantment and too soon to retreat into the shade. Girls in light bright dresses, their hair starting to bleach and their skins already tanning in this second week of June, and boys in summer suits, with golf collars and button-downs and fresh-pressed neckties, displayed themselves to their mutual gratification. They flirted in an offhand way, and observed each other, taking care not to lose the studied air of sophistication, and every participant was sublimely conscious of being an integral part of the rather splendid whole.

Young men waxed eloquent and boastful. They discussed jobs they would like to have one day or new ways to make a fortune in South Africa, in Texas, or in the Argentine; they speculated upon the sexual propensities of girls both absent and within earshot. Modern-day Alexanders, in their twenties already fretting for new worlds to conquer. They consoled themselves with a nebulous and implausible vision of a future. It unfolded itself before them as they talked, wider and wider and wider toward some rosy horizon, unindicated and unguaranteed but holding nonetheless all promise of placidity and contentment.

Years ago, before the war, they had heard Judy Garland sing a song:

> Somewhere over the rainbow,
>   Way up high—
> There's a land that I heard of
>   Once in a lullaby.
> Somewhere over the rainbow,
>   Skies are blue. . . .

Little land of lullaby. It was only a pretty song. There was no real substance to it, nor any guarantee, but it was comforting to hear. And they had gone on hearing it as boys and girls from infancy and through childhood, puberty, and adolescence. It took on all kinds of melodies as they grew older. It could have been a Christmas carol or a hymn, a medley of football marches or Glenn Miller's band playing "Sunrise Serenade." No matter how old they grew, it could still lull them just as when Judy Garland had sung it.

Like any tune with lyrics, it presupposed a certain outlook

29

without ever clearly defining what it was. Certain children went to certain schools and other children went to other schools. They came from different families and wore different clothes or they lived in different cities, different neighborhoods. None of this was to suggest for a moment that there was any question of superiority. Children assumed that it was superiority, but that was a child's selfish view. Though some adults held it, it was a ridiculous and outmoded view. Social distinction was a thing of the past; anyone knew it was dead as Henry James. One's children had simply been given "every advantage," and that was the politest way to put it.

In later years when these children were called to the Navy and Army and Marine Corps, their ears rang with these assertions of their elders who spoke of background and being the cream of the nation's youth. They were anxious, most of them, to forget these assertions and to forget about lullabies. They were not long in perceiving, from the attitudes of the men about them, that privilege carried a very formidable array of disadvantages.

(George Marsh when he reported to Fort Devens even saw himself as Harvey Cheyne, the pampered scion of a millionaire, the hero of *Captains Courageous*.) Except when conversing with each other, they were guarded about their past. They concealed all pertinent facts about themselves. But at Maxwell Field, or Quantico, or Fort Bliss this information was neither important nor impressive.

The most effective rule of conduct was rigid self-surveillance; for one to guard against disclosing his personality as scrupulously as he would conceal a sweetheart's posed photograph in the bottom of a sea bag or in the corner of a foot locker. One was as cautious about mannerisms and figures of speech as he was about using his own toilet tissue and scented shaving soap in the early mornings in a crowded latrine where others lathered their faces with Barbasol or Burma Shave, and used the rolls pegged behind the enlisted men's toilet freely and without concern over communicable disease. Once he had mastered these fundamental discretions, the pressures relaxed by themselves. He was absorbed and governed by the anonymity of the uniform.

Three or four years later they began to return. Now came a wild sense of achievement. They believed they had engaged themselves in an enterprise of proportions so tremendous that they could spend the rest of their lives appraising it. Now civic groups erected signboards at railway stations to welcome them. Wacs and Red Cross entertainers sang "Hallelujah, my guy has come back" from the prows of tugboats that piloted ships into the harbor. For a time it seemed to them that they had accomplished something of which no one else had been capable. When they thought it over, it had probably been more than their fathers had done. It had been a more Christian act, a manlier endeavor, than they had been conditioned for by any number of rectors, chaplains, tutors, or football coaches.

With this firmly in mind they cashed in their bonus checks and re-enrolled under the G.I. Bill of Rights at the same colleges they would otherwise have gone back to at their families' expense. Some became enthusiastic about the new veterans' organizations and for a time were civic-minded. To be a veteran was an elaborate and preoccupying business, an experience that offered an immense if transient satisfaction. The phase was not only significant but a lot of fun. It was a pity that it had to end.

It ended for them as unaccountably as it had begun, without their ever knowing when or how. Mysteriously they found themselves starting on a more vacuous existence. Yet it had an Elysian quality, something pleasurable and unspecific as a dream should be. The ruptured duck, which had enjoyed a fleeting vogue in 1945, had become an object of ridicule. To wear the parts of a discarded uniform was an ostentatious and pitiable gesture. Gradually they succumbed to a nostalgic torpor. They were returned at last to the charmed circle of old acquaintance. And softly, imperceptibly at the start, the strains of the old lullaby began, obscuring the grim years wearied away, the tensions and the anger and all the forgotten earnest resolves. This was the time the song had promised, for which they had crossed the rainbow.

"If it isn't Gus Taylor," somebody said enthusiastically, "returned from the dead."

"Hello."

"Don't you remember me—Tim Lund?"

"Timothy Frisbee Lund," I said, with desperate good humor. "How could I forget?"

31

But I had forgotten. He was some face, a face with a catchy name. Someone who had gone to college.

But Chee Wee Gibbons had deserted me and it was advisable to talk with someone. We went through the French doors into the ballroom where there was plenty of champagne.

Chapter Four

A bit later—I was keeping no track of time—I was sitting on the cement surface of the cement wall. This wall enclosed the eastern exposure of the terrace from a sharp drop of some sixty feet to the East River Drive which ran beneath. From this position, facing onto the terrace with my back toward the East River, I had watched the party grow. From time to time I heard the whistle of a tugboat as it passed another in the vicinity of Welfare Island. It was a deep, lonely sound, strangely discordant and ominous heard against the dance music and the babbling voices.

I had almost finished my drink when two of the three ushers emerged from the French doors and stood on the top step, on the side near to me. They surveyed the guests on the terrace below with a distant sultanic air. They wore their cutaways and pearl-gray waistcoats with a pride verging on arrogance, for they were important functionaries this afternoon. In recent days a series of parties had been given by friends and relatives of the bride and groom. As a result they appeared wan and tired and were relying upon the liquor served here to maintain the responsible façade of an usher. The humidity and the sunshine had left their faces shining, accentuating this way the circles beneath their eyes and the blemishes and razor cuts upon their faces. One of them, the shorter and frailer of the two, clapped a pair of dress gloves against the palm of one hand as he talked. The second was heavier and stood straighter and, catching a thumb on the bottom edge of each trouser pocket, tapped his thighs with extended fingers and the flats of his hands. Both beat time to the dance music with a posed and careful unconcern. They would be friends of Harry's, but I didn't recall having seen either one before. They had faces I found impossible to like instinctively and even before I heard them speak I was wondering if they didn't come from Southampton.

33

"Pretty close inside," the tall one remarked, without shifting his gaze from the people on the terrace.

"Pretty close," the shorter, frailer boy sad. "I suppose we ought to start dancing."

"With the bridesmaids?"

"I suppose."

"Bunch of trouts."

Presently the tall one smiled and pointed at a girl. "How do you like that? Why couldn't she have been a bridesmaid?"

"Anyone who goes shaking it around like that never gets to be a bridesmaid."

I saw that the girl in question was Chee Wee. She was talking excitedly to a group of young men and at this moment she tossed her head. I heard the shrill, unmistakable progression of her laugh, from falsetto to gasp, ring out above the other voices.

"She's an old pal of Tilton's," the shorter boy was saying. "She used to be around that apartment he lived in with George Marsh. You remember that apartment—and what was his name? The guy who was always playing the piano, trying to be everybody's pal?"

"That would be Taylor. I met him once. I had that pleasure. Whatever happened to Marsh?"

"You saw him last night. He was in the bag—as per usual."

"He's really been pouring it down lately." The tall usher paused in afterthought. He was pretty serious when he spoke again. "I don't know too much about Marsh. All I know is what Tilton tells me—"

"Tilton knows the whole story. Did he ever tell you about that Lila Norris? She was supposed to marry him last winter."

"I know," the tall usher said, looking out toward the river and the Queensborough Bridge. "I knew Miss Norris."

"She was something, I mean to say. Damned fine piece of scenery."

"Beautiful girl."

"I'll probably never see the like again, or you either. And she was crazy. The kind that will try anything once—for the bang of it. I don't know what she had but she had it. She was crazy.—Poor old Marsh."

"Marsh?" the tall usher said. "Wasn't he a treat? Wasn't he perfectly charming? And how about that speech about friendship

34

and what loyalty means? Every word he said it took him five minutes to think of the next."

"Tilton says he's been a mess since that girl."

"It wasn't the girl—you don't get gassed like that over a girl. There's more to it than that. . . . That boy's been on the skids for quite a while. He was born on the skids. I'm going to tell you what he is—he's a deadbeat. And to hell with him."

"That's kind of rough," the short boy said thoughtfully, stretching the pearl-gray gloves between his hands. "I think Tilton sort of hoped that Marsh never would get married. He and that other guy were living in the apartment. And making a fairly good thing of it, too. It got to the point where they were owing Marsh money and Marsh never cared about being paid back. So finally Tilton felt guilty about all that free-loading. . . . Even if he was having a swell time doing it, he didn't like the idea of living off of someone forever. Tilton says he tried to leave twice and Marsh took it as a personal insult, so Tilton never left. The one who left was the Harvard who was so nimble at the piano. One day this clown just upped and out, leaving Harry holding the bag. Tilton says this character owed Marsh more than three hundred dollars and Marsh never saw a nickel of it."

"What was that piano player's name again?" the tall usher said.

"His name was Taylor. Tilton says he's been laying low since February—and I can understand why."

Anyway, I thought, they didn't know me from Adam. Sitting there on the wall, only a few yards from them, I was glad of that. I might have lost my temper and started something. I was relieved that I hadn't had to.

As it was, I wanted to remember everything that had been quoted from Harry Tilton. Harry, as I might have expected, had misrepresented everything and he had done so on purpose. Harry knew that the rift between me and George Marsh had been over matters far graver than money. I would have liked to write his gossip down in pencil. I could read it over later on and refresh myself on what Harry Tilton was saying these days about all of us. Twice in my life I had come to blows with Harry and both incidents had been immensely satisfying. Even now I derived a quiet pleasure from Harry's appearance, which I had marred long

35

ago by slightly displacing the nose and more recently by scarring the lower lip.

What Harry Tilton's friends had to say counted for nothing of course. There would be no triumph in clouting one of them, and no purpose in challenging their aspersions.

"Tell me something," the tall usher was saying now. "I wish you'd tell me how you keep the polish on this patent leather. You can't just use polish—or is there a special polish you can get?"

"Get 'em rubbed with vaseline. Just a few dabs will preserve the finish."

They seemed happier now and more enthusiastic. They were much better qualified to discuss these matters than to mind other people's business.

All at once I was in a great hurry to get away from them.

Chapter Five

In the ballroom the reception line had broken up. The ushers and the bridesmaids were on the terrace posing for photographs. Indoors, a second photographer was popping flashbulbs at those dancing couples and seated guests that had been pointed out to him previously as relatives or close friends.

Several snapshots were taken of a local Congressman, of a coloratura soprano currently at odds with the Metropolitan Opera, and of a retired Rear Admiral who had served with Admiral Halsey. The Admiral and his husky blonde niece were warmly received at parties where he enjoyed some celebrity, half because of his flamboyant personality and half because he had stood in the platoon of exalted brass on the deck of the *Missouri* as MacArthur received the Japanese surrender. The Admiral enjoyed parties. He was an indefatigable dancer, an enthusiastic endorser of the bourbon highball, an amateur gymnast. At his undisclosed age, the Admiral was able to stand erect on his head and he was able to sustain that posture for a time sufficient for him to recite a ribald limerick about an old man from Port Said who persistently stood on his head.

As I came in the Admiral was on the dance floor and dancing the Mexican shuffle dance. Other couples kept a respectful distance and a small gallery of applauders stood behind the photographer as he popped flashbulbs at the Admiral in rapid succession. I watched the Admiral for a full minute before realizing that his partner was Chee Wee Gibbons.

Chee Wee danced with a poise and a restraint that was only natural to her under the circumstances. She hesitated properly between beats, stepping out and back with an emphatic switch of her pelvis, and she smiled in a logical sequence, from the Admiral's feet, to the Admiral's face, then triumphantly to the camera, and, lastly, back to the Admiral's feet.

37

Presently the Admiral burst into a harsh cough and, after no more than a second's pause, the five musicians in blue coats turned their deft attentions to a waltz. The coloratura soprano glided off in the Congressman's arms with a brilliant smile which the photographer hastened to record, dispersing the small gallery behind him as he did so. Chee Wee Gibbons and the Admiral were left alone and unnoticed on the edge of the floor. The transition was complete within a minute and the Admiral continued to cough.

Chee Wee wagged a painted finger at me. "Is there some champagne?" she called.

The Admiral rasped and expectorated into a handkerchief. He shook his head violently and signaled to Chee Wee.

"I forgot that he hates champagne," Chee Wee called to me. "But you've still got some of your drink."

"Here," she said, coming toward me and snatching the glass. "Can't you see the Admiral's choking?"

The Admiral folded his handkerchief into a small square and began to rub the perspiration from his balding forehead and from beneath his collar. When his coughing had subsided, he took the glass from Chee Wee and emptied it in one swallow, ice and all, grinding it down with his teeth the way a small boy eats an apple.

"Admiral," Chee Wee said, "I don't know if you've ever met Gus Taylor."

The Admiral and I exchanged a vigorous handclasp while he munched the ice.

"You smoke?" the Admiral asked, half opening his mouth so that some water dribbled down onto his chin.

"Yes, sir."

"Give it up," the Admiral said, his voice still hoarse from the coughing. "It's the worst thing for you."

"I know, sir. That's what they tell me."

"That's what Gene Tunney would tell you," the Admiral said. "Do you know Gene Tunney?"

"No, sir. But I know he doesn't believe in smoking."

"How do you know Gene Tunney?" the Admiral asked.

"I don't, sir."

"Were you in the Navy?"

"No, sir, I wasn't."

"Knock off that smoking," the Admiral said, and coughed briefly.

"Now take me. The smoking lamp is never lit for me as a rule. When it is I get to coughing. Now I had a cigar after lunch and I'm barking like a damned sea lion."

"But you've been dancing a lot," Chee Wee said. "You've been dancing the most fantastic amount."

The Admiral smiled at Chee Wee and pinched her arm just above the elbow. The Admiral turned to me and said, "I want you and your wife to be my guests at the Indian Harbor Yacht Club. Your wife's a regular honeybunch."

Chee Wee fingered her bracelets slowly while formulating her answer. "I hate to disappoint you, Admiral," she said. "We're not married. But we are very good friends and we'd adore to be your guests at the Indian Harbor Yacht Club any time you'd care to ask us.—I must admit that I don't know all there is to know about yachts."

"You know," the Admiral said, "I saw you grab that drink from him and I assumed he was your husband. Do you know the Indian Harbor Yacht Club?"

"No, sir," I answered.

"You live in Stamford, don't you?" the Admiral asked.

"No, sir. I don't."

"I'm thinking of buying a piece of property out there in Greenwich. That's what Bull Halsey suggested. It was my privilege to serve under Admiral Halsey. You didn't happen to be with CINCPAC by any chance?"

"I wasn't in the Navy, sir."

"How did you know Gene Tunney if you weren't in the Navy?"

"Sir, I've never met Mr. Tunney."

"Well, why in hell do you talk about him then, if you don't know him? I don't know what's the matter with you kids. You're nice kids. I know you don't mean to be fresh. But sure as hell you give that impression. All you kids can talk. But are you going to talk us out of the next war?"

"I don't see what you mean, sir."

"No. You don't see," he said. "There's a lot of things you kids don't see. I'm not saying you don't know how to face up to things when the chips are down. When the chips were down you were gallant. The Government placed a lot of confidence in you and spent billions of dollars on you. You were the best-fed, best-

39

equipped, highest-paid, best-trained fighting men in the history of warfare. We were very proud of you kids. We all felt that you had been gallant and that we did right to put our confidence in you."

"Thank you, sir," I said. "I didn't mean to be fresh."

"Nobody said you were fresh," the Admiral said angrily. "And I'd appreciate it if you didn't interrupt me. You are gallant kids and I love you, but I wish I understood you and I wish you weren't always sounding off and acting fresh. My nephew is Gunnery Officer on the *Nevada* and he's a swell, gallant kid. And so is my niece. My niece is here with me, and I wish you could meet her. She has a Chris-Craft and she keeps it at the Indian Harbor Yacht Club."

"We'd love to meet her," Chee Wee said.

"She's a swell, gallant, sweet kid, but she does a lot of talking. My nephew can talk circles around me if I let him. And that's what I worry about. When are you kids going to get squared away with yourselves? From now on you kids are going to run the team. If you don't care to listen to us that's not our fault.—Now, honeybunch, if you'll just get me a bourbon and ginger ale, I may stop sounding off. I'll tell your husband about the young man from Castile."

"Please don't send me away," Chee Wee said. "I love limericks."

"I think you'd better dance," the Admiral said. "Dance around and lallygag and slop up some cocktails. Whatever you do, enjoy yourself. But some day remind me to tell your husband about the young man from Castile."

Chee Wee and I danced a fox trot, moving cautiously to the side of the room opposite from where the Admiral had wandered off among the guests.

Twice I heard young men's voices exchanging bizarre Latin salutations:

"Hail, Praeceps!"

And then an answering bellow from the other end of the room.

"Hail, Piscator!"

I searched Chee Wee's face for some explanation, but evidently she hadn't heard.

"The Admiral wasn't exactly coherent," Chee Wee said after we had danced a little.

40

"You've got to give the Admiral a chance. He's new at this but he's fighting hard."

"I say he's plastered."

"The old guy's all right," I said. "He's very concerned with the young. I liked him fine." And then the thought struck me. "Who does he remind you of?" I asked Chee Wee. "I'll give you three guesses."

"I'll use just one," she said. "Lila's father. You didn't mean it complimentarily either. Oh, you're a stinker, Gus Taylor."

"Old Hadley Norris," I said, half laughing.

"You rat."

"I like Mr. Norris, sweets. Only he doesn't like me."

"Of course he always preferred George. George was polite to him."

"I saw him talking out there on the terrace. He looked the other way. I don't blame him."

"If he speaks to you, you be nice," she said.

"He won't speak to me."

"I'm warning you, Gussy. He's Liles' father. He adores Liles."

"He looked well," I said. "Better than I've ever seen him."

"Well he's lost thirty pounds."

"He's on the wagon."

"You be polite to him, Gussy. He's a very capable man."

"Let's get away from here," I said. "It's hot and there are too many people. I get tired of this bouncing around."

"You're not bouncing. You're one of the divinest dancers. You've always had a sense of rhythm."

"Thank you," I said. "But it's hot, and there are too many people."

We walked to a corner of the ballroom where there were two gilt chairs next the table that had the wedding cake upon it. When we had sat down, Chee Wee opened her purse and extracted from it first a small cigarette lighter, cased in black lacquer and with a red and green oriental design, then a gold cigarette holder with a bugle tip, and then a pair of black-framed, harlequin-shaped eyeglasses, studded with small semi-precious stones which made them look as if they had been designed by Salvador Dali. She placed the red plastic tip of the cigarette holder in her mouth and firmly clenched it in her teeth. Then she poked my arm and smiled. But when she saw that I had been watching her all the while, the

41

smile faded and for an instant, through the lenses, there was a flicker of resentment in Chee Wee's eyes.

"Well," she said. "Aren't you going to offer me a cigaboo?"

"Don't you carry them with the rest of that equipment?" I asked.

"Most men I know carry cigarettes. Even if they don't smoke themselves, they carry them."

"You know so many men," I said.

"You're the only one I've ever known who's difficult. I never believed it when Lila told me, but now I see it's true. Oh, don't have hurtie feelings. You tease *me*, you know." Suddenly she reached for my hand. "Gussy? Gussy? If you want me to, I apologize."

I was looking in my pockets for some cigarettes.

"Usually," she was returning to her confident, unapologetic self, "the person offers me a cigarette. It's embarrassing for a girl to always have to ask. That's a trouble of yours. You used to embarrass Lila in front of her mother. A girl doesn't like it when the person makes her embarrassed."

"Just what do you mean—'the person'?"

"You know damned well what I mean. I'm tired of playing up to you and of having to talk about something else every time Lila's name is mentioned. I don't see how you expect to be a lawyer when you insist on backing away from things."

But we did change the subject. I found myself telling Chee Wee about the two ushers on the terrace, and something of the conversation I had overheard.

"Did they think I was attractive? Which one thought I was attractive?"

"The tall one," I said. "And the other agreed."

"Was he really such a bastard, Gussy?"

"You wouldn't think so," I said. "They both looked familiar. I'm sure you've seen them before."

"Perhaps you're right. Perhaps they do come from Southampton. And in spite of what you think, they're probably very nice."

"I'm prejudiced," I said. "I never spent enough time in Southampton."

"I wish they wouldn't play all those tunes," Chee Wee said. "That's 'My Heart Stood Still.' I think it's a very beautiful tune and I think I'm going to cry."

"Well, don't cry."

"Did I tell you I ran into Gabriel Paster?" Chee Wee asked. "I talked to him for half an hour. It was a great surprise. But I guess it takes a lot to make me cry."

"It's all right if you cry," I said. "As long as it is not over Gabriel Paster."

Gabriel Paster was a little man with the reputation of being the most ambitious society columnist in New York. He had worked as a summer replacement to the regular gossip columnist of one of the afternoon papers and three years ago had graduated to the more ethereal realm of *Blythe*, where he edited a page of photographs and text entitled "One Meets the Most Beguiling People." Last autumn he had been a rather heavy beau of Chee Wee's.

"Forget him," I said. "There are plenty of fish in the ocean."

"Bat shingles to Paster," Chee Wee said distantly. "Have you got another cigaboo?"

"Here's your cigaboo," I said.

"Would you tell me why they play those soupy old songs?" Chee Wee asked. "They play them over and over, those lovely, soupy, silly songs. I don't think I ever heard you play this one."

"I never did learn it," I said. "I was just an East Northrup boy when that song was new."

Something had disturbed Chee Wee. I noticed that she was frowning, and I thought I knew what the trouble was.

"You heard me," I said. "East Northrup, Mass."

"You don't have to bite my head off, darling. It's a heavenly little town."

"Okay then," I said, but she remained disturbed.

"Did you know your *accent* changes? Did you realize? Sometimes you talk like a railroad clerk in Worcester. That gruesome drawl. Those frightful nasal a's. East Nawthrup, Me-yass."

"It's the same in Rhode Island, sweets. Nobody's exempt from their background."

"Mine's rubbed off," Chee Wee said impetuously, so impetuously that I smiled and she caught me.

"Isn't it a little boring," she said, "to be a professional hayseed? Really, Gussy, you're not a peasant."

"George used to call me a peasant."

43

"Well, you did pretty well. You mixed with the city slickers and you turned the tables on them—look at George Marsh."

"Okay, okay," I said.

Chee Wee squeezed my arm. "Then let's not be glib. Let's have a decent talk—we seem depressed. Why is that, Gussy? Why?"

"It's the atmosphere. We would have been happier at Jones Beach."

"You think I'm an idiot."

"When did I ever call you an idiot?"

"I like things to be romantic," Chee Wee said. "It's because I'm a woman, I suppose, and not a negative woman either. But I know there's nothing in the least romantic about us really. Instead it's just flat and, I suppose—negative. Oh, Gussy, I wish it could have been different."

"Now that's silly."

"I don't mean *us*. Not you and me. I'm thinking about our friends and everyone. I wish it could have been romantic for them all, the way it was for their parents. You don't know what fun it was to be lost and have people lamenting for you all over the place. And here we are. We've lived a third of our lives already.—Can't you see me, wearing beads and sequins and elephants and dinosaurs painted on my stockings, and with no bust at all? I wish I could go to a houseparty and not sleep for three nights or dive off a yacht with no clothes on. But if I did that nowadays, it wouldn't shock a soul. Instead I'd go to an analyst, and he'd tell me it was an aggression. You can have as many aggressions as you want nowadays—"

"Let's not cry in our beer," I said.

"In our champagne, you mean."

I'd made her smile, or rather I had made her make a sort of face, but a moment later she looked at me darkly. "I suppose you don't think it was fun to be a lost generation?"

"You are all a lost generation," I said. "Quote, unquote. Gertrude Stein."

"*The Sun Also Rises*," Chee Wee said. "I kept it on my bed table. It used to be my bible. I used to think I was Brett."

"It's a good book but it would make a lousy bible."

"You wish you could have been over in Europe with them. I know you do. You'd've loved it."

44

"Sure," I said. "Real disillusioned."

"Why shouldn't we be disillusioned? Who's got a better right?"

"It sounds pretty tempting, the way you talk about it," I said. But my words were coming out pompous, pretentious. I didn't want to preach, or argue.

"You think I'm being self-indulgent?" Chee Wee said.

"Forget it. They're playing a nice waltz. Hear it?"

"I could feel all they felt, everything, every feeling." And she added gently, "I wish you'd go on talking. It's good for me—and for you."

"You might as well forget it. You might as well stop identifying yourself with it. None of it was ever meant to be for you or me," I said. "Learn to say the hell with it. The hell with Gertrude Stein, the whole damned business."

"Gussy?" she asked in a thin voice. "Should we look somewhere else for our fun? If there's going to be any fun?"

"We can't look back at that dead business."

"Don't stop there," she said. "It's the first thing you've said that I really wanted to hear."

"I was being negative," I said.

"No—positive. I want to remember it. If that's what you really mean, you should say it more often, Gussy, and not be so—I don't know."

"Listen, you want to dance."

"Gussy, do you remember what you said? Or were you just making conversation?"

"Listen, I ought to speak to George Marsh. He must be here somewhere," I said.

"No, you weren't just making conversation," she said. "Did you ever talk that way with Liles? I never heard anyone say those things."

"Well, anyone could say them."

"We're all phonies, red hot phonies. All trying to crowd ourselves into somebody else's world where there isn't any room. That's the idea. Isn't it?"

"That's the idea," I said. "Chasing after false gods—something like that."

"You're terrific when you talk this way. I'm a terrific listener. Are you changing or what?"

45

" 'Tales of the Vienna Woods'," I said. "It sounds screwy without a violin."

"You are changing. You're growing way away from us, Gussy."

And in the car I had not dared suggest this to her. It was too soon to know if she was right, but I hoped so.

For more than a minute neither of us spoke.

"I do wish they wouldn't play those songs," she said. " 'Anything Goes.' I don't want to hear. . . . It's too much." Her voice, which had been faint to begin with, broke off completely.

"You know, Gussy? I've always had a lot of confidence in our generation, but now I'm not so sure. We seem so bogged down. I don't think we'd mind being bogged down, if we had a good time while we were at it."

"Chin up," I said. "A pip, pip."

And now I was sorry. It was a mistake to tease her.

"Funny man," she said crossly, and turned her head away.

From somewhere outside on the terrace the cry went up:

"Hail, Praeceps!"

"Hail, Piscator!"

"Hail!"

"Wow!"

"We never talked before," Chee Wee was saying. "Did you and Liles talk about these things? Or is it because the Admiral depressed us?"

"The Admiral loves us. We're gallant and he loves us. The best-fed, best-equipped, best-paid men in the history of warfare," I said. "Now watch out, they're coming over here. It's time for Harry and Doris to cut the cake."

"Gussy, you don't think I'm a fool for letting you make me cry? I don't think you ever saw me cry."

I hadn't noticed her dabbing at her eyes with a rouged piece of facial tissue.

Chapter Six

As by prearranged signal, the music burst into a crescendo and stopped abruptly. The players briskly disassembled their instruments. They tested violin strings and blew out silently into handkerchiefs the saliva that had collected in the trumpet and the trombone from two hours' playing; the worn reeds were removed from the saxophone and from the clarinet. They replaced their instruments in their cases, resting them on the blue velvet cushioned linings, and locked the cases so as to prevent guests from tampering, and lined them in a neat row beneath the piano. The pianist closed the top of the piano with a panel over the keyboard while the others filed past him, close by the terrace doors, and made their way through the guests to the washroom off the front lobby. "Hello, troops! You're looking mighty twosy twosy, troops."

Grinning and waving at us with a cheeriness that a photographer hastened to record, Harry Tilton invaded our corner. ("You've got to please the troops," he would say in moments of high exuberance. "Where's all the troops? It's party time.")

Doris was holding fast to Harry's hand and followed him from behind, gathering her satin train in folds above her waist so that she could move without tripping and in some way keep up with Harry.

"Hello, you two," Doris called. "Hello. Hello. We're going to cut the cake!"

For a moment Doris' face was lost in the swarm of guests that crowded around the table, and then she reappeared, wearing an anxious and determined look, as though Harry would forget her completely if she lost hold of him for a minute. Still more guests clustered about us, while Harry and Doris took their places behind the table on which the cake was standing. Chee Wee and I were forced to abandon the gilt chairs. "I must see this. Just this one

47

thing I must see," Chee Wee said. I lifted her onto my chair, where she watched the scene, supporting herself with one hand on my shoulder.

The photographer stood within several paces of the table, his camera poised, exhorting the guests to stand back, please, and coaxing Doris to behave as naturally as she would at home in her own parlor. On the photographer's instructions, Harry Tilton plunged into earnest conversation with his bride. Gradually, as Harry talked, brushing his hair into place, gently prodding with two fingers that glossy, black forelock so that it would not bulge too noticeably, he overcame her reticence. In a moment or two Doris was smiling and talking back to him and once she said something to Harry that made him stop a moment with his mouth open and his face puzzled as though he had forgotten the punch line of a joke.

"She said how much she loved him," Chee Wee whispered from behind. "I'll bet you anything that's what it was. And he's standing there like a simp. Why couldn't he tell her something sweet?"

At that moment Harry seized Doris and began to kiss her cheeks and nose and forehead, all glistening in the heat. Making guttural noises he nuzzled her neck and her throat while she writhed from surprise and from the tickling sensation and tried weakly to push him off with her hands against his face.

Amid laughter they cut the cake, Harry standing behind Doris and smiling at the photographer who was popping his flashbulbs again as fast as he could. They cut four slices, their right hands clasping each other on the knife handle. There was applause again and more laughter. Some of the friends and ushers were singing:

> The bride cuts the cake,
> The bride cuts the cake,
> Heigh-ho the fiddley-o,
> The bride cuts the cake.

A waiter and waitress relieved them and began to cut the cake rapidly. Mrs. Burke was the first to receive a plate. She made a great to-do, impulsively kissing the bride and groom on both cheeks and pressing their hands in hers. "I'll be running along now," we heard Mrs. Burke say. "And I mean to wish you all the happiness. And if you need anyone to help with the new apartment, you can always call me at my sister's."

"Mrs. Burke," Doris said. "Nanny." And she rested her head against Harry's shoulder, while he looked down at her with an uncertain expression and offered the pleated handkerchief from his breast pocket. Doris clutched at Harry's arm and looked up into his eyes with a doting, angelic gaze. She was as nearly beautiful as was possible for her, as nearly the June bride in a magazine advertisement for silverware. Her honest emotion cruelly transmitted itself to Harry. His face took on an awkward and startled expression and in that moment he was paralyzed, until she took the handkerchief and softly blew her nose.

"Cute," Mrs. Burke said, shaking her head and pulling away. "You look like Olivia de Havilland. Cute."

"Hey-o, Piscator," someone called.

"Hail," Harry called back. "Hail. Hey-o."

"Would you mind telling me," I asked Chee Wee, "what the shouting is? Or is that a thing that I shouldn't have to ask about?"

But Chee Wee was off the chair and talking to two of the ushers behind me. People were moving away with plates of cake and the bride was still standing there, blowing her nose.

George Marsh had not been there among the others to watch the wedding cake be cut. I had not seen him on the dance floor and though there must have been more than a hundred people in the ballroom who were not dancing, he was not among them, either. I went out again onto the terrace, which was not crowded now that the younger guests had been drawn inside. This time it was cooler, as the sun had settled on the western exposure of the building. Now the only shadows, on the farthest flagstones by the rail, were of the water tank and the ventilators on the roof and from an adjacent building a hedge that lined a penthouse wall also cast its shadows. It was quieter now on the terrace, with the tug whistles on the river sounding distinctly through the murmuring voices of the guests.

On the edge of the circle, standing three or four feet apart from the rest, I spied Ava Norris. She was listening to a man in a pale linen suit and a navy blue silk shirt. Heavy tortoise-shell spectacles rested precariously on his ears; their ends jutted deep behind to be lost in back of his head where the hair was longest and uncombed. He spoke rapidly, bobbing his head in an intense, im-

49

passioned way, and he fidgeted with a thick gold ring on his right forefinger, but Ava Norris seemed hardly to hear what he was saying. Being a tall woman, taller than he, she could look down at his face now and then and smile, perfunctorily. Ava Norris' gaze took in the entire scene, as she had trained it to, sweeping first to the left and back the other way, the full one hundred and eighty degrees; in one majestic swing she would scan the terrace, yet never fully depart from the conversation.

The moment I saw her I held still. I thought to turn back for the ballroom, but before I could move she had caught me with a turn of her head. She was arching her eyebrows and pursing her lips, so as to say "oh ho." Her companion turned toward me with a frown and adjusted his spectacles.

"Well, Mr. Taylor," Ava Norris called. "Augustus Taylor. As I live and breathe."

She wore light, off-color gloves and a stylized, salmon-colored dress, one that suggested Chee Wee Gibbons' dress and was at the same time more appropriate, more matronly. There was no doubt that this dress had not been duplicated either in New York or in Paris, whence Ava Norris had just returned from one of the frequent business trips that she called her "junkets."

Ava Norris had a reputation for being many things, just as she had many reputations. She was proudest to be known as a lady. Someone had written: "The only real lady in magazines." But she would admit that "lady" was an overworked word; the word she preferred was "gentlewoman." Not many people used it or understood what it meant, and I myself did not understand.

Ava Norris was saying, "Aren't you the cagy dog? I thought I'd never track you down. Look me in the eye, Taylor. And stop ogling my hat. It's nothing very swish."

It was a small, dark hat that sat on the back of her head, too small, I should have thought, for so tall and imposing a woman. It had a veil attached that covered the top of her hair and a part of her forehead. Yet what first struck the eye was the hair beneath, and this was always the case. People meeting Ava Norris for the first time invariably remarked on her hair. Even for those who had known her for years it held a fascination. It was done in a henna rinse, a conspicuous shade, without being an entirely vulgar one, and that afternoon it was arranged in a tight and immaculate upsweep, half-hidden beneath the hat and veil. *Time* Magazine had referred to her as "the russet-headed duenna of the nation's fashion-trenders," an emphatic but misleading tribute not merely in that it failed to define a fashion-trender. For truthfully there was more orange than russet in Ava Norris' hair and perhaps this explained why she was frequently taken, to her annoyance, for a professional actress in retirement.

Ava Norris said, "Aren't you going to say hello?"

"How do you do, Mrs. Norris."

"Well, how do *you* do, Mister Taylor?"

"Ava," I said. "All right. How do you do, Ava?"

"We don't have to be formal, Duck. Not you and I."

There had been just one period, a long time back and before the war, when Ava Norris and I had been formal with one another. But that had been just after we were introduced and it was the only time.

"You can relax, can't you?" Ava Norris asked. "You've always felt relaxed with me. Perhaps a little too much so."

I could only stand there on the terrace and look at her. I didn't think that anything I might say or anything she might say could make it easier.

But:

"I'm glad we're still friends, Ava," I found myself saying. "I was afraid we wouldn't be. You can't tell about these things."

"You never could," she said, smiling. "You never were worth a damn when it came to understanding people." She said this in a quiet voice, as an aside to me, because it was an innuendo and Ava Norris thrived on innuendoes.

"I don't believe you've met Myron Hervey," Ava Norris said, indicating the wavy-haired man she had been talking to. "He's having quite a success. Have you read *The Scourge of Chastity?*"

"I'm afraid not," I said.

"Really no reason he should have," Myron Hervey said obligingly.

"We've been discussing Myron's novelette," Ava Norris said. "It's about a ballerina, and all sorts of men fall in love with her. In the end she is about to marry the one she loves most, when she discovers that he is a panderer and a sodomist. And it's then that she finally decides to become a nun."

"Not a novelette," Myron Hervey said hastily. "A novella. Mine

51

is a thematic kind of thing. I had fun writing it, but of course anything like that is agonizing."

Myron Hervey, who had stood silently by while Ava Norris and I greeted each other, seemed near to bursting at the seams. He spoke, bobbing his head and working the gold ring up and down his forefinger. This was the first time I had met one of *Blythe*'s writers and I could contribute nothing to the conversation. I was glad to listen to him talk as I had no desire to exchange innuendoes with Ava Norris.

"Myron, don't frighten him away," Ava Norris said. She had seen me turn my head to watch a girl come through the French doors onto the terrace. "Myron is such a frantic young man. He loves to talk. But I won't let him scare you off, Gus, not when you haven't even kissed me. Aren't you going to give me a kiss?"

She kissed me on the cheek and I quickly kissed her back. "I didn't know you'd be here, Ava," I said.

"You know Hadley never misses a wedding. Of course I'd be here."

"I had no idea."

"You're so sensitive, darling. You know I'm glad to see you. You know I always like to see clever boys. Let me tell you about Gus Taylor, Myron. He really is a clever boy."

"Now there's a compliment," Myron Hervey said uneasily. "You must have a way with the ladies."

"He does indeed," Ava Norris said. "And that's what's amazing, when you consider that Gus is only a small-town boy. He's just an orphan."

"All right, Ava," I started to say.

"And such a clever young man, too. Gus is a lawyer, Myron, or he will be a lawyer if he passes his bar exams."

"Oh?" Myron Hervey said, wanting to be interested.

"Of course you'll pass them, Duck," Ava Norris said. "If you don't, you can always take them over again. But of course you can't miss, a deserving boy like you. It's been a long, hard struggle, with only your friends to watch over you. Just you and my rich ex-son-in-law-to-be, and my daughter, of course. You're just a rich little poor boy. . . . There's a clever line, Myron—rich little poor boy."

"Sometimes you outdo yourself, Ava. You honestly outdo yourself," Myron Hervey said.

"Gus and I haven't gotten together for a long time," Ava Norris said.

Myron Hervey smirked in my direction. "There are times when Lady Ava likes to play the virago."

"Myron, I resent that remark. And on the strength of it, you can fetch us two highballs. If you see my husband, tell him I'm out here with Gus Taylor, just relaxing. I think Hadley would be interested to hear that. Tell him that this is a great occasion and that I think I'm a little plastered."

Myron Hervey smirked and disappeared with no show of reluctance, leaving me alone with Ava Norris. She smiled, raised her nearly empty glass at me. "Here's how," she said and the talk began. Now we had things to discuss, and she very much doubted that her husband Hadley would disturb us.

Hadley Norris, she said, was the one whom she had been worrying over the past few months. But he was picking up. He was on the wagon and on a diet and she had persuaded him to take up squash again. He had said that it might kill him. He had said that between his gastritis and his blood pressure, he might die on the squash court at any moment. But he hadn't. It had been a perfectly dreadful winter for her husband and that had made the whole business doubly trying for her.

It had been enough for her to deal sensibly with Lila, to chase out after her all the way to California and to make sure that she would stay there. It had been enough doing all she could for George Marsh, though she had had to do it carefully and without compromising her position as Lila's mother. Somebody in one of the families had to handle the thing sensibly and realistically and not as a third-rate emotional orgy. God alone knew why, but she seemed to be the only person in either family who was prepared to meet that challenge. So the whole kit and caboodle had fallen into her lap.

She had thought, she had honestly thought, that George Marsh was going to fall apart last February. Old Marcus Marsh so sick and old, and Baby . . . Baby . . . what was her latest name? ("Ellison," I said. "Mrs. Ellison now." Ava Norris laughed gently. "Ellison. How silly. I thought it was still Seidel.") Ava Norris had gone on record years ago with the opinion, the very obvious opinion but somehow the more momentous for Ava's having voiced it, that Baby

53

was an infantile overperoxided blonde, a potential bottle baby. George Marsh's mother baby-talked and sang "Love for Sale" at cocktail parties; Baby didn't consider George a son at all; it was cozier to think of him as a kid brother, or a beau.

George was not famous as a Rock of Gibraltar. He'd needed support, somewhere to turn—but to a mother like that? No, you had to face things honestly. It was a miracle George Marsh hadn't fallen apart, completely.

She knew she might have done more for George herself. She had wanted to. (You could get exasperated with George, but it was hard to stay that way. He *was* helpless. Lost. Poor duck. You liked him, even though you didn't respect him.) But her hands had been tied in February because her husband, when he learned that the wedding was canceled, had gone to pieces also.

Hadley had stayed in the hospital two weeks this time, and it had done worlds of good. Now he was on the wagon and on a diet and the young doctor had said it would do him worlds of good physically and psychologically if he'd play squash again, three times a week. She would be taking a month's junket soon herself, to Buenos Aires; so he would have all that time to enjoy himself. And when she came back, she supposed Hadley would go on to Ontario where he could fish, in the interior of Ontario. He loved fishing. He loved all things that she took no interest in. But in return he left her alone with her job, didn't try to run her life, or interfere. A woman was lucky to have such a husband—one who let her have a little leeway in this man's world.

"I'm glad Mr. Norris is feeling so well. He looks fine," I said.

I had only to say this, lamely, and her whole tone changed back, the intimacy and the chit-chat forgotten.

"Why thank you. You complacent, considerate thing you. My bright penny . . ." She stopped it there. "What do you hear from my little girl?" she asked.

"Can't we leave her out of it?"

"I haven't seen you since that ghastly day. You never called me up." And here she was able to make a controlled, imperfect smile.

"That's right, Ava. I never did."

"Rich little poor boy. You're quite smug you know."

"Ava, don't give me a bad time."

She held her arms akimbo and drew herself up. She was about

my height this way. The muscles of her cheeks were taut and her breasts swelled large as I had ever seen them under the salmon-colored dress. The lady militant, the girded Amazon, Ava Norris of *Blythe*.

"It's a man's world," she said.

"Sure."

"What are you going to do then? It's time to get down to brass tacks, darling."

"No. No more brass tacks," I said. "It's our own business, we'll work this out by ourselves."

"You've had three months—four months. Do you think this is just a little game? Are you going to marry her or aren't you?"

"Lila won't be back till September," I said. "How can I tell at this point?"

"September. December. What difference does it make?" There was a pause while she eyed me dubiously, like a Goddamned Valkyrie, I thought, who isn't sure if I'm hero enough to get into Valhalla after all.

"Are you planning to marry my Lila or aren't you?"

"You know there are no plans. We're going to find out for ourselves. Ava, if you'd leave us alone—"

"Oh, how I'd like to ruffle just one hair on that complacent head of yours, just one hair." And again she cut herself short. "You can say something, you know. Stop us from having a scene. Why don't you say something bright?"

I could not have said anything, because Myron Hervey was standing behind her. He was holding three highball glasses in his hands and right away he was speaking to her: "Honestly, Ava, Hadley and I aren't much for talking together. Honestly, we don't have much in common. Did you expect us to talk all afternoon?"

"I'll give you a hand," I said, and took two glasses from him, and gave one to Ava Norris. "If you want to, we can talk some other time," I told her. "There's sure to be another time." As quickly as I could I turned and started toward the French doors and into the ballroom.

"You heel," I heard Ava Norris say. "Don't turn your back to me. You complacent heel."

"Darling," Myron Hervey was saying. "It's effective, but you're overdoing it, darling."

In a small clearing just before the ballroom steps a sunburned girl in a sleeveless, backless dress was straightening a boy's necktie. In one hand he held a champagne bottle and with the other her waist. As I got to the steps, he started to dance with her, waltzing her in a circle just in front of me and shaking the bottle upside down to show that it was empty. She dangled her left arm by her side and smiled at him self-consciously as he swung her around the circle, his coattails flying.

"Don't you think we might go inside?" the girl said.

They were blocking my approach to the steps and I had to stand for a moment. Then a hand closed firmly on my arm just above the elbow. That would be Myron Hervey, I thought. He wants me to go back to Ava Norris and smooth things over, but the hell with that noise. I jerked my arm hard and took another step forward, but the grip tightened. I felt a thumb press painfully on the nerve between the biceps and the bone.

"What's the rush, Sport-o?" a voice said, and I turned and saw that it was George Marsh.

Chapter Seven

"I was looking for you," I said. "I wish you'd let go my arm."

"Gibbons told me you came with her," George Marsh said, smiling, and he let it go. "But the question is, are you going home with her, now that Gabriel Pastrami has arrived?"

"Now what do you suppose?" I said.

"I didn't expect to see you here."

"I am, though. In a pretty big way. I just spoke to Old Lady Norris."

"So I noticed," he said. "It looked like quite a show."

"I shouldn't have come here in the first place," I told him. "It was a crazy thing to do."

"I hope you didn't say anything," George Marsh said. "You didn't make a fool of yourself?"

"I didn't have a chance to say anything."

George was puzzled, biting his lip, in that way he had when he was sure he was not being told the truth. His hair was trimmed closer and left his features more prominent than I remembered them. The black eyebrows stood out more heavily, accentuating the furrow between and the wrinkles on the forehead. He was tanned, and he had lost weight, but still he did not look well. The pupils of his eyes were dilated wide, the black almost obscuring the brown. His cheeks were hollow and the crescents beneath his eyes were darker and heavier. There was a tension that reflected from him generally. Part of it was in the way he held himself; the great broad shoulders tightly fettered by the cutaway that he had never had retailored because it had belonged to his father. Some more of it had always been there and it could be measured, that other part of his tension, as he stood there, towering apologetically above everyone on the terrace. There was a latent grandeur to him, but it was more difficult to appreciate now than usually. His necktie was

57

spotted and unstraightened and he wore a wing collar that dug too tightly into his neck. Something about him, some general appearance, was clumsy and farcical and not at all happy.

"I didn't tell you I've got a new car," George Marsh said. "I bought a Fleetwood and don't say it's repulsive, because it isn't. It's black and not so big. It's not such a bad car."

"Sooner or later it would have to be a Fleetwood," I told him. "Do you remember the first car? The Packard we drove to Florida? I guess this is your fourth new car."

"It's only the fourth," he said.

He had also gotten an air-conditioning unit and a television set for the apartment. Life was more comfortable up there now, what with these improvements, but it was lonely. He was tired, he told me, of going to the track and to Yankee Stadium and Ebbets Field by himself. Everyone was away. Either they were in Europe or they had gone West or to the seashore for the summer.

Why hadn't he gone to Europe? I asked. That's what he had planned.—It wouldn't have proved anything, he said. There wouldn't have been anyone over there that he couldn't see in New York in the winter. He hadn't wanted to go to Cannes again and not particularly to Antibes or Austria or to Lake Como and stay again at the Villa d'Este. Of course he had missed the Dublin Horse Show and the Fiesta at Pamplona. But those could wait for another year, a better year when things would be set and not such a rat race. Things should be set in another year, he said, providing we weren't all back in the Army by then, having our asses shot off. ("Yes, leave us not be gloomy. Andy Gromyko, flying saucers, Eniwetok, worlds in collision. What the hell?") He tried to keep his mind off things, off Lila too. He'd been to Nassau. He'd been to the Kentucky Derby and to the Middleburg Hunt and to the ball games and out to Belmont once or twice, but on the whole he had done absolutely nothing. "At least you went out and did something," he said. "Me? I'm tired of me. What's it like at Gracie Square?"

I told him it wasn't Gracie Square, but a block on East End Avenue and Eighty-ninth Street. I explained it was one of those blocks that Mr. Vincent Astor owned, but that it was cheap and very nice and that from the upper stories you could see the Mayor's house and hear the boats whistling on the river. "They say Mr.

Astor plans to tear down the whole block as soon as he gets a chance. He'd like to build something big there."

"When he tears it down, you'd better come back to us," George said. "We've kept the home fires burning, Manuelo and I." He went on, pretty embarrassingly, to imitate Manuelo. " 'Mr. Taylor no stay away long. Mr. Taylor forget everything and he'll come back right away soon.' "

"He's all wet," I said. "You spend too much time listening to Manuelo."

"I'd sooner listen to him by a damn sight. I'd sooner listen to him than to that silver-haired mother of mine."

He fell silent, with the mention of his mother.

"George, do I owe you money?"

"You don't owe me a nickel."

"Tilton is saying I owe you three hundred dollars."

"He's kidding."

"All the same maybe I do owe you."

"Jesus," George said. "Do we always have to go into this?"

We had been standing by the terrace steps with everyone milling around us, the boy with the champagne bottle still waltzing the sunburned girl, who was pleading to be taken inside. It had been a purposeless conversation in which neither of us had dared to say what he was really thinking. George had his hands in his pockets and was bending stiffly from the waist as though he were addressing the flagstones. He pulled up abruptly and gripped my arm again in a way that gave pain in the muscle just above my elbow.

We walked up the steps into the ballroom, and paused for a moment by the piano. Someone had opened the piano keyboard. With no particular thought in mind, I ran a finger down the keys. It made a crashing sound, much louder than I had intended. All the room, all the voices were suddenly still.

"Jesus," George Marsh gasped.

"What's wrong?"

"Look. They're all lined up. Jesus."

"Lined up for what?"

"The Serenade."

"How's that again?"

"Harry was a Chanticleer. Oh Jesus, it's no joke. They always sing at weddings. Let's get out of here. Jesus-pesus."

But at this moment Harry Tilton's voice broke in, carrying across the room to us with hearty assurance. "Think nothing of it, Gus-bo. It's merely the Serenade. The boys here were about to strike the note."

George called to him. "We're sorry, Harry. We didn't see."

We hadn't seen that the ballroom was cleared, that guests were lined along the walls, or that a group of nearly twenty, half of them ushers, had formed before the flower arrangement on the wall, where the receiving line had been only forty-five minutes before. Their leader stood before them, a long, spindly figure, with steel-rimmed glasses, gray flannels, an ostrich neck with a bulging Adam's apple. In his mouth he held a pitch pipe that he had been about to sound before I had struck the keyboard. He was staring at us, his eyes wide and bewildered. The bridal couple were enthroned on a settee. Doris was smiling rapturously and Harry sat regally beside her, his hair freshly slicked and combed. Everyone was hushed, awaiting something, and the awful sound I'd made continued vibrating on every eardrum in the room. It was too late to laugh or make a light remark or duck back again onto the terrace. There was nothing to do but stand there and make the best of the blunder like two abashed children in a Booth Tarkington novel.

Harry Tilton was on his feet, the master of ceremonies. He pointed his finger at me and cocked his thumb.

"Thank you, Gus Taylor," Harry Tilton spaced his words and enunciated carefully to show he was in complete control of the situation. Already there were audible giggles from several of the girls. "Laughing Gus Taylor, the clown of the keyboard. Put that pipe away, Howie. Gus wants to play something for the troops."

There was more laughter and scattered applause. George Marsh whispered hoarsely, "Play something. Don't make it any worse than it is."

"I've never heard the Serenade," I called. "Why don't I pitch them in myself?"

"Okay. You do that little thing."

I sat on the piano bench and ran my fingers over the keys.

"Just be perfectly pleasant," George Marsh was saying in my ear.

"High C," Harry called. "We usually pitch it there. Put the pipe away, Howie."

"Just play the note," George Marsh was saying. "He'll forget about the rest."

I hit the note twice and sustained it with the pedal, as Howie raised his arms. The singing began.

"Thank God," George Marsh said. "That's using your head. Now don't move. Don't do anything."

The Serenade was a medley that I had heard before often enough, wherever there had been a New Haven atmosphere:

> They call her Lady Louisville Lou—
> Oh, what that vampin' baby can do.
> She's the most heart-breakin'est,
> Shimmy-shakin'est,
> That the world ever knew.

There followed another, the most familiar, which described how a woman goes from man to man as a silver dollar goes from hand to hand. These were easy songs, adaptable, to be sung either melancholily or boisterously, as the party mood required. They were five in all. The chorus sang them lingeringly but with precision and in such a way that it was clear to all that there was something sacrosanct about their music. From the way the singers placed arms on each other's shoulders it was apparent that they were all great friends, good-naturedly indulging in a little postgraduate bonhommie. In spots, they harmonized egregiously, but the over-all effect was nice. There were several solos, one of them was delivered in a tremulous tenor by the thin dark usher I had overheard talking on the terrace.

George Marsh was leaning on the piano top. "Do you see, it isn't so bad? As long as you didn't start anything with Harry. They're almost finished now."

"How well they sing together," I said. "What clean-limbed young fellows they are. This is the first breathing spell I've had all afternoon."

"If you really want a breathing spell," George Marsh said, "wait until this song is over and then take a look behind you, over by the door. There's Fuzzy Eaton. He was asking for you."

"Where's Fuzzy?"

"He's right over there with a drink in his fist," George said. "Now take it easy. They haven't finished this song."

Fuzzy Eaton. The first image that came to mind was Fuzzy at a dance at the Longwood Cricket Club in Brookline. He had contrived to steal the tablecloth from beneath the punch bowl and a cushion from the settee in the ladies' room, and when the party was over and we had come to get our coats, we had found Fuzzy bedded down on the coatroom floor. It had been impossible to arouse him. A charwoman had wakened him at ten, the story went, and Fuzzy cheerfully removed himself to the men's locker room. He had had time to shave and shower and put the whisk broom to his dinner jacket before returning to his family's house in Chestnut Hill to greet his parents on their return from church.

That had been during college and just after the war, but one was constantly hearing stories about Fuzzy Eaton. The course of his development was charted by a series of breezy, collegiate peccadilloes and roguish encounters with a cast of stock characters. Invariably it was Eaton versus the father of a debutante, Eaton versus the Dean's Office, the headwaiter at the Ritz Bar, the Commissioner of Motor Vehicles. Any of these events made a story suitable for regaling one's friends, all of whom were bound to ask after Fuzzy Eaton sooner or later. This was a form of general entertainment, since everyone was fond of Fuzzy Eaton. "A drinker of note," the saying was.

However difficult to accept, the facts were that Fuzzy Eaton had flown sixty-three missions as a pilot of a B-17, that he had been shot down over southern Germany and that, though he had been officially listed as killed in action and so had been widely mourned throughout Chestnut Hill and Brookline, he had escaped from a Stalag Luft north of Weisbaden to American lines at the time of the Rhine crossings. In May of 1945 Fuzzy returned to Cambridge, a RAMP, the first of the bona fide veterans. He returned in such a storm of glory that the Dean's Office, which had seen fit to expel him four years previously, permitted Walter Baxter Eaton to re-matriculate at Harvard College as a dropped freshman.

This was an impressive array of feats. The reluctance of strangers to accept them was nonetheless understandable. Fuzzy Eaton had begun to bald. He was markedly casual about his dress and personal appearance. Furthermore, he had perfected a way of speaking that was offensive to many, combining the colloquialisms of Mt. Auburn Street with an accent that was classically Grotonian. It was difficult for someone who had not known Fuzzy a considerable while to believe that he had achieved anything as a warrior or that he would achieve anything as a civilian. Yet Fuzzy had friends and they stuck to him.

"He was asking after you," George said again. "I know he wants to see you. Hey, don't wave until they've finished the Serenade."

A moment later they had finished singing. There was applause and whistling and again:

"Hail, Praeceps!"

"Hail, Piscator!"

Fuzzy paused to unload two tall drinks from a passing tray and headed toward us, carrying his own drink in one hand and the two fresh ones in the other, as though they were ice cream cones.

"Is that Santa Claus without his beard? Or is it Jimmy Savo?" George Marsh smiled, for this was an old joke of his.

Fuzzy did have a round and puckish face like Jimmy Savo. He was squat and jocular enough to pass as a premature Santa Claus. Today he wore a plaid bow tie and was perspiring through a rumpled pink shirt.

"Hello, Gub. Gopher." Fuzzy never forgot nicknames. "I brought you both some sauce." He sat down on the piano bench, between me and George Marsh.

"You're fat. You've got a hell of a sunburn," George Marsh said.

It was as if we were sitting around the room at Adams House, swapping the old fancy insults, calling one another by the obsolete nicknames. Spiritually Fuzzy had never left Cambridge. His was the narrow, complacent, unenergetic attitude for which a Harvard man is criticized. It was not aggressive, or positive; it had nothing to do with the disquieting intangible known as campus spirit. It was particularly dangerous when Yale men were at hand, since Fuzzy Eaton felt that all Yale men were fundamentally hypocrites, and he would go to any length to antagonize them. This was why Fuzzy Eaton set about antagonizing the members of the song group just now dispersing throughout the ballroom.

"Blue boys. Blue boys. True-blue blue boys," Fuzzy was singing softly to himself. But as two members of the chorus passed directly in front of us, he lost his detachment and burst into full voice, "Abullashit—abullashit—a bow-wow-wow. EEEEli Yayul!"

The two singers glowered at us, then walked away.

63

"I'm not sticking around for this," George said. He went off, with an apprehensive frown.

"I wish you'd tell me what this Serenade is all about." I meant it as a leading question, one that should have distracted him. "Is it an institution? Or is it just an old Yale ritual?"

Fuzzy was delighted for the opportunity I had unwittingly afforded him. "Thah's a ticket," he seemed to be saying, in that exaggerated accent. "Hah's a fine old ritual idea. A songfest type of thing, whenever a boy gets married. Lots of fine old songs, fine and glorious old true-blue songs always sung by the Chanticleers at the time of the ceremony. And this afternoon, Gubber, we happen to be surrounded by Chanticleers. Isn't that nifty? Don't you wish you were a Chanticleer?"

"I thought it was a kind of rooster," I said.

"I'll let you in on a little secret, Gubber, I'll give you a little indication. This is such a happy occasion, and there are so many Chanticleers around, I think I might tie one on. What would you say to that, Gubber? We can't all be Chanticleers, or Whiffenpoofs or O's and B's."

"What about O's and B's?" I said. "I wish you'd talk so I could understand you."

"Orpheus and Bacchus. 'We supply the Orpheus and you supply the Bacchus.' That's their little motto. Cute? Cute as a gnat's ear. And in great demand, I'm told, at fashionable gatherings both in New Haven and elsewhere. I wish I could be a gentleman songster. I wish I could have been a Whiffenpoof, or a Whif, as they're affectionately called. Or a Poof."

Fuzzy was capable of pitching his voice to any direction, at any range. He climbed up on the piano bench and stood there, gesticulating at the Chanticleers.

"Hail, Praeceps! Hail, Piscator! Hail! *Ave atque vale. In hoc signo vinces.* And *semper fidelis.* Hail!"

"For the love of God, will you sit down?"

"Just a few old Latin mottoes, Gubber," Fuzzy said, smiling down at me, manorially raising his glass. "You cut no ice with the Chanticleers if you don't know the password. Stick with me, Gubber, and you'll learn about the Elis. Take the Bonesmen. Any loyal member of Skull and Bones is honor bound to leave the room if ever that name is mentioned."

His hands forming a megaphone to his mouth, he began to chant in the manner of an auctioneer. "Oh, Skull and Bones. Hey! Oh, Skull and BO-HONES! Hey, SKULL AND BO-HONES!"

He was impervious to protest and beyond restraint, and I was helpless.

"Not one of the bastards moved an inch. I always said they were fakers. I thought there'd be at least a few loyal Bonesmen at Tilton's wedding." Fuzzy stepped from the bench at last. "I suppose I've behaved atrociously," he conceded. "I don't imagine Tilton was amused."

"Look, I don't know you," I said. "I've never seen you before in my life."

"Let's not take it so strenuously, Gubber. We're all having a bang-up time, just being boys and girls together."

"By the time you count to ten," I told him carefully, "someone is going to clout you. And I'm not going to raise a finger, because I don't know you. I've never seen you before in my life."

Two ushers did come over, either just then or a moment later, to suggest that this was as good a time as any for Eaton to go home. It appeared for the moment that Fuzzy might be ready to apologize, but he was not. Rather, he extemporized on "the joyousness of the occasion" and, by way of parenthesis, assured them of his deep feeling for New Haven tradition.

"Funny Boy," one usher said.

"Let's go, Laugh Riot," said the other.

They laid hold of Fuzzy's arms roughly and began to pull.

"I can take care of him," I said, shoving.

"You butt out of this."

"Don't. Say, don't!" A shrill voice interrupted. "Mrs. Slater says to leave him alone. She doesn't want any trouble." This was Howie, the angular director of the Chanticleers, come to avert disaster. "The bride and groom have gone to dress," he said, a restraining hand on the chest of each usher. "All members of the wedding party wanted upstairs. On the double!"

Fuzzy Eaton brushed the sleeves of his jacket, as with an injured look he watched his assailants depart.

"That Mrs. Slater sounds like a high-type lady," he said to me ruefully. "To think of ejecting me—at the height of the festivities."

"The festivities are about over," I told him. "Let's you and me look for some coffee."

"I suppose I was atrocious?"

"Atrocious."

Fuzzy beamed. "Don't let it get you down, Gubber. Every day's going to be Sunday by and by."

I had outgrown him, I supposed, but it was nice to see him again, happily carrying on his futile battle against the status quo—Don Quixote and the windmills. Perhaps he was an ass, but he was the most honest ass I knew. Running into him, I was quite confident, had been the one happy event of the afternoon.

Chapter Eight

In a bedroom on the second floor the bride and her eight attendants would have foregathered by now. I pictured a sisterly nucleus, fragile and more demure than similar gatherings at the Water Club during the June wedding season. If the young ladies assembled this afternoon, clutching bouquets and rustling tulle, were timider than most, it was because they were closest friends of Doris Slater and every one from Hartford, Connecticut, come to New York for a spree. In contrast to other, less self-conscious young women who went there to help the bride dress, these girls would be soberly impressed by the surroundings, which were not to be duplicated in Hartford. But what they lacked in sophistication they compensated for, quietly, with earnestness and dedication.

I pictured them at first perching upon the beds in silent communion and waiting for the brightest to speak up and relieve the uneasiness. After a lapse of time one of them would begin the first faint sally toward informality, a joke perhaps, stirring the first tremulous giggle. A pause again, and more dainty rustling, and then, ever so hesitantly, the questions and the polite replies. What had been Harry's wedding gift? Did they know where they would be living? Had Harry been promoted again at the ad agency? When would they be coming back to Hartford? A placid stream of inquiries slowly welling the atmosphere to a prim, not wholly positive gaiety. A maid would enter with champagne and a tray of glasses and sandwiches would be sampled and someone might offer around a box of chocolate peppermints.

I pictured Doris at the dressing table, applying in frightened dabs the unfamiliar perfume that Harry had beseeched her to wear. (Harry had never cared for sulphur soap.) The bridal gown would hang on a chair beside, forgotten in anticipation of the new costume to be put on at any moment. The "going-away dress," the nightgown, the silk underclothes, the slippers, the fitted toilet case, and all the alluring accouterments of the wedding-night trousseau would be appraised and handled and exclaimed over. Here, for a few uncomfortable moments, an incursion of the less charitable, less vestal instincts of covetousness. But this could not last for long; soon there would be tears and laughter all over again and a good deal of apologetic kissing. The little litany of encouragement and well wishing could begin anew. Thus far my private assumption, doubtless biased, conjured up from hearsay and a passing glimpse of the wholesome misfits who had tended Doris Slater's train.

Meanwhile, three doors down the corridor, in a second bedroom, a contrasting spirit would prevail. I knew it well:

Harry Tilton, his fifteen ushers, and a large number of Chanticleers and other nonorganized admirers would be meeting there, amid the spilling of drinks and the breaking of glassware, to perform the great marital rite. There would be a second repertoire of songs too lusty for inclusion in the Serenade. Toasts would be drunk and glasses smashed in honor of the groom, the bride, the groom, the ushers, the groom, the bridesmaids, the Chanticleers, and again the groom. There would be a toast to the bride's father, who would have made a self-conscious appearance, smiling as well as he was able in the interest of good fellowship. Another toast to the groom. Those recently married would banter with Harry Tilton as he undressed, offering suggestions as to wedding-night procedure, the fallibility of the diaphragm, of all contraceptive devices in general, and there would be elaborate instruction for the handling of a frightened bride, the dangers of selfishness and obstinacy.

Once the groom was in the shower bath, his consorts had the opportunity to play the traditional pranks. Wet bath towels could be snapped against his flesh. The shower curtain could be ripped and torn and the bather deluged with champagne, hair tonic, tooth powder. Discomfort could be further assured by sporadic flushings of the toilet which caused the shower to fluctuate between chill and scalding temperatures. Eventually the groom would be carried, naked, dripping, kicking, to a bed, here to be held on his back while with lipstick, mercurochrome, or shoe polish his body was emblazoned with bold circles, arrows, and inscriptions calculated to embarrass him in the marriage bed. The shouts and bellowing would subside eventually as the consorts turned their attentions toward the evening ahead. The groom would be left to hunt his wallet, airplane tickets, his traveler's checks and whatever other essentials to the honeymoon had been hidden from him. He would undo as best he could the knots into which his shirt and trousers and shoe laces had been tied.

This was the ritual. It was performed by rote, but up to the very end it demanded the energies of every participant. When it was over, it was no longer of interest to anyone.

To the management of the Water Club it was purely an annoyance. It put the dressing room into disuse for several days and entailed the preparation of a statement of damages which the groom's father was obliged to settle by the end of the month. The groom, however, would recall it in the days to come with a special poignance, for it was consummate proof of acceptance by his fellows. The very sadism with which they discharged him from their circle was all the stronger an indication of their esteem. When Harry had finally dressed and left his room to join his bride in the hallway his original identity would be irretrievably lost. Henceforth he would face the problem of reingratiating himself with the tribe on a different basis. An altogether different basis, since now entered upon monogamistic existence he could never again be accepted as the footloose contemporary of old. It was a turning point in the life of Harry Tilton, an irrevocable moment vastly more important than the wedding ceremony had been. He would remember it in many an interlude of solitary reflection as he led out his life with Doris.

While these twin dramas were being acted out upstairs, guests were gradually leaving from below. The musicians had returned to play a few final tunes and Fuzzy and I had had to leave the piano. Perhaps twenty people remained in the ballroom, grouping about the hall entrance so as not to lose sight of the staircase upon which the bride and groom were expected at any moment. Maids and waiters were clearing away the plates and cups and empty glasses. The tea service was being disassembled and the tablecloths folded. There were positively no more drinks, a waiter told us; the only way to get one was to speak to the house manager. So Fuzzy set out in search of the house manager.

69

It was all over but the shouting and somehow I had weathered it all. The thing to do was find Chee Wee.

She was in the hallway, by the coatroom, talking excitedly with Gabriel Paster, her bracelets jingling.

"You're not getting squiffy, are you, Gussy? Why didn't you stop Fuzzy from making an ass of himself? You could have stopped him."

"Boys will be boys," Gabriel Paster remarked. "But hasn't it been a swell party on the whole?"

"Don't ask him," Chee Wee said. "He'll only make some horrid answer. It hasn't been my fault, has it, Gussy, that you haven't had a good time?"

"I had one hell of a time," I said. "I wish I were getting squiffy."

Gabriel Paster smiled at me anxiously, twitching his upper lip and the thin line of black bristles that simulated a mustache. He was smiling at me out of politeness, contorting his face into a shy grimace that resembled one of the talking rodents in a Walt Disney film. He was a man of very little charm, but his livelihood depended on his charming people, though people seldom liked him. George Marsh, for instance, called him Gabriel Pastrami. He looked hunted, too, I thought, and that was because he was a gossip columnist, eternally damned to the dodging of libel actions and threats of physical violence. "It's been such a swell wedding," Gabriel Paster said exploratorily, since he was not sure of me. "I'm enjoying it so much. I met Mrs. Slater and liked her so much."

Chee Wee took my hand, in a way she meant to be playful, girlish and coy. "Don't be surly," she said. "The ordeal's over. You don't even have to buy me dinner. Gabe has invited me to have dinner with him and Myron Hervey and these people who are friends of the Norrises, and they live in California, in La Jolla, and they've been seeing a lot of Lila. They say that she hasn't got much to do out there and that she's always out on the beach. They're very amusing people and we're meeting them at Voisin. You can come too."

"I couldn't afford Voisin."

"I don't think we need worry about that," Gabriel Paster said. "After all it was my invitation."

"Thank you, but I'd better be going home."

"You don't mind my making off with Miss Gibbons?"

"Of course he doesn't mind," Chee Wee said. "And don't you apologize to him either."

"I feel rather awkward," Gabriel Paster said.

"Gussy, if you won't come with us," Chee Wee went on, "you might arrange to do something with George Marsh. I know he's been looking for you."

"I've already seen him," I said. "But maybe we'll catch a drink on the way home."

"Well, good-by, darling. And thank you for bringing me. Have you got the keys to the car?"

Doris appeared at the top of the stairs, wearing a light gabardine suit, her "going-away outfit," and a small red hat fastened at a devilish angle to the side of her head, like a favor at a New Year's Eve party. She held her bride's bouquet before her, as though it were a candlestick too heavy for one trembling hand. The bridesmaids stood at the foot of the stairs, hidden from me by a barrier of anxious spectators. This was the answer to a schoolgirl's promise made in the rosy, uncomplicated past when to catch a bride's bouquet was a guarantee of marriage, as all life had been based on guarantees, in those days when the Water Club was something from a distant and unreckoned world. There was a moment's silence as the bouquet fell, and next the bridesmaids' light cries and laughter. People crowded closer in the hall, some making for the doorway, some shoving energetically toward the stairs to catch a last harried glimpse of the bride and groom.

"It's like the B.M.T. at rush hour," a girl was saying in back of me.

"It's worse," a boy said. "A hundred times worse."

"Whoops!"

"Whoops, madam!"

This was the end of a long afternoon and I wanted to get away as soon as I could.

"Hail, Praeceps!" came the call.

"Hail, Piscator!"

"It's the Chanticleers," the girl behind me said. "They're always using those Latin words at initiations and at weddings. Don't you think it's priceless?"

"Hey, hey, hey," someone called, and a loud roar followed.

Between the people ahead, I had a quick glimpse of George Marsh at the foot of the stairs. He was smiling sheepishly, both fists filled with yellow confetti, and waiting for Harry and Doris Tilton to dash down the stairs, out onto the sidewalk and into a black limousine.

An expectant hush came over the crowd and lasted just long enough for one to hear, like a dying sound of love, the melancholic whistle of a tugboat.

Chapter Nine

At a quarter past seven, while it was not yet dark, George Marsh and Fuzzy Eaton and I hailed a cab at the corner of Fifty-sixth Street and First Avenue and asked to be taken cross town to Park. When we arrived at our destination, George, still wearing his cutaway, paid and tipped the driver. The driver, had he turned to thank the donor of so ample a tip, might have wondered at our retracing our route a half a block north along the west side of Park Avenue and at our turning beneath a green awning into the doorway of a brick building that occupied an entire block front. It was no secret to Fuzzy or to me that we were being taken to the Squash and Quoit Club; and it probably was no secret to the taxi driver since that, after all, was the only building in the vicinity which one was likely to enter in a cutaway. But George Marsh was as embarrassed by his membership in the Squash and Quoit Club as by most other benefits of his inheritance, and he went to ridiculous lengths to conceal them.

We went up to the barroom on the second floor, where George Marsh ordered club sandwiches and mint juleps. We sat in a booth at the north end of that great and nearly abandoned room, beneath the mahogany paneling and the canvas mural that depicted sporting scenes in old Manhattan. Twilight was still visible from the two tall, many-paned windows and we could look out onto Park Avenue where the first cars were switching on their parking lights and where the first lights were beginning to go on in the apartments all along to the east side of the avenue as far as we could see. Inside was the long oak bar. A gentleman with a tired and angry look on his face carried on a slow and muffled conversation with one of the bartenders. Close by at a table two other gentlemen played backgammon, talking quietly and rattling the dice in their hard leather cups. These and the occasional clatter of plates and glasses behind the bar were the only sounds, for it was late on a spring evening when few members used the bar. The wall lamps behind us, burning beneath their parchment shades, cast a yellow glare on our table. A waiter in a white duck uniform brought us our order and for a short time we sat without speaking and drank the mint juleps in their frosted chrome cups and ate the sandwiches and some salted pumpkin seeds out of a cut-glass bowl.

When conversation began, it centered on Fuzzy Eaton's retarded graduation from college, his brief stint in the sales training program at Filene's in Boston, his abortive efforts to enroll in a school of veterinary medicine (one thing Fuzzy loved was animals, dogs and horses, horses and dogs, but not cats—Christ!), his incipient baldness, his failure to impress the bridesmaids. Beads of perspiration coursed from the cropped crests of his hair down his brow and temples. "Hah wahs one of those dollies," he seemed to be saying, "who had me dead to rights. I asked for a dance. She said she didn't know me and she didn't like what she'd heard. She said I had a big bad reputation."

George ordered up another round of mint juleps. He was laughing at anything Fuzzy had to say. The plan was to make a night of it. First we would return with George to Seventy-first Street while he changed his clothes, and we would sit around and have a few fast friendlies; and then head for Fifty-second Street and drop in on the joints and hear the music, cut up a few touches. Later we would pile into a cab and go out to La Guardia Field and wait around until we could get ourselves on a flight for Bangor and taxi it from there to Bah Habbah. In Bah Habbah we could spend the weekend, Fuzzy said, at any number of friendly homes. Everyone would be glad to see us up there and George ordered up another round on the strength of it.

"Don't look at me," I said finally. "You know I can't do it."

"Now, Gubber, don't *you* crap out on us. There's plenty of pianos to be played in all those friendly homes. You've never seen such pianos," Fuzzy said.

George Marsh looked at me, rubbing a big hand over his cheek. "What are you talking about, Sport-o? We'll be coming back Sunday night."

"Sunday night, hell," I said. "I've been on those weekends."

74

"So Gubber is a big boy now," Fuzzy said. "I wouldn't press the point. I wouldn't twist his arm, if he finds us immature." He got up from the table and seemed even sulky for a moment before he smiled. "And now if you'll both excuse me, please, I am going above to take a small shower. It's a warm evening and one should be feeling fresher, looking neater. Maybe when we get to your place, Goph, I can borrow a shirt."

Fuzzy was gone for a full half hour and all this time George Marsh and I spent talking while the street lamps went on up and down the Avenue. It was the last talk I had with George Marsh.

I could never be sure of all that we had said or whether either of us had entirely lost his temper. What I was to remember best was a series of impressions which were imperfect and not all reliable. There was the still unfestive atmosphere of that great empty room and the humidity and the gradual nightfall and the lights going on outdoors, but strongest was the impression of finality. We both must have realized that there was no common ground left us.

If George didn't know this, it was time that I told him. It was time that I thanked him for all that he had done for me and time that I wished him well and took my leave. I wanted him to know that I wished there had been some other way for me to act but that there was no other way.

It was too painful at this juncture to look back. All afternoon I had been looking back and I had found, even in that short space of time, that looking back annoyed me. And the people I had seen this afternoon, the ushers from Southampton and Ava Norris and now, it seemed, even Fuzzy Eaton belonged with George in some enigmatic puppet show. I had met with them in the past, as a stranger on their home territory, where I was at a disadvantage. The best and wisest thing I could do was to meet them on neutral ground, and meet them there as seldom as possible.

I asked him, "How's your mother?"

"She's just fine," George said. "But I wish you'd call her Baby. She could never understand why you stopped calling her by her name."

"I stopped when she married Mr. Ellison," I said. "Someone said he was touchy about those things."

"He's not touchy, and the name is William," George said. "Or Zip. . . . They called him that at Princeton. They call him that at

Kenyon and Eckhardt. Who are you to be so formal?"

"Old Zip," I said.

"Don't laugh. He's my stepfather. He's a big wheel, big man on the Kellogg Account."

"Very affable guy."

"Balls," George said. He seldom used the word. Generally he was fastidious about his language.

"She's happy then?"

"Happy as a clam, she says. She really loves him, I suppose. She keeps house." George sighed. "That silver-haired mother of mine."

"Where is she?"

"They've rented a summer place, at Watch Hill. Zip goes up for long weekends, and Baby keeps house."

"Why not Fishers Island?"

"She never went back there after my old man died. You know better than to ask."

"Have you seen much of her lately?"

"Not too much. Every time, she gets started on Lila . . . and that tees me off. My mother hasn't any use for Lila any more."

"Wasn't that to be expected?" I said, smiling.

Without batting an eyelash, he leaned toward me and said in a low voice, "You damned well better decide about Liles, Sport-o."

He must have known I would be unable to answer him.

"We're pretty much of a closed corporation, you and Liles and I," he went on softly, even apologetically. "We can tell the truth to each other. No grudges. No hard feelings. I should think you'd understand by now."

And he must have known that this nobility, while so desperately honest, was irritating, and that I'd never learned to deal with it. Just once, I thought, would you mind *not* turning the other cheek?

"You think I'm corny?" George said.

"I think you're mighty damn sorry for yourself."

He ordered another mint julep and I refused one. He told me that he'd been drunk the night before, at the bridal dinner; he was sure he had made a fool of himself. He had tried making a speech to the bride and groom, but when he got on his feet he had been drunk as an owl. Now he had no idea of what he might have said; he only wished someone had made him sit down.

"Listen, Sport-o, you should have another julep," he said, when

76

the waiter had cleared the plates away and had brought him another frosted chrome cup. He had had enough to drink today too, I could tell by his eyes where the pupils had dilated wide, giving them a moist dark glaze. He gripped the cup between both hands and pressed with his wrists hard against its sides as though it were a beer can he was trying to crush. "The trouble with you is you're losing your sense of humor. And the trouble with me is I'm losing my nerve. You don't see how funny it could be if I ran into Lila again, and I don't know that I have the guts to."

"Don't try it," I said. "I don't think it would be so funny."

"There's one thing I'd like to ask," George said, scooping some of the salted pumpkin seeds into his big hand and spilling some on the table. "Do you hear from her? Does she write you letters?"

Then he asked how did I think she was, was there any truth to the rumor she was coming East in the fall, or did I think she'd marry some creep and spend the rest of her days in California? I answered all he asked me clearly, trying not to hurt him, thinking carefully of what to say, and without lying. The sum total of my answers was nothing that he had not known before; and this he realized quickly.

"You think I'm a chump?" he asked.

"That's a dumb question," I said.

"*You* don't know what this is like. It's such a fierce, fierce feeling."

"Let's not talk about it," I said.

He scooped up more of the salted pumpkin seeds and began arranging them in orderly circles on the table top.

"How's the export business?" I asked pleasantly.

"What export business? That dumb crazy scheme? I wasn't interested in it anyway."

"That's too bad," I said. "What will you do this summer?"

"Not too much," he said. "Nobody uses the *Excalibur* any more. She's moored off Seawanhaka. Gathering barnacles, or she would be if the Captain didn't look at her every day or so. It's a shame."

"Can't your uncle use her?"

"The old gent can't go outside the house."

"I'm sorry."

"But we could use her," George Marsh said. His face brightened, and this was the last time I'd ever see that hopefulness. He spoke

77

rapidly. "We could be in Bermuda in a week. You could take your vacation."

"I can't take a vacation," I said.

"Fuzzy could come. We'll have a hell of a time."

"I told you—"

"It will be like the old days. Please," George said.

"No."

"Why? If you could—"

"Shut up!"

"What's the matter?"

"Will you ever stop groveling? What do I have to do to make you mad? You ought to hate my guts."

I could remember beyond that only the last fragments of the conversation, for the flow had stopped right there. I had the feeling that everything we said was said for good and all, that there was no conceivable chance of our going over it again.

"I'm sorry about all these things that have happened," I remembered saying. "But there's nothing you or I can do about any of them. It wasn't your fault about Lila or about any of the things that have happened. You've had a hard time, and if you want you can tell me you had a lousy childhood, the way Chee Wee Gibbons would say it. You can't help who your mother marries, or how often. I'm sorry about your father, but what do you expect to do about him?"

George took some more of the pumpkin seeds and patted them with his fingers on the table into the shape of a square. "There isn't one thing you can tell me that Lila hasn't said already," he said. "Or else her mother has said it."

"Sure," I said, "and it's all true."

"Don't you fret about me. I didn't come here to have you psychoanalyze me or to listen to any of that old crap. Gee." Something about a mild expletive appealed to George Marsh. When he combined it with the coarser language that some situations demanded of him, the mild expletive had a paradoxical and sometimes a farcical effect, as if Lord Fauntleroy had erred and been sent to reform school. "Gee," he said again and added an obscene expression he had learned in the Army.

A fistful of pumpkin seeds scattered crazily over the table.

78

"I appreciate the kind words," George said. "Thanks a lot, pal." He signaled the waiter.

"Do you remember," I found myself asking for no reason, "when you were Crucifer of the choir? You remember the school hymn—'Oh, God and Father of mankind, forgive our foolish ways'?"

"I remember another one they sang in the Army: 'If you've got a buddy, tried and true . . .'"

"I don't need another drink," I said, as the waiter came.

"I'm only ordering for myself," George said to the waiter. "Mr. Taylor will be buying his own drinks from now on."

"I understand I owe you three hundred dollars," I said. "Tilton has been noising it around that I don't pay my debts."

"You don't owe me anything," he said. "And why should it be Tilton all of a sudden? Why pick a fight with everybody? Or have they made this Screw Your Buddy Week?"

"I'll send you the money," I said. "That's one thing that we can clear up."

"You know what you can do with that money," George said.

He set his cup down on the table.

"And now I guess you'll be running along."

I had never seen this cold anger in him, and that gave me to think that I might have accomplished something.

"Good-by," I said.

"Stay loose," he said. "Gee. You're one in a million. Stay loose, Hot Stuff."

Later I remembered that I had turned when I reached the doorway and I had seen George Marsh, one last outpost of empire alone in the Squash and Quoit bar, toss off his mint julep and with one wild sweep of his hand wipe the cut-glass bowl and all the salted pumpkin seeds onto the paneled floor. Times without number I would remember watching that.

Going up my stairs, the three narrow, lint-laden flights to my apartment, I felt my head aching. Twice I lost my balance and fell, first against the iron railing and then on my hands on the carpet when I came to the second-story landing. I was full of Scotch and champagne and mint juleps and angry with myself for not having come home sooner and angry with Chee Wee Gibbons for having brought this on me. I ran up the next two flights as fast as I could, impelled by a deep-rooted collegiate notion that any violent exercise before retiring would send blood to the head and so reduce the likelihood of a hangover.

I turned on the bedroom light, expecting that Mrs. Rowe had been in that afternoon for her weekly housecleaning. But the bed was unmade and my laundry lay by the door where I had left it unwrapped, beside a pile of the last week's newspapers. Some shrunken socks and an old sweater and three wrinkled neckties lay across the bed pillow.

I undressed, hung up my clothes, and went to the bathroom and there took two aspirins and a soda mint from the medicine cabinet. Then by the light of the lamp that shone in the bedroom I made my way through the kitchen to the icebox. A tugboat whistled as it passed Randall's Island and below the Triborough Bridge, a longer and lonelier sound now that I was hearing it in the night. There was a cardboard container of milk in the icebox and three tomatoes wrapped in a cellophane package. I took them both to the kitchen table and sat there on a wooden chair, washing the pills down with the milk and biting into one of the tomatoes that I had sprinkled with salt. The janitor's buzzer rang just then.

"This is me, Mr. Taylor," Mr. Klaus said through the speaking apparatus. "I do hope I'm not disturbing you, but my wife said she thought she heard you coming in."

"Did I make a lot of noise going up those stairs?"

"Of course not, Mr. Taylor. We never have trouble with you. Mrs. Klaus was saying just yesterday what a nice-mannered gentleman you were."

"What's on your mind, Mr. Klaus?"

"There was a special-delivery letter came tonight. I told them to leave it with me for when you came in. Dolores will bring it up. She's just in from the movies. My little girl will bring it up."

"Well, thank you for your trouble, Mr. Klaus."

"Okeydoke, Mr. Taylor."

I went into the living room and lit the lamp by the desk and searched among the papers for my checkbook. It was the middle of the month, but I had just enough in the bank. Or, I would have enough, when I had cashed in my last war bonds. I had never cashed in a bond yet without a sense of humility and regret, and not without faintly uncharitable recollections of my uncle Torbert

Case. I found a pen beneath the papers and wróte my check to the order of George Warwick Marsh III in the amount of three hundred dollars. I had stamped and addressed and sealed the envelope with the check inside by the time little Dolores Klaus knocked on my door and delivered me my letter.

Standing by the desk in the living room, I lit a cigarette and watched out the window the lights of automobiles crossing the Triborough Bridge and the neon display lights that shone from the tops of buildings across the river in Queens. Perhaps I would be better off living in Queens, incognito, where I'd hide from these letters, hide from her—and from the thousand voices calling on me to *decide*.

It was no more than a note, written in pencil on blue notepaper, and Lila had written it hastily and impulsively so that her scrawling, complicated hand was more than usually difficult to read.

Wednesday

Darling, darling,

I know I shouldn't give in to these moods. But they come so often I hardly know what to do about them.

I feel like a woman of the world—which is what I always wanted to be, but now that I am one in a way, I find that it's awful and I don't want to be at all.

I wonder if you are going to Harry's wedding and if you'll see George there. He writes such long letters and they're filled with plans and such impossible things. I mean to write him, but keep putting it off with almost any excuse. He's one of the dearest people in the world and I want him to be happy, but if I was to go on hurting him, I would be even more of a terrible person than I was. Do you think he'll ever stop?

Will you ever call me, Bug? I know it's wrong to ask, but I keep praying that you will. I've got your new telephone number (RE 7–3214). Chee Wee sent it to me. I'd call you, except that you'd say I was being brazen. I want to call you almost every night, and especially tonight. Will you meet me when I get back? Will you still be there, or won't you want to even see me? September seems such a long way off.

I can't bear to think sometimes what I've done to people. It wasn't all my fault, was it? You said it wasn't all. Mummy and Pappy had a lot to do with it, I guess. So did you.

I'm not always blue, but when I am I take long walks down the beach alone and watch the sandpipers. It helps to do things like that and I always feel much better afterward.

Please don't think I'm being hammy, because I'm not really. Miss miss miss you.

Darling, what is going to happen? Will things be different in the fall?

BOOK II

Part One ~ "Haec olim meminisse iuvabit~"

Chapter One

"Consider, Gus, which is the finer quality? Patience or diligence? For myself, I'd hesitate to say."

It was the middle of a late September afternoon, the last afternoon I would spend as a true East Northruper. My Uncle Torbert Case was taking this opportunity to press upon me some extraneous, last-hour bits of counsel. This was a day that he had looked forward to for years; it was that September day in 1936 when I entered Emmanuel Academy as a Fifth Classman.

"In many ways you could say that both qualities were one and the same," my uncle was telling me. "You could say that one is the complement of the other. It's a satisfaction, fellow, when you've lived as long as I have, to one day discover that both these attributes can dwell harmoniously and auspiciously within oneself. . . . Now would you pass me that trowel?"

For the past half hour my uncle had been laying brick at the edge of our front lawn. The sun was not hot that afternoon and a cool wind was blowing toward our house from the direction of Simple River. My uncle had been doing nothing strenuous, but beads of perspiration had formed about his throat and neck, and his yellowish white hair already was tangled and matted about the temples, where he had rubbed dry his moist forearms. He had not bothered to change his clothes or to wear an apron to protect them. Working as he did, there was small chance of his dirtying anything. He wore cotton workman's gloves and a pair of yellow doeskin trousers, patched below each pocket and along the seams, the area most frequently torn.

He had bought the trousers in Bermuda, at Trimingham Brothers', but that had been in some time long ago, while he was still active in the law and could afford expensive vacations. The trousers had been worn and torn and patched many times since, but they remained unmistakably Trimingham doeskin and not shabby. The years had yellowed them to a buttery shade that blended handsomely in the afternoon sun and, with a perverse elegance, to the yellowish tint in my uncle's hair. True, his appearance would have been more arresting had he thought to match the doeskin trousers with something other than a dollar-fifty belt with its scarred chromeplate buckle and a faded and brownish sweat shirt. He was able to accommodate these contrasting elements of costume without apologies or remorse. There was no reason for him to feel self-conscious, because he was busy at being himself, a middle-aged gentleman of small means, a man of background and of cultural attainment, diverting himself for the nonce with a touch of manual labor.

My uncle considered himself solely responsible, both as architect and as artisan, for the construction of the brick wall now not yet totally encompassing our front yard. The lightness of his labor was made lighter still by the co-operation of Mr. Di Sportini, who was at the present moment in back of the garage, mixing mortar. Mr. Di Sportini was a familiar figure about our house, though as Dr. Kew's handy man, employed for the upkeep of the Headmaster's House, he owed first allegiance to Emmanuel. He worked extensively about the Academy's grounds and in September and October was placed in charge of a ten-man leaf-disposal squad. Also, he did odd jobs for faculty families who lived in the village.

He had been made available to us through my uncle's connection with Dr. Kew and with the Emmanuel faculty, a connection which had been strengthened through the years by my uncle's unflagging efforts as arbitrator and middle man in a multitude of jurisdictional disputes which had arisen between the Academy and the Township of East Northrup. Nearly every improvement about our house and garden had been made by Mr. Di Sportini, though my uncle claimed credit for each of them. I looked upon Mr. Di Sportini as perhaps the most important of all the advantages that accrued to our household as a result of my uncle's long-proven devotion to the Academy. "No school could have a stauncher ally, nor any town a more conscientious citizen," Dr. Kew had once written in his semiannual Headmaster's letter to the school's alumni, "than Torbert Case, '04. No one has made a more earnest endeavor to break down unfortunate and outmoded barriers between Town and Gown, which, we fear, have too long been an East Northrup tradition."

Given this sort of encouragement, my uncle felt a title to the services of Mr. Di Sportini as he did to the use of the Academy's tennis courts, its stationery, its gas-driven lawn mower, its library, and to a number of other facilities of which he had been availing himself for almost as long as I could remember.

My Aunt Connie appeared twice on the porch, leaning on the trellis that held the vines of Dutchman's pipe. She called to us across the lawn: "Don't dirty your trousers, Gus. We haven't much time. We honestly must start soon, Torbert, if you're to be changed and fresh for the drive. Do we have gas in the car? Gus has got to be there in time for Evening Prayer."

At the longest it required fifteen minutes to get from our house to Emmanuel, but my aunt had anticipated this drive for so long that it had become an event to her, as important as the Friday trip to Boston to hear Mr. Koussevitzky, whom she revered as "Koussie," conduct the Symphony Orchestra. She had already dressed herself for today's event. There was a touch of bluing in her hair, which she had put up in pins against the back of her head, loosely, so that it would not be taken for a bun. She wore a gray silk dress, printed with tiny white flowers, and a cameo brooch and a cultured pearl necklace. My aunt was not a handsome woman in the way that my uncle was a handsome man. She lacked his veneer; on seeing her for the first time one did not feel as one felt upon seeing him, that this was a figure who had stepped out of a Van Dyck portrait. She was close to my uncle's age, but she looked younger, stronger, and less at odds with life. Though she was not given as he was to philosophizing interminably about any such thing as contentment, she had known contentment all her life. She was a clean, fragrant woman. On the hottest day she seemed to have stepped out of a scented bath.

"Hurry," my aunt called each time she appeared by the Dutchman's pipe. "Oh, Torbert, please hurry. You're covered with perspiration."

And each time he would wave the trowel cheerfully at her. That was precisely what he would not do, he said. Hurry. He had hurried all his life. Turning back to the wall and to the mortarboard that lay beside it, he began again where he had left off.

"To put myself in your place, fellow," he went on, "I'd first seek out a patient person as a friend. Learn patience from him, and you may learn diligence too, if you are lucky. One day you will find yourself building a brick wall. You might say that each of us must build his own brick wall. And we would do well to remember that exterior patterns do not matter, so long as the foundations are deep."

The wall toward which my uncle turned his attentions that afternoon was the end product of a series of setbacks and frustrations that had beset him all summer. Its alleged purpose was to separate our front lawn from the concrete sidewalk which the Board of Selectmen had laid that summer as a public way—to extend the entire length of Elm Street, on its northern side, from the Simple River and directly through the Elm Street residential section as far west as the Congregational Church and the village mall. The brick wall was a project that had lingered in my uncle's mind throughout the summer, while from the porch he had gazed upon dogs and small boys in the act of desecrating the Euonymous hedge that bounded our two and one-half acre property to the south along Elm Street.

At the last town meeting, in the month of March, he had protested vociferously, as an owner of property on Elm Street, against the laying of the concrete walk. He had vigorously resisted the selectmen's resolution. But the angry voice of Torbert Case had rung out before in the Town Hall, and when the issue of the concrete walk had been officially placed on the town warrant, his final outcry was granted the same brief attention that had been granted the previous ones. The moderator had scarcely put the issue to a vote when the ayes thundered through the hall, the heartiest possible endorsement of the cement walk and the sharpest rebuke that Torbert Case had ever suffered in a public place. Never since his retirement from the law, since he had settled in East Northrup, had my uncle been in a position from which there was so little retaliation.

He was frank to say as much to the meeting. He had but two recourses, he concluded in a burst of eloquence that had been quoted widely that summer throughout the town and as far abroad as Worcester and Framingham. He could do one of two things, and he would surely do one of them. Either the board could vote him an appropriation for the purchase of chamber pots which he would place by his hedge to accommodate the natural urges, whether canine or puerile, of all those who would sate themselves upon his Euonymous. Or, failing this, he would have no choice but to uproot the entire hedge, and he would undertake to replace it with the most unsightly brick wall possible, and thereby deprive Elm Street of a handsome hedge, perhaps the most satisfactory horticultural specimen of its kind in western Massachusetts.

We had not believed my uncle would make good his threat and for a time, toward the end of August, he appeared to have forgotten it entirely. This delighted my aunt, who had made me promise never to mention the matter in my uncle's presence. On the evening of Labor Day, however, the bubble burst. It was an especially sultry evening that had come at the end of a sultry day, unrelieved by any cloudburst. The East Northrup Whippets had lost, decisively, the last game of the season to the team from Northrup Center and had dropped to an ignominious fourth place in the Twi-Lite League. Three boys, whom I knew but slightly from the grammar school (I being a seventh grader and they two grades below), had left the game in its late innings to restore their holiday enthusiasms with a swim in Simple River. They had taken with them a dog, a fat, low-slung dog that wheezed and coughed after exercise, and was claimed by its owner as a "spaniel." Of all the pets in East Northrup, it was the least beguiling, but none had a prouder owner.

When their swimming was done, and its aftermath of acrobatics and dare-deviltry executed on the underhanging spans, they headed up Elm Street, walking barefoot on the Tarvia, their wet hair tight against their foreheads. The spaniel loped ahead of them, sniffing intermittently the trunks of the elms, its porous, lavender-hued tongue lolling a bare inch above the ground.

This procession arrived before our house at the precise instant that Mr. Roger Frapp, a bachelor who taught Classical Studies at Emmanuel Academy, turned between the clumps of the hedge and into our gate, arriving for dinner, as was his custom, ten minutes earlier than he had been invited. At that instant my Uncle Torbert was crouched in the vegetable patch beside our house, gathering mint for the iced tea. Aunt Connie was on the front porch, enjoying the sunset and the evening air, and smoking the second cigarette of her daily quota of three. I sat on the porch step, watching her. I had reached the conclusion that I was already a more accomplished smoker than my aunt would ever be, when I heard the gate latch open for Mr. Frapp.

I did not hear it close, as all other sound was obscured by the staccato shriek that Mr. Frapp let out. Aunt Connie leaned forward in her rocker; the cigarette slipped from her fingers. I saw my uncle rise and start toward the gate, where Mr. Frapp stood frozen on one foot, holding his other ankle tightly in one hand and his face contorted in pain.

"He drew blood," I heard Mr. Frapp say. "He bit me."

"Yuh kicked him, did'nya?" A small figure in loose-fitting overalls had stepped belligerently forward to challenge Mr. Frapp in a voice more sharply pitched than his own. "He bit back for fair trade. We all seen ya kick him."

There was a shrill chorus of assent. His allies lined up behind him in resolute defiance of Mr. Frapp. Nor did they break their ranks before my Uncle Torbert. Nor waver as he charged toward them across the lawn.

"Kick again," my uncle shouted. "Kick as hard as you possibly can, Roger. We'll have him impounded. Impounded and chloroformed!"

My uncle piled threat upon threat, with waggling fingers and brandishing arms. He poured out his wrath in waves that broke one by one against the intrepid phalanx beyond the gate.

I wanted no gesture and no word to escape me. Leaning on the porch railing, I watched in fascination. And my aunt, who feared for my impressionability, packed me off upstairs, to fetch iodine and gauze from the medicine cabinet in the bathroom. Reluctantly I obeyed, and when I returned to the porch the despoilers had vanished and their pet with them. Mr. Frapp sat in the rocker, his bitten leg bare to the knee. I found my uncle and my aunt in the parlor, where she was gently disputing the wisdom of his outburst.

As they caught sight of me in the doorway holding the iodine and gauze they withdrew to opposite walls like guilty children and pretended to search the sofas and bookcases for my aunt's misplaced eyeglasses.

"Never mind it, Torbert," my aunt said finally. "They're sure to turn up."

My uncle said, "If you'll excuse us, Con, Gus and I have something to discuss."

"It would be so much better," my aunt said, "not to make it an issue, dearie. If it has to be done, then it has to be done. But it would be much better to do it inconspicuously. . . ."

"There are certain sacrifices," my uncle said, "that must be made for the sake of principle."

Aunt Connie let it go at that. Mr. Frapp was calling from the porch that he had begun to feel a touch of nausea.

I sat in the leather Morris chair, drawing my knees up under my chin and fingering beneath one kneecap the scabbed wound that had been left by a bicycle accident some days before. Uncle Torbert shut the door.

"A moment ago," my uncle said, "I made mention to your aunt of a question of principle. Principle often entails sacrifice. I made that point to your aunt so that you would take note of it. You did take note of it, I am sure."

"I took note," I said. "Thank you."

"You are now twelve or thirteen years old, is that correct?"

"Thirteen in November."

"I wish your father could see you now."

Again I said "Thank you," since I could think of no more appropriate reply. I had no recollection of my father and mother who had been killed in an automobile crash when I was two years old. At times I had doubted whether they had lived at all and I had speculated as to whether my Aunt Connie might have borne me without my uncle's knowledge. When I said so to my aunt, she had been so thoroughly alarmed as to enlist my uncle's powers of dissuasion. He had painedly outlined the facts of life to me and by way of substantiation had produced my birth certificate from some locked drawer. My aunt had uncovered a framed photograph taken of my mother and father while they were on their honeymoon. It showed them waving from the sundeck of the *Mauretania*, two curiously youthful figures in unfamiliar costumes. Both wore smiles so wide as to distort their faces and leave no impression of what either looked like. They did not seem adult to me or capable of parentage but rather like a pair of smiling twins from a story book, neither much older than I. To discuss my parents was a chore of emotional archeology that I loathed.

"Imagine, if you choose, that it is not I, but your own father who

91

is talking to you. I want you to speak with me honestly. Now certain of these town boys are your friends—"

"Ned Sellers is my friend. But those kids were just fifth graders."

"Ned Sellers," my uncle said. "Would Ned have a dog?"

"It was his father's collie bitch that had that litter over the Fourth of July. Mr. Sellers keeps them locked up at the garage."

"Would that be Wendell Sellers' son? I can't place Ned Sellers."

"He's been around," I said. "Lots."

"I wish you'd consider that expression—'been around lots.' When you are at Emmanuel, I hope you will learn to express yourself in some less colloquial way. Let's say that Ned Sellers has been at the house a good many times and that I don't happen to remember him."

"He's been at the house a good many times," I said.

"Perhaps I should remember him," he said, "but I don't believe I do."

"Because you don't like Mr. Sellers."

In East Northrup it was common knowledge, even at my age level, that Mr. Sellers and he were opposed politically, that Mr. Sellers had sponsored the laying of the Elm Street walk.

"Mr. Sellers and I have always respected one another," my uncle said, "whatever our differences."

"You don't like Ned Sellers, either," I said.

"Personal feelings do not enter into questions of principle, but that is neither here nor there. It has nothing to do with the inconsiderate treatment of our property by a band of vandals, some of whom must be known to you."

"I know who they are," I said. "They're fifth graders and Ned wasn't one of them. You're trying to make me say it was Ned's fault."

"Don't be antagonistic. You know your aunt and I were fond of that hedge. We took great pains over it, and we did not want to see it destroyed. . . ."

"Ned Sellers didn't hurt the hedge and the collie hasn't been anywheres near here with her pups. You're trying to blame Ned because it was his father that wanted the cement walk."

My uncle heard me out with a strained equanimity; a faint grimace played about his nose and lips.

"In many ways I am sorry, fellow, that so many associations you have formed in this town will be curtailed if not broken entirely.

92

But also I am glad for the opportunity that Dr. Kew and the Trustees are offering you at Emmanuel."

"I'll still know Ned Sellers," I said. "On vacations and in the summers, won't I be living here?"

"You'll make new friends. There will be other situations, other problems. You'll be caught up in them soon enough. There'll come a time when you will lose interest in our local dilemmas, though you can scarcely appreciate that now."

"I won't ever," I said. "I've always known Ned Sellers."

I sat in my chair and heard him out, crossing and uncrossing my bare legs. My uncle was not capable of expressing himself without first clouding the issue with vagaries. They were his tissues of protection and he spun them about him like a cocoon.

"In the final analysis," my uncle said, here indicating that the last issue had been scrutinized out of existence, "it makes no difference whether the boys responsible were friends of yours or whether they were sons of men who resent my position in this community. It's only a small community and yet as I have often said, what we say and do here is a measure of our self-respect."

"You mean what you said about setting out the chamber pots?"

"That statement," my uncle said, coughing, "was an extreme one. I have since regretted it, although it was meant facetiously." He paused. "I haven't the vaguest inkling of what may or may not be being circulated about the town. Nor do I care. My only concern is that you not be influenced by biased and propagandistic assertions."

"I heard Mr. Sellers talk about the hedge," I told him. "He calls it the Eyesore of Elm Street."

This and other symptoms of ill will had come to my attention during the hot idle afternoons that Ned and I had spent lying in the shade of the East Northrup Garage, Lubritorium and Automotive Appliances (Wendell Sellers, Prop.), listening to Mr. Sellers talk to his trade.

My uncle paused, searching for his thoughts as though they had flown through the open window and were hiding from him out there in the foliage.

"The Eyesore of Elm Street, is it?"

"It was only a joke," I answered nervously.

"Yes, only a joke. Only a local dilemma. What we do and say here, fellow, is a measure of our self-respect."

93

He coughed, looked at me sidelong for a moment, and I knew he was on the verge of a great pronouncement.

"I brought you in here," he began, "to explain the bearing of principle upon what I have resolved to do. I am going to uproot the hedge. I am going to replace it with a brick wall, a construction which will no doubt be ugly, which will no doubt be interpreted as a willful desecration of the handsomest street in the village. However, I can't help that."

"Is it just on account of that old dog that bit Mr. Frapp?"

"You may consider that the straw that broke the back of the camel. Consider it the final turn of the screw. It is not, however, the central issue. You realize that I do not do things out of vengeance. I am known to be a man of my word. When I say publicly, as I did in the last town meeting, that if circumstances compel me to take a step I cannot compromise, I take it. I will not shillyshally, you understand."

"I understand," I said.

"During supper we had best not discuss this before Mr. Frapp and your aunt. But afterward I want you to take your bicycle and pedal down to Mr. Di Sportini. Ask him to be here in the morning at half past eight, no later. I am going to let him help me with the digging."

Next morning he breakfasted early in his gardening clothes and by a quarter past eight he had gathered the garden tools from the cellar, shears, a spade, a hoe, and a light pick. He had laid them out on the lawn and had stood over them, with his hands on his hips, his yellow-white hair freshly combed and his long face turned eastward up Elm Street, the direction from which Mr. Di Sportini would arrive. The early morning sun had cast itself in patches through the elms onto his white shirt and face, and I had watched him hold that Barrymore pose for a long while, as though he were indignant that there was no response from the waking village.

Gradually, like an elongated red anthill, the wall took shape and grew, eating away the best September days. I could clock what time remained before the Academy opened simply by the growth of the wall. It did not matter to my uncle how long the project took; it could take forever, for all my uncle cared.

He did not discuss the details of the project further, either with me or, as best I knew, with my aunt. If there had been any difficulty, I had no idea of it. Yet I was surprised momentarily by something Ned Sellers said to me the morning of the day Emmanuel opened. Ned had been back at the Woodman School for nearly ten days and I had gone over there on my bicycle at recess time to say good-by to him and the others.

"How's your uncle paying for that wall?" Ned asked me.

"He's just paying for it, I guess."

"My father says a wall like that costs money. If it's any kind of a wall at all, it comes to around six hundred dollars, my father says." Ned put his hands in his pockets and made a clicking sound with his tongue. "I suppose your uncle gets all the bricks and stuff free from the Academy? Well, who pays Di Sportini? My father says Di Sportini don't work that way for his health."

"He's paying for the material," I said. "He's taking care of Mr. Di Sportini."

"Your uncle's no rich man. He's not near so rich as he lets on to be."

"You don't have to tell me about my own uncle," I said.

"It don't matter," Ned said. "Have a good time for yourself at the Academy, and keep your nose clean. There's where you'll meet the rich boys."

By then the others had closed in around me, full of questions and suggestions. The word had got round in the summer about my winning the Meeker Scholarship. The Meeker Fund was available every year to the most deserving boy from the township. It guaranteed six years' tuition at the Academy plus limited expenses. In the fifteen years of its existence, only two other boys had taken advantage of it and it was no surprise that I had won the scholarship, as my uncle was so bugged on the Academy and my uncle, as anyone knew, was the Administrator of the Meeker Fund.

Nonetheless, my schoolmates could not suppress a deep inquisitiveness as to my future. They thought the Meeker Fund a gilt-edged passport from their own environment to the alien realm of the Academy, and, subsequently, to some outer sphere that bore the label, High Society. Would I be allowed to see them again, or visit with their families? Would I be allowed back inside the Congregational Church? Would I be allowed to play them in football or baseball? Would I be expelled if I were caught fighting? Was it

95

true that I would have to change my clothes three times a day? That I would get fifty dollars a week allowance? I answered what questions I was able, but my information had a deflating effect. In their eyes I saw the admiration of me and the curiosity receding.

But they had caused me to forget Ned's questions. My uncle's brick wall and the matter of his solvency were furthest from my mind that day.

It was four o'clock, Aunt Connie called to us, this time from the front bedroom window upstairs. Four o'clock and my uncle would have to change his clothes. There was no time to lose, she called, and my uncle perfectly well knew that we had less than two hours before Evening Prayer.

"I'd better go up and help her close the trunk," I said.

If I had made no move, my uncle would have made none either. He would have held forth till sundown, explaining the selection of friends, the rewards of industry, the price of cowardice.

Uncle Torbert said, "Very well," smiled, and stood up himself, ready to forget the trowel and the mortarboard. He removed his work gloves and searched his pockets for his watch, the gold chain that had belonged to his father and that he had promised to leave me in his will. "It's getting on," he said. "Well, we must get your aunt organized and ready for Evening Prayer."

He laughed slightly at his own joke, but I sensed that I had disappointed him by not having been properly attentive to what he had been telling me. He inspected the fresh blue shirt and the new gray flannel trousers I had put on only an hour before. "Don't forget your jacket, that bright blue jacket your aunt bought you. I wish there'd been time to get your hair cut. I'd like you to go up there with a proper military haircut. Do you have a proper necktie?"

"It's on my suitcase in the hall," I told him. "I think you'd better tie it for me, though."

"You should know how to do that yourself. You'll be tying a lot of neckties from now on."

"I guess I will," I said, taking pains to say it cheerfully. For the unsureness and the fright at my going, that all day I had held as a knot in my stomach, had begun to spread.

96

Chapter Two

Not quite a mile from the firehouse in the center of the village lay the buildings and grounds of Emmanuel. They covered closely four hundred acres and included meadows, playing fields, Packard's Pond, and the woods surrounding, the largest single landholding in the district. The buildings and dormitories occupied the most prominent of these acres, along a wide rising expanse that was known among the old inhabitants as Birch's Rise and the highest altitude in that otherwise flat terrain. Seen from the firehouse, they cut against the northern horizon and formed an incongruous, immodest backdrop to the village itself. Excepting the Wythe Gymnasium, every one of them was visible from the cement apron before the firehouse doors. The tallest trees, the hemlocks, elms, and willows, older and more expensively groomed than any trees in the township, did not obscure the Academy's complicated silhouette. The only imperfections in the firehouse view were, to the west, the spire of the Congregational Church, which seemed to cleave the yellow clapboards of Headmaster's House and, eastward, where the second stories of the Woodman School and the East Northrup Public Library had from this perspective an effacing effect upon the neat white-over-brick Georgian pattern to which all but two of the Academy's buildings conformed.

The ascent from the village to the buildings themselves was made by the winding macadam drive which passed at a gentle climb through a series of carefully leveled lawns and playing fields, and between the tallest, most ornamental of the trees until, on a green plateau on top of the rise, it forked to the right to form a wide oval where cars were parked. The dormitories, the classrooms, the dining hall, the laboratories, the chapel, and the infirmary were within short walking distance of one another and of the oval, which had been laid to accommodate them. Though all but the Headmaster's

House and the chapel were of brick with white cupolas, white porticoes and wooden steps with white railings, they lost much of the energetically standardized appearance so evident from a distance. Despite the firm intent of the trustees, alumni, and two Boston architectural firms, it had not been possible to infuse into the newer buildings the same quality of venerable Anglicism or the antiquarian atmosphere the older buildings had.

My knowledge of Emmanuel, her history and tradition, was limited to the definitive chronicle of the Academy, the chronicle which enjoyed the endorsement of the Right Reverend Emmet Cavender Wash, Chairman of the Board of Trustees. It had been prepared in his second year of residence by the newest headmaster, Matthew Kew, A.B., Bowdoin College, A.M., Ph.D., University of Pennsylvania. This volume occupied a prominent shelf in my uncle's study, and understandably so, since in its preparation Dr. Kew had enlisted the talents of Torbert Case, '04, long a professional alumnus, friend of the school, and—I was not to appreciate this for many years—an untiring aspirant to one of the very occasional vacancies on the Board of Trustees. My uncle amused himself by dabbling in belles lettres. He was an occasional contributor to the *Atlantic Monthly* and to noncommercial publications, notably that of the Society for the Preservation of New England Antiquities. Uncle Torbert had indeed laid claim to the actual writing of *Emmanuel: The Birth and Growth of a Private School*. Those who knew my uncle and were familiar with the prosy authority of his pen did not dispute him. In Chapter 1, for example, the account of the discovery of Birch's Rise by the Founder, a widowed Boston merchant of Scottish birth who had migrated to Worcester County in 1820:

Bidding a reluctant "adieu" to the marts of trade, Josiah Birch looked forward to the comparatively idle life of a scholar and country gentleman. Writing "finis" to the concluding episode of a career that has drawn respect (dare we say envy?) in the annals of maritime New England enterprise, it was his intent to live out his days in some pastoral community, surrounded by his sons and by the books he loved. Looking westward, his admiration was captured by the then small but already industrially forward-looking community of which Worcester is the center. Some fourteen miles to the south of that budding city, in a township called Northrup, there lay a proud crest of ground and some four hundred acres surrounding. From its summit Josiah Birch surveyed such countryside as he had not imagined. . . . Not since he had stood as a boy on the purple heathered fields near Inverness had Josiah Birch as deeply sensed the unfettered wonder of Nature, or felt himself so purged of the besetting cares of commerce and metropolitan life . . .

And yet the Founder had not remained purged for long of worldly cares; no sooner had he built his home on Birch's Rise than he encountered disaster. The chronicle goes on:

It will be remembered that in the second and third decades of the nineteenth century many of New England's industrial benefactors were attracted to the then undeveloped state of Maine. Thither also Josiah Birch. It was as a true progressive that Josiah Birch invested his savings in the region of Augusta, in certain land grants known as the "Maine Townships." . . .

The chronicle did not brazenly state so, but it was easily deduced from ensuing paragraphs that the Founder had met his financial Waterloo in Maine; and hence it was clear even to me when I reread this account some years afterward that the Founding had been motivated less by altruism than by desperation. The Founder, a graduate of Edinburgh, and scarcely blind to the cash rewards of piety, undertook to educate his sons and, at a fee, the sons of prosperous neighboring farmers into a fierce barrel-thumping form of godliness. He scoffed at the suggestions of mercy, absolution, and other Romish mollycoddlings of the New Testament and reveled in the terrors of the old Jehovah, requiring his pupils to memorize whole chapters from the books of Daniel. This explains why Emmanuel Academy—an "academy" in name only—is the only church school in New England which bears an Old Testament name.

The Founder taught his classes in a row of converted box stalls in the stable behind Headmaster's House. (The brick building which stands on that site is known as "Old Stables" to this day.) When a group of students petitioned for a stove to heat them from the winter chill in the hayloft which served as a dormitory, the Founder had dismissed them with a Latin phrase. "*Haec olim meminisse iuvabit*—One day even these tribulations will be a joy to remember. I would commend each of you those words of Aeneas who thus addressed his men in time of great peril and hardship." Thus spake the Founder, and hence the Academy motto which has been Gothically reproduced ever since wherever the Academy crest is shown.

Emmanuel declined to a state of desuetude after the Founder's death and so had remained until the arrival of young Edgar Trimble in 1893. To continue from the chronicle:

99

The resuscitation of the Academy in an era when the stern concept of the British public school was at its greatest vogue, when Spartan ideals and militant piety took root in a prevailing atmosphere of pelf and mammon, was a mighty challenge to one who was a graduate of the Harvard Divinity School, ordained in the Protestant Episcopal Church, and an apprentice of the Reverend Endicott Peabody of Groton.

In 1893 the chapel was completed, an imposing graystone building of neo-Gothic lines. For thirty-nine years the Academy prospered. Its enrollment grew from a few score castoffs unacceptable to the Rector Peabody to three hundred, the maximum number presently allowed by the trustees. Endowments skyrocketed, scholarship money poured in, and serious attention was given to the selection of a faculty. All the fine new buildings were built, each faithful to the spanking white-paint brick Georgian pattern. Dr. Trimble was beloved of the alumni, who named him, after Dr. Peabody, "the Little Rector."

When, upon his reaching seventy, the trustees voted the Little Rector his fifth Sabbatical leave, they must have forgotten the evangelical fervor of his young manhood, for they were smitten dumb on Dr. Trimble's return to learn that he had spent six months at an island retreat on Lake Michigan and had joined the Oxford Movement. Bishop Wash searched nearly a year before finding a suitable replacement.

The replacement was of course Dr. Kew, an unfaltering Episcopalian who pledged himself to the preservation of the traditions of the old Academy, about which alumni could read at the end of *Emmanuel: The Birth and Growth of a Private School:*

What has survived are not merely the niceties of the Founder's religious convictions, nor simply his vast contribution to the educational cause, but the respect for industry, the reverence for duty, the pursuit of truth, and the regard for individual integrity. Puritan qualities all. All have survived in the fullest measure at Emmanuel through the change and turmoil of more than a hundred years.

Uncle Torbert was very proud of that concluding paragraph.

I sat in the back seat of the car, resting one arm upon the black suitcase my uncle had lent me. Tomorrow Mr. Di Sportini would deliver my trunk. The breeze from the open window blew to me the scent of lily of the valley which my aunt was wearing just for the

100

afternoon, because it was a proper occasion for fragrance and fresh clothes.

"I'd take it out of second gear, Con," my uncle said, when we were heading up Elm Street. "There's no need to strain the differential."

He was as concerned for the car as she was. They wanted to preserve its musty dignity and what remained of the waxy elegance it once had had. My aunt had bought it in 1932, a year of particular trial, to bolster their morale. Setting aside "a few little things" of her own, she had sold them, over her trustee's objection, at the bottom of the market, and the proceeds had bought a gray Chrysler sedan. It was a fine old car, my uncle explained, without specifying exactly why; it represented something. It gave him security and it always would, so long as my aunt would go on driving him about in it, and driving carefully.

"Slow, now, Con," my uncle said, and relit his pipe. "We haven't far to go, but we should remember that for Gus it's a long, long journey. If we go slowly, that much more of it will stay with him."

She drove as slowly as it was possible to drive in high gear without stalling the engine. Past the Congregational Church and turning left at the Mall, over the flat stretch of road by Miller's Hill and left again at the intersection, by the pine trees that lined the reservoir. Then straight along, the first raked and burning leaves on the fields beside us, and the brave bluster of September colors on oaks and beeches and poplars.

And most of it did stay with me. The breeze was cooler from the window, even cold, and in it the burnt leaves, my aunt's lily of the valley scent, my uncle's pipe tobacco, and the odor of automobile exhaust that clung to the gray velvet seat cushions and that had made me carsick as a child combined into a momentary something I smelled for the first time and would not smell again. Fright sprang from the knot in my stomach and shot through me suddenly, and, as I sat beside the battered suitcase, my shirt still open at the neck, and my necktie hidden in the pocket of the bright blue jacket my aunt had picked out at Rogers Peet, it was soon beyond my control.

"Gus. Now listen to me, Gus," my uncle was saying. "There is something that I don't believe we've touched on before. It has to do with your scholarship."

"I certainly appreciate what you did for me," I said.

101

In June my uncle had told me about the Meeker Fund. I was sure I had thanked him then, in June, as soon as he had told me.

"I don't see what you're thanking me for. I don't know what you think I had to do with it," my uncle said. It seemed as though I had insulted him.

"Your uncle is proud of you," Aunt Connie said quickly. "You won the scholarship by yourself, and you should be proud, too, and not for a minute feel ashamed or embarrassed."

"I am proud," I answered her, but I did wish that we could talk about something else.

"There's nothing to be ashamed about," my aunt repeated. "You're not to feel that you're different from the other boys."

"Dr. Kew knows about it, doesn't he?" I said.

"Of course he knows. But you're not the only boy who has a scholarship. He knows it's nothing to be ashamed of. . . . But it's your private business and Dr. Kew isn't going to let on to a soul."

We drew toward Birch's Rise and began the slow, winding climb up the drive. Parked on both sides and on the edges of the playing fields were cars many times more glittering than our Chrysler, with their chrome finishings and white tires and curved contours as polished and arresting as cutouts from a motor company's brochure, wide, fat cars, and as we drove between them I could plainly read the Landon-Knox stickers on their windshields.

Mothers and fathers in tailored suits, now and then with duck or pheasant plumage in their hats in salute to autumn, milled among the cars and strutted across the oval drive. Their sons went before them; overgrown, undergrown, graceful, gawky, with clear and pimpled faces, shrill and husky voices, these were the current Emmanuelers—assorted as to growth, unpruned and unadjusted. Carrying suitcases, or clothing, or pieces of light bedroom furniture, they paraded before their parents; so many show dogs straining at the parental leash.

My uncle faced back toward me and tapped on my knee for attention. I had been gripping the window's edge in a sort of stupor.

"Look them over, fellow," he said. "This is a day you'll remember as long as you live. You're going to make a lot of friends here."

My uncle gave instructions. We would park where Matthew Kew parked, by the garage behind Headmaster's House. Matthew never minded my uncle's taking liberties, provided they were taken discreetly. And we would go inside where it would be relatively quiet and remain there with the Kews until the chimes rang for Evening Prayer.

"Just back up there, Con, beside that magnificent automobile, and try not to dent its fender or break the lattice."

There was a lattice frame behind Headmaster's House, overgrown with ivy and honeysuckle to shield from visitors the back porch and the unsightly trash cans. Already parked beside it was a huge black limousine. Its lines were square and imposing, as though it had refused to compromise itself to air currents; its proportions were the antithesis of streamlining. A chauffeur in a dark uniform and a visor cap worked over it with a chamois cloth.

"That's the good girl, Con, ease back gently on the lattice, gently, gently. Now. That's the good girl. . . . Isn't that a perfectly magnificent car, Con? Gus, can you tell me what kind of a car that is?"

I had never seen a car like it.

"That's a Rolls-Royce. And the man polishing it is a liveried attendant. Think of that, Con, a Rolls-Royce with a man on the box."

"I wonder who that car belongs to," my aunt said. "It couldn't be Matthew Kew's."

Uncle Torbert went into the house ahead of us.

"He forgot to tie my necktie," I said to my aunt.

"Come sit here, Gus." Aunt Connie patted the cushion behind her, and I climbed over the back of the seat.

When I had a knot, she bent to straighten it. Her scent of lily of the valley hung between us, a comfort to smell. A dear old-lady smell.

"Dearie, that jacket does seem so awfully bright. I hope you won't wear it too often."

"I've got two suits in my trunk, and both of them are dark."

"You mustn't be vague about those things, Gus. Try to be like the other boys. Your mother's one fault was that she was vague and I never thought your father understood that terribly well."

"Aunt?"

"Dearie, what is it?"

"Did I get the scholarship because of Uncle Torbert?"

"You know better than to ask silly things."

"I was only wondering," I said.

103

"Dearie, everyone wonders sometimes."

"I suppose I could have stayed on at the Woodman School?"

"I suppose, if it had been absolutely necessary. You've been a lucky one, Gus."

I nodded.

"You're going to make new friends. You'll be getting to know new people."

She talked on, reiterating this and that and paraphrasing my uncle. You're a brave boy, she seemed to be saying, but you'll need to be braver.

We went to the side door and Aunt Connie rang the bell. While she waited for a maid to answer, she took time to rearrange my necktie.

"There's a smudge on your chin," she said. "Did you bring a pocket handkerchief?"

"Don't spit on it, Aunt," I said. "I can wipe it off myself."

"You spit, then. You can't go to Evening Prayer with a great smudge. I wish you weren't quite so vague about these things, darling. You spit, if you don't want me to."

"Isn't this a fine old Federalist house?" Aunt Connie asked, folding my handkerchief and putting it in my breast pocket. "Do you know about this house?"

"Josiah Birch built it," I said. "In 1821, before he lost all his money, and Dr. Trimble built on the kitchen wing."

"I think it's wonderful," she said, "the number of things your uncle has taught you."

In the Headmaster's parlor, Dr. Kew's wife, Martha, was attending to the final details of the tea. She hovered between the two full-length, thirty-paned windows on the west side of the room, in the bay that had been designed for the Founder by no less an architect than Charles Bulfinch, and that was the parlor's front exposure to the lawn, its sprinkling system, and the bustle and traffic about the oval drive.

Opening Day Tea was one of her happy chores, happily accepted. The tea service, all of it Academy property down to the least consequential sandwich fork, was arrayed upon the good Headmaster's House linen. It covered two substantial serving tables that had been borrowed from the dining hall and stood now in the bay. Plates of sandwiches had been placed on one end, beside other plates of raisin cake and chocolate brownies, and the covered plates of hot codfish balls, Bisquick muffins, and miniature sausages. The opposite end accommodated the large plastic trays, good, utilitarian trays that had weathered many a buffet and faculty tea. On them the Academy china was carried, an uncountable number of teacups nestling in their saucers, and each bore the inescapable inscription: *Haec olim meminisse iuvabit.*

Martha Kew's shadow, caused by the late afternoon sun streaming through the bay windows, danced up and down, the length of both tables. She straightened cups and plates, adjusted the flame beneath the silver tea vessel, or hastened to attend to some other bit of incompleteness. All must be ready by Evening Prayer; the parents would be coming here direct from the chapel.

"Go right on with whatever you're doing, Martha," Aunt Connie said. "We're not here to interrupt."

"Connie, excuse me. I didn't see you. Isn't this exciting?" Mrs. Kew turned to concentrate her smile on me. "And when I think of all the glorious days, the start of a brand new year. Gus, isn't it about the most exciting thing in the world, to be starting something?"

I replied I guessed that it was.

"My, isn't that a handsome coat?" Mrs. Kew said. "My, oh my, Gus."

"Torbert was to meet us here," my aunt said tactfully.

My uncle had joined Dr. Kew across the hall in the study and Mrs. Kew expected he was in there still, talking and no doubt sampling the sherry that Mr. Marsh had brought with him from New York. "Mr. Marsh is quite an elderly gentleman," Mrs. Kew said. "And Matthew makes it a point to handle him with kid gloves."

"Would that be Marcus Marsh," my aunt said, "who owns that magnificent car outside?"

"Marcus Marsh is the only trustee who comes to pay his respects in a Rolls-Royce, Matthew says." Mrs. Kew raised her eyebrows naughtily. "Torbert knows him, Con."

"They're old friends," Aunt Connie said. "Or they used to be."

"George Marsh came to us last year," Mrs. Kew said. "Let's see. You're a Sixth Classman, Gus?"

"I'm in the Fifth Class," I said.

That was nice. George Marsh was also in the Fifth Class, and he was new last year.

"I don't know the Marshes," Aunt Connie said, "but Torbert likes them. He says they are terribly rich, but in a perfectly nice way."

"Matthew thinks the world of George. He's turning out splendidly, for a boy as young as that. It's been a hard family situation."

From the hallway beyond the parlor door came the sound of masculine voices, and a burst of Dr. Kew's heartiest laughter. Mr. Marcus Marsh was the first to enter the room. He walked with a limp, supporting himself on a pair of matched malacca canes. I noticed his lustrous black shoes and the lavender rosette in his lapel. Though he stooped as he walked, he held his head doggedly erect, resisting the ingloriousness of that posture. My uncle and Dr. Kew followed at a respectful distance, and my uncle's eyes were fastened upon him with something close to reverence.

Mr. Marsh held in his distended stomach with a waistcoat of white linen material with deep blue piping, a waistcoat my uncle would have worn proudly. But my uncle did not own such a waistcoat.

Dr. Kew bounded toward me, clapping his hands together and beaming like a bountiful provider about to carve the Christmas turkey.

"Well. We've caught up with him at last. Well. Well. Well."

As I had anticipated it would, his hand settled between my shoulder blades with a resounding slap.

"Well, well, well. How many wells make an ocean, Gus?" It was Opening Day and Dr. Matthew Kew was at his straightforward, shaggy best. It was Opening Day and he was being Father Flanagan, Spencer Tracy, and a boy's best pal all in one. "That's quite a coat you're wearing, Gus. Say now."

But for superficial similarities, the heavy brows, the thinning, reddish hair, the tendency toward freckles and obesity, Dr. Kew was no Spencer Tracy. He was, by his own terminology, "an academic trail-blazer." And his zeal was camouflaged beneath a bland and bookish exterior.

"It's pretty bright, I guess," I said.

"Pretty bright, I guess, *sir*," my uncle said sharply.

"I mean sir," I said.

"Oh heaven," Dr. Kew said. "We either say 'sir' or we don't say 'sir.' There are ways and ways of showing one's respect; we don't insist on anything. We're not Elizabethan as all that. As long as Gus respects me, he can call me what he wants. This isn't Groton, after all."

Dr. Kew broke into a chuckle. A divergence from the pattern of Groton School was a trail to Dr. Kew, and petty laxities of discipline like the one just touched on were achievements he would have himself known by. It required ingenuity, after all, to blaze fresh trails in a pedagogic forest and yet remain taint-free of the infectious under-shrubs and ivies that sprang from progressive and experimental doctrines. He had abolished the six-year Latin prerequisite for the diploma. He discouraged the hazing of new boys. He permitted First Classmen in good standing to spend four weekends away from the school and to smoke pipes in his presence in the Headmaster's study after the evening meal. These were the trails he had blazed, while in no wise jeopardizing the spirit of the Academy or the Puritan tradition on which it had been founded.

His jocularity, however, was wasted on Mr. Marcus Marsh, who now addressed himself sternly to Dr. Kew. "Whatever it is you're talking about, I don't think any of us is in a position to carp at Groton."

Dr. Kew hastened to excuse an innocent quip. He had not meant to carp, Dr. Kew said. He was not a disingenuous man. And, to look at his brown worsted suit and plain wool necktie that had been handwoven by natives at the Grenfell Mission in Labrador, one might well believe that Dr. Kew was not a disingenuous man. He begged to amend his casual remark. He had the realest respect for Groton and for the Reverend Endicott Peabody. To be quite honest, he often said to Bishop Wash that one of the realest satisfactions of his job was that it afforded him a healthy, competitive relationship with Dr. Peabody.

My uncle chose to intervene right here. "What Matthew is telling us, Marcus, is that he is a traditionalist, of the same sort as you and I. Did you ever read, for instance, our history of the school? I'd say there was some rather formidable evidence there, Marcus."

"Should I read it?" Mr. Marsh asked. "I don't find much to read these days."

"If you haven't already, I recommend it heartily."

107

"Well," Mr. Marsh said, "I don't think any of us is in a position to carp at Groton."

The chapel chimes rang out the completion of an hour. The clock tolled. It was five, exactly, and time for Evening Prayer. My aunt and Mrs. Kew began the exodus toward the door, Mrs. Kew with a last glance at her tea tables. Dr. Kew followed them alone, and Mr. Marsh, my uncle and I brought up the end of the procession. We walked slowly, careful not to hurry Mr. Marsh.

"I wonder," Mr. Marsh said at length, "if anyone has news of Edgar Trimble? It's curious that all this chimes and chapel business should make me think of him. I wonder if he's still alive."

"I'm sure he's very much alive," my uncle said brightly.

Mr. Marsh acknowledged him with a grunt.

"I have a great-nephew, you know. Do you know my great-nephew George?"

"No, sir."

"I thought you might be friends. George and I motored up here today all the way from Great Neck, Long Island. We stopped for lunch at Hartford. It was an extraordinarily long drive."

"The going gets better," my uncle said, "once you get out of Connecticut and onto Route Twenty."

But Mr. Marsh was addressing himself quite definitely to me. "George rode in front with Williams; so I was able to sleep, fortunately. It's a very long drive, you know."

"It's a small world, Marcus," my uncle said. He was obliged to lower his voice slightly, since we were approaching the chapel doors and other boys and their parents were converging upon us. "To think we should both have nephews starting in where you and I left off."

"My great-nephew George is my brother's grandson," Mr. Marsh was saying to me. "Not every old bachelor has a great-nephew. Now what would you say to that?"

"I hope George will look Gus up," my uncle said, I felt a little desperately. "Gus, there's a tradition for you. Three generations of Marshes."

108

Chapter Three

I sat in back of the chapel, between my aunt and uncle, in one of the elevated pews beside the vestry that were reserved for visitors. From this vantage point I watched approximately two hundred and fifty boys file into the central pews, flop to their knees, and drop their heads into the crooks of their arms, in prayer. These were the Old Boys, from thirteen to eighteen years old, taking up the places assigned to them the year before. Formal worship held no novelty for them; they carried it off as they might a meal or a set of tennis. I knelt upright on a knee cushion and watched through loosely clasped fingers, wondering if ever I would acquire that casualness. Possibly the day would come when I would be as untroubled by the chapel's austerity, the Bach Prelude softly descending from the organ loft, the white marble altar beneath a Florentine triptych, the exquisitely stained windows, and the vaulted stone ceiling.

It was a short service, in which Dr. Kew had read the lesson and the Chaplain, Mr. Coates, who had a heavy head cold, delivered the prayers and the Twenty-third Psalm in a phlegmy monotone. He lasted no more than twenty minutes, while I explored the pages of my hymnal in search of the school hymn which every good Emmanueler was expected to know by heart.

Afterward, on the chapel steps, we encountered Mr. Frapp wearing a sharply creased suit the color of dark mustard and a tightly knotted lavender necktie. It was a hurried conversation, since my uncle was anxious not to lose sight of old Mr. Marsh. But he talked long enough to establish two facts of my academic future. I was to live in Old Stables, Number Three Dormitory, and the Supervising Master of Number Three for that year was to be Mr. Frapp, none other.

"Roger," my aunt said, "would you be an angel and show Gus to his room?"

Mr. Frapp smiled winsomely. You did not think of Mr. Frapp as having any age at all. He moved in an aura of Melachrino cigarettes and Sappho, a mildly opiate exoticism. Besides being the Academy's most competent classicist, he was its only James man and had done translations from George Sand, attainments which were in the main unheralded at Emmanuel. Notwithstanding, he had a pugnaciousness that centered in a pug face that suggested that he was not entirely fragile as his slender body might indicate. Also, his hair was clipped short on the top of his head, giving him quite a Teutonic look.

"You could hardly call it a room, Con. Gus won't have an honest-to-goodness room until he's a Third Classman," Mr. Frapp said and added, with a small intrepid laugh, "that is, if he behaves himself."

He agreed to show me the dormitory, but we would have to hurry. My aunt knew of course that he was expected at the tea party, too. Mrs. Kew expected him. Again Mr. Frapp gave a slight, high laugh, and he and I went behind Headmaster's House to take my suitcase from the Chrysler.

I followed Mr. Frapp down a set of wooden steps and a gentle incline that separated Headmaster's House from Old Stables. We approached the old building from the rear, and there a handsome, black-haired boy in shirt sleeves was bouncing a tennis ball off one of its walls.

"Tilton," Mr. Frapp said, "I see you're not neglecting your daily stint of exercise."

The boy caught short before his throw. "Sir?"

"I take it you spent a pleasant summer."

"Yes, sir."

"And that you did not curb your splendid appetite for recreation?"

"Sir?"

"But that amid all the sport and pleasure there was time to prepare for your make-up examination in Latin?"

Tilton fit the tennis ball into the hip pocket of his trousers and jauntily began, "Took the make-up this afternoon, sir, and I did my best. Wouldn't be surprised if I failed it again, sir."

"That's straightforward of you, Tilton, but I'm confident that it was mere modesty on your part. Much as they become you, I suggest you withhold your apologies until I've read your paper."

"Sir, it wasn't an easy exam, sir."

110

"Examinations are not meant to be easy."

"I left some sentences blank, sir, and wrote in the margin to explain that I was sick last spring when we were doing the subjunctive and past conditions and all that."

"That was a misfortune you had the three summer months to compensate for."

Tilton was about to hurl his tennis ball against the wall again. He poised himself petulantly for the throw, but was stayed once again. "I don't think that's fair, sir."

"Let me caution you not to vent your rage against the dormitory wall. The dormer windows are breakable, as windows have a way of being. I think that if you can contain yourself till tomorrow when the handball courts are open, all of us who lodge in Old Stables will thank you."

I trailed Mr. Frapp indoors, through a dark corridor and up two flights of stairs carpeted with brown linoleum and smelling of creosote. On the third-floor landing we turned to the right and down a lighter, more cheerful corridor whose walls were hung with black on white reproductions of Renaissance art and photographs of the Sistine frescoes, of the Acropolis, the Parthenon, and of lounging youths with footballs and striped jerseys who had played on the Academy teams long ago in the Little Rector's heyday.

This Mr. Frapp was a perplexing contrast to the excitable man who used to come for supper at Elm Street. He strode through the corridor, explaining its facilities. "Here's the fire alarm. In case of emergency, you simply break the glass. But woe unto him, Taylor, who tampers with it unnecessarily." In the same precautionary tone, he called my attention to the fire escape—"For fire, Taylor, and not for frolic"—his own quarters which, not being one to dodge a Mr. Chippsian cliché, he called his "sanctum sanctorum"—an inviolate place, particularly during examination week, the laundry room— "fresh bed and body linen, Taylor, each Friday morning"—and the washroom.

We stopped and Mr. Frapp pushed open a swinging door. A strident voice carried out to us, a voice in full song that quavered, but with a proud determination:

> Tonight, tonight, I must *for*—get,
> Mu—sic, mae—stro, pul*eese*. . . .

Mr. Frapp held the door ajar, cleared his throat loudly, and stepped inside. I remained in the hall, listening.

"Who dat? Who dat man?" A comic, rasping voice.

"Good afternoon, Eaton," I heard Mr. Frapp saying. "I'm pleased to see you've lost none of your ebullience since June."

"Excuse me, sir. . . . Sir, I thought you were somebody else."

"Exactly what are you doing, Eaton?"

"Taking a shower, sir. I was pretty sweaty."

"Do you find the water warm enough? Or do you plan to make this room into a Turkish bath?"

"I like plenty of hot water, sir."

"Look at this room, Eaton." Mr. Frapp's voice was virtually a squeal. "*Look at this room!*"

"It was this way before, sir. I didn't do—"

"Eaton, come out of that shower!"

"Sir, I've got soap in my eyes. Honest. *Sirrr—*"

"Pick up the towels, Eaton. Do I make myself clear? Pick up your mess."

"*Sirrrr—*"

Now I opened the door myself, and beheld through clouds of steam the spectacle of Mr. Frapp, my uncle's friend, clutching the ear of what appeared to be a small, fat, pink boy. The head was a mound of lather. Set against the vivid flesh it looked like a bonnet on a cherub. Mr. Frapp's thin arm was extended rigid, his face contorted only slightly less fiercely than his victim's.

"Yow, sirrr!"

"March!"

"*Sirrruh!*"

"March! You will pick up these towels one by one."

Eaton's dripping body stumbled to and fro upon the wet tiles, retrieving the sodden towels singly wherever they lay, by the wash basins, the urinals, the toilet stalls, depositing them into a white metal hamper. I watched motionless, a fly on the wall.

"Taylor," Mr. Frapp said abruptly, "this is Eaton. Eaton and I often find ourselves at cross purposes, but the result is always the same. I hope you will profit from his unfortunate example."

I followed my Supervising Master down the hall, at considerable distance. His breath was coming in quick gasps and he had not recovered himself completely when we reached the dormitory. He stopped to consult a mimeographed paper, his body still trembling.

"Seventeen," he said. "That's a double cubicle. Taylor and Vale. The only new boys to grace our dorm."

Old Stables Three was a cavernous hall, illuminated sparsely by hanging lights and dormer windows high up on either side. At dusk it was a somber, shadowed place. Along its sides the cubicles were set, thirty of them, with initials of forgotten boys scratched onto their varnished walls. Each cubicle was fitted with a canvas curtain with the familiar colors, green on white, in broad stripes. Number Seventeen, which we approached through a maze of trunks and open suitcases across a scarred oak floor, was freshly swept and tidy. There was a dormer window overhead to ventilate it and the adjoining cubicle. I saw two steel beds, their mattresses in rolls upon the springs, and beneath each was a white enamel chamber pot, or thundermug, as I later learned to call them. One plastic-seated chair, two battered chests of drawers, two clothes racks, some hangers, and a wall mirror completed the picture.

I dropped my suitcase onto one of the beds.

"I wouldn't recommend that for the springs," Mr. Frapp said. "Each boy is held responsible for damages to school property."

The cubicle had a musty smell, and it was cold. As I listened to Mr. Frapp striding away on the creaking floor, I felt a little sick to my stomach.

In the dim light I took the sheets and blankets my aunt had packed on top of my suitcase and made up one bed. This is the good bed, I told myself grimly, and it's nearer to the window. Where is what's-his-name? Where are you, roommate? A steamer trunk stood outside our cubicle. A new black trunk with roommate's initials— C.U.P. Vale, Jr. That was a name and a half. I'd have to tell it to Ned Sellers sometime. There'd be a lot to tell Ned Sellers.

When my aunt and uncle left, it was about dark. Call them up, Aunt Connie said, if I felt lonely or if something was on my mind. I waved them off, and watched the old, old, fine old car, our Chrysler, till it reached the fork of the drive and disappeared.

It would be suppertime any minute now, though I wasn't hungry. I thought how it would be to sit in a dining hall alone with three hundred boys and masters and not to know one of them but Mr.

Frapp. I was a mass of interior dreads and tensions that no one must ever know about. I put my hands in my pockets and started toward the school.

Behind me I heard a firm voice, with more than a hint of arrogance, calling, "Where do you think you're going?"

This boy looked indignant. Therefore, and because he was taller than I, I thought he might be one of the proctors, those student administrators my uncle had told me of, who supervise the younger boys. He was too tall, too straight, too neat, to be a contemporary of mine. His dark hair was trimmed and ruly in a way that mine would never be and he was dressed flawlessly in an ink-black suit striped with white threads barely visible. It seemed only right and natural that one like him should address me in reprimand.

"You can't walk over there," he said, "new kid."

I frowned at him. I was a new kid. So what?

"You've got to be set straight. The first thing is not to be a fresh new kid."

"How was I fresh?" I said.

"I'm only telling you not to be," he said. "There are some rules around this place. You can't walk on the oval grass unless you're a First Classman."

He went on to define the rules. I didn't think that he meant to condescend. It was as though he thought I would be glad to hear them:

Call the masters "Sir" and the First and Second Classmen "Sir" and don't try to put on airs. New kids ran errands for First Classmen. Took their suits to the cleaner's and shined their shoes and such as that. And cleaned up the library. They didn't ask you to do much, but when they did you had to jump. And keep to the side of the halls when you walk through and keep one hand almost touching the wall. Don't ask why, because it just was that way. It wasn't bad, except in the first few weeks, and by spring everybody forgot the whole business. Just remember that if someone hollered "new kid" you had to run as if you wanted to get there first.

"It sounds like West Point," I said.

He did not seem to have heard me. His eyes were fixed in the distance on the chapel clock. "It's almost six-thirty. We eat at six-thirty."

The dining hall was in Brockaway, a little to our left. We walked

114

to it slowly, carefully skirting the oval. A bell sounded inside, a high, vibrating ring.

They were always ringing bells, he said. About a million times a day, and each one meant something different. That one meant there was three minutes before supper. There would be another, two short rings, to let you know there was just one minute before the doors are closed. Six times late in a week and you were on Saturday Disciplinary. Somebody would have to explain to me all that.

He rubbed an oversized hand over his cheek in speaking. He was no surer of himself than I, I soon saw, merely proud about concealing it. He said things categorically, even the simplest things, as though he expected you to argue them.

"What class are you?" I said.

"I'm in the fifth class. I might as well ask what class you are, and what your name is, and how old you are, so we can get that over with."

"I'm in the same class as you," I said shyly, "and I'll be thirteen in November."

"I'll be fourteen in February," he said, "but that's because I went to school in Switzerland. I missed a whole year."

In a sudden surge of friendliness, I told him my name and that I had never been to Switzerland. I had been to New York a couple of times, and once to Maine on a fishing trip, but outside of that I hadn't done much traveling, though I meant to one day. I intended to travel one day, but mostly I had stuck around East Northrup where my aunt and uncle lived.

He rubbed a hand to his cheek.

He gave me no more, save that his father had once been a partner in a brokerage and that he spent his summers at his great-uncle's house in Great Neck, Long Island. So by the time we reached the dining hall, I knew without his saying so that he was George Marsh.

115

Chapter Four

The impressions of months that followed are fragmentary but not blurred. I was not a timid boy. Rather, I was more inquisitive than I should have been. With my aunt and uncle living not a mile away, I could hardly have succumbed to homesickness. And the anxieties that had gripped me on Opening Day, while they paraded before me in the small morning hour that I lay awake waiting for the rising bell, retreated, once the bell rang, to the back of my mind and lurked there. I was usually too busy to worry about them. I pushed myself hard, harder than I needed to. I was eager to conform and I wanted to acclimatize myself as quickly and thoroughly as I could.

I wasn't confident that I could be the best, and so I told myself I did not want to be. I only wanted to give the impression that I could have been the best, if I had cared to try. With that margin for safety, I could always exempt myself from absolute failure. This required a double effort: first to excel, and then not to. I had to push and curb myself at the same time and the results were sometimes bewildering.

My studies were uniformly more complex than any I had undertaken at the Woodman School. Latin was hardest, as I could not camouflage my ignorance from Mr. Frapp. ("Words, words, words, Taylor. Kindly stick to the material, and if you don't know what you're talking about, do say so. You have the distinction of being the only member of the class not familiar with the prepositions requiring the accusative: *ante, apud, ad, adversus. . . .*") I learned more of the eccentricities of Mr. Frapp—his squealing voice in tantrum, his fetish for kicking the unprotected shins of those who had provoked the "Jovian wrath" against which he delighted to warn us.

And Medieval History was hard, owing to the forbidding character of our instructor. Mr. Flemister was a bald Vermonter, dourer than Calvin Coolidge, a man of boundless pessimism. ("Medieval

116

history is not forgotten history. I must warn the class that failure in daily preparation constitutes a grade of zero for the week, and hence zero for the term, zero for the final examination and zero for the College Board.")

English was easier, as Dr. Gregore practiced a less vehement tyranny. He was an abstractionist, a speechifier, a hypochondriacal bachelor with cheerless plump cheeks. Dismal Gregore had set his sights high as a younger man; he had spent his summers fulfilling the requirements of his doctorate. This achieved, he had formally resigned from Emmanuel to accept a post at a women's college in Ohio. But fate had brought him back to the creosote-smelling classrooms, to spotting his clothes with powdered chalk, to pointing out to distracted Fifth Classmen certain weary apothegms in *The Autobiography of Benjamin Franklin* and "Sohrab and Rustum," to coaching small boys to declaim "The Road to Mandalay" for the annual Declamation Contest. Dismal Gregore's doctor's dissertation, six hundred and thirty-one pages, including bibliography and footnotes, on *Dryden and the Restoration Tragedians*, had been bound and presented to the Library where it remained unread, leaning upon the only other occupant of the faculty publications shelf, a chronicle entitled *Emmanuel: The Birth and Growth of a Private School*. Dismal Gregore had been his nickname for years; boys mimicked him sadistically and advanced tantalizing theories of his failure in Ohio. And he was aware of this, and bitter. He took revenge deviously, by vaunting his erudition in the classroom, belaboring his pupils with aphorisms which he was quite certain they would not understand. He was celebrated for quoting Arviragus' song from *Cymbeline*. ("Oh no, gentlemen, oh no, no, no. I will not hear your fevered exculpations. A lesson unprepared remains unprepared—withal. I assigned you work, and you did not do that work. I cannot help you, gentlemen. You are pampered. You know our saying, I suppose?

> Golden lads and girls all must,
> As chimney-sweepers, come to dust.

Did you hear it, gentlemen? *Chimney sweepers!* Think that over. . . . Apthorp, I regret to inform you that impertinent noise will cost you three weeks on Saturday Disciplinary.")

Athletics gave me a greater feeling of adequacy. New boys were assigned to the Academy's three intramural societies, of which mine was Ithacan. Five afternoons a week that autumn I wore a deep blue jersey with scarlet rings about the sleeves and played in the backfield of Ithacan Seconds. I was no taller or heavier than my classmates, but at the Woodman School I had played a rougher and readier game than most who had come from polite country day schools.

The modestly advanced status I enjoyed on Ithacan Seconds was my surest social entree. It brought me into contact with the several aspiring athletes in my class who also had been elevated from the Third teams to face more strenuous competition. We were not friends as yet, but since we were the only Fifth Classmen so privileged, our close association was inevitable. Walter Baxter Eaton played against me on Jason Seconds in a tattered crimson jersey which, when new, had had sleeves unsoiled and had been resplendently ringed in gold to connote the Golden Fleece. Despite his tubbiness and slothful disposition, he was surprisingly aggressive and already Mr. McTeale of the First Squad had predicted he would be a likely lineman in his day.

I was a little better acquainted with Howard Tighe Tilton, Jr., who was then the highest-touted player in our class, having lasted on Spartan Firsts for over a month against boys weighing twenty and thirty pounds heavier before he returned to the second team. He was his team's kicker and passer and also its quarterback and thus in a position to name himself pass receiver as well. He was quicker and more agile than I, but when I did block a pass, or intercept one, he never failed to congratulate me. "That's the going," he would say. "That's my boy." I enjoyed tackling him hard. There was a satisfaction in cracking my shoulder pad against him. He was a good ball runner, but I discovered he did not like to be tackled. After I had knocked him down, he would tug at his needlessly huge shoulder pads and would remove his helmet, flicking his long black hair into place with a snap of the neck. He had sharp brown eyes and a handsome face with high, Balkan features, and that he should be an athlete in the bargain was a heavy pressure on his unformulated personality. Before the huddle could begin again, he had to replace his helmet and saunter back to his waiting teammates as casually as he could.

I had to struggle to give the impression of a potentially brilliant but casual scholar, but it was not as taxing to achieve the same effect athletically. As in class, I was content with a suggestion of excellence while avoiding the positive demonstration of it. This was relatively simple to do, since as an athlete I was better than mediocre. My advantage lay in experience. Eaton and Tilton and a half dozen others were better than I, though they weren't aware of it yet. The only one to suspect me was George Marsh.

We played together on Ithacan Seconds, where he was steadier and less dashing than Harry Tilton and yet our best player, a unanimous choice for captain. He called signals in a quiet voice and from any backfield position could buck the line and sweep the ends. We experimented with one or two reverses that Mr. Welling, a pleasurably vague physics instructor who was assigned to coach Ithacan Seconds against his wishes, had borrowed from the notebooks of Mr. McTeale of the First squad. They were elementary plays, the crudest attempts at deception, but they were exciting for us. In one sequence Marsh would feint toward the line and spin to hand the ball to me who would carry it around end. This and a lateral play we were most proud of, and usually I handled both of them.

"You don't strain yourself, do you?" George Marsh said to me one afternoon. "Maybe you've played more football. Maybe you went to public school and maybe we didn't."

"So what?"

"Just don't think it makes you any different from anyone else. You'd better start playing football here, because you're no better than we are."

He was extraordinarily sensitive. It puzzled me why anyone so mild beneath his pride should be driven to belligerence by the thought of my having less advantages than he. It was a perverse reaction, since in a normal course of resentments I should be the one to feel belligerent toward him.

Our common bond was the progress of the team. We would discuss it in the dormitory before the lights went off. He had high hopes of our winning the series against Jasons and Spartans that fall. He kept a scratch pad of projected plays and memoranda and hints he thought might help the players. He thought we needed someone who could drop kick as well as Harry Tilton. "You could do it," he said, "if you wanted to. You could practice with someone on Sundays."

"I study Latin on Sundays," I said.

"I'll help you with your Latin if you'll learn to drop kick."

"I hate to borrow other people's footballs."

"Buy your own," he said. "For thirteen dollars you can get a pretty fair football. You don't have to be so cheap about it. Just write them out a check."

"A check?"

He looked at me curiously. "That's what I said."

I confessed that I had no checkbook, no bank account, and that my allowance for two months would not come to thirteen dollars.

Even in his splendidly adult silk dressing gown, he looked awkward and ashamed. "Listen," he said at last, "I can lend you thirteen dollars."

And before I could collect myself he had led me to his cubicle and from a pigskin billfold counted out the money into my open hand.

When the lights were out I whispered about the incident to my cubicle companion. He was a tall, spindly boy who lived with a widowed mother in the town of Canandaigua, New York. In the first months of our living together, C. U. P. Vale, Jr., and I had communicated with a mutual diffidence brought on by our uncertain position as the lone initiates in a dormitory of veterans. Faced with the necessity of asserting ourselves against such a formidable barrier, neither of us had taken more than a polite interest in the other. He wore neckties with the heads of hounds and foxes printed upon them and he fastened them to his shirts with a gold clip in the shape of a riding crop and kept them, when they were not in use, on a sterling silver stirrup which served as a tie rack. The wall by his bed was adorned with brightly-colored hunting prints and with two photographs of himself in a derby and riding habit posing by a horse that had a prize ribbon fastened to its bridle. I had drawn no conclusions about Vale and had talked with him only sparingly. But that night I knew that I must discover something about him, if I were to sleep at all. Mr. Frapp had a rule against talking after lights, but I paid no heed to it.

"Could you afford yourself a football, if you wanted it?"

"I suppose I could," Vale whispered apprehensively.

"You'd just pay for it out of your allowance?"

"Or I'd write home for the money."

"Your mother would send it to you?" I said.

"Why wouldn't she?"

"Do you have a bank account? Do you have your own check-book?" I said.

"I will have."

"When?"

"As soon as I'm sixteen."

I was silent in my bed for a minute or more, considering the importance of what he had just told me. But when I questioned him further it was plain from his measured breathing that C. U. P. Vale, Jr., was asleep, or pretending to be.

My finances were simply understood.

Last winter Aunt Connie had driven me to Boston to consult with Mr. Jennings in the Post Office Square Branch of the Legatees' Trust. I had sat on a hard pine chair by Mr. Jennings' desk and had waited while a clerk brought in a sheaf of papers for Mr. Jennings to ponder over. Mr. Jennings, a serge-suited man who had been my father's trustee and was my aunt's as well, made a puffing sound with his lips on turning each page. Upon finishing the lot he swung toward me in his chair.

My father, said Mr. Jennings with a benign smile, had of course had no formal estate at all at the time he died. But—and what a fortunate "but"—he had left a twenty-five-thousand-dollar-life-insurance policy in my mother's name, and since she had died with him, the policy reverted to me, amounting after lawyers' fees to nearly twenty-four thousand dollars. And—quite a big "and" it was, too—that was not all. My mother had not managed to spend every last cent of her principal before she died, though, laughingly ventured Mr. Jennings, who had been fond, so very fond, of my mother, she had certainly been headed in that direction. My mother had never taken the trouble to draw up a will, but the residue of her principal came to ten thousand and some odd dollars, which were incontestably mine. In a manner of speaking, then, it was a disguised blessing that I was their only child. For thirty thousand dollars conservatively invested by Mr. Jennings and his associates ("we people," Mr. Jennings said), could yield no more than four or four and a half per cent under the most favorable circumstances. I must understand that Mr. Jennings and his people were not of a mind to fritter away my principal on random speculations. Hence, I did not have, as it were, the stars to thank for the twelve hundred dollars that came to me annually, but such other more accessible of God's blessings as oil, electricity, and natural gas.

I left Mr. Jennings with happy impressions of my father's providence, of my mother's elfin charm, and of the potent natural forces which the Legatees' Trust had harnessed in my behalf. (It seemed to me that his estimate had been more than generous and that he had expressed it with modesty and restraint.) Twelve hundred dollars a year could have been twelve million. This being the case, I could not appreciate Mr. Jennings' repeated allusions to economy. Nor could I understand what timidity had caused my aunt, who had known the glad facts all along, to conceal them from me. Why, I wanted to know, was I limited to five dollars per month pocket money? Why, given such a limitless pool to draw from, should there be an allowance at all?

Aunt Connie assailed my misconceptions during the drive home— "Do you know what it costs us to feed you, Gus? Do you know that every little thing you ever had, every piece of clothing and every sickness has been paid for out of that money? We've had to budget and plan. You're not very realistic, I'm afraid, dearie. You sound like your father"—so that in the end I was thoroughly ashamed of myself.

On Sundays, when I returned to Elm Street for lunch, my aunt tirelessly inquired why I had not brought a friend. "I think it's mean of you not to ask someone to your home on Sunday."

"I don't know anyone that well, Aunt."

"Surely you know someone. Don't you have a roommate?"

"He never talks," I said.

"That's ridiculous, darling. I'm sure he'll talk if he's comfortable."

"Why don't you ask the Marsh boy?" my uncle would ask, too anxiously.

"I don't know him that well," I would say quickly.

If there were no one else left on earth, I would not ask George Marsh for Sunday lunch at Elm Street, where Aunt Connie shrieked questions at me from behind a kitchen door and my uncle fiddled with his food and talked endlessly of the grand houses he had lived in as a boy. Life was changing for me and I was angry that neither of them realized it. I was struggling beyond the hinterlands of East Northrup toward a dim horizon that had no resemblance to the past.

But Vale's presence in our Elm Street parlor was at least thinkable. And I did ask him. The next week we walked down Birch's Rise on a cold November noon, and tried to be friendly.

I said, "You've never seen anyone like my aunt and uncle."

"You've never met my mother," Vale said.

"They ask an awful lot of questions. You'll see."

"So does my mother."

"You'd think I'd been away to China for ten years," I said, "the way they ask the questions when I come home on Sundays."

"It can't be that bad," Vale said, and laughed.

"You've got a string of names," I said, further on.

"Charles Upman Pratt Vale, Junior. Isn't that some string?"

"At home do they call you Charley?"

"At home they call me 'Cup.'"

"C-U-P, Cup?"

"Or 'Cuppy,'" he said. "It's embarrassing."

Our simple buoyancy lasted until we reached Elm Street, but when we caught sight of my uncle's brick wall and I explained its story to him, Vale fell silent. At table he looked pained and frightened. He sat stiffly at my uncle's right through lunch, staring at his plate for long intervals and responding to my aunt's conversational sallies with a bob of the head or a tortured smile.

I tried to think of subjects that would amuse him. I spoke of Old Stables Three, of Mr. Flemister, of Dismal Gregore. Vale never smiled; he was poking his fork into a mound of mashed potatoes. Uncle Torbert took his turn, giving an analysis of the Academy's recent games with Milton and Saint Mark's, but Vale was not a football enthusiast. My aunt brought dessert, butter pecan ice cream and, for Sunday treat, butterscotch sauce. My uncle, talking uninterruptedly about old Mr. Marsh and his nephew George, had started to embarrass me. I hardly knew George Marsh, I told my uncle quite severely—and then it was that Vale uttered his first coherent sentence.

"You must know him pretty well," Vale said, "if you borrowed thirteen dollars off him."

I saw Uncle Torbert swallow deeply from his water glass and replace it on the table with an exaggerated delicacy, reach to his vest pocket for the ancestral gold watch and quite unaccountably start to wind it. My aunt had been surprised half-risen from her chair in the act of offering Vale more butterscotch sauce. She sank back.

Vale sat upright, his thin fingers clenched to the table's edge, and swallowed.

"Dearie," Aunt Connie said. "Dearie, why did you do it?"

"Fellow," my uncle said, "is this true?"

"I had to buy this football," I told him. "I'm going to pay it back."

"Oh dearie," Aunt Connie said, "couldn't you have bought a cheaper football? Couldn't you have paid for it yourself?"

My uncle had pushed himself out from the table. He stood up, fingered his watch a moment, and stuffed it into his vest pocket in a deliberate manner.

"If you will excuse me, I have matters to attend to in my study."

He left us, muttering, and stamped into the hall and up the stairs.

"Gus," Aunt Connie said, "you've hurt his feelings."

"I didn't mean to, Aunt."

"Dearie, borrowing money is against your uncle's principles. I think he was truly shocked—"

"I'm sorry," Cuppy Vale said dully. "I always make trouble."

My aunt set down the ice cream dish. She raised her eyes to the ceiling, guiltily. We could hear him walking around up there in his study.

Afterward in the kitchen as I helped with the dishes, my aunt spoke to me privately. She beckoned me toward the china cupboard and advanced me thirteen dollars from the tea box which contained the household funds. She got my solemn promise to repay George Marsh immediately, and not to trouble my poor uncle with the matter.

"Now you go upstairs and talk to him," Aunt Connie said. "I'm afraid we've hurt his feelings."

"But how?"

"You talk to him, dearie. Your uncle is a remarkable man and I hope you always will respect him."

I found my uncle at his desk, ordering a debris of letters, envelopes, and paper clips. He brushed a spray of tobacco crumbs into the wastebasket. "Hello," he said. "Sit down. I was about to send for you."

The walls about him were hung with framed mementos of an earlier, more purposeful existence: a photograph of the Case mansion in Lynn, built in the 1850's from the early revenues of the Case Shoe Manufacturing Corporation, a panoramic photograph in three sections of the American Field Service unit with which he had journeyed to France in 1917, and the diplomas from Emmanuel, Harvard, and Harvard Law School. On his desk was a silver canister inscribed to him by his partners with the date of his retirement. Beside this was the reference book which he had sworn by in his days as a trustee: *Short Selling, For and Against,* by Richard Whitney and W. E. Perkins. He had only to look back on these appurtenances of an active life to reassure himself. He became a lawyer again, a trustee once more negotiating the estates of a handful of admiring widows.

"Do you see these blotters?" he asked. From a drawer he produced a pair of folders in red morocco leather, old and tattered and marked in gilt: Paid and Unpaid. "I keep bills in these. Which would you say was the thicker?"

"The Paid," I said.

"Exactly. There is just one bill that I haven't paid this month, and that was an unexpectedly large one from that mason's supply firm in Worcester—for the materials that went into our wall. That was a big order."

I nodded dutifully.

"But it's a debt," he said, "that I'm liquidating by degrees. Do you know how I could pay it all off very easily if I chose? I could pay a call on our friend Mr. Gillis of the Merchant Farmer's Bank. Perfectly easily, and he'd be glad to make me a demand loan at four and a half per cent. But do you think I'd approach Mr. Gillis? Do you think for one minute I'd do that?"

He rose abruptly from his chair and drew a long frame from behind his desk.

"I would not. And here's the reason why." He handed me the frame. In it was a simple strip of cardboard, yellowing at the edges. I read in bold print: THE BORROWER IS SERVANT TO THE LENDER: *Proverbs xxii, 7.*

"When I was in college my father gave me that," he said. "It hung in my room there and afterward for almost ten years in the State Street office. I want you to have it for your cubicle."

125

"Couldn't I hang it in my room here?"

"In your cubicle at the Academy," he said, "where you can look at it every day. If I can pay for the wall without putting myself in bondage, you should be able to pay for a football."

"Yes," I answered him. "Thank you."

When it came time to go, Vale started out the front walk ahead of me. I waited till he had gone several yards, and asked my aunt, "Do you think Uncle Torbert will ever finish paying for the wall?"

She smiled uncertainly. "If not this year, then next year. Dearie, you pop up with the most ridiculous ideas." And she kissed me.

Chapter Five

I hung my uncle's framed slogan on a picture hook from the molding of the cubicle wall. Vale, with whom I was growing friendlier, confessed it made him nervous. He made a joke of counting his pocket money in the evenings. Only to make sure he hadn't lent me anything that day, he said.

I approached George Marsh several times, putting aside my misgivings, and made it known that I was prepared to reimburse him. Each time he looked at me with a puzzled frown, as though I had said something vaguely outrageous.

We settled at last in the closing weeks of the term, in a way that was a surprise to both of us. It was during the examination period that preceded the Christmas holiday, when football was over and there were long afternoons of study. Mr. Frapp had instituted a rule that year, a rule most deliberate in its purposelessness, against entering the dormitory before nine o'clock at night without his express permission. Hence, for diversion, the more adventurous of our number took to spending as much time there as possible. However, you would not have expected to find George Marsh doing so. It was startling to come upon him one afternoon, the paragon of rectitude in this atmosphere of clandestinity.

George Marsh was in his cubicle, pulling open a warped bureau drawer and making a dangerous lot of noise in the process.

"Keep it down to a dull roar," I told him. "Do you want to fix us both?"

He grinned and said he was very sorry.

"I have your money," I said. "I've been lugging it around all week."

"You'll need it for Christmas. You could pay me next term."

"I have to pay you now," I said.

127

He accepted the money, my aunt's crumpled bills, and tossed it carelessly in the open drawer. It was as if I had insulted him.

"Have you seen Frapp?" he said cautiously.

"He's not in his room," I said. "What are you doing here?"

"Don't you fret."

On the bed was a packet of letters bound by an elastic band. He picked it up and weighed it in his palm.

"I came up here to read my mail in peace," he said, something of his arrogance coming back. "I get about three of these per week."

He moved the envelopes slowly under my nostrils. They had a provocative smell, rather scandalous against the mustiness of Old Stables Three.

"Show you something," George Marsh said, and he plucked a letter. "Grab a gander at this."

The envelope was postmarked Providence; it was addressed in a flourishing hand to George W. Marsh III, Esquire—which seemed a monstrous affectation. The envelope was daintily lined with blue tissue and a thin watermarked sheet protruded from it.

Suddenly I was annoyed. "Is it from your mother, or what?" I said.

"Read it," he said.

"I don't want to read it."

"That's your loss," he said and took back the letter. "You're jealous," he said. "You're love starved."

"That's what you think."

Yet I was not going to divulge my private life. Muriel Delas had awakened something in Ned Sellers and myself at the Woodman School. Muriel had exhibited a warm inquisitiveness in the opposite sex. Being less advanced scholastically than physically, Muriel had remained three years in the seventh grade, where to unsuspecting boys she made herself a familiar guidepost on the path from puberty to adolescence. Ned and I had had our fling with her as two skeptical experimenters, each a bit cowed and jealous of the other. Muriel Delas had been an experience in her own way irresistible, but there had been no devotion, no watermarked notepaper, and no perfume.

"You don't know what it's like to be in love," George Marsh said.

"Who wants to be in love?"

"Show you something," he said.

128

He extracted from his pigskin wallet the snapshot of a girl in a tennis costume. Her figure was far less provocative than Muriel's. About her bare arms and legs there was tragically little flesh, and her small body which the camera had caught from the side was flat as a youth's, but her face, smiling beneath the wide ribbon and low bangs on her forehead, was eager and serene, vibrant and composed, part girl, part woman. It was a defiant, impertinent face. A girl too young to be kissed and too old to be spanked; she had no right to look as she did.

"Her hair gets almost red in the summers," George Marsh said. "I took that picture myself."

"How old is she?"

"About the same as you and me. She goes to Miss Eustis' School."

"Does she live in Providence?" I said.

"No." He was scornful. "New York."

Now he was bored, as though I were incapable of understanding him. He's said all he's going to say, I thought sadly.

My eyes were on the bureaus that were below the dormer window. There his personal possessions were arranged in a regal square of light—silver-backed brushes, a leather-handled clothes brush, a leather box for collars, a leather stud box. They were marked with his initials, strange, expensive things, like the girl in the snapshot.

"Haven't you ever seen a hairbrush?" he said. "You brush your hair, don't you, like anyone else?"

His words tumbled out upon each other in an angry rush, and there it was, the deep hostility. That I should be different, which meant be different from him. He must have known as I did that he was the different one, so much a contrast, but wanting badly to conform.

"I was looking at the photographs," I said.

"Take a good look. They won't bite."

I bent over the bureau and looked closely.

"That's my father," he said. "He shoots skeet. That's him at our place in Long Island, holding his shotgun. Is that so extraordinary?"

But I was looking at the other. He moved beside me and paused at my elbow where I could hear his breathing. "Well, what about it?" he said.

It was a portrait photograph of a young woman in profile, taken from behind so that she posed looking into the camera over her

129

shoulder, her head tilted coyly downward. I examined the dark hair, cut short against her neck and done into tight spit-curls, her thin black eyebrows and pouting lips, and the bare back and the bare arm upon which her chin was resting.

I gave out a long whistle through my teeth, as Ned Sellers did when he was reading *Spicy Detective Magazine*.

"She looks like Betty Boop," I said, "and she's naked."

"That's a picture of my mother."

"But she's absolutely in the nude," I said.

An arm flared toward me in a wide arc. The heel of a hand caught me on the cheek and I fell onto the bed, in a fiery blindness. He lurched upon me and, panting furiously, seized my shoulders. I had not guessed how strong he was or the great advantage of his weight and height. He was battering my head against the cubicle wall.

"Take it back!" I felt his hot tears falling on my neck and hands and heard a voice of desperate hurt and anger.

A sequence of previous battles flashed across my mind, battles won or lost or drawn in back village lots, in the dusty yard of the Woodman School. There had been nothing like this savageness, but it was just. Intentionally or not, I had done him the Supreme Dishonor.

"You don't say that! Son of a bitch! You peasant! Peon. . . ."

I had no will to fight, only to take my beating.

When the rage had spent itself, he pulled away and wiped his nose and eyes with a pocket handkerchief. He turned his back to me and I had the feeling that he was ashamed.

"I'm sorry. I didn't know," I said.

"I'm sorry," he said gently.

"I deserved it."

"I have a disgusting temper."

The photographs had been knocked from the bureau, a chair was overturned and the mattress and covers had been torn from the bed. Together we repaired the damage.

"Hell," George Marsh said. "Your head's bleeding. Now take this towel."

I put a hand to my scalp where there was a throbbing welt and drew it back soaked with blood.

"Better go to the Infirmary. I'll go with you."

"They'll only ask questions."

"I don't care," he said seriously.

"The nurse will report it to Frapp. We'll get on Saturday Disciplinary," I said.

"I've never been on Disciplinary," George Marsh said.

When we were on the front steps of the Infirmary, he took my arm above the elbow. "Nobody's seen me act that way."

"You had the right," I told him.

"I can't talk about my mother," he said. "Just let's never try. I'll take you out for lunch sometime, if she comes up. If she ever does. . . . Are your parents divorced?"

"They're dead."

"That's right," he said. "That puts us in the same boat—in a way. We could say that we're both victims of shattered homes. That's great, isn't it? I read it in the *Reader's Digest*. Mrs. Kew showed me an article, 'New Hope for Children of Divorce.' Do you feel unloved, unwanted?"

I smiled bewilderedly, and he was waiting for me to say something. So I attempted to laugh.

"You'll make out all right," he told me. "But you're an awful peasant. I think I'll have to set you straight. You have a lot of Bostonian ideas."

My wound was healing nicely beneath a large white plaster the next Saturday afternoon, which found me and George Marsh doing penance in the coal yard. We shoveled coal down a chute for three hours, replenishing the Academy's boiler supply under the beady eye of Dismal Gregore. Rebuke came heavy and punishment galling to George Marsh, but it only came that once. He received a Deportment Award in June and I was the only one to remember his single lapse. In time I would have forgotten it myself, as George Marsh perhaps forgot it, had it not been for the fight in the dormitory and that odd admixture of gentleness and fury.

The process of setting me straight began thus with a welt on my head. Thereafter, tentatively, we began to know each other; he got to be more tolerant and I less of a peasant. Vale and I continued to live together and were friends, and I could not yet claim Marsh as a friend. Vale, though he was conquering his shyness, was essentially a peasant too, but he showed no inclination to be set straight. He was not, for example, much impressed with the great event that took place in our Fourth Class year. George Marsh on the other hand was extravagantly impressed. He spread the story about the class, gilding details with a flair that startled me. I didn't look on it as a heroic act at the time. It also was a scene of violence, but it occurred in public and it won me prestige:

For on Packard's Pond in February of 1938, in a crucial and hard-fought game, I blacked the eye and broke the nose of Harry Tilton. That I did so in a fit of temper for which Mr. Flemister, who coached us hockey as severely as he taught a history class, penalized me with a month's Saturday Disciplinary did not detract from the celebrity of the occasion.

George Marsh pulled us apart before Mr. Flemister could get to us. George had seen, even in last year's football season, the first traces of antipathy between Harry Tilton and myself. He repeated remarks that I had made, about the crease in Tilton's jersey, the spotlessness of his pants, the unnecessarily huge shoulder pads, the shin and rib protectors, and the dozen other idiosyncrasies for which Tilton had won his reputation. Harry Tilton could skate circles around me, yet seldom dared to charge me or check me into the boards. On that memorable afternoon, George Marsh played defense with me. He heard the remarks that Tilton, playing left wing for Spartans, called to me over his shoulder while stealing a puck from under my nose. Harry was the flashy loud-mouth with everyone that afternoon, but for some reason he put the bee on me. It was a wonder, George told everybody, that someone hadn't taken a poke at Harry before. But Harry usually kept away from fights. This one started when Harry's stick caught in my skate and flicked me over. Standing right beside the Ithacan nets, George saw the play, and he had to admit that Harry hadn't tripped me on purpose. It really had been an accident, but no one had blamed me for blowing up. Quite a few had cheered, in fact, when I had got up and gone for Tilton. George said it had done his heart good, honestly and truly, to see somebody grab Harry's stick from him and then just lay into him against the boards, fists and elbows flying. It surprised George so that he stood gaping at us for a good two minutes before he got hold of my shoulders and pulled me off. It was really something, George said. Laying into Harry Tilton had been the biggest thing I'd done so far. George told the story excitedly and spoke rapidly, pacing his words with the action like a sports announcer.

Tilton was unable to play the remainder of the season and for football and hockey ever afterward his magnificence was marred by a large and ugly noseguard. Yet he took no reprisals against me and did not demur to class opinion which had swung for a brief time so wildly in my favor. He accepted my apologies more heartily than I offered them and was, in fact, quite friendly.

Fuzzy Eaton, jubilant, proclaimed that he had known I'd had it in me all along. Fuzzy reigned undisputed creator of all class nicknames. It was he who, taking from the phrase "game as a gopher," had nicknamed George Marsh. It was he who had bestowed upon one Alfred Means who, as a new boy in an early siege of homesickness, timidity and maladjustment, had regrettably wet his bed, the life-lasting title of Soaker Means. When after the Packard's Pond episode, improvising on my own name, he addressed me widely as Gubber, I accepted the modest tribute with pride.

So fortified by a new sense of belonging, I began a warmer association with George Marsh. He continued to joke at my expense, but in a tone that was mild and even complimentary. We could speak together without the mutual defensiveness that had stood in our way the year before. He took pains to inform me when a letter arrived from Miss Eustis' and mentioned that there were other girls there that I might like to meet one day. From me there were confessions of the inadequacies of East Northrup and from him more allusions to a world apart, from which he seemed committed to return for nine months of the year like a young Olympian to mingle among mortals. He learned what had been my secret—that I took piano lessons three times a week in the chapel crypt from Mr. Eaves, the choirmaster and organist whom my aunt had prevailed upon to teach me at an almost negligible fee. I had an ear for music, a fair gift Mr. Eaves had just discovered and that was faintly disturbing. It was nothing to boast over and bore so slightly on the social sphere that I had sworn the malleable Mr. Eaves to silence.

Then at last George Marsh found out. "I wish I could play the piano. It never hurts to know a thing like that," he said. "You're lucky." Thenceforth I practiced my scales with something close to zeal and was not ashamed who knew it.

Early one morning of that same February we learned that George Marsh's father had died. The news did not come in the usual way.

No notice, mimeographed in the Alumni Office on black-lined stationery, appeared on the Academy's bulletin boards. At Evening Prayer no mention of the memory of George Warwick Marsh, Jr., Class of 1915, was made by Dr. Kew. No verse was quoted and no hymn sung. The Academy ensign flew as high as any other day from the flagpole on the oval. The death was never recognized officially.

We read of it in the newspaper on the way to breakfast, seven or eight of us, including Harry Tilton, Fuzzy Eaton, and myself. Harry Tilton's eye was colored and puffy over a carefully bandaged nose, but it gleamed impudently upon a prominent column head on the first page of the second section of the New York *Herald Tribune*.

"Oh-ho," he said. "Anyone seen Gopher?"

Fuzzy was reading over his shoulder. "That's no joke," Fuzzy was saying. "No joke at all."

"Gopher doesn't know," somebody said. "I saw him in the can."

"You mean he has to find it out by reading the paper?"

"Maybe it's some other Marsh."

"Yeah," Harry Tilton said. "How many people do you suppose there are named George Warwick Marsh, Jr.?" He poked a finger at the story's lead:

"*George Warwick Marsh, Jr., of 270 Park Avenue, a former stockbroker, died yesterday in Doctors Hospital of injuries received in a fall from the fifth-story window of a West Side hotel Monday night. Norris T. Heink, Publicity Director of the Hotel Neptune, 121 West 53rd Street, affirmed in a statement specially prepared for the press that the death had been accidental.*"

Harry Tilton pursed his lips to a whistle. "The affluence of incohol, no doubt."

We others stood silent in the cold, and watched the ungloved finger trace inexorably down the page as though controlled by some spirit, watched it pause and tap upon the last paragraph.

"*A near witness to the accident was Marianne Phelps, an entertainer, who gave her address as in care of the William Morris Agency. Miss Phelps told reporters that the room from which Mr. Marsh had fallen was one of a suite that she has occupied in temporary residence since the first of the month. The forty-three-year-old heir of the late George Warwick Marsh, former high executive of the Imperial Carton and Can Corporation, had been dining with her at the time of the accident. Miss Phelps revealed that Mr.*"

*March, who had been in poor health, complained of dizziness and
nausea and had opened the window to 'let in a breeze and freshen
himself a little.' Miss Phelps said that at this point she had excused
herself from the room and had returned to find the window open
and Mr. Marsh vanished. 'He wasn't feeling himself,' she told news-
men. 'I am sure it was only a very tragic accident.' Miss Phelps
described herself as 'upset.' A Police Department spokesman today
confirmed the opinion that the death had been 'presumably accidental.'"*

"The Goph—poor old Goph," Fuzzy said.

"Poor Miss Phelps," Harry Tilton said. "One of the old Philadelphia Phelpses, no doubt."

"You're a real funny fellow," Fuzzy said. "Now shut up."

And everyone else told him to shut up.

Chapter Six

Cuppy Vale was not as horrified as I by the cruel news and the cruel way it came to Gopher Marsh.

"How is that any of your business? Why do you always butt in?" he said glumly, dismal as Gregore. "Anyone would think it was your father that died."

In our Fourth Class year Vale and I shared a cubicle in Old Stables Number One. Vale was unobtrusive, bound by a harder self-reliance than I, and felt no compulsion to seek out friends. He remained steadfastly loyal to his home town of Canandaigua and looked on me as a fellow peasant in danger of being led astray in a maze of uncertain values.

"You don't need to preach to me," I said.

"Why should I preach to you? You're not as dumb as you make out to be. You're okay in Latin now. You're good at math, and you're some kind of an athlete. You're good, only you're so dumb about yourself."

He would say something like this, cutting through all my careful subterfuge, in the same precise way that, at the start of the autumn term, he had walked into the cubicle and straightaway observed that my Uncle Torbert's long framed placard was nowhere to be seen. It was exasperating that a gawky contemporary should know me that well.

"I'm not worrying about myself," I said. "If you're looking for something to worry about, why don't you worry about those hickies on your face? That's a real crop."

Vale only grinned. "A healthy hicky now and then is relished by the best of men."

We all had tried, but none of us had been successful in goading Cuppy Vale. He closed his eyes, and grinned again, wryly, without losing a shred of composure. "You go right ahead and hang onto

Gopher Marsh's coattails. You can't tell but maybe you'll have a swell free ride. Maybe you can ride on his uncle's yacht."

George Marsh's father had been cremated and his ashes buried in the back garden at Great Neck. It had been a simple funeral at the old family place with only himself, his Uncle Mark, and a Filipino, Manuelo, who had been his father's valet, in attendance. Compared to what he had expected, it had been a cinch and he had been just as glad to have it that way. Helen Marsh, who until two years before had been his stepmother, had planned to be there too. At the last minute she had called from New York to say that she couldn't bear to, much to his uncle's relief and, George was frank to admit, his own.

Though he wore a black band about his sleeve and a black silk necktie, he shunned sympathy and special consideration wherever it was offered. He kept desperately busy. He went to the tryouts for the next year's hockey and was accepted for the first squad, an uncommon feat for a Fourth Classman. Dismal Gregore made the unprecedented offer of excusing him from a one-thousand-word book report, and George had done the paper anyway. He spent no idle time by himself. Wherever he went, he took a companion; from building to building or to the village for candy and an ice-cream soda, one of us had to go with him. It didn't seem to matter who it was, if he would talk and come up with something to laugh about. Given these circumstances and this trend, it was not surprising that George Marsh invited me to have lunch with his mother.

"They'll be up on Sunday, and you better come along. I haven't seen Baby since last summer, but she'll want me to bring a friend anyway. Baby always wants to see my friends," he explained. And, seeing the trace of a question upon my face, "I don't know why I call her Baby. I've always called her that and so does everybody except my stepfather who calls her Barbara. . . . I'm only telling you this to save you the trouble of figuring it out for yourself." He rubbed his hand, in the old apologetic gesture, over his cheek. "Don't be frightened by my mother. She may carry on about the Old Man and that kind of stuff, but Bert Seidel is pretty good with her. My Uncle Mark claims she married him because he's Jewish and she wanted to get back at the family. I think I like Bert. He's some kind of a lawyer. He works hard, and he tries to keep Baby on her toes."

The Seidels arrived shortly after noon that Sunday in a Driv-Urself Ford they had rented in Boston. The drive had taken almost three hours, all because of Bert, who thought he remembered a shortcut to avoid traffic on the Worcester Turnpike. Mr. Bertrand Seidel, a heavy-set man of extreme composure who drove cautiously and spoke with authority of routes and highway improvements, ventured that a man was entitled to make a mistake once in a while and placed his great hand, in its gray dress glove, affectionately on his wife's fur-draped shoulder.

"I take it all back," his wife said. "Seidel, you've got the patience of Job."

She had been gaily prattling with her son. She had placed George on her right beside the window, so that she might enjoy the coziness of being bundled between her two men. They had taken the midnight from New York, a great relief to her, since it had meant a small victory over Bert. For once she had persuaded him to knock off from the office early enough—"and on a *Saturday* afternoon, mind you, when everyone else's husband is home sleeping"—to take her out to dinner. They had gone to Jack and Charlie's and on top of that she had wangled some tickets to *Du Barry,* where they had laughed themselves silly. Before he could catch his breath, she had whisked Bert in a cab back to the apartment, where the bags were packed and waiting in the lobby, and had whisked him down to Grand Central.

"Squire?" she said. "How old would you say your silver-haired mother was? Think carefully and tell Mama her age."

"Thirty-seven," her son said carefully. "Or thirty-eight."

"Thirty-eight," she said triumphantly. "Why should an old grass widow hide her age? Sometimes, looking at myself, I think I'm sixty, and above all in the mornings. Fortunately Seidel's at the office by the time I wake up, so he's spared that fright. We're getting on, Bert and I." A glance at her husband. "Here I am practically past the age of parturition—and a very damn good thing too."

Mr. Seidel brought the car to a full stop before an intersection and peered patiently to the left and right. "All right, Barbara," he said firmly and as firmly shifted into low gear.

"One thing about being married to Seidel," she said to her son, "you don't get embarrassed. He keeps his opinions to himself. . . .

138

I think he thinks I'm an infant. Do I look like an infant to you, Squire?"

I recognized the pouty bow of the lips I had seen in the photograph and the round face, which was fatter, with a fold beneath the chin, and less pallid under a layer of rouge. Her hair was the same deep black, but it bore no trace of a curl, being combed in a looping wave, and tied up in back with a bright pink ribbon that did look juvenile. She had on a full beaver coat that had fallen loosely about her when we had been introduced on the steps of Old Stables; the figure beneath it had been full and on the verge of plumpness, although the legs had been trim and pert.

"What do you think, Squire Marsh? What do I look like, anyway?"

"Baby," George Marsh said to his mother, "you look fine to me."

She grabbed his ears and pulled him to her, covering his face with kisses. "Love you, love you, love you to death, Snook."

She took a piece of tissue from her purse and set to wiping his face with matronly satisfaction. She appeared to notice for the first time that I was in the back seat.

"How's he been behaving himself, Charlie?" she said. "Has he been giving you any trouble?"

"His name is Gus," George Marsh said.

"Well, Gus, where do you suggest for lunch?"

"The Northrup Manor's easiest to get to," I said. "In Northrup Center."

"God, the Northrup Manor!"

"All right, Barbara," Mr. Seidel said.

George's mother was not the first parent to protest against the Northrup Manor. A sprawled assortment of wings and ells attached to a two-story building with a gambrel roof, it was neither comfortable nor aesthetically pleasing. But because it was owned by the Academy, having been acquired in the Little Rector's boom days, to accommodate a growing influx of relatives, it had never been wholly abandoned. The trustees had leased it to an elderly couple named Flynn who had moved recently to Northrup Center from the city of Worcester.

When we arrived, the large dining room was, as it was almost invariably, barren. Place settings and white tablecloths shone funereally on more than thirty tables and Mrs. Flynn, at being interrupted in reading *The Woman's Home Companion*, escorted us to a round one in the center of the room.

"I wouldn't call this the warmest room I ever dined in," Mrs. Seidel said.

"Mr. Flynn's in the cellar putting some steam up now," Mrs. Flynn said.

She passed us each a carbon-typed menu on which alterations in price and entree had been made and remade in ink and pencil.

"These are old," she explained, redundantly.

Baby Seidel tugged at her husband's sleeve. "Don't be cheap, Seidel. Can't you tell that this is an occasion? Let's get some champagne splits."

Mr. Seidel neatly unfolded his napkin. "Now," he said. "Now, Barbara."

His wife nipped grimly on a red-tipped cigarette, inclining her head for George Marsh to light it. "Let's see," she said, blowing copiously at Mrs. Flynn. "Have you a nice pâté?"

"Don't serve patty," Mrs. Flynn said.

Mrs. Flynn served us the soup, the meat, and a Waldorf salad in a laborious progression, but there was no hurrying her. George Marsh listened politely to his mother, nodding his head and speaking only when spoken to directly.

A look of concern crept over his stepfather's face. "George," he began gently, "I can't tell you how sorry we were about your father. Your mother is an emotional woman—I thought it would be wise for her not to get in touch with you right away."

George Marsh stared dumbly at the tablecloth.

"Do you love me, Snook? Do you think I'm a horrid mother?"

"Of course I don't."

"I thought your Uncle Mark would break the news. He's so damned competent about these things. Seidel said not to call you, and he's so *damned* competent. . . . If I could call you, I thought naturally your uncle had. And of course no one had." Her chubby hand crept up George Marsh's sleeve. "Snook . . . Snook."

"Don't," George said. "Please, do you have to cry?"

"It takes guts to go through a thing like this," Bert Seidel put in suddenly. "Believe you me. I'm proud of you both."

His wife snatched another red-tipped cigarette and lit it herself. "Seidel, don't try to be fatherly. You're a he-man, and a real sweetheart, but it happens that George hasn't got a father. The Squire is all on his own."

"George and his mother don't see each other often enough," Mr. Seidel said to me. "It looks like you were roped in to pretty much of a family affair."

I couldn't look at her, at her husband, or at George. They were talking some more, and soon Mr. Seidel was asking me to tell him all about the Dramatic Society and hockey and winter sports. It seemed that Mrs. Seidel had started to cry and George kept calling her Baby and she kept calling him Snook. Mr. Seidel wanted to know where my home was and what I did in the summers. I wanted to get away, to run home to Elm Street and never come back. Then I began being frightened, and I couldn't look at my food. George Marsh was saying something incoherently and his mother was saying that she loved him very much.

Eventually Mr. Seidel said, "Don't you feel so hot?"

"No, sir."

"What would you say to a quick drive in the car?" he said. "You can show me around the town."

The Ford meandered down High Street, past the stores that lined its either side making it the nucleus of commerce in Northrup Center. I felt much better now.

Mr. Seidel was smoking another cigar, holding it away where the smoke was drawn out of the car through the little flipper window on his left. He was a man built heavily enough to have played football at college, bigger than Mr. McTeale of our football squad.

"How about taking a spin over there and you point out to me the points of interest?"

He had a deep voice. It seemed to originate somewhere in the center of his chest and flowed with a mighty calm, with something of the authority Mr. Sellers had when he was demonstrating a car to a customer. But Mr. Seidel was not like Mr. Sellers or Mr. Marsh or my uncle or quite like anyone I'd ever met.

He admired the snow and ice of Millers Hill, where the tiny figures of boys skiing in the sunshine reminded him of beetles scrambling on a cake of ice. I called his attention to the scenes I knew best. "This is Simple River," I would say and he would think that was a pretty good name for a river and wonder if I swam in it in

141

the summertime. "Here's Elm Street," I was saying. "There's the library and the Congregational Church at the end, down by the mall. And here's where I live."

He slowed the car and shifted gears. "That's a nice old house," he said.

"That wall is new," I said.

"It's a nice-looking wall."

We took a wandering drive through East Northrup and over the Meadows Road back to Northrup Center. The car skidded once or twice on an icy stretch in back of Millers Hill.

"I don't suppose you get so much snow in New York," I said.

"It snows, but they try to shovel it off in trucks, but they only get part of it and the rest stays there all winter long getting dirtier and dirtier. This is good clean snow. When I was your age I lived in a little town but it was too close to the city. It was a little town in New Jersey, near Rahway."

"Oh sure," I said. I knew there was an airport in Newark and a boardwalk in Atlantic City; and that was as well as I knew New Jersey.

"Tell me, what does your dad do, Gus?"

"He's dead," I said quickly. "My uncle used to be a lawyer but he's retired."

"That's what I am," Mr. Seidel said. "A lawyer. Do you ever visit New York?"

"No, sir. Not yet."

"If you're ever there," Mr. Seidel said, "call me up and come downtown on the Elevated. That's a nice ride, and we'll have lunch together."

The Ford nosed reluctantly into the drive before the Northrup Manor and we climbed out. Walking up the creaking steps to the creaking porch Mr. Seidel said off-handedly, "How do you suppose George likes Northrup?"

"I think he'd like it O.K.," I answered, "if he didn't have to come here to school."

"Are you and George pretty good friends?"

"Pretty good."

"Did you ever think of asking him to stay with you?"

"I don't think he'd like it much."

142

"No," Mr. Seidel said quietly. "I don't suppose he would. George is a fine boy, but he misses a lot."

My attitude was different when Mr. Seidel and I returned. I was not as tense, as frightened. And George and his mother looked peaceful in an empty parlor, he reading, and she plucking out "Love for Sale" on an ancient square piano.

"He could play it for you," George said of me proudly.

"Why, Charlie," his mother said. "Do you play?"

"Baby, his name is Gus."

I was able to laugh, and easily accept her; she wasn't half as weird. Although she must be crazy. I thought that it might be her and not George Marsh whom you should pity.

Chapter Seven

Late in March, through the press of books and examinations and packing that were the prelude to the spring vacation, I was conscious of a closer pressure from Cuppy Vale. He liked to ski. While he confessed to being naturally awkward, he believed that if he kept at skiing, it was the one sport he might some day master.

A few days before the vacation he gave me an invitation. "Maybe you could come up to Canandaigua. We have some not-half-bad slopes there, or we could go to Stowe or North Conway if there's some decent snow left. If you think you could afford it."

"I'll be going to New York," I told him casually. "Thanks all the same."

"How can you afford that?"

I faced him resolutely, with a feeling of rebelliousness. "Because I'm staying with Gopher Marsh, that's why."

"Reason enough," Vale said. "You'll be staying at his uncle's. I call that very nice. Very well played."

"He invited me," I said.

"You'll have a good time and you won't have to worry about its costing you. . . . Too bad it isn't summer. You won't be able to ride on the yacht. You should have timed it to take a pleasure cruise on the *Excalibur*. Have you got the train fare?"

It was useless to talk back to him, for he would too well understand my anger.

The question of train fare was more bitter than he knew. My aunt was determined that I spend my holidays at home. ("We never see you, dearie. You never come for Sunday lunch any more.") And she was not at all sure, judging from what Mrs. Kew had told her, that she approved of the Marsh boy's mother. Uncle Torbert, however, very highly approved of the Marsh boy's uncle, Marcus. I was advanced twenty dollars and given permission to remain in New

York one weekend. Friday to Monday, Aunt Connie insisted, was time enough to spend in New York.

She drove me in to Boston. At Read and White's on Summer Street we rented a tuxedo, a stiff shirt, a collar, a pair of patent-leather pumps, and even studs and cufflinks. At the South Station, while my aunt inquired if the price of a round-trip ticket could not be adjusted to a three-day limit rather than thirty days, I made some furtive purchases of my own. A copy of *The New Yorker* Magazine, the *New York Times*, two packages of Old Golds, and a thirty-nine-cent cigarette lighter.

Aunt Connie walked with me through the gate and down the track, instinctively past the diner and parlor cars until we reached the line of coaches, halfway to the engine. Aunt Connie straightened the collar of my overcoat and stepped back admiringly.

"I can't get over it. You're a grown young man," she said.

It was the one o'clock, a very snappy train by her standards, and we had done well to get there ten minutes ahead of time. As I climbed aboard she rushed to plant an impulsive kiss on the edge of my cheek, where my head was turned. Settling myself in a seat, the bulky suitcase in the rack overhead and my overcoat and long knit scarf with the green and white stripes of Emmanuel dangling beside me, I looked out the window and saw her. A small, gray figure bundled in fur to the tip of her chin, smiling vaguely and intermittently waving the fingers of one hand. I unfolded the paper, started to read, but felt her eyes through the sooty window and so, minutes later, turned again. She was pointing to her chest and mouthing a message at me. My tie needed straightening.

"Good-by, dearie," her lips were saying. "We'll see you on Monday."

She was standing there as the train pulled out, waving bravely and calling something against the impossibility of the engine's roar. I can take care of myself, I thought. I'm old enough.

The train waited ten minutes in the Providence station, but I decided not to get off. From under the roofs that sheltered the platforms by the tracks I saw the white dome of the capitol, partly covered with snow and looking like a design on a postage stamp.

There was another stop, a briefer one, at Westerly. Through the window I watched a girl, with a small red hat and a trim blue coat with brass buttons, being bid good-by by her parents. A conventional scene at a rural station, the family car in the background, the honest, middle-aged faces of man and wife smiling hard to conceal the sorrow of parting, the cheerful conductor helping with the heavy bags. It could have been, given brighter colors, a poignant bit of Americana from the brush of Norman Rockwell; it could have been a cover on the *Saturday Evening Post,* warm and universally touching—but for the expression on the face of the girl. She faced them impassively and cringed from their kisses and fidgeted as though the train would pull off at any moment without her. She approached the adjoining coach, her parents following. The girl turned to them only once and then to snatch from the hand of her mother a folded magazine, a tangible possession, it seemed, and so more valuable than any farewell blessing. Then, perhaps cruelly, the train was in motion once more, giving the final, inexorable cleavage, and I watched Dad and Mother turn, Mother dabbing her eyes with a hankie, join arms, and walk back to the car.

When the magazine and candy butcher who had boarded at Providence made his rounds with a basket of sandwiches, I bought a light lunch at my seat. Milk in a cardboard container, a ham and a ham-and-cheese, and a porous apple, I leaned back when it was eaten, and dozed.

Yawning, I lifted the window shade and saw that the train had stopped at New Haven. I collected the apple core, the milk container and sandwich wrappers, placed them secretly beneath the seat. Inside my pocket I felt the bulge of the cigarettes, which I would try when the train was rolling again.

As it gathered speed I made my way to the door of the coach onto the cold outside platform. Standing on the flooring over the steps by one door the conductor had just fastened, I saw a girl by the door opposite, smoking. She wore the small red hat and the blue, brass-buttoned coat that had caught my eye at Westerly. The magazine was tucked beneath one arm. She wasn't so old, I satisfied myself, not any older than I was, though with the matching scarlet shoes, lipstick, and nail polish it was clear she wanted to be older. Yawning again, I took out a cigarette and tried to light my brand-new lighter.

I had clicked it several times unsuccessfully, when I heard the girl's rather sharp voice say to me, "Smoke much?"

146

I smiled at her, superciliously as possible. "I guess I was smoking when you were in diapers."

"I'll give you a tip," the girl said. "Try matches. Later when you're a big shot, you graduate to a lighter, but a good lighter. Not something out of Liggett's."

I looked at her and tried hopefully to arch my eyebrows, wanting to keep a cool, collected distance, wanting to look quizzical.

"Catch," she said, and tossed me a card of matches. It dropped to the metal floor and the lighter dropped after it.

"We're all thumbs today, aren't we?" the girl said. She allowed the smoke of her cigarette to curl for a moment about the lashes of her gray-green eyes, and then the sting forced her to shut them, inelegantly.

"Smoke much yourself?" I said.

"Smoking is forbidden at Emmanuel," she said archly.

"We all learn to smoke at home."

"Where's home?"

"East Northrup," I told her. "Massachusetts."

"That's where Emmanuel is," she said. "Can you answer one simple question? Where's home?"

"East Northrup."

"Oh, God give us strength." She rolled her eyes upward and sighed, to indicate great patience.

"I go to school in East Northrup," I said. "And I live in East Northrup. Catch on?"

"Why didn't you say so?" the girl said. "Aren't you wondering how I know you're from Emmanuel?"

I paused, surprised by this sudden naïveté. She had sounded almost delighted by her powers of observation. "Anyone can look at a necktie," I said. "I guess there's just one tie with these green and white stripes on it."

"You don't need to be snobbish about it," she said hurtfully, in a way that made me regret all this witty business. "When did Emmanuel ever have exclusive rights to green and white? Have you heard of Dartmouth?"

"This is a lighter green."

I smiled, hoping we could stop playing games. She was an attractive girl, with a firm little figure; yet because of a nasal, Yankee

147

determination in her voice, she seemed always defensive, implacable.

"You go to New York often?" I asked.

She gave a brittle laugh. "I practically live there."

"But your home's in Westerly."

For an instant she frowned, because I had said this baldly, as an incontrovertible fact. "Did you see me get on the train?"

"I saw the conductor carrying those heavy bags," I told her. "I saw your mother kiss you good-by, and I saw you steal her magazine."

She smiled, much more softly. "It was my *Blythe,* the April issue. I simply can't go anywhere without it, my pappy says. I think it's a much better magazine than *Vogue,* don't you? Or wouldn't you know?"

I laughed.

"Do you know a boy at Emmanuel named Alfred Means?"

"We call him 'Soaker' Means."

"That's horrid," she said. "Do you know Peter Fern?"

"Frazzle Fern," I said, laughing. "You know all the lulus."

"Well, I'll admit—but they're both sweet boys. Do you know Roger Comstock? Colton Cutting?"

"They're in the class above."

"Bunny Bolting?"

"We don't call him 'Bunny.'"

"I don't care to know what you call him," the girl said. "Do you know George Marsh?"

"I'm coming down to visit him, matter of fact."

"Really?" she asked, and brightened. "I'm going to visit Lila Norris."

I nodded blankly.

She was breathless, tapping the magazine under her arm. "You know—*Lila Norris?* Her mother's editor of *Blythe?* George Marsh is mad for her, she's my best friend. Whenever I go to New York I stay with the Norrises."

"I've heard about her," I said quietly. "I've seen a picture of her."

"It's a small world," the girl said. "Are you going to the Get-Togethers?"

"I don't know what we're going to do. Is that a dance?"

"Are you going to the dinner before, at Linda Parkhurst's?"

"I wouldn't know," I said.

"She's a friend of ours from school. I know she asked George, he's taking Lila to the dance. There'll be quite a Eustis crowd at Linda's. You better tell me who you are."

"Gus Taylor."

"I'm Chee Wee Gibbons—don't laugh. That's what they call me." We shook hands across the platform in mock formality.

"I love New York, don't you?" she said childishly, and her brittleness vanished. "I'm going to live there one day. I can't abide Westerly."

Back in my seat, as the train passed Stamford, I asked myself what had made Chee Wee Gibbons seem a pathetic impostor. It might have been that she refused to admit to herself that she was a Westerly girl. Beneath her array of affectations that were incomprehensible to me, I recognized this, the impostor in her—we were quite a bit alike.

At 125th Street, where Aunt Connie had warned me against getting off by mistake ("It's the same as Back Bay Station, dearie, but it's in Harlem"), I took down my suitcase and put on my overcoat and scarf. The lights and the gilt on the black sign of the Hotel Naomi disappeared and the coach dropped underground, into darkness, and hurtled through the track and switching lights to the journey's end at Grand Central Station.

Mr. Marsh, and the house he lived in, which George had likened to "an old brownstone museum—way up on Fifth Avenue," had been long a legend in my mind. Yet I had not imagined that on each side of it I would see identical buildings of brownstone, standing drab and abandoned, "To Let" signs on their walls which in the light of a street lamp were thick with pigeon droppings. In an era when wrecking firms competed for their destruction with private philanthropies and European consulates, it was appropriate that the one private home on the block belong to a Marsh. It was the lone survivor, loftiest and noblest of the forest, the fruits of an antediluvian acorn, nourished through gnarled iron roots by the vigor of a forgotten age.

I had had no preconceptions, either, of how I would feel upon setting foot inside. I had not known that there was still a place on earth where a clean, neatly-dressed boy of sixteen, wearing the Em-

149

manuel tie and scarf, could feel as a chimney sweep from a London slum felt a century before upon blundering into the great fireplace of his lord's manor.

I had been told, of course, of Pitney. The wart on his nose and the silvery thatch of hair that identified him the moment he opened the iron-grilled inner door. I had been told of Pitney, the oldest household retainer, older than Mr. Marsh himself, who clung fiercely to his prerogative of exercising Mr. Marsh's paired Dalmatians twice daily in Central Park. If it seemed indecent to me that an arthritic septuagenarian smaller than myself should hang my coat and haul my suitcase to the elevator car, it seemed sheer crudity to Pitney that I should protest. When I struggled to relieve him, he drew back, fairly toppling against the marble stairs under the weight of my bag.

I was shown my room, my closet, and the bath across the hall. Pitney emphasized that Mr. Marsh was expecting me downstairs and so I dallied only to wash my face and hands and to change my shirt. Pitney unpacked my suitcase. With a rush of gratitude I saw him stuff into a pocket of his livery the receipted slip which the clerk at Read and White had improvidently pinned upon my rented dinner clothes. While the elevator crept downward, he informed me that Mr. George was not at home but that he was expected shortly.

I was led without a word across the long carpeted hall to the drawing room and there, close to a grate of glowing coals, I was presented to Mr. Marcus Marsh.

"It's time we shut the night out, Pitney," Mr. Marsh said. The blinds were drawn over two wide windows and across the lights of Central Park. "I feared at first that George had invited Mr. Tilton. How glad I am to have been mistaken."

"I'm very glad to be here, sir."

"Mr. Tilton is constantly bothering us over the holidays, constantly on the telephone. George is entirely too polite to his friends." Mr. Marsh appraised me from his armchair. "What's the good in having friends it you can't be rude to them once in a while?"

"Tilton was going to Florida this vacation, sir," I said. "Maybe he's not back yet."

Mr. Marsh puckered his lips. "We may thank God for small mercies," he said. His face loosened under the parchment-shaded reading lamp, slowly assumed a kind of merriment. "I'm glad you could stay with us. With one or two reservations, I think I can safely say I enjoy George's friends."

A second man, slightly Pitney's junior, approached with a coal scuttle, stooped stiffly, and replenished the grate. Pitney reappeared with a tray upon which were three sherry glasses, a decanter, biscuits, and a bowl containing radishes, celery, and raw carrots.

"You'll take sherry, I expect," Mr. Marsh said.

"If you don't mind, sir."

"Why should I mind?" he said. "George's father took whiskey at the age of twelve. Do you remember, Pitney, when Mr. George's father got onto a quart of your Jameson's?"

Pitney grunted, bestirred by the memory. I took a glass of sherry and two biscuits but left the vegetables untouched.

"Pitney and I thrive on raw vegetables," Mr. Marsh said. "You quite possibly have heard of Bernarr Macfadden. Many believe he's an impostor. I think I should explain from the outset that Pitney and I emphatically do not."

Pitney's arm quivered beneath the tray. He snorted, and I saw by his face that this was not a seizure of senility but of mirth.

"At least," Mr. Marsh was saying, "at least we're not the recalcitrant fossils that George's friends assume us to be, but we resort to the most outrageous nonsense to prove it."

I was at home there, though I could not have told why. The leather-bound sets of Thackeray and Carlyle, the tapestries, the brocaded satin bell cords above the mantel, the portrait of the school of Gainsborough were familiar as the antimacassars in our Elm Street sitting room. My uncle, in one of his many intimations about the Marsh family, had suggested that Kipling and Lloyd George and John Galsworthy had been entertained in this house. My uncle said that Marcus Marsh was all that Soames Forsyte was not and all that Soames would have liked to be.

"I am awfully glad you could stay with us," Mr. Marsh was saying. "I never had a son, I never ventured marriage. But I think I understand the young. My brother was the great progenitor. He had a son, George Junior, and a grandson—George. He left the boys money, to be sure, but among all his obligations he had little time for them. I don't know who's responsible for my brother's grandson, if I am not. George's grandfather is buried in the back garden at Great Neck and we've buried his father there—a Southern custom perhaps. I was fond of George's father. I'm fond of George. I wonder if he realizes that when I die he'll be the last of us—I'm afraid I'm boring you."

"No, sir."

And so he told me, for the first of many times, the story of the birthing party at which George Marsh had made his delayed entrance into the world. I did not ask him a single question and yet he was talking to me freely and telling me things I had no business to hear. He was confiding in me with the rare directness by which age communicates itself to youth, with the mutual sympathy that bypasses the generation in between.

At length he turned his attention back to a copy of *The Spur*. He held a wide reading glass over each page and read, chuckling over something or other. His white hair, which had been agitated by laughter, was as unruly as it had been that day in the parlor of Headmaster's House.

I walked quietly about the room trying to identify objects. In the light of a great lamp with a Nanking china base a whole corner of the room was revealed, together with an alcove that connected. Here were more volumes, the Furness edition of Shakespeare, the works of Meredith, de Tocqueville, and in a shelf of nautical miscellany, Maclay's *History of the Navy* and *The Influence of Sea Power upon the French Revolution and Empire* by Mahan. A bronze bust of Socrates rested on top of the case, and on a pedestal nearby, in marble, a small bust, hatless, of young Napoleon, the First Consul.

I entered the alcove through its dark velvet portieres and switched on the light. Its walls were covered with Marsh family memorabilia. Here were a photograph of Mr. Marsh and his brother George in two canvas chairs, wearing Panama hats, seated on the afterdeck of the *Excalibur*, and a photograph of a coach and three pairs of horses which a faded inked label identified as the July, 1924, Excursion of the Coaching Club of New York to Marshmain, home of the brothers George and Marcus Marsh, Great Neck, Long Island. And there hung the oars with which the Marsh brothers had rowed on college crews, the whips and riding crops which the brothers once had wielded, the mounted shoe of a Marsh stable entry which had won the Preakness, and here more photographs of the Marsh brothers posing with horse, fish, and game, of George Marsh as a small boy in bathing trunks poised upon his father's bare shoulders as if to dive from the *Excalibur's* stern.

I looked again at the photograph of father and son and was struck by the incongruousness of it. It was the only indication on those walls that George Marsh had ever had a father. I wondered about that father, of whom the whimsical old gentleman in the next room had told so much, much more than I had a right to know. The ashes of Andy Marsh now lay under the sod in the family burial plot at Marshmain. The same plot, I had been told, to which Andy Marsh invited a hundred friends, carrying flasks, for a midsummer's eve party, in deliberate disobedience of his outraged father. There was no rancor in Uncle Mark's tone as he told me this scandalous story, and yet I was embarrassed to have heard it. And I wished I hadn't heard about the Sixty-fourth Street birthing party, or the things Uncle Mark had said, again with no rancor that I could notice, even about his niece by marriage. ("I'm going to be a *mother!*" Baby Marsh announced one morning that Uncle Mark never forgot. "Can you imagine anything so preposterous?") Baby Marsh, I thought, Baby, Betty Boop with no clothes on. "Forever the flapper, a rouged anachronism in a pink bow ribbon," old Marcus Marsh described her. "Now on her number three hubby, she persists to struggle by a numbed mechanism of instinct. One day you'll comprehend these things, Gus."—I wished he hadn't told me that. Especially since my own uncle Torbert Case kept talking about the Marshes and the aristocratic mold. That's some kind of a mold, I thought. But I remembered, just now, a thing I'd heard George Marsh say often, and that I hadn't understood before. Uncle Mark was the only person he trusted as a kid, George had said often. Uncle Mark was the only reliable person in the world, even if he was a little cobwebby. Then, that was a pretty lucky thing for George. At least he had Uncle Mark to cling to.

A small organ console was half hidden by the velvet curtains, its pipes built into the wall above. I sat on the hard wooden stool be-creak.

Mr. Marsh called from the sitting room, "Can you play an electric fore it and carelessly pumped one of the pedals, which gave a dry organ? Can you play a good rousing hymn?"

"I can play 'Oh God and father of mankind,'" I said.

"Poor Edgar Trimble's hymn. I find it depressing. Can you play 'The Son of God goes forth to war, a kingly crown to gain'?"

I turned on the light and the organ switch, and he called that the pipes would warm up in a minute or two. To encourage me, he began humming. Slowly, I followed him, finding my way about the unfamiliar keyboard, testing the various stops and settling for Vox Humana. When I found the tune, he shouted approvingly and sang along with me. It was a deep, vibrating voice that rose at the start of each new stanza above the wavering sound of the pipes. We went through it once and were bursting into it again when George Marsh entered the room. The young lord of the castle, returning to his own. In his black tie and armband in that dark room he made a melancholy prince.

We took chairs in the drawing room and pulled them close to the old man. Having sung so lustily, he could not be bothered to raise his voice in simple conversation. "Where have you been all day?" he asked George.

"This afternoon I was skating. On Fridays you can skate at the Garden." In the light George looked healthy and relaxed, his cheeks a cheerful pink from exercise. It was strange that he should also seem sad.

"What garden?" I asked him.

"Madison Square Garden." He smiled at his uncle. "First time in New York," he said.

"I know all about him," Mr. Marsh said. "He's a fine boy."

"You know his uncle," George said. "Mr. Torbert Case."

"Of course I remember Torbert Case. I remember that day at Emmanuel. It was Opening Day. I remember how exhausting that was." Mr. Marsh crossed his arms over his stomach, contentedly. "Tell me, did they ever name him Trustee?"

"Not yet, sir," I said.

"What was the name of that extraordinary volume?"

"*Emmanuel: The Birth and Growth of a Private School.*"

"That was the most extraordinary book. . . . Why do you suppose he did it?"

"My uncle is very interested in the Academy, sir."

"Yes," Mr. Marsh sighed. "He certainly is. . . . I always thought he should have been named Trustee."

"He sends you his regards, sir, by the way."

"Well, you tell your uncle Torbert Case that I send my regards. And ask him—well, you'd better not ask him."

"Sir?" I said, eagerly.

"Ask him if he still believes in the infallibility of Kreuger and Toll."

"How do you mean, sir?"

"You tell him that Marcus Marsh sends his regards and asks if he still believes in Kreuger and Toll."

"I'll tell him, sir. But I wish you'd tell me."

"I think," Mr. Marsh started, then paused. "I think he'd rather tell you himself. All things being equal."

"What's Kreuger and Toll?" George Marsh said.

The old man pushed to the edge of his chair. "If you boys will give me an arm," he said, "I left my canes downstairs."

He continued to talk as we helped him down the hall. "I wish I were going to the theater with you tonight, but I am never able to sit through it these days. It's hard to get an aisle seat any more and you've got to sit on the aisle if you've got sciatica. I thought of having you both dine with me at the Union Club, but I find the food indigestible at the Union. I prefer to dine here with Pitney. When you get to be as old as we are, you appreciate your raw carrots and your yogurt. The old man's ambrosia, we call it. We're great admirers of Bernarr Macfadden."

That night we went to *The Boys from Syracuse*. We rode home from the theater in the town car with Mr. Marsh's chauffeur sitting serenely in the front.

"I'll bet we bored your uncle stiff," I said.

"Listen, nothing bores the old gent," George Marsh said, and he must have been smiling in the darkness.

"He's something, your uncle."

"Yes," George said. "He is a great old gent."

Chapter Eight

We had a late breakfast Saturday morning. There was no sign of Mr. Marsh or of Pitney. In the daylight, without them, the house was lifeless, a brownstone mausoleum. Even the water had flowed slowly into the great bathtub on the third floor and when finally enough had collected to bathe in I had found that it was cold. George said that his uncle had probably motored out to Great Neck for the day, rising at dawn, which was his habit, so as not to miss a minute of daylight. And Pitney was exercising the Dalmatians. It took him an hour each morning to walk them on their leads through Central Park to Sixtieth Street and back, though this was Saturday, and Pitney was not likely to have walked so far because of the crowds at the zoo. The house only came alive at night when his uncle sat before the drawing-room fire before dinner and for the few minutes afterward that he remained awake and talkative. The rest of the time it was a lonely house, George Marsh said.

"What do you suppose your uncle meant about mine?" I asked. We stood, buttoning our overcoats in the front hall, in a pool of chilly blue light that fell from the stained-glass panes above the door.

"I expect he has some joke," George said. "I think your uncle used to ask him for business advice. Let's get out of here."

We caught a Fifth Avenue bus at the corner of Seventy-ninth Street, climbed to the open deck, and rode slowly through the Saturday traffic. It was a brisk, sunny day that carried no hint of the season. Riding with our coats buttoned to our necks and the cold wind at our faces, it seemed like a morning in autumn, too vigorous for spring. I watched the figures in Central Park, hoping for a glimpse of Pitney and the dogs. There's the Frick Museum, George Marsh was saying, or that's the Knickerbocker Club, the Hotel

Pierre, and that's the Plaza. (This was his New York and if I wanted to see Grant's Tomb and all that, I would have to see them by myself on a rubberneck tour.) He pointed out the hansom cabs by the Plaza. One night he had ridden in one, all over the park, on New Year's Eve and he had been with Lila. The driver had taken them all the way to the East River, and afterward to Sutton Place where Lila's family lived. They had watched the boat lights blinking, traveling up and down. George must have been pretty tight from champagne he had taken at the dance they had been to earlier, for he had kissed her.

He related this last to me reverently.

"You mean that was the first time you ever kissed her?" I said, astonished.

George was smiling proudly.

"You've known her three years," I said. "More than three years." My mind flashed back on Muriel Delas of the Woodman School, that signpost of my own adolescence. I had achieved as much and more with Muriel in one summer evening.

"You're kidding me," I said.

I recognized a flickering in the dark eyes that was not pure anger, but the old dread of criticism.

"Lila's not the kind of girl you neck with. Hell, you can always neck with girls." He spoke like a knight in defense of his lady.

"I didn't mean anything by it," I said. "It just seemed a pretty long time."

We left the bus at Fifty-seventh Street and walked silently down the Avenue, threading through the crowds in front of the big stores. It was impossible to tell from his expression if I had hurt his feelings. We walked several blocks thus, uncommunicatively, until a thought struck him, a pleasant thought that lit his face. "I nearly forgot. Lila's birthday's this week." He turned. "Let's get her something nice. Let's try Cartier's."

In the store I wondered at the clerks, who were elegantly dressed, and the silver and watches and jewels in the showcases, brilliantly lit from within. The clerks eyed us indifferently at first and moved off as we approached. I would have gone up to them obsequiously, but George Marsh stood his ground.

"Is Mr. Holz here?" There was the proper sharpness in his voice, the proper insistence which clerks and headwaiters understood.

157

"I believe he's downstairs. He'll be here in a jiffy, Mr. Marsh."

And in a jiffy Mr. Holz was coming to us pleasantly over the carpeted floor. "Why, Mr. Marsh. Your uncle was in to see us the other day, about some cufflinks."

I was embarrassed by Mr. Holz, who had such a personable memory for names and faces, and then I was strangely ashamed of George Marsh, who seemed to be showing off. Mr. Holz showed him a selection of pins and clips which he said were not only charming but popular. George settled at last for a small gold clip, in a four-leaf-clover pattern, set in the center with a small transparent sapphire. Mr. Holz was enthusiastic about it. It was a modest gift, charming, popular. It was appropriate for a birthday, and Mr. Holz seemed to be saying that it was precisely what he would recommend to a young man in danger of exceeding himself. It cost sixty-odd dollars; George paid by check. I had never seen a blank check.

We left the store and walked south for a block or two, then turned to the left toward Madison Avenue. The gift was very much on George's mind. "I wonder if she'll wear it for the party tonight. I bought her a coral necklace in Bermuda—which she never wore."

"If she doesn't wear it," I said, "give it to me and I'll sell it."

He looked at me as though I had said something vaguely outrageous. "If she doesn't wear it," he said, "I'll buy her one she will."

"You're really in love?" I said.

"Damn right."

We strolled through the bustling pedestrians on Madison Avenue, having no part of them. We were quite unique in ourselves, in the blaze of our youth and tasting the delight of being on a holiday, a brisk, glad, purposeless time. No one else on the sidewalk had the perceptiveness we had or the appetite.

The mood shifted in the mid-forties where we began to see faces. They were faces we recognized without associating names with them. We felt a kinship with them which we would not admit and which a common code prohibited us from displaying. It required a mutual tolerance, even a forced apathy; the code demanded further that no iota of poise be sacrificed. If close physical confrontation was inescapable, a greeting was permitted, but it must be a clean, quick greeting that would compromise neither party. Beyond this there could be no communication, for a vacationtime meeting on

Madison Avenue was not an ordinary event. To be openly friendly in a public place would lay us bare before the world.

Being together, George Marsh and I could share the responsibilities of detachment. We held scrupulously to our own conversation, greeting none of the faces, and so we managed to traverse a vital section of his New York, and to mingle with the vacationtime users of college club pools and squash courts, those being shepherded by parents through lunch or the matinee, the youngest crop of charge-account customers of Tripler's, Brooks', and Abercrombie's, and the Putnam County-Westchester exodus from Grand Central Station, without exchanging a nod. We saw ourselves in all the adolescent shapes, the clear and pimply faces, the neat and rumpled clothing, the slouched and ambling gaits of half a hundred contemporaries. We concentrated on our own thoughts, preserving our individual identities against the anonymity that descends on this rarefied quarter of Manhattan twice yearly, at Christmas and at Easter, wih a brigade of hatless, open-coated, callow tourists wearing on their knit wool scarves a score of different colors. Kent, Choate, and Hotch-kiss, Pomfret, Exeter and St. George's, St. Paul's, Groton, and St. Mark's. Emmanuel, Andover, and Middlesex; these and a dozen more are recognizable to the practiced eye. But to the uninitiated onlooker, to whom one scarf is no more emblematic than another, to whom there are no school colors and kids are simply kids, these are a brash and pampered group, the sons of the rich and the would-be-rich. The boys are themselves conscious of this prejudice, and react according to their temperaments, either aggressively or, like George Marsh, bashfully.

"You'd think they'd have the sense not to come out all at once, making clowns of themselves on the street," he said.

"What the hell. It's vacationtime," I said. "What do you care?"

"You care," he said simply, and I knew that he was right. I cared for appearances as frantically as he.

"You're a damned snob," I said helplessly.

"Didn't I tell you I was going to set you straight?" he said, and now he was grinning. "Let's get some lunch," he said. "We might take in a movie."

This peasant made his first approach to the apartment play-grounds of the East Sixties entirely alone. That evening the arrival at Linda Parkhurst's, hostess to the Miss Eustis crowd, was achieved with many a frightened misgiving.

I had been assisted into my boiled shirt by George Marsh. His shirt was quite different, a silk the color of rich cream that was pleated about the chest in comfortable, casual folds. I was quick to perceive that my own selection from Read and Whites rental department had been an unhappy one. The egregious, opalescent cufflinks protruded well below the sleeves and the corrugated material of which the lapels were finished, beside the inky satin of George Marsh's lapels, was no more fortunate. The nadir had been my snap bowtie. George Marsh was obliged to lend me a tie of his own, and there he had left me, with a hundred urgent questions coursing through my mind, and went off to pick up Lila.

At the apartment house there was a telling contretemps with the elevator man. The name Parkhurst meant nothing to him at first. The apartment I wanted belonged to Mr. and Mrs. Crowe. It was thus I learned that in these precincts the best little boys and girls did not necessarily have the same name their mothers had.

A maid in a fresh white apron received me with a startled look and led me into a bedroom where I was to leave my overcoat. I was depressed by the absence of other coats and the near sepulchral quiet of the apartment. I was ushered into the empty living room and sat uncomfortably on the sofa's edge. A mantel clock ticked the minutes away; there was no other sound but the bustle and clatter in the kitchen. A grand piano stood in the corner, inviting me. I ran a hand gently over the keys and tried a chord or so, softly. I was interrupted then, by the voice of a girl.

"Please play. Play anything."

"I can play 'The Happy Farmer,'" I said.

"Oh, please play. I'm furious with Mother."

She was a burly girl with a full freckled face, tightly curled, taffy-colored hair, and a pair of tense blue eyes that looked piercingly about the room as she spoke.

"Aren't these minutes ghastly?" the girl asked. "Don't you hate giving parties?"

"I never gave one," I said.

"It was all Mother's idea. She says it's the way to meet boys. Then she and my stepfather cheerfully skip out and leave me holding the bag." She was taking short, frantic tugs at her belt. Her dress was baby-blue, of thick tulle, and an underslip was visible beneath it. Two gardenias were pinned in a corsage upon her chest. "Mother decided to bunch me herself, because if she didn't, who would? And I could only get to the hairdresser this morning, so the permanent refuses to set."

"It looks fine," I said.

"What are we going to talk about?" she said. "It's three hours before the dance and I've got to entertain twenty people. Promise you'll stay right here and play the piano."

We introduced ourselves and shook hands formally, she with a limp warm hand. George Marsh had said that Linda Parkhurst was a jolly girl. Linda Parkhurst, he had said, was sure to be field-hockey captain at Miss Eustis' in her year, and was a dear friend of Chee Wee's and Lila's, though a different type, and they called her Huggy, for a reason I did not yet perceive.

"At the dance you'll have to dance with me, you know," she said. "Everybody has to dance with his hostess."

The doorbell rang. "Pray for me," she said, clasping her hands. "And don't you dare leave that piano."

Guests arrived singly or in threes. The singles were unattached stags, like myself. Each girl came escorted by two boys, whose dance subscriptions had been underwritten by her father as guarantee against her being forsaken and other vicissitudes of the evening. Some of them I recognized. Colton Cutter, from a class above at the Academy and Larry New and Roger Pervis, also in that class. They made their way to a sideboard where tomato juice, sherry, and canapés were served. A diminutive brunette arrived, convulsed with giggles, and her escorts followed her, an incongruous pair, Harry Tilton, who had just returned freshly tanned from Florida, and Soaker Means, whom the girl introduced as Alfred. Chee Wee Gibbons appeared in bright fingernail polish and a green satin gown. Gaily oblivious of her escorts, she flung herself upon Linda Parkhurst, then upon Harry Tilton with a cry, hugged him, and kissed the air by his cheek, in imitation of an honest kiss. Harry responded in kind and the two embraced before all eyes. Larry New, who was one of Chee Wee's escorts, looked on sullenly from the sideboard.

"Want you should meet an old friend," Harry Tilton said, leading Chee Wee toward me. "The piano player."

161

"Friend!" Chee Wee shrilled. "Don't *tell* me! He's awfully clever —and a pianist to boot!" She rushed to me with her hands extended, palms downward, arms stiff, the picture of delight. "You have everything at Emmanuel. This one tried to pick me up on the train."

"Now let's not be playing hymns," Harry Tilton said to me. "This is a party."

"The West Northrup wonder," Chee Wee said.

"East Northrup," I said and rose from the piano.

Harry pressed a hand on my shoulder. "Let's not go sneaking off. Not when we want you should be playing the piano."

Chee Wee came behind me and hovered over my shoulder in a flurry of musical interest. "I can play 'The Happy Farmer,'" I said.

"Wonderful. We'll make it a duet." She crowded beside me on the bench and fumbled through the high keys.

Harry Tilton spanked her wrist. "This here's a piano, not a harpsichord."

"Play 'Scatterbrain,'" Chee Wee begged.

"I don't know it," I said.

"You *don't*? It's just as popular as 'Oh, Johnny.'"

"You play by ear, don't you, Maestro?" Harry Tilton said.

"I play by ear," I said, annoyed. "Why don't you get off my back?"

"This is one talented boy," Harry said.

Harry was leaning over the piano top, smiling directly upon us, all white teeth and suntan. "Like you should meet young Taylor," he said. "A most talented boy, and Gopher Marsh's guest."

"I'll sing it for you," Chee Wee interrupted.

Chee Wee hummed a few bars, and I followed her on the piano. "You've never seen Lila, have you?" she said. "This is her song."

"I've seen her photograph," I said.

"You can't miss her." There was a ray of doubt in her greenish eyes. "You're not embarrassed, are you?"

"Takes more than that to embarrass the maestro," Harry Tilton said. "That right, Maestro?"

"Go chase yourself," I said.

"Boys," Chee Wee said. "Boys."

And Harry chucked her under the chin, and walked off jauntily to the brunette giggling on the arm of the sofa.

"Maybe you don't like him," she said.

"I like him fine. Did you notice how his nose is crooked?"

162

"I heard about that," she said coolly. "Not much happens at Emmanuel that I don't hear about." She watched the brunette brighten at Harry's approach. Soaker Means stood by unnoticed, holding out to her a glass of tomato juice. "He is handsome," Chee Wee said. "I've never seen a boy who looked so divine in dinner clothes. . . . Well, will you look who's here?"

George Marsh was standing stiffly in the doorway.

"Gopher!"

"It's the Goph!"

Chee Wee reached him ahead of the rest and affectionately kissed the vacuum beside each of his cheeks. He smiled shyly, unconscious of the impression he made on an entire room simply by standing in its doorway.

"Where is she?" Harry Tilton called. "What did you do—drown her?"

There was no answer, for now Lila stood beside him, radiantly, in a deep blue gown. She could have been a movie starlet, Deanna Durbin in bangs, but she was prettier. Her face and arms were tanned, for she too was just returned from Florida, and a scarlet flower adorned her hair.

"Birthday Girl," Harry called. "And loot, too. . . . Diamonds, no less." He nuzzled her neck, just under the hair.

Lila Norris stood in the center of them, tossing her sun-streaked hair. She was a tiger lily, a tanned, technicolor vision, the writer of impassioned notes, she whom George Marsh had but lately dared to kiss, his cherished, impudent angel.

Now came a burst of admiration for a slender bracelet of diamonds her parents had given her, and for the clip which was fastened on one shoulder.

"Huggeeee!" Lila cried. "Hug meeee!" and for a moment bent like a willow stem in Linda Parkhurst's arms.

Now George Marsh took her by the hand and was leading her toward the piano.

"Here he is," I heard him say. "Here's Gus Taylor."

I pretended to be studying a sheet of music. I couldn't bear to look up when I knew I was blushing to the roots of my hair.

"He's not very social," she was saying. "Is he?"

"This is Lila Norris," George was saying. "Aren't you going to say hello?"

Her hand felt tiny when I took it; it seemed a doll's hand, but it was warm. She had a smile ready for me, but it seemed unreal, too practiced. And it wrinkled the tip of her nose.

"You went to Cartier's," Lila Norris was saying. "You helped pick out my birthday present. You play the piano beautifully. I've heard so much about you."

"I've heard so much about you," I said.

Dinner was served in the adjacent dining room, a composite of gold chairs, linen-draped card tables, candles, and bridge lamps. Soup, string beans, chicken à la king, green salad, rolls, and sherbet. It was eaten slowly, accompanied by prattle and an occasional effort at sober conversation.

To be at the dance at a respectable hour, it was absolutely necessary to be out on the sidewalk, hailing taxis by ten o'clock. Those were not Huggy Parkhurst's instructions; they were her mother's. So no one was to blame her if they seemed rude. She made the announcement standing at her place, after Harry Tilton had silenced the company by ringing his fork against an empty glass. She tugged at the belt of her gown as she spoke, and her anxiety renewed itself. She raised a chubby hand to beckon the girls to the powder room. The boys were to make themselves at home. Take care to blow out the candles. Stags were asked to help with taxis.

Five of us who were from Emmanuel sat around one table, leaving a minority rump to fend for themselves. "Pardon us for living," one of them said. "We didn't happen to go to Emmanuel."

"Let's get all gonged up," said Harry Tilton, aged sixteen.

He unveiled a fifth of Old Crow which we felt compelled to drink, from the water glass. It took a courage we did not have to deny Harry Tilton, who had run the risk of smuggling it in. One who looked wan even in the best of health was Soaker Means and this evening his pallor, induced by the amounts of sherry and rye that Harry had pressed upon him, was close to phosphorescent. To no one's surprise, Soaker vanished into the night shortly afterward and Harry had the giggling brunette to himself.

We took our time about getting into our coats, and when we joined the girls in the hallway and they remarked on the smell of our breaths we were rather pleased.

I was to ride to the dance with George and Lila. At first I could not find them downstairs in the lobby, and I searched the sidewalk where the others were shouting for taxicabs. I did not find them until I went back inside. They had just stepped out of the elevator and Lila was standing before a tall mirror, settling the bright artificial flower in her hair.

"Don't be silly," she was telling him.

"If you don't like the clip I gave you why didn't you say so?" His face was twisted and unhappy.

"I told you I adored it," Lila said. "But it doesn't go well with this dress. So I took it off."

"Is that flower gadget something someone gave you?" George said angrily.

"George, it was only Tommy *Gates*."

"Where did you see him?"

"I told you, in Palm Beach," Lila said, dwelling upon her tanned image in the cool glass. "I don't see why you carry on over nothing."

"I don't see why whenever I give you something you never wear it."

"You're impossible," Lila said. "Gus, tell him he's impossible."

Lila continued smiling at me, wrinkling her nose. It was as if she could move mountains simply by wrinkling her nose.

Chapter Nine

Lila had invited us for Sunday lunch at Sutton Place. She opened the front door of her family's apartment and greeted George with a contrite loving look. The sapphire clip was strategically pinned to the corner of her blouse, and George was smiling.

"What a shame you missed Mummy," Lila told us. "She took Mathilde out for lunch. . . . And Pappy doesn't feel well. He's going to eat off a tray."

"It's an Easter treat for Mathilde," Chee Wee Gibbons said, although no one had asked her.

"Mummy's so busy she hardly sees Mathilde any more. They were planning on spending the day together, but Pappy has a cold."

"You won't miss them," Chee Wee said, again gratuitously. "They'll be back by three to be with Mr. Norris."

"So we'll be by ourselves," Lila said.

"After lunch we thought we might go to Radio City," Chee Wee said.

Chee Wee stood courteously behind her dearest friend, but she was not one to be ignored. She was an inch or two taller than Lila and when she spoke she waved her wrists. Whether from habit or contagion, Lila was gesturing also. Together they produced fairy tinkling sounds; I observed that they were wearing identical bracelets with miniature gold charms. However they might strive to effect it, it was not a convincing sisterliness. Chee Wee was the heavier and had dark coloring, but, being untanned, her complexion contrasted sallowly to Lila's. And where Chee Wee inclined to languor, Lila gave out an uncontrolled effervescence that demanded your attention.

"Come," Lila said quickly. "Come say hi to Pappy."

Mr. Hadley Norris sat in his study in a deep leather armchair, reading a confidential newsletter called *Capitol Facts.* This was

166

still, technically, vacation and so he was sitting as far from his desk, as far from anything that reminded him of the investment counseling business, as possible. His back was turned to the desk, where his office correspondence waited in large manila envelopes sent daily by his secretary, where one of three telephones, one connecting direct to the Chicago branch, one a private connection with Norris, Brion and Heath downtown, might disturb him even on a Sunday. When the girls brought us in, he rose with some difficulty, for he was a heavy man, if not a large one, and judging from the peelings on his face, he had suffered a severe sunburn.

"This is Gus Taylor, Pappy," Lila said. "A friend of ours."

"Staying for lunch, I expect," Mr. Norris said, rather flatly.

"Pappy, of course."

"I'd like to offer you a cocktail," Mr. Norris said, and shook my hand.

"No, sir," I said politely.

"As a rule we offer cocktails, but my wife is away just now and she neglected to say where the key to the liquor closet is hidden. No one can tell me where it is. Often I wonder why I employ all these people when none of them can tell me anything."

"Now, Pappy," Lila said.

"I seldom touch cocktails," Mr. Norris went on. His daughter smiled nervously. "But Liles has so many friends that when I'm left to entertain them I sometimes bust off the wagon. You're all too old to play pin-the-tail-on-the-donkey, I don't see why you can't have one cocktail. If you're as grown-up as you let on to be, you might as well do everything that grownups do. Now my wife won't look at it that way."

"Oh, Mr. Norris," Chee Wee giggled.

"George," Lila said. "See if you can't get Pappy on some other train of thought."

Mr. Norris lowered himself by degrees into the folds of upholstery and settled painfully against a fat cushion. He pulled the lapels of his quilted blue smoking jacket about his neck and looked hostilely at the windows beside him. There had been a hoarseness in his voice and a vague faltering in his movements to and from the chair. While noticeably overweight, he appeared to be a sound man, with only the first vestiges of grayness at the line of his thin, pomaded hair. And yet I was disturbed for Mr. Norris.

167

Suddenly he buckled his knees against his stomach and sneezed three times resoundingly. "Every time I come north from Florida," he said, mopping about his nose with a loud foulard scarf, "I start one of these damned colds. No vitamins, hormones, liver injections or doctors have the slightest effect on my constitution. . . ." Again he sneezed, and George Marsh dashed to the windows. "Never mind it, George," he said.

"There may be a draft, sir."

"No draft. It's just a cold getting under way. You can depend on it like the morning tide." His head and shoulders racked with another sneeze. "Just let me sit here in the sunshine, Liles."

Lila draped herself fondly on the arm of his chair. "Promise me, Pappy, you won't be a grouch."

Mr. Norris's newsletter lay at his feet on the carpet and he struggled to reach for it. "You're not going to read us any more of that dreary business," his daughter said. "George, please don't let Pappy talk about Washington."

"George," Mr. Norris said gruffly, "are you boys aware of what's happening to the country?"

George Marsh smiled indulgently.

"I wonder if you have any idea of what we're coming to. I'm glad I'm not your age, George. I hope you won't think I'm a bleary old man if I tell you I feel sincerely sorry for you boys." He turned his head slowly, bringing me into his range of vision. "Are you going to inherit something?"

"I don't expect to, sir."

Mr. Norris coughed asthmatically into his fist. "Then I can't feel so sorry for you," he said. "There'll always be some college where you can learn to be an economist or a poultry farmer, and then you can go to Washington and tell them how to run the country."

"Pappy!" Lila said. "That's gloomy. If you talk that way you'll spoil our lunch."

Mr. Norris knotted and unknotted the tassels of his smoking jacket and stared forlornly out the window. "I wonder why it is that you and your mother are determined to prevent me from expressing myself. How do you think it looks to strangers? Your friend here is going to leave thinking I'm a bleary old idiot."

"He's not going to think anything of the kind, Mr. Norris," Chee Wee said.

Mr. Norris nodded gratefully. "It's nice to have an ally. There's enough conspiracy in the world, and enough right here in our Government, without having to contend with it at home."

Lila bent over him and ran her finger lightly across his forehead. "Silly old Pappy," she said. "You know that Mummy loves you and Mathilde loves you and I love you. And George loves you."

As we went in to lunch, we left him immersed in *Capitol Facts*. "Perhaps someone would be kind enough to bring me some sandwiches and orange juice on a tray." There was more of plea than command in his voice, which broke now into a barely coherent grumble. "Just leave me here in the sunshine, Liles, and let me thaw out."

We four ate lunch in the dining room. A maid in uniform served us, pussyfooting over the heavy carpet that was a light beige in color to match three of the walls, of which a fourth was white. Chee Wee pointed out the centerpiece of plastic flowers, and the Haitian woodcarvings over the sideboard. All these were accomplishments of *Blythe*'s home-designing staff, who had been responsible for the unusual mirror effects in the hall and other triumphs of *décor* which Chee Wee enumerated with pride. At one time or another all the rooms of Ava Norris' apartment had appeared as paradigms in *Blythe*.

"There are only two things that bother Pappy," Lila declared toward the end of the meal. "He hates President Roosevelt. And he's embarrassed because Mummy has a career that she doesn't need to have."

When lunch was over Lila tiptoed into her father's study and emerged with a finger pressed against her lips.

"Let's go out quietly," she told us. "He's taking a nap in his chair."

Very quietly we gathered our coats and prepared to leave the apartment. Before we could we heard a key turning in the door. A small girl came in holding a box of animal crackers.

"Mathilde!" Chee Wee said, as though she were actually a member of the family. "Mathilde Norris, aren't you going to give us a smile?"

"Mummy's cross," Mathilde said.

"Shhh," Lila said. "You'll wake up Pappy."

"Mummy's cross at Pappy," Mathilde said. "He got sick and

spoiled our day. He promised we could go to the Botanical Gardens."

"Where *did* you go?" George Marsh asked her pleasantly.

"We just had some puey lunch," Mathilde said. "Mummy, those are *mine*—"

Five tapering, manicured fingers had snatched the box from the child's hands.

"I said no eating between meals. I meant no eating between meals," a stern woman said.

"Mummy, I was going to *play* with them!"

"You are going to your room, young lady. Hannah will take you."

Hannah, who was the maid, took Mathilde's hand and led her wailing from our sight. The animal crackers remained on the card tray on the hall table.

"Mummy," Lila said, in a heavy whisper, "Pappy's sleeping in the study."

Her mother was removing a hat with an enormous brim to which a brownish veil was attached.

"Mummy, I promise he's all right," Lila said. "He had two glasses of orange juice, and his green pills and his nose drops, and he ate almost all his lunch."

"Did you give him anything else?"

"*No*, Mummy!"

"You know what happens when he comes back from Florida and he's by himself."

"He's not going to the office tomorrow," Lila said. "Couldn't you stay home with him?"

"How can I, Duck? I have to be in Havana, for days and days."

"I forgot that," Lila said.

"You know how to get Dr. Sloane if you need him. And if there is an emergency, you may call Miss Ballou at the magazine and she will cable me."

"It's not serious," Lila said. "He's tired. He should have stayed on for the sailfishing."

Mrs. Norris plumped her hat and veil on the table, beside the animal crackers. Her movements were precise, managerial. She spoke in the inured tones of one accustomed to calamity. By removing her hat she had revealed a vast head of hair of a startlingly reddish coloring that was a good deal more vivid than her daughter Lila's. She was explaining why it was that she couldn't back out of

170

the Havana junket. Two copywriters, ten models, and an obdurate Greek named Telemachus to take the photographs. That was handful enough. But while she was in the area she wanted to sound out Hemingway about a contribution to the *Blythe* Symposium to be published next winter. In France last autumn she had sounded out Picasso. Picasso was contributing five hundred words on the meaning of freedom. "It sounds i-*deal*," Chee Wee exclaimed, and George Marsh, on whom Mrs. Norris was bestowing an odd flirtatious smile of greeting, seemed transfixed. Optimistically, I assumed that anyone so busy had no time for formal introductions. However, I had done a poor job of being aloof, for now undeniably she had spotted me.

"And who on earth is this?" she was saying to Lila.

"This is my mother," Lila was saying. "This is Gus Taylor, George's friend."

"How do you do, Gus?" Mrs. Norris said. "I'm sorry you've been subjected to this domestic scene."

"How do you do, ma'am?"

Chee Wee giggled. "He's blushing," she said.

"No, I like him," Mrs. Norris said. "He has manners and a nice open face. I hope George will bring him around often."

"I'll bring him around," George Marsh said pleasantly. "You can bank on that."

All four of us had supper that night with Uncle Mark. We sat in the drawing room for a long while after supper. Lila said there was another dance, the Junior Holidays, that was being given on Tuesday night, and when I told her that I would not be going, since I'd promised to be back in East Northrup by Monday, Chee Wee said that was ridiculous. She had no intention of returning home until Friday at the earliest.

"You'd better stay," George Marsh said.

"You get right on the telephone," Lila said, "and tell your family we're not letting you go home until Wednesday."

"My family's fussy about promises," I told her. "It wouldn't do any good."

Mr. Marsh looked at me over the top of his newspaper. "You're going to make a telephone call?" he asked.

"He's going to call Boston or somewhere," Chee Wee said. "He's going to call his uncle or somebody."

"Your uncle Torbert Case?" Mr. Marsh said. "Let me speak to your uncle."

"They made me promise, sir. I don't think it would do much good."

"You let me talk to your uncle. We're old friends," Mr. Marsh said.

Lila placed the call and when the lines were clear she passed Mr. Marsh the telephone. Aunt Connie's voice carried shrilly from the receiver to across the room. She was repeating, "Yes, what is it? Yes, what is it?" in a sort of paroxysm. It was how she always sounded when the telephone rang unexpectedly at Elm Street and it was a long-distance call.

"Mrs. Case?" Mr. Marsh was saying. "This is Marcus Marsh, in New York. I wonder if Torbert is there?"

Then the voice of my uncle, embarrassingly pleased: "What can I do for you, Marcus?"

"I can't tell you how we're enjoying Gus's visit," Mr. Marsh was saying. "I'm taking it upon myself to ask if it might be extended a day or two more. . . ." The room was silent but for his voice. George and Lila and Chee Wee stared tactfully at the wallpaper.

"We made great friends here these last few days and I'm wondering if I haven't been a little indiscreet with Gus. . . . I was surprised that Gus had never heard of Otto Kreuger. But then I don't imagine he's quite the household word he used to be, what? The fact is, I may owe you an apology, Torbert."

I thought: For the love of God, don't make a sap of yourself, Uncle. But let me stay in New York.

"Of course I meant it jokingly, Torbert. But I clearly owe you an apology."

Chee Wee, Lila, and George allowed themselves to smile now and I rested easily in my chair, because it was apparent that Mr. Marsh had taken care of everything.

Mr. Marsh handed me the receiver and Aunt Connie was talking. "Gus, you are coming home on Monday. You gave me your word."

"It's only a couple of days," I said. "I'll be home Wednesday, Aunt. I'll take the ten o'clock. I absolutely promise."

"Dearie, you broke your promise. I'll have to take back the twenty dollars."

"Aunt, I don't think it's fair."

"I don't think it's fair, either. But you gave me your word, and

172

that's the way it is, dearie." She was silent a moment. I wondered if we had been cut off. "Dearie, we'd better hang up. This is Mr. Marsh's call. Good night, dearie."

"I'll see you Wednesday, Aunt. I'm taking the ten o'clock."

"I don't understand what's happened, Gus."

She hung up first. I put the telephone back on the table, moving slowly, not quickly or brightly as I should have, having got what I wanted. Part of life was over for me on Elm Street, ended just as surely as another part had ended once in September when we had taken out the old Chrysler to drive to the Academy on Opening Day.

Chapter Ten

Probably I learned too much about my uncle too early, and if there had been any fault in that, it was Aunt Connie's, because she told me.

It was a complicated story and had to do with stocks and bonds and two old maiden sisters named Perkins who owned real estate in the South End of Boston. Uncle Torbert had been handling their affairs.

"Did he invest their money in Kreuger and Toll, Aunt?"

She looked at me sternly. "I don't know what Mr. Marsh may have told you when you were in New York."

"It had something to do with Kreuger and Toll," I said. "Didn't it?"

"That was a very popular stock. There was absolutely no reason why your uncle should not have followed the advice of a very famous banking house—in spite of Mr. Marsh. Marcus Marsh always did have a tendency to mind other people's business."

It had happened in nineteen thirty-one or two; Aunt Connie remembered that it had come after the crash. Uncle Torbert's clients had been ladies, rather elderly, most of them, and in many ways the most valuable clients and most difficult to deal with that the firm had. Uncle Torbert had a manner and distinction that his partners did not have. Uncle Torbert was the only partner who understood ladies and was gentle and considerate of elderly ladies. They had had complete faith in Uncle Torbert and it was no reflection on him if the old Misses Perkins, who were known to be disagreeable, and one of whom later became a Roman Catholic, held a grievance against him. Uncle Torbert had been concerned with the Perkins sisters and had made a special point of investing for them in only the soundest and most reputable securities. The stock he had bought them in greatest quantity had of course been a reputable

174

stock, thoroughly analyzed and recommended by a sound firm. It was perfectly true that Marcus Marsh, when Uncle Torbert happened casually to mention it, had advised against the transaction. Aunt Connie held nothing against Marcus Marsh, but he was a very rich man, inclined to be meddlesome and free with advice. She realized Uncle Torbert admired him, but she had reservations of her own about a man who made such a display of his wealth. And Aunt Connie had thought it presumptuous of Marcus Marsh, a man in his position, to give advice on any matter when it had not been asked for. When Uncle Torbert had ignored what Mr. Marsh told him, Aunt Connie had been proud. She had felt then and she felt still that Uncle Torbert had done the only dignified thing. Trusting himself, he had bought for the irascible Misses Perkins twenty thousand shares of a Swedish match concern called Kreuger and Toll.

Certainly Uncle Torbert was not to blame for the catastrophe in Sweden. He was not to blame if Otto Kreuger was not an honest man. Uncle Torbert had followed the advice of a famous banking house, as many another had. It was unfair of Marcus Marsh to chide him, and it had been hideously unfair of the Perkins sisters to request his resignation.

This had been the cruelest blow to Uncle Torbert. He and Aunt Connie had taken a week's motor trip through Quebec while he thought about the future and had a fearful bout with his conscience. Then they had returned to Boston, and my uncle had made up his mind to retire from the law. His partners had been reluctant to see him go, but they were wonderfully generous. My uncle's most proud possession was the cigarette box they had inscribed and presented to him at a small dinner in his honor.

She had never regretted his decision and was sure that their lives had been the richer for it, because it had led to their moving to East Northrup. She had never regretted buying the house. She had never regretted buying the Chrysler. Uncle Torbert planted the gardens and the hedge and had time for his reading, for his antiques, and for his writing. It was the first time in his life that he had been able to do the things he had always wanted to do. He joined the Massachusetts Historical Society, began addressing the Garden Club of Worcester, and a year or two later Mr. Sedgwick bought for the *Atlantic Monthly* his first article entitled "Botany in My Back Yard." There had been the Academy and his interest in town affairs. The whole investment had been worth while.

"You mean it's your house, Aunt? You bought it?"

Yes, she had bought the house and she had bought the car with some things of her own that Mr. Jennings was watching out for at the Legatees' Trust. She had been lucky with Mr. Jennings, who did things slowly and who had not had time to buy Kreuger and Toll. To bring Uncle Torbert to East Northrup, to watch him flourish here, had cost a great deal, but it had been a price worth paying.

"You mean you support us, Aunt?" I asked her. "You paid for the brick wall?"

Foundations laid in childhood were collapsing all together like a house of cards.

The following Sunday when I came for lunch alone Uncle Torbert met me on the porch. He was only sorry that I hadn't come to him directly, as he had nothing to conceal. I was entitled to have heard the story from his own lips, but as long as I had elected to ask my aunt, no matter. I was certainly old enough to know about that sort of thing and to understand. He knew I would profit from it in some way, as it had been one of the turning points in his life. We walked through the front yard, feigning admiration for the crocuses that were in bloom beside the brick wall. Learning hard facts and adjusting to them was the process of growing up, he said. He was impressed with how I had met the challenge, he said. He was proud of me.

I found that because I did not wish to listen it was possible for my mind to wander and to return at the appropriate interval. "Yes," my voice would say. "That's the way the world goes, I guess." But I would be concentrating on the crocuses Aunt Connie had planted.

Lavender, yellow, and crimson crocuses. They were blooming where she had put them, beside the wall Torbert Case fancied as an emblem of his integrity, yet even this Aunt Connie had had to build for him. She had stood aside, waiting for the bills to come in. When they did, because every man should have at least the illusion of paying his own debts, she had gone to Boston to talk with Mr. Jennings and a few days later those magic extra dollars had appeared in my uncle's bank account.

"One of the most extraordinary things," Uncle Torbert was saying, "was the man Kreuger himself. Whatever else may be said of him, he was an unforgettable person. Some time ago I prepared an article for the *Atlantic* on the influence he might have had on our economy. Ellery Sedgwick was afraid the subject would be unpopular, but I still think it was an interesting idea. Remind me to show you the paper sometime, fellow."

When he placed a comradely arm about my shoulders, I pulled away. "Will you please stop calling me 'fellow'?"

"Now, come back here," he called. "You know I'll not tolerate insolence."

He called again, as though I hadn't heard him. I walked up to the porch steps and straight into the house without turning my head.

For more than a month I avoided him, not trusting the silent fury that came over me when he was near. In my trunk I found his framed slogan—The Borrower Is Servant to the Lender—and wondered whether to give it back to him. I ended by hurling it into one of the huge wicker trash baskets at the Academy.

For Fourth Class English Dismal Gregore required us to read *Huckleberry Finn:* " 'Golden lads and girls all must,' " he addressed us of an April morning, " 'like chimney sweepers, come to dust.' Did you hear me, gentlemen? Like chimney sweepers. Or like Huckleberry Finn, gentlemen. I don't imagine you have ever met anyone like Huckleberry Finn, and therefore when you read this book you will be exposed to certain human experiences hitherto quite undreamed of. It will be an adventure—Apthorp, you will remove your filthy fingers from Bockling's collar and prepare to read. Chapter One, page one—"

Cuppy Vale and I did not agree with our instructor. We believed that there was something of Huck Finn in each of us. Nor was Pap Finn an unfamiliar character; we feared and hated him as Huck did and like Huck, when he saw his father lying drunk in the gutter, we could not but admire him somehow. Pap had been one of the last of the free men, a victim of progress, and in this respect he resembled other men we knew, men like Mr. Hadley Norris, like some of the fathers who had sent their sons to Emmanuel. Looking about us, we could spot many Huck Finns, of a species new since Mark Twain's day. We had friends who would have seemed fancy pants to Huck. And yet they had something in common with Huck, for if they had been pampered, they had been punished also. Few had even seen the Mississippi. They had no opportunity to run away on a raft. They had come to Emmanuel instead.

Cuppy Vale derived a wry satisfaction in thinking he was one of them. Vale scarcely recalled his father, who had blown his brains out when Vale was six years old, and yet it amused him to fancy his unfortunate parent as having been an incarnation of Pap Finn. Even I, smarting from the discovery of my uncle Torbert Case's degradation, sought to include myself in the same category as Vale and the others. However, Vale did not agree that I belonged.

"Your uncle's harmless," Vale told me. "You can't qualify on him."

"He's a bum," I said defiantly.

"He's not exactly a bum."

"He's a fraud," I said.

"You're feeling sorry for yourself," Vale said. "You're not near as bad off as some. Take Frazzle Fern—"

Frazzle Fern had a father who now raised orchids in New Jersey, subsisting on alimony paid him by Frazzle's stepmother, and contributing little to Frazzle's support. Frazzle owned only two suits of clothes, but that was not the reason for his unpopularity. Frazzle sucked up unabashedly to masters and First Classmen and was notorious for his tactlessness. Or take Boo Hoo Beemer, Vale said. Boo Hoo Beemer, always bellyaching, might have been a better sport, were he not dogged by the whispered scandal of his father's having been barred from the courts at Forest Hills as a tennis cheat. Yes, Vale said. You could argue that most of the screwballs at Emmanuel had gotten that way at home. And it wasn't just the screwballs, either. Take Gopher Marsh.

And I had had to agree with him on Gopher Marsh. Better than any of us he resembled Huckleberry Finn. I was then in the process of becoming the close friend of Gopher Marsh, closer even than of Cuppy Vale. And I was learning the facts which dovetailed into a theory that splendidly refuted Dismal Gregore.

At about the time Vale and I were doing our conjecturing George Marsh was deep in the matter of his father's will. Dr. Kew allowed him a three-day extension of a Christmas vacation to confer with lawyers in New York. Lawyers wrote him long and unintelligible letters which they drove all the way to the Academy to explain.

178

George might not have been so conscientious about listening to them, had his Uncle Mark not required him to. Uncle Mark said George was old enough to take the responsibility of his own affairs. Thus he first learned about corporations and indentures, about Consolidated Imperial Carton & Can, about money, and about what his father had done with his money. Looking back on the weeks of consultation and the mountainous suits, claims, agreements, writs, and affidavits, George was inclined to agree with his uncle that the ultimate of his father's negligence had been his failure to die intestate.

The mourning was long past, but the specter of the father returned to haunt the son. It was a form of exorcism when George talked about his father. There lived in New York an old friend and classmate of Andy Marsh's, an obstetrician named Gummering McClough. The same doctor who, as "Gumdrop" McClough, had once courted Baby and who, having lost her to his friend, had generously officiated at the East Sixty-fourth Street birthing party. Gumdrop McClough remembered so many things about Andy Marsh's college days.

Andy had stuck it out for a year and a half with the class of '22, and that long only to make his father's club. He achieved this ambition easily, because a young man like Andy Marsh was in demand as long as he stayed young. He was popular at college and during the first years of his marriage when, a crazed Peter Pan in a raccoon coat, he had vowed never to grow old, had sworn he didn't care what happened after the age of thirty.

Of all his friends, Gumdrop McClough was the only one who took Andy seriously. Seven of them had rented one of the rathouses on Plympton Street, and Andy divided his time between there and the club. He spent his mornings sleeping or teeing golf balls through an open window onto a vacant lot behind. It was a special satisfaction to Andy when he smashed the windows of a rival club across the lot. Whenever this happened, Gumdrop McClough was sent around to make Andy's amends and it was Gumdrop who had given Andy his first serious talk about drinking. Andy had thanked Gumdrop elaborately for his concern, but the result had been negligible. After all, it was a considerable feat to have undergone delirium tremens before the age of twenty-one. No one but Gumdrop paid attention to Andy's Oriental fatalism. Only Gumdrop had followed Andy out of the club one February night to investigate what the

179

others had taken for just another episode of drunken bravado. He had found Andy lying across the trolley tracks on Massachusetts Avenue, his hands clasped across his chest in prayer and his head resting on a mound of dirty snow. "Don't you bother me," Andy Marsh had mumbled. "If the car comes, it comes. If I'm going to die, I'm going to die. *Kismet.*" A delegation had pulled Andy back into the club and laid him out on a pool table. There he awoke in the morning, retching dryly, two hours late for the mid-year examination in which he had invested six hours of work and nearly a month's allowance at the Widow Nolan's Tutoring School on Harvard Square.

George had other, happier tales of his own to supplement what Gumdrop McClough told him. He had memories of baseball games and visits to a ranch in Wyoming. Sometimes he had had fun being with his father. Even at the very end, when his father was staying at hotels and asking all the time if his mother was happy, they had had some good times. There was a Dr. Mills, who made a specialty of people like his father. In the summer George had taken a fishing trip to Ontario with his father and Dr. Mills had come along. He had been a good guitar player and George was glad of his company. When Dr. Mills played "Dardanella" or "Don't We Have Fun?" George's father would come to life and sing right along with the music, though afterward he would get surly, and not talk for hours at a time. George's father had told him that Dr. Mills was all right and that he had tried. George hoped so later, because among the bills to be paid one turned up from Dr. Mills, for $7,500.

"I wish you'd keep this stuff under your hat," George would tell me.

"Naturally," I would say.

And I did not even tell Vale. The bonds were solidifying between me and George Marsh. That Fourth Class year which had brought the renunciation of Uncle Torbert, the Huck Finn theory, and the saga of Andy Marsh was the most crucial year.

George Marsh kept a radio-victrola in his room at Phelps House. That was in the academic year 1939 to 1940, when he had shared a room with Fuzzy Eaton. One of the privileges of being a Second Classman was that you had a room with closets, bigger bureaus, a desk to study on, and you were excused from study periods if you

180

were passing all your courses. During special hours you could also play your radio, or, if you had one, your radio-vic. George Marsh had a magnificent portable radio-vic, finished in cowhide. It had buttons for controlling wave length, for modulating the tone, a luminous eye that became a full green circle when the reception was perfect, and an arm that turned records over and another that tripped them into a slot on the side. It played up to twenty-four records, both sides if you wanted them. It was the only machine of its kind in all of Emmanuel.

On the long, overcast Sunday afternoons in February when there was no hockey practice, I would listen to the radio-vic. George Marsh had six thick albums of Artie Shaw, Benny Goodman, Claude Thornhill, Eddie Duchin, Ted Straeter, Bix Beiderbecke, all the songs and all the singers that mattered to us. I passed up many a Sunday lunch at Elm Street to sit in George Marsh's room, listening to the vic.

George would be at his desk, probably writing a letter to Lila, and he would have her picture in front of him. Lila was standing against a glass dressing table in a polka-dot dress that showed in a mirror behind her, smiling into space, her chin tilted upward at the photographer's direction, and George Marsh's sapphire clip fastened in her hair, big as life. Now and then, when a particular tune came over the vic, he would gaze at the picture in a way that nauseated Fuzzy Eaton. Fuzzy would groan from his bed, roll over to the wall, pull the comforter over his head and return to his slumbers. I would stretch out on his bed and study the ceiling while the music played. There were three tunes that winter that turned up in every record batch, "These Foolish Things" by T. Dorsey, and someone not half as good as Billie Holliday singing "String of Pearls" and "I've Got a Right to Sing the Blues." I was getting just a little tired of all three.

Four or five others might barge in on us; and I would have to pull myself up into a corner of the bed so someone could sit there. They would loll around for an hour or so, First Classmen mostly, mostly athletes, friends of Gopher Marsh's. Playing on all the teams as he did, Gopher knew them as well as his own classmates. Big Rog Pervis, the pitcher, who would blow up that coming spring in the ninth inning of the Middlesex game and spit his chewing tobacco on the mound before the coach would call Gopher Marsh from first base to save the day. And Soggy Miller and Pete Hal-lowell and Crabs Cotherman who had played in George Marsh's backfield in the fall. They admired Gopher, much as Lower Schoolers admired him. ("But we'll get them next year," the little Fifth Classmen had said, the week after we lost to Middlesex in football. "Gopher Marsh will be back next year.") The First Classmen did not begrudge him these kudos. They did not begrudge him the precedent of being the first boy in Academy history to have been football captain in his Second Class year; they had even elected him to succeed himself in the year to come.

Yet it was on one of those Sunday afternoons that I learned to my astonishment that not everyone felt about George Marsh as we did.

Big Rog had been gregarious that day. He had wrestled with me on the bed for a while, complimentarily. Likewise, Big Rog had flattered Fuzzy Eaton's sleeping form by swatting it firmly on the buttocks. He had left us shortly, taking his companions with him, for the purpose of catching a butt in the chapel crypt. He had paused to beg Gopher's pardon. As a representative of Student Government, Gopher was not supposed to know about those things. Big Rog tweaked Gopher's ear and slouched out the door, giving us all a final horse laugh.

I stretched out on the bed and yawned. Covers were half torn off the bed and some loose records were strewn about. A Cole Porter album had been ground to pieces when Crabs Cotherman had fallen on it accidentally. Fuzzy was asleep again, snoring gently underneath the comforter, and a heavy languor was setting in in the wake of the bull session. George Marsh rested his chin on the back of his fist and stared broodingly out the window at the grounds and buildings, lifeless in the gray afternoon. The letter was in his other hand, stamped, sealed, and addressed. He tapped it slowly in time with the vic. It was Artie Shaw, Helen Forrest singing "I'm in Love with the Honorable Mr. So-and-so."

The room was silent except for the low grind of the vic mechanism and the flipflop of the ejected records.

"Sometimes don't you think you're about going nuts?" George Marsh said and slipped his mouth over his fist, gnawing. The remark was uncharacteristic of him, since it could have been interpreted as a criticism of the Academy.

182

He brought his fist down hard on the desk. "I tell you. We'll get a car and drive to Gentian Cove. Lila's going to be there with Gibbons," he said.

"The family going to be there?" I asked, suspiciously.

"The family's renting a cottage through the Mariposa Inn. Naturally, Gibbons had to tag along too."

"Who's asked us?" I said.

"Who had to *ask* us? Can't we show up accidentally on purpose? We can stay at a boarding house, or sleep in the car. God, we can sleep on the beach. Don't be so damned Bostonian."

"What car?"

"We'll buy a car."

"You don't just buy a car," I said.

"Who's asking *you* to buy it?" he said. "Don't be so damned Bostonian."

"I've never been to Florida," I said.

He grinned, so as to say, "You peasant."

"I know where you can get a car right in the village. You could get it today," I said.

"Not on Sunday."

"I know where there's a car you can get for four hundred dollars, a 1937 Packard convertible. If you want it, it's yours by Evening Prayer."

"We can't skip Evening Prayer!" He made a face of dismay. The thought of breaking a rule.

"Who said anything about skipping?" I said. I was very glad to have the upper hand for once.

Fuzzy Eaton was asleep. We tried to bring Cuppy Vale, but he was working on something for the Academy magazine, *The Beacon;* he was competing to be editor-in-chief next year. Harry Tilton, who knew all about cars, would gladly have come, but as we came to his end of the corridor and heard the caterwauling and conga beats coming from his room we hurried past. It was a balmy afternoon for February, the kind that would ruin the hockey rinks, and we wore no coats, only our football sweaters, with the blocked white letter woven on a green background. We wore the sweaters inside-out, with the E's showing on our backs. It didn't occur to me until we approached the center of the village that this would be the first

time I had ever worn an Emmanuel letter in the presence of someone like Ned Sellers.

He spotted us from the back door of his house. "If it ain't the
football hero," Ned Sellers said. "Stover at Yale. Hiya, Stover!"

"I brought you a customer," I said.

Ned Sellers slipped off the back stoop, hands in his pockets, wearing a green cardigan jacket with black squares. His face was fat
and puffy with its map of freckles and his red hair had grown
brighter over the years. He was six feet tall and the heaviest man
at Northrup High. When he had outgrown the Woodman School,
he had moved to Northrup High, and there he played right tackle.
George Marsh and I had scrimmaged against the team from Northrup Center three times that fall, on Wednesdays. The reason we
never played a real game against Northrup High was that we were
practicing for Saturday's game, not because we were afraid of getting hurt. Even so, George Marsh had broken a wrist in one of those
scrimmages and Ned Sellers had noisily claimed credit for it.

"You want some licorish candy?" Ned Sellers said, his mouth full.
"I just got finished dinner. What time do you eat your dinner up at
old E-man-yu-well?"

It was a short walk from the Sellers' house to the Garage. When
we got there I studied the old sign, East Northrup Garage, Lubritorium and Automotive Appliances, Inc., Wendell Sellers, Prop. It
was a little weatherbeaten, but it was the same old sign. The pumps
had been painted a few times and had new tops to them, since Mr.
Sellers had switched from Shell to Esso, but they were the same old
pumps.

"Any you fellas wanta use the rest room?" Ned Sellers said.

"No," George Marsh said. It was the first word he'd spoken.

"Don't have to bite my head off about it," Ned said.

"Sorry," said George.

Mr. Sellers was inside, under the elevator jack. He was working
on a rush job, some faculty car that had to be greased and tuned up
for Monday. So Ned drove the car out and parked it before us, with
the motor idling. A sturdy little Packard, black, with a ragged canvas top.

"It used to belong to Mrs. Higgins, over to Meadows Road. A nice
job, only twenty-three thousand miles on her," Ned Sellers said.
"She's a little rattly."

"That's putting it mildly," George Marsh said, and moved to the rear of the car to examine a dented fender.

"By the way," I remembered to say, "Ned Sellers, this is George Marsh."

"Yeah," Ned said. "I know him. I know who he is."

George was squatting in the road, trying to pound a loose hub cap into place.

"Where're you planning to take her?" Ned asked me, pointing at the car.

"We were thinking of going to Florida," I said.

"Ooo, Florida," Ned said to me privately. "Now ain't that hotsy-totsy?"

Ned Sellers never picked up new expressions. Ever since we were kids at Woodman, when he wanted to heckle someone he said the same thing. "Hotsy-totsy" or "You're full of what makes the grass grow green." I'd never heard him use a different one.

George Marsh was pulling at a torn canvas strap that dangled from the roof of the car. "You'll have to get a new top."

"We're not charging for the top," Ned said. "You can get one for yourself in Boston, at the Packard Motor Company."

George asked him to lift up the hood and jazz the engine.

"New plugs you'll notice," Ned Sellers said. "We gave her the complete overhaul. The works." He pulled the accelerator band and the engine roared.

George turned calmly and circled the car two times, tugging at the collar of his football sweater. "How much do you want for it?" he said finally.

"Seeing it's you that's asking, about five or six hundred dollars," Ned Sellers said slowly. "You better take it up with my dad."

"Look," George said in a curious tone. "I know about cars and this one isn't worth half that."

"You take it up with my dad," Ned Sellers said.

"I thought he was asking four hundred."

"You take it up with him," Ned said.

While George talked to Mr. Sellers, Ned took me inside the shop by the back door. He found a key on the shelf beneath a box of washers and opened the coke machine beside the cash register. Ned and I drank coke alone in the shop and talked, the first time in we didn't know how long.

"Boy, you sure pick 'em," Ned Sellers said.

"He's a good guy. He's a hell of a good guy," I said.

"You betcha," Ned said. He offered me a smoke that I refused because George Marsh was outside.

"He run the school?" Ned said. "He must be a real big shot."

"I don't want to smoke anyway."

"Such a big shot," Ned said.

"You'd like him, once you got to know him."

"You betcha."

"Everybody likes him. It's not just me."

"You betcha."

All Ned Sellers wanted to know was if what he'd heard was true, that we were going to play real games next fall with Northrup High. Ned hoped so, because he'd heard that we were going to have a pretty hot team. He guessed it was going to be a really hot team, if I was only a substitute end and my buddy was captain again. My big buddy buddy.

"What you going to do next?" Ned was asking. "Your aunt told my dad you're going to Harvard."

"I suppose I will."

"That's where most of 'em go, ain't it? Harvard?"

"A good many go to Yale and Princeton and different places."

"How d'yuh mean *different*? What's different about Yale and Princeton?"

"They're not the only places," I said.

"Anybody going to Holy Cross this year? Anyone going to Notre Dame?"

"No."

"Yeah," Ned said. "That's what I thought."

We were silent while he reached out two more cokes. When he gave me mine, he stood beside me and ruffled a hand through my hair. "Your name's Gus Taylor, ain't it?"

"Sure."

"You're the same Gus Taylor used to mess around old Muriel Delas?"

"Sure I am."

"Same Gus Taylor used to work those pumps with me?"

"Hell, Ned, you know I am."

"That's all I wanted to know," Ned said. "Don't look at me in that tone of voice."

"When are you going to grow up?" I asked him.

"Ignorant old me," Ned said. "Your buddy going to Harvard, too?"

"Yep."

"You going to be roommates and all?"

"Ned, you could lay off," I said.

"You tell your buddy next fall I might break a leg for him. I just might."

"I said you could lay off."

"Oop, sorry," Ned said, and looked in back of him. "We almost had an argument, Dad."

"Hello there, Gus," Mr. Sellers said. Mr. Sellers was standing behind Ned, waiting to say that there was a crazy kid from the Academy who had a New York license and was ready to pay five hundred dollars for the little Packard.

I was quiet as we walked back up Birch's Rise. George Marsh whistled and talked on about the car and the trip, in which I had suddenly lost interest. I was angry with myself for something.

"You didn't have to be snotty," I said at last.

"What do you want me to do, ask him home for Christmas?"

"You didn't need to be snotty."

He laughed. "Everyone has a townie friend somewhere."

"You'd better take that back."

"If you say so," he said, and paused. And then, "You know, when you get sore, your voice changes? You sound like a townie yourself."

Chapter Eleven

Gentian Cove is a key that lies off the west Florida coast. To reach it you drive through the town of Sarasota and out to the ferry landing. It was past eleven o'clock at night when George Marsh and I arrived, wearing the clothes we had driven and slept in for forty-eight hours, our hair matted from the last hundred miles of having the top down, our mouths coated with the residue of cigarettes and stale coffee. I had expected it would be difficult to persuade Aunt Connie that I should take this trip. Since the Fourth Class year I had been spending as many vacations as I could manage away from Elm Street. Two years had passed since the first New York visit, almost two years exactly, for this was March again, in 1940, and I was approaching seventeen. Aunt Connie would say to me, "Dearie, we never see you," which was almost the truth.

In March of 1940 a number of vacations lay ahead of us still, but I had discovered a formula for intimidating Aunt Connie. There was hardly a demand she would not accede to, if I alluded to world events and the possibility that I and thousands like me might soon be dead. The prospect was remote enough to be alluring to me, having recently discovered Rupert Brooke, and to George, then detecting within himself traces of his father's romantic fatalism, but it was nightmarish to Aunt Connie. The result was that she allowed me to do whatever I wanted to do with but a token of protest. This time she had merely sighed and kissed me good-by, wishing myself and George a good time, extracting a promise to drive carefully. We drove as carefully as we ever did, spelling each other, rushing more and more recklessly along the narrow Carolina highways, driving feverishly through the night. Over the dark stretches while George Marsh slept in the back seat, I had time to regret bamboozling my aunt. I thought of her alone with my uncle at Elm Street. She would go on cooking his meals, washing his socks, listening to him talk day in and day out, and nights she would lie exhausted at his side in the four poster and endure his monstrous snoring, waiting for the lull which would permit her to sleep. But I could not think of her for long. Elm Street was a long way from Gentian Cove.

"I guess we could have made it faster," George was saying as we rolled off the ferry ramp, onto the pier, "but forty-eight hours isn't too bad."

"How long are we going to stay?"

"A week, two weeks. What's the rush?"

"Where are we going to stay for two weeks?"

"Don't you fret," he said.

Rooms were twenty dollars a day at the Mariposa Inn, but I knew he would have taken one if it hadn't been for me. "Are the Norrises expecting us?" I said.

"Why should they expect us? We're not staying with them."

He was peering over the wheel, trying to identify something in the darkness. We slowed down on the side of the road. "There ought to be a church along here where we take a left," he said. "Lila said it was about a quarter of a mile from there to the cottage."

"To what cottage?" I said.

"The one they're staying in, jerk."

The whole purpose of taking the cottage had been to get away from Palm Beach to a quieter place and a different kind of people. Last Christmas when I had been back to New York Mrs. Norris told me about Gentian Cove. No one but Boston and Philadelphia and Wilmington people went to Gentian Cove and life there was simple and unpretentious. When Ava Norris was on vacation she liked to relax, cook meals herself, and try to forget that she was Ava Norris. One hour a day she did her mail and her secretary called her from New York every morning at ten, but that was all. She would see no one she did not choose to see and she refused to answer the telephone. Lately it had become impossible to do this in Palm Beach where they owned a house, and so this year they were sneaking off to Gentian Cove, where they would see nobody but a few quiet people who had never heard of Ava Norris. She only wanted to hide and recapture her femininity to her heart's content and not have to cope with things.

George Marsh and I were driving slowly down a narrow road,

189

looking for a coral pink cottage with a hibiscus hedge and a row of conch shells on either side of the front walk. Wherever it was, and Lila had said it was just a quarter of a mile, Ava Norris was asleep inside, recapturing her femininity. Her husband Hadley would be asleep also. It had been a bad winter for him and he was very tired. He had hardly been downtown at all since Christmas. She and her husband always went to bed before nine o'clock. He insisted on it; it was a man's world.

"Lila's a great one for directions," George Marsh was saying. "She said watch for a clump of palm trees on the right. What in hell is a *clump* of palm trees? I wish we had a spotlight."

"And wake up the neighborhood?" I asked.

"The girls would see it."

"Are you going to wake up the girls?"

"What do you think we came down here for?"

"You're going to make a big hit with the family," I said.

We were creeping along in low, because there was a hibiscus hedge just ahead and several upturned conch shells gleaming in the headlights. The engine had loosened considerably during the trip and at this speed it squeaked and rattled, a deafening noise in the quiet night.

"I only want to know one thing," I said, knowing this would be my last chance to ask it. "Is it essential to see Lila now?"

He was peering at the house and seemed not to hear me. The car stopped and he opened the door abruptly. He got out to investigate, leaving the motor running. I turned off the ignition and the rattling stopped. The whole island was asleep.

There was a sound of footsteps on the path and a murmur of girls' voices. Before I opened my eyes the door burst open and Chee Wee and Lila were throwing their arms around me, warmly kissing the empty air by my cheeks.

"We expected you this afternoon," Chee Wee squealed. "We were desolate."

"Welcome," Lila was saying. "Welcome to the land of the orange blossom."

"Let's keep it down to a dull roar," I said.

"Stuffy, stuffy!" Lila teased, and her nose wrinkled in the light of the dashboard.

It was a clear, windless night that Chee Wee thought ideal for staying out in. Neither of the girls was sleepy. They could have stayed out all night under the stars and listened to the surf washing the beach, the surf whose dampness reached out to us from somewhere not far off. The girls were in pajamas with their hair tied in by bandannas, because they had been afraid a wind might come up suddenly from the sea. They brought us tuna-fish sandwiches and lobster salad from the icebox, tiptoeing softly in and out the kitchen door. We sat on broad towels which Mrs. Norris had ordered for beach use only, their gaudy stripes quite visible in the starlight. The girls slid their feet back and forth across the stubbled, sandy grass to warm them. But they were still not comfortable. They scurried off for sofa cushions and blankets from their beds which smelled of soap and perfume as we pulled them about us. There were three blankets, one which George and Lila shared and the other two for Chee Wee and myself. Lila remembered that in the kitchen was a jug of wine, muscatel, that the cleaning woman had left behind. The muscatel and cigarettes were all we would need, now that we were so comfortable. We could sit out all night, as long as we were careful not to wake the family.

The girls weren't crazy for the taste of muscatel and one swig was enough for George Marsh. It was too sweet. I liked it, however. Not for the taste, but for the effect it had of waking me and for the mounting joy it brought at having got here at last.

"I've never been to Florida before," I was telling Chee Wee. I sensed that we were true friends now. It was time for a few confessions.

"Me neither—but I'm going to come here lots from now on," she said. "I can't come next year, because I promised my family. But I'm coming the next year. Lila's invited me, January 2nd to 9th, 1942. We're going to Palm Beach. I've got it marked in my diary."

"Do you keep a diary?"

"Not really. It's a sort of engagement pad. A long-term engagement pad. I used to keep scrapbooks, too. They weren't ordinary scrapbooks, because they were all about the future. The life I was going to lead, not the life I was leading. Nothing about life at home, needless to say."

"Like me and East Northrup," I said. "I couldn't keep a scrapbook about East Northrup."

"Are you going to finish that whole jug by yourself?"

191

"Maybe. I hadn't thought about it."

"That's no way to drink wine," she said.

I was sitting up, the blanket around me, and tilting the jug to my lips, with my index finger to the handle, using my bent arm as a lever. "Where I come from, this is how we drink sweet apple cider."

I saw that she was looking at me with pursed lips and giggling faintly.

"You're sozzled," Chee Wee said.

"Don't be ridiculous."

"Let's see you get up."

I got to my feet very easily. To prove how easily, I posed on one foot, then on the toe of that foot, stretching my arm with jug in hand high up toward the stars. My other foot extended well out behind me. It made a striking pose, George Marsh told me later.

"Whoopsie!" Chee Wee shouted, and pinched the calf of my supporting leg just above the ankle. "Whoopsie—do!"

I started forward and tripped, falling on my chin in a furrow of sharp grass roots and sand. Some muscatel had splashed on my face, leaving a sticky layer of sand as I righted myself.

"Very funny," I told Chee Wee and started toward the cottage, turning my back to her.

"You're not going to upchuck, I hope?" I heard Chee Wee say, and she fell into a dainty convulsion.

"Don't be ridiculous," I said. "I'm going to wash my face."

I heard George Marsh say something, and Lila called softly that the bathroom was the first door on the right after the kitchen and Chee Wee called to Lila that I was obviously going to upchuck. I turned once to request them to keep it down to a dull roar and continued defiantly toward the house.

There were no lights in the kitchen, nor any switch that I could find, and the same was true of the hall and the living room beyond it. An endless row of doors led off the hall to left and right, but not one in the vicinity of the kitchen. I opened a broom closet, a linen closet, and then, angry that my stomach should be churning with a warm, sugary nausea, angrier than ever with Chee Wee, I seized the handle of a third door and pulled hard.

I was to hear later in the most minute detail the consequences of my deed. Yet at the time, as images careened across my mind, the scene had a ghastliness of its own that needed no refreshing. I was

192

aware then, without anyone's telling me later, that I was in a woman's bedroom. A clock was ticking and I smelled the powders and cologne even before I lurched against them and they clattered to the floor. There was no need to tell me after that I had cut my cheek against a jagged edge of glass, for I felt the blood with my own fingers as I raised myself off the floor. If, when the bed lamp was snapped on, I tottered in its light, a stupefying figure in a bloody shirt with a bloody, sand-caked face, a pallid face, the shabbier for a three days' growth of whiskers, there was no need to describe it to me. I had seen it all in that hideous instant when I confronted the dressing-table mirror. And I had seen in a corner of the glass the frozen, beauty-creamed features, the curler-studded, henna-rinsed hair, and the fierce eyes staring.

"What do you want?" A numbed and frightened voice at first.

"Huh?"

Then a pause, more dreadful than the crash.

"What do you want?"

I told myself that I must avoid panic and, with a view toward rallying my own composure, I sat down, thinking to find the dressing table a suitable support. It was tragically unsuitable, having conspired to dance away from me, as though on tiptoes, and before I could catch it, the triptych paneled mirror lay in splinters at my feet.

I raised my arms in a pacifying gesture. "Please don't scream," I said. "You'll wake up the family."

The figure was erect beside the bed, clutching the bedding to her bosom. "Where did *you* come from?"

"East Northrup," I said. "Where do you think I came from?"

"I think you'd better get out of here."

"I'm looking for the bathroom," I said.

"Gus Taylor," the voice said evenly, icily. "I told Lila you boys were not to come here unless you were invited. My husband and I are trying to get some rest."

"Mrs. Norris. Nobody told me that this was your room. I had no idea it was you, Mrs. Norris."

"Get out of the house."

"I can't this minute, Mrs. Norris. I think I'm going to throw up."

Chapter Twelve

It had been unforgivable, Ava Norris said in a memo that Lila brought over to us at the boarding house the next morning. Ordinarily she could be a good sport; she had been young herself. Adolescent drunkenness was another matter; there was no need discussing that, Ava Norris would only say that I had behaved like a hoodlum, frightening her out of a night's sleep and destroying expensive glass. She hoped we would find ways of amusing ourselves on the island. We should have no trouble finding some other little boys to play with. Under the circumstances, we would understand how it was impossible for us to go to the cottage. Her husband had laid down the law. We would understand also why she had been forced to forbid Lila and Chee Wee to see either of us.

Lila dared linger only briefly in our room. "It's been sheer hell," she said. "If you could have seen Mother at breakfast . . . I've got to run, George. I'm so afraid when these rages come over Mummy. She tries to cover up by being *calm!*"

I was too weak to hold the paper in my hand, so George read it aloud. It was difficult to comprehend, for the merciless throbbing in my brain. When he was through, I rolled over on my pillow and closed my eyes. All I could think of was the bluish memo paper, on top the *Blythe* logohead, and the printing just below it, *Memorandum from the Desk of Ava Norris.*

George crumpled the paper into a tight bluish ball and flicked it under the washstand. He watched forlornly as it bounced into the enamel slop bucket underneath. Probably he had never been given a room without running water before.

He moved from his bed to the window and stood for a time silently, glaring between the cheesecloth curtains, leaning his strong forearms upon the rickety frame.

Then he swung viciously from the window and, catching a metal

194

wastebasket on his toe, sailed it against the wall with a crash that threatened to split my head into sections. He stood over my head and bellowed: "You did it up brown, didn't you? . . . Boy, I hope you're satisfied."

He scarcely spoke for the rest of the day.

We ate a supper of eggs and coffee at a small lunch counter, and after that found a barroom in the basement of a resort hotel. It was a dark room, lit only by the spectrum effect of a jukebox, and deserted but for a honeymoon couple who sat at a table, their cheeks on their hands, and cast wan, resentful looks at us. At the bar I ordered two Alka Seltzers and George took Cuba libres, specifying in the stern tone reserved for those who waited on him that he wanted fresh limes and Jamaica rum. We emptied our glasses without a word, George leaving his stool at intervals to play the jukebox or the slot machine. I watched him empty five dollars in fifty-cent pieces into it before an ineffable wave of remorse swept over me and I left for the boarding house alone.

"Tonight's my turn to get fried," George grunted as I left him. "Tomorrow you can nurse me."

Whatever his intention, he came back an hour later perfectly sober, and so was doubly disconsolate in the morning. During breakfast at the lunch counter he told me, "I'm going to the beach and you'd better come, too. It'd be a hell of a note to come all the way to Florida and not even get a swim."

We changed to bathing suits and I drove him to the beach while he deplored the rents in the car's canvas top. He promised himself half aloud to get a new top in Miami. He had decided in the night to leave for Miami and from there take the plane to Havana. He had never seen Havana, but his mother had often gone there with Bert Seidel. He had his traveler's checks that he could cash anywhere. As for me, I would leave him at Sarasota and make my way north on the bus.

We got to the beach at ten and parked in the public area in a spot close to a pole, upon which a sign proclaimed the neighboring beach to be private property, for the use of guests of the Mariposa Inn. When he read the sign, George Marsh forced a vulgar belch.

A handful of early swimmers were splashing off the public beach. George swept through them haughtily, with the careful eight-beat crawl of which he was as proud as he was of his furious forehand smash in tennis. He pressed inexorably out to sea, knifing through the slow rollers with his face rising for air on alternate strokes. I lost interest in following him and when I waded to the beach he was headed for a sand bar some fifty yards ahead of him, where the adamant breakers dashed against the outgoing tide. The hell with him, I thought. Let him take out his grievances against the whole damn Gulf of Mexico.

The lifeguard beckoned me over to his stand on the private beach. He was pointing at George, who was buffeting among the whitecaps on the shoal.

"Can he swim good?" the lifeguard asked.

"Don't mind him," I said.

The lifeguard was combing his hair, looking into a small mirror nailed against a post below his stand. A bottle of Vitalis rested on the sand beneath. "He's not my lookout," the lifeguard said. "If he's off the public beach. I was out there a while and I mean there's a drag to that tide."

"He'll be all right," I said. I watched him comb his hair the way Harry Tilton might comb his, lovingly, as though each hair was brittle and might break off if pulled too sharply. He had a sun tan and was blond and wore a flesh-colored sweat shirt, his Red Cross emblem stitched on the front of it.

"I'm not going after him," the lifeguard said. "It's not my jurisdiction off the public beach. I'm not about to go after nobody off the public beach. I don't like wettin' my head up unless I have to. I got this sinus trouble."

"Thanks for the kind words," I said. "I'd better get back on my side of the line."

"Just thought I ought to tell you," I heard him answering behind me, and then in a surprised tone, "Howdy-do, Mathilde. You're early for your lesson."

I looked around at Mathilde Norris, in shorts and a halter, smiling coquettishly at the lifeguard.

"I don't feel like swimming today," Mathilde told him. "The water's stinky."

"Your mother told me one half hour," the lifeguard said.

"Let's not and say we did."

"That's okay by me, Mathilde. I don't know how Mrs. Norris would like it."

196

"You'll get your old money," Mathilde said listlessly. "I'll tell Mummy we went in anyway. I can sit down in the water and come out wet. She'll never know."

"Well," the lifeguard said.

"You want to play some gin rummy?" Mathilde asked. "My sister and her friend have a pack of cards."

The lifeguard had been wiping between his toes with a towel but now he looked up at Mathilde with a guileful expression. "They want to play? We could set up one of the beach umbrellas."

"They want to be alone," Mathilde told him. "You and I can play without a beach umbrella."

The lifeguard looked vexed. "I owe your sister a dollar and a quarter for yesterday's game."

"That was yesterday," Mathilde said, toying with a pigtail.

The lifeguard was surveying his kneecaps and thinking very hard. "I'll tell you what, Mathilde. I'll play you one game if you'll run over and bring your sister back," he said.

"She won't come," Mathilde answered. "She's in the middle of a sulk. You don't know what my sister's like when she gets in one of her sulks."

I walked behind Mathilde and pulled her other pigtail. "Hey," I said. "That's quite a little get-up you're wearing."

Mathilde turned her round, chalky face up to mine and squinted in the sun, registering nothing. "You vomited in Mummy's room," she said.

"Mathilde," I said, "what do you say we go look for some sea shells?"

"That's dumb," declared Mathilde. "Who cares for stinky sea shells?"

"We can sit in the sun. With a bathing suit like that it's a shame not to have a suntan."

"It's not a bathing suit. It's a playsuit that my sister used to wear before she got big in the fanny and the front."

"She's not so big," the lifeguard said. "She's just right." He rolled his eyes at me and winked. "Nice," he said.

"She's bigger than she used to be," Mathilde said.

"Let's walk down the beach," I said. "I want to talk to you, Mathilde."

"I'm not allowed to talk to you. Mummy will send me to bed at half-past five."

"Mathilde," I said sternly. "What would your mother say if she heard you'd skipped your swimming lesson?"

Mathilde looked up and down the beach furtively, and then gave me a judicious glance.

"Don't you think you might as well take a little walk with me," I continued. "Just to stay on the safe side, Mathilde?"

"Oh, all right," Mathilde said. "If you're going to use blackmail."

Mathilde was prejudiced against the public beach, having seen the grocery boy in swimming there two or three times. I explained that beaches were organically the same, composed of the same sand, and fronted by the same ocean.

"It's a puey beach," Mathilde said when we reached it. "People do things in the water."

"That's ridiculous," I said. "Don't be ridiculous, Mathilde."

The child giggled. "That's what you kept saying the night you vomited. You kept saying 'Don't be ridiculous.'"

We sat on a bath towel and watched George Marsh make his way back against the tide, using the same relentless crawl. I wondered how much it cost to learn to swim like that. How many lifeguards, beach boys, summer camps and chlorinated swimming pools had played their part in this enviable creation?

He touched shore and bounded toward us, pausing only to pick a bright shell.

"Hi, Mathilde. What's new?"

"Hi, George. What's new?"

The private password. The familiarity I could never share.

He crawled to the child on his hands and knees and shook his wet hair over her.

"Stop, George. Stop it!" Mathilde shrieked delightedly.

He laughed and held her shoulders in his fists. "What's the good word? Has your mother changed her mind? Can we come around after lunch?"

"You'd better not," Mathilde said, faintly.

He shook her, his face stiff and uncomprehending.

"I said you'd better not come," Mathilde sounded frightened. "Mummy is madder than six wet hens. George, you're hurting my arm. George!"

He dropped her shoulders and rose, fingering the flat shell. In final protest he wound back his arm and flung the shell ruthlessly over the water. He squatted in the sand, the football crouch, the balls of his feet and his right fist supporting him, and charged. He crouched and charged, time after time, up and down the sand, against a host of invisible defenders, lashing out at them with his elbows that he had trained to use as flippers. And suddenly he was the ball runner, the line bucker, tearing off tackle, head and shoulders down, arms to the body, a cannon ball, knees pumping cruelly into the faces of a hundred phantom tacklers.

"Why don't you relax?" I called to him. "We'll work something out."

"Yeah," he called back. "You're a real genius, you are. Thanks."

I watched him crouch once more and charge in a last helpless frenzy that propelled him far down the beach.

"Wow!" Mathilde said.

"Mathilde," I said suddenly. "Would you like some nice jelly beans?"

"I'm tired of jelly beans," Mathilde said. "What do I have to do?"

"I want you to take a note to your mother."

"You have to take me to the movies," Mathilde said.

"I promise," I said. I stared forthrightly at the child, assuring her I was as good as my word. "Meet me here at two o'clock."

"At two o'clock," Mathilde said, "I have to take my nap."

"At three then. Right here by the sign."

George set out after lunch to cash some traveler's checks and I had time to deliberate over my note:

Dear Mrs. Norris,
What happened in your room that night was all my fault and this is to apologize. I do not expect that you can forgive me for a thing like that. I don't know how I did it, but I did not mean to. I know you don't want to see us any more; and so I will go home tomorrow.
However, I don't think you are being fair if you blame George for what I did. He did not have a thing to do with it and he doesn't deserve your being angry at him. He was looking forward to this trip. He is terribly low and ashamed. Please ask him back to your cottage after I am gone. It was all my fault and I am ashamed of myself. But you are being wrong and unfair to George.
                                        Sincerely yours

We planned to leave late in the morning of the third day, as soon as the car could be oiled and checked. The two o'clock bus left Sarasota for Jacksonville and there I could make connections with Greyhound that would take me all the way to Boston. When George left for the garage I told him I would walk to the beach for a last swim.

It was an overcast morning and the public beach was deserted. There was consolation in the warm sea water but the weather was raw and foreboding. I walked along the hard sand, shivering in my wet bathing trunks and wishing I had not come after all. In the distance I saw my friend the lifeguard huddled beneath a blanket in the seat of his high stand. I headed for him at a quickened pace, momentarily brightened by the prospect of his company.

"There's a sign over there," he greeted me. "Says this beach is private property."

"I wanted to be in your jurisdiction," I said. "I feel safer knowing you're here to watch over me."

He lifted his head and frowned. "Are you kiddin'?"

"Gee whillikers. Yesterday I thought we made friends."

"I called you over yesterday, so you wasn't trespassin' then. I don't remember askin' you to come today."

"Maybe we could play some gin rummy."

"Are you kiddin'?" he said.

"Maybe you got something to tell me this time. Maybe you could tell me about sharks and sea pussies and the dangers of the deep."

"You bother me," he said, and went back to picking at his hand. "I got a splinter climbin' up the steps and I have to get it out before it's infected."

He kicked angrily at the wooden ladder. "I *told* 'em they ought to sandpaper these steps. There. . . . I just remembered," he said, "Mathilde left you a note."

He poked a foot toward the corner of the platform and I heard a scraping of paper.

I scrambled up the ladder and grabbed the bluish envelope.

"Watch it!" the lifeguard yelled. "You'll spill the sun tan lotion."

I dropped to the sand and tore open the note. It was short and puzzling and at the end the initials appeared in lavender ink, inside an executive little circle:

Gus,

I want to talk to you at noon today. I shall be waiting on our verandah.

A.T.N.

At the boarding house I unpacked a gabardine jacket and a pair of shorts from my suitcase and borrowed an open-collared tennis shirt from George Marsh.

Outdoors the sun had begun to break, as though presaging something, and, as I walked to the Norris' coral pink cottage, it was shining brilliantly upon the hibiscus hedge and the upturned mouths of the conch shells.

Ava Norris stood on the narrow verandah, attired in grayish beach pajamas and with a dab of grease on the end of her nose. She looked a little less tall than usual, but that was only because she was wearing flat, open-toed sandals.

"Twelve on the dot," she said. "Nobody can say that you are not a punctual young man."

I followed her silently down the verandah to where it turned at the corner of the cottage onto a wider platform furnished with glass-topped tables and modernistic canvas beach chairs.

"Of course you're a monster," Ava Norris said, settling herself in one of the chairs. "And I'm not in the habit of consorting with monsters—"

Here she raised her sharp face and tittered. When she wished to break the ice, Ava Norris reverted to this titter as a sort of condescension to her sex. It was the same nervous outlet that Chee Wee Gibbons or her own daughters used and with Ava Norris it did not ring true.

Sometimes it was impossible for me to believe that Ava Norris was Lila's mother. It was impossible to believe that she had ever shared a bedroom with Hadley Norris long enough to perform anything as uncircumspect as the act of love and the reproduction of the species.

At this moment the last of Ava Norris' tittering died in a draft of warm and salty air that wafted between us across the verandah. "I can tease as well as scold, you know," she was saying. "Gus, I'm afraid you have a lot to learn about women."

Within her reach, on one of the glass-topped tables, stood a tray with a single cocktail glass, a dish of hearts of onion, and a blue thermos from which she poured a pale fluid consisting predominantly of gin. I was surprised to see her tapering fingers bare of jewels and nail polish, and then I remembered she had come here to relax. Without lipstick her mouth was a thin line. Her skin, salved by devoted fingers with an assortment of subtle compounds, coolly awaited a sun tan.

"It was beginning to be glorious on the beach when I came up," Ava Norris was saying. "I hated to leave my husband in the middle of our morning's gin rummy."

I watched her suspiciously from my chair.

"What's the trouble, Gus? We're on speaking terms, aren't we?"

"I just don't know what there is to say, Mrs. Norris."

"We could talk about the water. There's been delicious swimming lately." She fingered an edge of the Ava Norris hair which was wet where it hadn't fitted into her bathing cap, and made a dark contrast to the legendary henna rinse above.

"Gus, I hope one day I can teach you something about women, believe me. One day you may be an attractive young man. You never can tell."

"Thanks, Mrs. Norris," I said.

But she wasn't giggling or smiling.

"Now George is a sweet boy, but George has reached his peak. I know all about George, and I knew his father too. But you, you're quite a different proposition. I think I can make you this one hesitant prediction: take ten years and you'll be head and shoulders over the George Marshes of the world. If you only use your head. Do you ever use your head, Gus?"

"I try to, Mrs. Norris."

"Are you interested in becoming an adult?"

"Yes."

"That's nice," Ava Norris said. "I've been thinking about you since I got your note."

She poured another glassful from the bottomless thermos. This was quite a change from the kind of talk I was accustomed to hearing from my uncle Torbert Case.

"That note was a rather dubious piece of composition. Disorganized, schoolboyish. The point is, you wrote it. You stood up to me and told me I was wrong and I like that. That's what a man should do in this man's world. . . . I like to have a man assert himself," she added quietly.

As there seemed to be nothing more to say, I struggled to disengage myself from the enveloping canvas seat.

202

"I'm glad I saw you, Mrs. Norris. I have a two o'clock bus to catch."

She was not looking at me but at a design of mounted sea horses and star fish that hung on a placard over the living-room door.

"Why, darling," she said, "you're expected for lunch."

"Mrs. Norris," I said uncertainly, "you didn't have to ask me."

"Nonsense. I told Lila this morning that you and George are welcome at the cottage at any time."

I watched her belt down the last of what had been her fourth or fifth Gibson cocktail. Now that the business had been done, the ground covered, she was dismissing it from her mind and sealing the top securely on the thermos. She would not take another. Ava Norris knew where to draw the line. Already the sound of laughing voices came to us from the path that led upward from the beach.

"You're welcome to stay. We'll say no more about it. We'll not mention anything to George."

She lay back in her chair and began her nearly biological metamorphosis back to femininity. There was a perceptible sweetening of her expression. "Why haven't you found yourself a girl of your own?"

There was no time to continue, for Lila and Chee Wee burst over the verandah steps and were upon me in a rush of wet bathing suits and streaming hair. Their cheeks pressed mine and their lips resounded tenderly against the air beside my ear.

"You did it," Lila cried. "You've brought Mummy to her senses!"

"Our hero!" Chee Wee cried.

Like two penitent kittens they dashed and huddled in the embrace of Ava Norris, the complete, surfeited mother. It was a tender pose, but some thirty seconds of it were sufficient for Ava Norris.

"Lunch in twenty minutes," she said abruptly. "Liles will wear the taffeta skirt."

"Mummy, I promised it to Chee Wee."

"Mrs. Norris, I've never worn the taffeta." Chee Wee's disappointment was faithfully registered upon her face.

"Lila will wear the taffeta." The girls vanished obediently; it must always have been as simple as that.

Ava Norris moved about the porch, emptying the scallop-shell ashtrays. "Liles is terribly generous," she said, "and Chee Wee is a darling. But enough is enough."

There was a scuffing of bare feet upon the wooden porch steps. Hadley Norris came in view, his arm resting paternally on the shoulder of George Marsh.

"Our bronzed Adonises of the sands," Ava Norris said.

In bathing trunks Hadley Norris was rather more red than he was bronze. And of the two, George Marsh was vastly the more credible as Adonis.

I had not recovered from the impact of seeing Mr. Norris in bathing trunks, but I rose to shake his hand politely. "How do you do, sir?"

Mr. Norris made a perfunctory barking sound and turned to his wife. "Mother, since George is back on board, we're going to have to break out the rum ration. Don't worry about anything, Mother. It isn't every day that George gets off probation."

With a cheery wink at George he whisked away, beneath the sea horses and star fish and through the open door. Ava Norris followed him, but at a distance.

George Marsh held the clothes he would change into over one arm; white flannels, navy blue shirt and white buckskin shoes. He had carried them all the way from the boarding house and over the beach, yet there was not a wrinkle on them and not a grain of sand.

"I don't know how you swung it," he told me, "but I really want to thank you."

"Nothing to it," I said.

"You must have gotten quite a going-over." He smiled. I knew he would have liked to tell me more, were he able to express such things.

"It wasn't too bad," I said.

"You must have talked fast," George said.

"I didn't do much talking. It was all in a note I sent her."

"Old Man Norris told me you were really going to get the works," he said and grinned.

I was suddenly suspicious. A moment ago it had seemed so natural for George to appear in bathing trunks, Hadley Norris' arm about his shoulder. "He went down to get you, didn't he? You had the news before I did."

"If you want to know the truth," George said, "as soon as he heard the freeze was off, the old blade came down to hunt me up.

You know he gets pretty lonely up here by himself with only the women."

"And he told you I was really going to get the works?" I asked.

"He just said she was good and mad."

"You mean that's what he hoped."

"Don't be so damned Bostonian," George said. "The old blade doesn't feel at home with you yet. That's all."

"You can say that again. He didn't bother to shake hands."

"But you made a big hit with the old lady?"

"Yes," I said. "Now she's calling me darling."

"No kidding?"

He laughed and slapped my shoulder. Then he too had gone inside to dress.

I stood on the edge of the verandah, looking down the steps at the path and the grass which was scrubby and brown in the sunshine, with none of the enticement it had held that first night. I was bewildered by Mr. Norris' indifference toward me. It was bitterly true that only George could speak his language. And on the other hand, Ava Norris and I had made our alliance so easily, almost as though we were conspiring against George and Mr. Norris. I did not like the idea. Why was it so hard to identify myself with George Marsh? There were inviolate areas, I was beginning to recognize, where he and I could meet only as strangers.

Ava Norris came out on the verandah to fetch me. "Gus, why are you looking so woebegone?" she said and without waiting for an answer led me into the living room.

Hadley Norris was tickled to death to have George back aboard. If he had said so once, he had said so a dozen times, as he concocted the rum drinks, adding the maraschino cherries, and the slices of orange and pineapple. He was dressed to match his mood, in a maroon silk shirt printed with a yellow Hawaiian motif of ukuleles and outrigger canoes that was pinched unmercifully into the folds of his stomach by a pair of pink linen trousers. He urged a second and a third drink on George and harangued the room with stories he had picked up from friends in Washington. His head bowed in mock prayer, he recited the Roosevelt version of the Twenty-third Psalm. ". . . and I shall dwell in the poorhouse forever." A carbon copy had been mailed him by a friend in New York.

205

Lila was quietly smoothing her taffeta skirt. "Mummy, can't we get Pappy on some other train of thought?"

We ate lunch in the breakfast nook that separated the living room from the kitchen. On one side of the table Ava Norris stubbornly pressed her conversation with me:

"Two attractive girls under one roof, Gus, and you're as aloof as the Prince of Wales. Aren't you a little young to be playing hard to get?"

"I like Mathilde," I tried to say. "Why isn't she eating with the family?"

I was sure she could not hear me, for opposite us in his corner of the breakfast nook the man of the house had launched into a story about the three doctors who were dining together, the Frenchman, the Britisher, and the American. Mr. Norris was endeavoring to imitate the accents of each speaker.

"Eeet ees marveluss what our French colleagues can do . . . why . . . we take the livehr of a peeg, put eet een a dying womahn and, mon Dieu! now she is back walking the streets. . . ."

As long as Mathilde refused to take her swimming lessons, Ava Norris was saying, Mathilde would spend her days in her bedroom.

". . . veddy int'resting, I'm sure, but in England we also have achieved a surgical miracle. We have inserted the pancreas of a male goat into a dying peddler and now he is back, er, walking the streets!"

But Mathilde and I were great friends, I was trying to say. Mathilde did not deserve this punishment.

". . . and the American doctor said, 'Let me tell you about the astounding surgery we are performing in *this* country. . . .'"

Ava Norris touched my arm, but we were approaching the punch line:

". . . in this country, the American doctor said, we have put a horse's ass in the White House, and now *all* the people are walking the streets!"

Our raconteur, who had been standing for the better part of the story, now sat and pounded George on the shoulder, roaring and coughing.

"Pappy!" Lila cried. "Maybe it was funny the first time!"

The briefest flicker of antagonism showed in Ava Norris' eyes, but she would not move her head. A chill settled over the breakfast nook. Hadley Norris excused himself and returned bearing a fresh planter's punch. George and Chee Wee and Lila talked in snatches; Ava Norris prated determinedly about the Florida climate. Isolated with his unflagging good spirits, the man of the house mumbled and coughed and laughed by himself. At the meal's end he remembered a story that was not for ladies' ears. Leaving his plate untouched, he rose, glass in hand, and proposed that George accompany him out-doors. George Marsh appeared apprehensive, glanced at Lila and at her mother. Then as his host lurched from his seat and upended the bowl of salad dressing, he saw his duty.

Lila, looking disconsolately after the men in her life, would not speak until the door banged on the verandah.

"Pappy's being horrid. Haven't you *any* reason for not liking President Roosevelt, Gus?"

All was silent in the breakfast nook. Ava Norris' spoon stirred in her iced-coffee glass. From outside came the sudden sound of break-ing timber, followed by a hoarse cry, and George Marsh was calling for me to lend him a hand.

Ava Norris was already on her feet. "You stay here," she said to me, "and talk to the girls."

Her pajama legs bustled militantly as she made for the open door.

"It's all right, Mrs. Norris," we heard George Marsh saying out-side. "He was a little dizzy and then a board gave way beneath him and he fell onto the conch shells. I think he's hurt his side, but he'll be fine in a minute. If we could find some brandy."

The door slammed shut, closing out the voices, and Lila was sobbing recklessly on Chee Wee's shoulder.

"He's all right," Chee Wee was soothing her. "You heard George say he was."

Tears coursed down Lila's cheeks, symmetrical, spherical tears that dripped and ran like raindrops. Her eyes, seen through tangled locks, were enchanted springs from which her maiden's sorrows flowed, apparently with some regularity.

"Don't you see? Don't you see it always happens when Pappy is with George? I know he can't help it. I know George can't help it. But why must it always happen in *front* of people?"

She loosed a torrent of woe onto Chee Wee's shoulder. "Oh why? Why? Why?" She beat upon the table with her fragile fist. So she remained, in an infant's tantrum, until her mother reappeared.

"I'm sorry, Mummy. It makes me so mad."

"If you can't control yourself you had better go to your room," Ava Norris said and that was all of the passion and the drama.

Lila dried her eyes and swallowed and promptly lost herself in her mother's instructions. Mother and daughter were as a team long drilled in domestic emergency. The name and number of a doctor who had been recommended was on a bluish memo slip within reach of the telephone. The doctor came on schedule with a hypodermic and an Oldsmobile sedan into which George and I helped the unresisting form of Hadley Norris.

It passed too quickly and too mechanically for me. But before the doctor had driven off, Ava Norris was busy at her desk with the day's mail and the girls had changed back into bathing suits for the afternoon.

Chapter Thirteen

X-rays showed that Hadley Norris had broken two ribs and further tests indicated the recurrence of a liver condition. He spent two weeks in the hospital at Sarasota. And we saw no more of him in the eight days that George and I remained in Gentian Cove.

They were swift, tranquil days. George found another tourist home where he was more comfortable and where we had a bath to ourselves. We took meals at the Norris' cottage. We swam and played tennis on the courts belonging to the inn. There was no set schedule to the days. Ava Norris, wishing to relax, was not a demanding hostess. Each day one of us would retire to the verandah with her an hour before lunch to play gin rummy, while she kept score and served herself at intervals from the blue thermos. She would draw me aside in the evenings to ask about East Northrup or about what, if anything, I was learning at school. And she was curious about my future. She didn't mean to pry, but she couldn't help being inquisitive.

On the last afternoon, George Marsh drove Ava Norris into Sarasota to the hospital and Chee Wee went with them. So I came to spend some uninterrupted hours alone with Lila.

We lay in the sand and Lila rubbed my back with the sun lotion that had done wonders for her and Chee Wee. She and Chee Wee were sun worshipers and proud of it. Why come all the way south if you couldn't go back to school absolutely black?

She lay on her back, her eyes closed to the sun which beat down upon her, bestowing ever more of itself to her browned face. I watched her face and body in profile, not knowing what to make of my closeness to her, nor of this primordial feeling.

"You might pay attention while I'm talking to you." She moved to me, resting ladylike on one elbow, and poured a baby's handful of sand upon my back. "I get so many queer ideas. You could help me to keep the right ones and make me forget the crazy ones. I wish you'd tell me what you think of George."

"What are you worrying about?" I said. "You're in love with him, aren't you?"

"Of course. I love him better than anyone in the whole world."

"Then I don't see what your problem is."

"You never talk about anything serious, Gussy. I wish I knew what went on in your mind."

"Not very much," I said.

"You're shy, aren't you?"

"Let's talk about something else," I said.

"Let's play a game," Lila said. "Let's play trade lasts. You're awfully nice and Mummy is simply goofy for you."

"George is simply goofy for you."

"You've got to give me a *real* T.L."

"If you really want to know," I said, "I think you're pretty as all hell."

"That's no T.L. Aren't I unusual or anything?"

All her life people had told her she was pretty and all her life she'd had the idea that pretty girls didn't have brains.

"George told me to build *you* up." She lowered her eyes coyly and gave me a little smile. "George says you're like Chee Wee, you have some sort of a complex about where you come from. What's the *matter* with East Northrup?"

"You don't need to build me up." Digging my chin into the crook of my arm, looking hard into her face, I returned the smile. "Why say what George says? Why don't you think up something of your own for a change?"

"I hate you for that!" Lila cried. "I'm utterly original and unique!"

She knelt and scooped sand rapidly over my back, then rubbed so that it would adhere to the coating of sun lotion. When I tried to seize her, she scampered off into the surf, glancing once over her shoulder to make sure that I was chasing.

The sea was high that afternoon and breaking within only a few yards of the beach. Lila plunged defiantly into a tall wave and allowed another to wash over her as she swam. Standing up to her chest in the water, she waved both arms at the sun, fell backward and floated, arms outstretched, over the crest of a roller, laughing at the sky. I swam to her, a tanned, slender figure in two bands of scarlet cloth, inert upon the sea.

We dove through the breakers one by one and made our way beyond them to where the gentler waves rose and fell about her shoulders. Her hair was wild and pressed in snarls against her cheeks or forehead, wherever the sea might wash it. "You look like Medusa," I said.

"Put me on your shoulders," Lila said. "I want to feel the breeze up there."

She rode my back and shouted incoherently into the wind, pulling my hair to left and right like a horse's mane to indicate direction. I stumbled under the surge and floundered once, letting her slip forward over my head.

"You clumsy!" She plowed toward me with both hands splashing water in my face. I reached to duck her but she dropped beneath my arm and lost her balance, falling against me. She caught an arm about my neck and thus we drifted for a long moment in the trough of a wave.

"Pretend I'm drowning and you've rescued me from a watery grave." And she placed her other arm about my waist. "You pretend to be towing me in."

I swam easily with the waves and she gripped tighter when we reached the breakers, and there, with a little shriek, she was carried from me to land on her back in a wash of frothy water. As she raced for the beach an arm reached out for her.

"You all right? He didn't hurtcha?"

The lifeguard stood before us, wet to the ankles, in a pair of snug purplish Jantzens. A plastic whistle dangled about his neck from a piece of twine.

"How many times I have to tell you to read the signs?" He advanced toward me menacingly. "If you wanna drown, do it off the public end." He looked protectively at Lila, who was covering her mouth with her hands and giggling like a naughty child.

"Roy, don't be such an old woman."

"So long as you swim off this beach I'm responsible for your safety. Din'tcha hear the whistle? There's bad water out where you was. I don't know what you thought I was blowin' for. I din't come down here for my health."

Lila danced away from him and up onto the sand, and as she

211

passed him she flung her tangled hair prettily onto her shoulders. "Sometime we'll play gin rummy, Roy. You ought to have a chance to win your money back."

Roy plodded after her. "You wanna play some now? I got nothin' special doing."

But her back was turned and the wind from the sea dashed the words back into Roy's open mouth. He hung his head and his eyes avoided mine.

We took a long walk over the sand, letting the sun dry us. Lila practiced her best posture. She pretended to walk with a book on her head as the dramatic coach had taught her at Miss Eustis'. That spring they were doing *Holiday* and Lila's heart was set on the role Katharine Hepburn had played in the movie. She walked stiffly, pulling in her behind which she felt was bigger than it ought to be. Farther on, she extended her arms in front of her, pressing her fingers against each other in a bust-developing exercise. That and swimming the breast stroke were the two surest ways.

"George says I worry too much over my figure."

I was starting to notice the plaintiveness that crept into her voice when she mentioned George. "You know I don't think he likes me even to wear a two-piece bathing suit? He never says anything, of course."

We passed the beach umbrellas and the reclining forms of the Boston and Philadelphia people her mother was cultivating. They waved at Lila and she waved back gaily, being a gregarious, outgoing girl.

"He never says it," Lila said, "but he has his way of letting you know."

"I guess everybody has to mind something," I said.

"You mind all kinds of things. I can tell."

"I didn't like you handling the lifeguard."

"You mustn't mind Roy. He was just being himself." Her voice was softening, losing more of its happy edge. "You know I don't think George would have cared at all if he'd seen me with Roy?"

"You were flirting with him, weren't you?"

"Only a little. I couldn't help it. Before you and George came we were alone here for days. Do you think George sees any other girls?"

"Now don't start worrying about that."

"I wish he would. It isn't fair that he doesn't. I see boys if I want to."

"What boys?" I said, teasingly. "Roy and who else?"

"I don't think that's your business exactly."

"Do you see Harry Tilton?"

"I think he's a very nice boy," Lila said.

"Well, suit yourself."

"I do flirt. I flirt terribly."

"As long as you don't mean anything by it," I said, lamely.

"You could have kissed me in the water," Lila said. "I'm glad you didn't."

"It was just as well," I said.

"Mummy says it's all right for girls to be silly when they're sixteen." She was walking slowly and watching her incredibly tiny feet make shallow dimples on the sand. "Mummy says I shouldn't be tied down. I don't feel tied down. I want George to need me. I like having somebody absolutely need you the way he does. Sometimes he frightens me, but I need to have someone love me and he loves me best of all. I think I like it because it's sad and scary, like Romeo and Juliet . . . and then I get scared because of the family. I don't want to do to George what Mummy's done to Pappy. Just the same I *would* do it, to any boy. I know I would unless he can stop me. I think it's a terrible thing I have inside me. I have to have somebody who's strong, strong!"

Her eyes were a deep summer blue and she was staring fiercely at the sand, with a look of violent beauty as though her thoughts were powerful as the sea. If she were a silly girl, you felt that it was a deep and wanton silliness, that beneath it ocean currents were pulling this way and that.

"I never saw you look that way before," I said. "What is it?"

"I don't know what. I think I want to grow up too much. I don't have any business thinking some of the things I do."

"You're wild," I said.

"Don't say that. I don't want to be wild."

"George showed me a snapshot of you once. You wore a tennis dress and a ribbon in your hair. You didn't look like a little girl at all."

"I feel like running," Lila said. "Let's run all the way to the steps."

For nearly a quarter of a mile I paced her until we reached the steps that led from the beach to the cottage. At the end she was running ahead of me and waited for me to reach the steps, smiling brightly, and breathless, the worry burned from her eyes.

"You know what?" she asked. "I feel we know each other very well. I feel I can trust you."

"Can't you trust George?"

"Of course, but that's for different things."

George Marsh and Chee Wee were waiting when we reached the verandah of the cottage.

"Gussy and I had the most glorious time," Lila said to him.

"Gussy?" George sat on the balustrade and as Lila went to him, he drew an arm around her. "I don't think anyone has ever called him Gussy."

At ten in the morning, George Marsh and I set off for East Northrup with the top down. We had allowed ourselves fifty-five hours before the deadline, which was Monday by Evening Prayer. The girls stood about the car and chatted. It had been a fun time, a perfect, peaceful fun time, and none of us would ever forget it. When George started the motor, they dashed and embraced us from the running boards. I knew that Lila and George had kissed the real good-by somewhere inside the cottage, and yet as she bent over me I felt the unmistakable press of her lips against my cheek. Had it been the mere courtesy kiss that Chee Wee Gibbons gave, I would have felt an awkward jealousy.

Chapter Fourteen

Fuzzy Eaton's father generously lent him a Ford runabout for the summer of 1940. In it we journeyed many times over the Worcester Turnpike from East Northrup to Chestnut Hill. Though my aunt wasn't sure what to make of Fuzzy, who sat about our front porch and drank her iced tea with monosyllabic indifference, she was happy that I had a friend from Chestnut Hill. Her approval was not diminished by the fact that, when Fuzzy spoke at all, she was at a loss to understand him. He had adopted a new way of speaking, as though he had a hot potato in his mouth, which Aunt Connie said was not the way most people spoke in Chestnut Hill. I tried to explain this idiosyncrasy:

"It's his imitation of a Groton accent, Aunt. He started to talk that way as a joke and he's never managed to shake off the habit. You'll get used to it in a while."

But Aunt Connie was not satisfied.

"There's no such thing as a Groton accent. Proper speech is proper speech, not accent. When English is properly spoken there's simply no accent at all. When your uncle talks, he hasn't a trace of an accent—I'm sure I don't understand why you call him Fuzzy when his name is Walter. Walter Baxter Eaton is a distinguished name. I should think he'd be proud of it. He has a nice family that have never been divorced. I used to know his mother. She was in my sewing circle."

The lack of morality being so deplorable among the parents of my other friends, Fuzzy Eaton quickly became in Aunt Connie's eyes the ultimate in social desirability. Though it was the last entire summer I was to spend in East Northrup, my aunt encouraged me to see all that I could of Fuzzy. When the Eatons invited me to spend the month of July in North Haven, Maine, and Aunt Connie received a note from Mrs. Eaton confirming the invitation, her joy was unconfined:

"Perhaps conventional people aren't exciting to you, Gus, but you'll grow to realize that that is exactly what makes them worthwhile."

The conventionality of the summer was sabotaged, however, when word reached us that the *Excalibur* was lying off Bar Harbor. Fuzzy and I sped there as fast as the Ford would carry us, to find Uncle Mark and George Marsh in a paralysis of gloom. Baby had surprised everyone by divorcing Bert Seidel.

Bert Seidel was not the first stepfather that George had lost, but the amputation of Bert from the family tree was the more painful for Bert's having been a nice guy. Bert's predecessor, a Californian health addict named Judson Sturgis, nobody had had much use for, and George had not grieved after Judson. So he took it upon himself to grieve doubly after Bert, who was still very much alive and the best stepfather he would ever have. One of the world's great men, George kept saying.

Uncle Mark spent a week ashore with friends. As a gesture of consolation, he made the yacht and crew available to his nephew. Fuzzy and I accompanied George on a cruise down the Maine coast to Buzzards Bay and back, agreeably sharing his bereavement. The day scarcely passed that George did not eulogize his lost stepfather.

"Cheer up, Goph," Fuzzy Eaton would intone on the somber evenings we spent below playing poker with the captain. "Every day's gwine to be Sunday by and by." But it took more than Fuzzy to resuscitate George Marsh. We left him aboard the *Excalibur* in much the same state we had found him. It wasn't until we went back to school in September, as First Classmen now, that George fully recovered.

In that last year at Emmanuel no one worried about George Marsh. Whatever might have troubled him that year, whatever interior sorrow, he showed it to no one; he was the serenest, the securest of us all.

He led the choir as Crucifer, wearing a white surplice over a red cassock each Sunday, save during Lent when the cloth was white over black. He bore the great brass cross through the chapel aisle, measuring his pace to the slow beat of the Academy hymn. He towered over the little sopranos, hymnals in hand, their eyes glued to the back of his dark hair, who followed piously in his footsteps as he led them into the presence of God. So, in one capacity or another, he led us. Head proctor, president of the First Class, chairman of the Missionary Society, football captain. From September to June, he was a figurehead, the property of the school. He had no self to indulge with grievances or torment with anxieties. All private pains were allayed by the supreme absorptive anodyne of being Gopher Marsh.

He broke his wrist in October, in the game with Noble and Greenough. In twenty-four hours that wrist, the same trick wrist he had broken the year before in scrimmage with Northrup High, dominated discussion at every table in the dining hall. With it bound in plaster of Paris and sponge rubber, he played for half the next Saturday's game against Boston Latin. We lost but one of a seven-game schedule that season and we beat Middlesex. The score was recorded in white paint upon the football used at the opening kick-off. It is on exhibit today in the trophy room of the Wythe Gymnasium: *E—27, M—6; 1940, G. Marsh, Capt.*

That night George Marsh stood on his chair at the head of the football training table and addressed the school, the faculty, and the alumni, who had gathered for the victory banquet: "I still don't know if it's real. When we were coming off the field I had to ask Fuzzy Eaton to pinch me to make sure I wasn't dreaming. I couldn't even find my locker when I left the showers, but there was Mr. Morris Opdyke. We've all heard of Mr. Opdyke. He was captain of the undefeated, unscored-on, Opdyke eleven of 1922. I'll take Mr. Opdyke's word for it, because he knows how it feels. He told me I would always remember the two happiest days of my life—today and the day I get married!" He raised his arms, endeavoring to quell the rage of applause. "I want to lead a long cheer to the man who deserves all the credit, Coach McTeale! And I want to follow it with a long cheer for Mrs. Kew, whose patient and generous efforts have made this wonderful banquet possible!"

Again, on a cold February night, as Lila Norris smiled up at him from the throng, he climbed to the steps of Headmaster's House to lead the First Class men and their lady guests through a long cheer for Mrs. Kew, without whose patient and generous efforts this dance

217

weekend, which we would remember always, would not have been possible.

Chee Wee Gibbons, who had come on my invitation, huddled in her borrowed furs and squeezed my arm. "I can't believe it's George, but it is George. The way he was born to be. I'll never ever forget tonight. Doesn't it make you proud, proud that he's your friend?"

It was but one in a procession of scenes, one of a hundred cheers a head proctor leads, a single episode in the legend of Gopher Marsh. It was but a fragment of that happy interlude when the Academy was a playground and the world was our oyster.

In June on our very last night in the playground, on the eve of Awards Day, our yearbook, *The Lexicon*, was distributed. The members of the graduating class sat up late complaining about it. Our yearbook chairman, C. U. P. Vale, Jr., swore he had done his damnedest to liven up *The Lexicon*, but that Dr. Kew was determined to keep it as monotonous as his pride and joy, the *Archivi Emmanuelenses*, notorious for its flatulent obituaries and thumbnail alumni notes. Anyway, we did not blame Cuppy Vale; 1941's *The Lexicon* was no better than the usual dull compendium of athletic and scholastic statistics, class photographs, quotations from Bartlett; and the caricatures that art editor Pansy Peters had inserted in the hope of levity (Boo Hoo Beemer, a bawling infant in diapers; Soaker Means, sheepishly eyeing a water spigot) were at least unusual. Perhaps that was the neatest way to tie up six formative years, perhaps Dr. Kew was right. But we felt cheated.

Fuzzy Eaton in particular. He, *The Lexicon* recorded, had played on all three teams, been four times a letter man, but that was not enough. "Not a word about my scholastic achievements," said Fuzzy, who had rarely got a grade above C-minus in his life. "Or my qualities of leadership," he added with a merry cynicism that was intended to draw me as an audience and did. "Take the hot shots," Fuzzy said. "Gopher Marsh—damn near a full page of statistics." And, pointing to me, flipping farther through the book, "Hell, even you, Gubber. Six lines at least. Captain of the debating team. And valedictorian. How did you swing that?"

"I didn't want it," I said. "Dr. Kew appointed me."

I was sensitive about my task as valedictorian, and acutely dissatisfied with the speech I had prepared.

Four evenings of that week I had repaired to the Harold Manter Benjamin Memorial Auditorium with Dr. Gregore of the English Department. Dismal Gregore had sat in the back row of the empty chamber and I had stood in semidarkness on the platform, my arms clasped behind my buttocks, and we had rehearsed the speech. Dismal Gregore coached me on my delivery and recommended certain additions and deletions. My theme was suggested by Dr. Kew. Tentatively titled "The Responsibilities of the Sons of Emmanuel," the message derived from the series of paternal talks Dr. Kew had been giving us First Classmen in his study since the month of May. I had not escaped the ringing clichés of the traditional valedictory. I was to begin my address with an anecdote, salt in the customary classical allusions, and conclude it with an expression of gratitude to Dr. and Mrs. Kew and to the entire faculty for having given us six such happy and valuable years. Dismal Gregore cautioned me to avoid swaying by distributing my weight evenly on both feet. Then he congratulated me in advance on an honest and cleanly thought-out speech.

"Why fret about it? It's just a speech." Fuzzy yawned and flung *The Lexicon* into an empty chair. "This is the last night, Gubber. Let's give the old place the once-over. Let's check the Discipline Room. See how many times we got racked up this year."

The bedtime regulations were not enforced that night. Fuzzy and I wandered through the darkened buildings in moods of premature nostalgia, paying our last respects to the classrooms, catching one farewell butt in the basement of Phelps House. When we came to the Discipline Room, a narrow chamber on the ground floor of Terrance where the punctuality and deportment records were kept in ledgers, Fuzzy switched on the light. "Bet I got racked up more than any guy in the class," he said proudly, and drew out the volume for the current year. We thumbed through the long alphabetical listings, running our fingers down the ancient dates and penalties.

Abbott, Allgood, Apthorp, T., Beemer, Billis, Bockling, Bolt . . . What words could match the simple rhythm of the names? Stop a finger on any one and the parade of memories began. Here was the real class album, the true valedictory. Fifty-seven printed words cramped at the margin of the page to accommodate the penciled entries of an offended faculty:

Peeper Bockling had received a term's suspension for studying the interior of the female servants' quarters with a spy glass. Frazzle Fern. Naughty Neddy Napham, the mimic, whose imitations of the faculty were the most accomplished in the school. Rope Rumson who had kept charts in a betting pool on the dates when faculty wives most probably would give birth. . . . *Stoughton, Stowe, B., Taylor, Tilton, Topping, Towle, J. C., Upton, Vale, Wampole, Wild.*

"We had some awful simple tools," Fuzzy Eaton was saying, fondly, writing them off already in the past tense. "They weren't such bad guys, were they, Gubber?"

"I'd like to sit up all night," I answered. "I'd like to write my whole damn speech over again."

I, who had been named spokesman for fifty-six of my best and only friends, would the next day betray them with ten minutes' worth of platitudes. Tonight, though, the way was open to flay the glum, borrowed prophecies about standing on the threshold of a chaotic world. The mothers in the audience might dry their tears. We were not concerned with time nor with worry about the world beyond, about which Dr. Kew was worried, to enter which Bishop Wash would give us his benediction, to which the Congressman guest of honor would surely devote his entire commencement address. We would defy death and the trustees and the Deans of Admissions, and Adolf Hitler and Benito Mussolini, all of whom seemed to have the same dour designs upon us. As best and only friends, emerging from the cloister where we'd led a third of our lives together, we must stick together and take care of ourselves, and forbid the pompous frauds to louse up our future. If the future belonged to us, as they were forever saying it did, we could handle it very nicely, thanks.

It would have been quite a speech and so easy to say.

At approximately twenty minutes past eleven the next morning, I mounted the speaker's platform in the Harold Manter Benjamin Memorial Auditorium, waited out the scattered applause, and made my bows. "Bishop Wash, Gentlemen of the Trustees, Dr. Kew, distinguished guests, classmates, friends. Coming before you this morning, I am reminded of that favorite story of Dr. Kew's about the Athenian and the Spartan who met by accident upon the road. . . ."

In white flannels and blazers that had the Academy crest and

220

Haec Olim Meminisse Juvabit stitched on the pockets, my classmates faced me from the two front rows. It had been a grueling commencement on a particularly hot day and several besides Fuzzy Eaton were dozing. Others fidgeted in their seats, tapping diplomas tied with the green Academy ribbon. Now and then as I paused a curious face would turn up to me, then turn to the floor once more when it was evident that I had my thoughts well memorized and that the pause had not been accidental. When I stepped down from the platform and took my seat amid the dying applause, Cuppy Vale tapped my shoulder from behind to say that it was all over now and that as valedictories went, mine hadn't been too bad.

The Awards Day luncheon that followed the graduation ceremonies was the most mammoth of the annual undertakings of Mrs. Kew and the kitchen staff. Guests were to serve themselves and since there were a thousand-odd mouths to feed on Headmaster's lawn, the process was a drawn-out and congested one. Mrs. Kew and Mrs. Bruce, the housemother-dietician, looking harassed and feverish, chivvied and darted in and out of the pack like sheep dogs.

The sun beat down on the uncovered grass and drove large numbers to the shade of the great maples that lined the drive. Under these classmates gathered to lay summer plans; the new graduates bade friendly farewells to the most antagonistic of their former masters. Each square yard of lawn was the scene of a minor drama of forgiveness and well wishing.

Old Mr. Marsh was listening good-naturedly to my uncle, who had buttonholed the old gentleman for a long talk about the future of the school. "No, Torbert," I heard Marcus Marsh saying. "To be perfectly candid I don't anticipate that there will be an early vacancy on the Board of Trustees. You realize, Torbert, we can't deliberately *create* a vacancy. . . ."

Aunt Connie threw her arms about me and kissed me, her face moist with tears. "Dearie, why didn't you tell me? Nobody told me you were going to make a speech. And you won the Debating Prize! I wish your father could have seen you today." She hadn't cried so since Lindbergh landed at Le Bourget Field.

Mr. Flemister congratulated me on what had been, after all, a creditable showing on my college-board examination and Mr. Frapp presented the members of his First Class Greek section with pocket editions of the *Iliad.*

By this station wagon and that convertible second husbands and their predecessors unbent over paper cups of fruit punch discreetly laced with alcohol. Estranged couples approached each other wistfully, out of years of hostile silence. "Alice, you're looking terribly well. I simply wanted to say what a fine job I think you've done with Billy. Could I interest you in some raspberry ice?"

The first cars drove off in the early afternoon and the flurry began to subside. I had exchanged a happy handclasp with Dr. Kew, promising to drop by often whenever I was at home. I was making my way to Headmaster's parlor where Mrs. Kew waited to bid us all good-by, when I saw George Marsh. He was walking across the oval grass, laden with books and silver awards, having waited until now when the crowd was thin to carry them publicly to the car. His great-uncle's chauffeur appeared to relieve him of the booty, and he was free to go with me to Mrs. Kew.

"I liked your speech," he said. "It made me feel sad about everything. It was a great day."

"Yup. A great day."

"Don't you feel sad?"

"Not especially," I said.

As we approached the yellow clapboards of Headmaster's House, the chapel chimes struck the half hour and he stopped a moment, immobilized by that familiar sound. "I wish we were new kids. Jesus. I wish we were starting all over again. Is that a stupid thing to say?"

On the steps we waited in line for Mrs. Kew to receive us and they came up in groups to shake his hand:

"So long, Gopher."

"Take it slow, Gopher."

"Sure you don't want to change your mind and come to Yale with the white men, Goph?"

"Look us up in Grosse Point, Gopher."

"See you around the campus, Goph."

He shook hands and gave all the proper answers, but as they drifted off one by one his smile left him and he gazed on the oval drive as though each car that drove away were deserting him personally. In this past, most glorious year I had forgotten how bewildered he could look.

The captains and the kings depart.

222

BOOK II

Part Two — The World Beyond

Chapter Fifteen

The objective of the Harvard Summer School, in which we were registered within three weeks, was to achieve a semester's work in one six weeks' session. The objective of the acceleration program under which hundreds of freshmen were admitted that June was to shunt them along the assembly belt of higher education at the fastest pace the traffic would bear. This was done in deference to the Selective Service System and the National Emergency. It was accepted by us as a necessary evil. It was the first of a long line of necessary evils.

Fatherly freshman advisers, sitting in their narrow stalls at University Hall, advised us to make the best of it, and we proceeded to do just that. It would have been easier had we not been required to carry an intensified schedule at the start. Relatively few of us had shown the foresight to confer with brothers or friends in upper classes before accepting the ponderously sensible recommendations of the Deans. Thus we found ourselves taking five courses instead of the minimum four. Because we were too cowed to cut classes extravagantly and because many a freshman course merely duplicated work we had already done at Emmanuel, not one of us was placed on probation after the first marking period in September. Fuzzy Eaton got five straight C's, a singular achievement in itself in that it had been accomplished almost entirely on Cuppy Vale's lecture notes. It was the more remarkable for the fact that George Marsh, who at Emmanuel had frequently led a class in which Fuzzy often finished in last place, received only four C's and a D.

We three lived in Wigglesworth in a three-room suite that overlooked Mass Avenue. We had a tiled bathroom with a shower stall where Fuzzy kept a supply of ice that came in packaged blocks from the vending machine in the parking lot beside the Harvard Provision Company on Mt. Auburn Street. A Mrs. Walsh made our beds and endeavored to tidy up the sitting room from time to time, though we tended to discourage her from this on the theory that we liked to know where everything was. (Somewhere in the array of bottles that lined the mantelpiece and book shelves were presumed to be several not entirely empty.) Through the auspices of Eddy Shawn, the Mt. Auburn Street tailor who had been making up suits for George Marsh since his Fourth Class year at Emmanuel, a telephone was installed and waiting there in the room. Our monthly bill averaged fifty to sixty dollars. It was as well that George Marsh was there to pay the lion's share, which he in fact did owe—for the hours' long conversations held regularly with Lila Norris at her family's summer home in Far Hills, New Jersey.

Mr. Eaton's battered Ford had gone to Fuzzy by default as a graduation present. George Marsh had traded in the old Packard against the price of a 1940 Pontiac, and gas coupons, again through the auspices of Eddy Shawn, were obtainable in reasonable quantity. Thus we were assured of a pleasantly mobile summer.

Since whether he ate them or not he would be charged for them, George Marsh took most of his meals in the Union. Though he was always agreeable with those who shared the tables there, he faced from the start a problem of social relationship that many a son of Emmanuel had faced before him. He was not alone in his predicament, though, being sensitive to psychological tensions, it troubled him more than most. When George ate at the Union he sat at a table that might accommodate as many as twelve of his classmates, and so it was a mathematical certainty that some of George's dining companions would be strangers. One would anticipate that over a period of time, over, say, a semester's worth of communal meals, George would begin to make friends in the Union. Granted he would not make a great number of friends, for he was not exceptionally gregarious by nature. And yet, of the hundreds of unknowns that George must have dined among between June and September, how could he have escaped becoming friendly with some? It is a fact that he did escape, that not one of the strangers whom he met in the Union ever became a friend to George Marsh. To understand this phenomenon it is necessary to depart from considerations of mathematics and weigh instead the subtler motivations of instinct.

Years before he came to Harvard George Marsh had sown the seeds of friendship on the playing fields of a dozen different schools.

226

In the catch-all of a great university a tiny side pocket exists, atrophied, isolated, inexplicable as the appendix in the digestive tract. Into this pocket fell the seeds of such friendships as George Marsh had formed, to flourish with another few happily and unmolested, through a trammeled, unconventional experiment in Harvardiana. Hank Barthelmess, the catcher of the Middlesex team, would become a friend. Daisy Morse, the former Groton break-away runner, would become a friend. As would Tanker Terhune, the Saint Paul's goalie. Each of these would in turn meet us who were friends of George's and thus by controlled multiplication a self-contained nucleus would form.

Like the appendix in the human animal it gave nothing to and took nothing from the undergraduate body, yet it never ruptured and it could not be removed by surgery. It was impervious to the crusades of President Conant and the Dean's Office. It had suffered from but had survived one inroad after another: the outlawing of the rathouses in which Andy Marsh and his contemporararies had reigned supreme, the establishment of the house system with its communal dining halls, the outlawing of the tutoring schools. And it was likely to survive as long as the principles of free thought survived at Harvard. For want of a name, some called it the "St. Grottlesex Crowd." Others, more succinctly, called it "The Clubmen."

We asked only to be let alone, wished only to avoid hostility on the part of the great body of classmates whose names we had not troubled ourselves to learn. Yet among us were some extremists who made a mockery of themselves. Their actions reflected upon us all; they were the tarnish on our armor. Since they owed their existence to us, we could not entirely ostracize them, and still we could never forgive them for having coined an expression which made us wince—the "White Men." In the Union and in all public places we did our best to avoid them. Privately, among ourselves, we disowned them. They were loosely christened the "Jerks."

One hoped for a limit to the chagrin which the Jerks heaped upon us but there was none. There were many accommodations for freshmen in the Yard but Wigglesworth, the Jerks would say loudly, was where the White Men lived. White Men, they would say, were never seen in Widener Library. White Men, if they carried books at all, never carried them in the green canvas bags on sale at the Harvard

Coop, and White Men did not try to get better than the minimum three C's and a D.

The Jerks would tell you very seriously that it was not wise for a freshman to be seen in the Ritz Bar in Boston, and yet those who were seen there constantly were the Jerks. They didn't seem embarrassed about having to forge false birth dates on their drivers' licenses to show that they were over twenty-one. They wore crew cuts and white shoes and bowties wherever they went, so that they looked exactly like the cartoons in the *Lampoon*. As a matter of fact most of the Jerks went out for the *Lampoon*, believing it to be the one White Man's organization open to freshmen. (The little essays about life inside a martini glass and the advice to freshmen about how to behave on the Gold Coast and the cartoons about White Men encountering the green-bag set made the *Lampoon* embarrassing to read and they had all been thought up by Jerks.) The Jerks were always telling you about what clubs their fathers had belonged to or about their chances of making the Dickey. No one else ever talked about those things; only the Jerks. The Jerks were sloppy and noisier than ever when they were drunk, and when they weren't drunk they generally pretended to be, because they had an idea that a White Man ought to get drunk at least three nights a week. Few Jerks went out for athletics. Almost none for crew. Whenever possible you tried to avoid the Jerks.

Two of them lived across the hall in our entry at Wigglesworth. We never learned their last names, though they were engraved on calling cards outside their door. They were the type to own calling cards, and they had gone to Belmont Hill. They tried to make friends with us and knocked on our door in the afternoons to borrow an icepick or to ask if we wouldn't join them in a few martinis, which they called "tinis," or old-fashioneds which they called "ofies." They asked us to call them by their first names, but behind their backs we referred to them as Horace and Allen Horsebun.

We made faster friends with a trio on the floor above. For several weeks we had nodded at them as they passed us in the entryway. At last one night there was a heavy knocking on our door. George Marsh opened it cautiously, fearing it to be the Horsebun boys, but when the door swung open we saw that it was the friendly, chubby fellow from upstairs.

He stood in the middle of the room and surveyed the walls, as

228

though we had invited him in to appraise the *décor*. He was cocky and blasé, but there was nothing offensive about him. He looked at the large green and white banner that covered a part of the wall and the minute he spoke he made himself welcome.

"Emmanuel," he said, in tones of conventional disgust. "If this were our room, we'd have that draped over the toilet seat."

Our guest sprawled himself on the brand-new sofa that George Marsh had bought at the Coop. His name was Moses Beach. Probably George wouldn't remember, but they had met once in New York, and he had seen Fuzzy Eaton somewhere, and he knew who I was and that I played the piano.

Fuzzy gave him a drink from the fresh Fine Arts bottle in the bookcase and used the last of the ice in the shower stall. We talked for a few minutes about courses and the number of cuts it was safe to take and about what happened when you got on Pro. Fuzzy gave a description of the Horsebun boys at a "tini" party and our guest rolled about the sofa hysterically.

"Let's go into town," he suggested finally.

"It's ten o'clock," George Marsh said.

"You can sleep in the morning. I'll rout them out upstairs and we'll go in town in a taxi. We'll take in the Coconut Grove. Let's go, gang."

So we made the first of our new good friends, these from St. Paul's School. Danny Guile and Lou Tremaine, the roommates of Mo Beach, happened to be in the same Gov. I section that I was in. Starting together, we learned nearly all that seemed worth learning. It was a form of knowledge, but again of a particular kind, and we found little of it in Plato's *Republic* or behind the carved wood benches in the classrooms of Sever Hall.

We learned to hop the subway turnstiles and ride to Park Street free when we couldn't find a taxi, how to squeeze two at a time into the revolving iron gate of the side entrance by Hazen's Lunch and thus ride two for the price of a dime. We learned in back alleys by McBride's or the Oxford Grille that there was fierce resentment toward us on the part of Cambridge youth. We learned about a public dance emporium on Huntington Avenue called the Rae-more-Playmore and, through an experience that Mo Beach had, discovered it was not advisable to escort young ladies one met there to a festivity so far afield as the Labor Day Dance at the Essex County

229

Club in Manchester. We learned our way to Scollay Square where Sally Keith did her tassel dance at the Crawford House and learned where to find other, coarser entertainment in the saloons nearby. At Dad's Tattoo Shop between Scollay and Bowdoin we watched Dad's electric needle trace an inky, bloody pattern on the bare forearm of Mo Beach and held our breath for Mo when Dad slopped a rag moistened with a dirty, milklike solution he called disinfectant upon the finished wound. We learned that if you treat a tattoo properly with Lysol and cold cream, the scabs will wear off sooner and leave a cleaner, clearer mark, later that there was something contagious about tattooing and so returned to Dad's while Lou Tremaine had some colors added to the butterfly on his shoulder and Fuzzy Eaton, whose mother was very much alive and active on the Grounds Committee of the Longwood Cricket Club, had the flesh over his biceps decorated with a simple wooden cross encircled in a wreath of sunset and inscribed to her memory. We learned the exact taxi fares to Fenway Park and Suffolk Downs and of a driver who lurked in the shadows of a bowling alley near Kendall Square who, for a consideration, was willing to run us across the Mass Avenue Bridge to darker regions still, the fringes of Back Bay and the lower reaches of Beacon Hill, where vice blossomed nightly under the not totally observant eye of the Boston Police Department.

Now and again George Marsh would lament the lassitude he knew was creeping over him. He received an E in Anthropology on the November Hours, and deservedly; he was the first to admit that he had not cracked a book. George would ask himself what had become of his ambition. Five straight C's were all he hoped for. To achieve them, he must atone for his failure in Anthropology, and so he drove himself for an entire week before the mid-year examinations and got the A that was necessary. He managed this by following the example of Fuzzy Eaton, who was flunking not only Economics A but Geography as well and had signed up with a private tutor in Melrose. They refused to divulge the man's name because of the risk involved. Since the tutoring schools on Harvard Square had been outlawed, the consequences of outside tuition not sanctioned by the Dean's Office had become disastrous. Fuzzy Eaton observed that a healthy C average was about as expensive to obtain as an abortion.

Danny Guile and I never made the trip to Melrose because we

couldn't afford the tuition. We were not proud of having to do our work; had we had ample allowances, we would happily have commuted to Melrose with our roommates. I did most of my studying in Widener, at a far-off table by which few familiar faces passed. And when I found I'd got a B and a B-minus at mid-years, I didn't tell a soul.

A former captain of Emmanuel could not escape the pressures of the freshman coach, and so George Marsh went out for football that September. But when his wrist gave out after the second week of practice, George was just as glad. There was no arguing with a fractured wrist. He could call his time his own now and take a drink or two at football games. He took his exercise on the squash courts four afternoons a week and on the fifth he drilled with the R.O.T.C. in back of Soldier's Field. Mo Beach and I were in the same platoon with him. We wore high boots and blue lapels on our blouses with the Harvard insignia, a bogus uniform which caused us to burst out laughing when we saw one another.

At least once a week it was party time, generally in Mo Beach's room upstairs. They would ask me to play their piano for them, against all the noise. "I Got Spurs that Jingle, Jangle, Jingle." Through the ever-obliging Eddy Shawn it was possible to engage the services of a handy man and barkeep. Hammertoe was the favorite choice. A repressed musician, Hammertoe would relieve me on the keyboard and play like a stupefied Fats Waller, for the noxious gin punch that Hammertoe was known for had a more rapid effect upon Hammertoe, sampling it straight from the bowl, than on the guests whom he served with Dixie cups.

The girls who came were those whose debutante parties we would be attending throughout the fall and winter, or a scattering of the freshman classes of Wellesley and of Radcliffe. I could not conceive what it was they enjoyed so about the parties. They were pawed and spilled upon and jostled from lap to lap and only the renegades among them took more than two drinks. Every advantage of upbringing went to naught in these crowded, potato-chip-littered arenas where the balance of popularity was held by the looser types or the out-and-out maladjusts. It was a sad commentary on our taste that, to insure herself against neglect, a girl's best course was to achieve nausea in the bathroom or a moral lapse in plain view on the sofa.

Lila Norris came all the way from Miss Eustis' to be at the climactic party of the season that we threw in our room after the Yale game. She milled about that afternoon in a bright yellow sweater. Boys crowded around her wherever she paused, teased and laughed with her, but always with deference, never touching her, for she was George Marsh's girl. The Boston girls in plainer, more washable colors looked on tolerantly. Lila Norris, when she finished Miss Eustis' in June and even when she came out the following winter, would not be the kind of girl they need worry over. The flamingo does not compete with the turtle dove.

Save through long distance, Lila had been at school and inaccessible since September. She was a great addition, George confided to me as we helped Hammertoe move in a fresh cake of ice from the shower stall. It did him good to show her off.

"It's a pretty good party," I said.

"Yes," he said. "It's one big stink, all right."

Harry Tilton had the knack of hitting parties at their peak. He blew in with a half dozen friends from New Haven, most of whom knew Lila and greeted her warmly, more warmly than our Cambridge friends were accustomed to greeting their mothers or sisters. An uneasiness stirred in corners of the room as Harry Tilton squatted beside Lila's chair and nuzzled her neck underneath the auburn hair. It subsided in a moment when Harry spotted George Marsh and rushed from Lila's side to goose his old friend. They fell on each other with back slaps and arm punching and the party was good for another hour at least.

No one kept count of the numbers that drifted in and out of the room on their way to and from other parties, or the breakage, or the strangers and their strange girls who stood by the punch bowl availing themselves of Hammertoe's concoction. But sometime after nine o'clock it was definitely over. George Marsh took Lila in town for dinner at Locke Ober's, but before going they lingered on the threshold, arms locked affectionately, and took in the wreckage.

"It was a big stink," George said proudly, "the biggest of the year."

That night we went to bed in spirits of high self-congratulation. For all the loss and breakage, for all the cost, our reputation for hospitality had been established.

George Marsh made up his mind to go out for freshman hockey

and did so seriously for several weeks until again his wrist betrayed him, and he did not so much as win his numerals. Again George was just as glad. This time he was settling down, he told me, beginning to work at last. What was more, he would not be wasting his time and money on tutoring. And yet it was noted that George continued to show up pretty regularly in Melrose. Even on Sundays. The news of Pearl Harbor broke upon George and Fuzzy on a Sunday afternoon, from the radio in the Pontiac, when they were on their way out to Melrose.

An immediate effect of the war was that we took to reading the *Crimson* at breakfast. In the past it had seemed an innocuous sheet, valuable mainly as a guide to the movie schedule at the university theater. But when the news bulletins quoted Senators and Congressmen who were unalterably opposed to the lowering of the draft age, and when that age dropped from twenty-one to twenty and dangled there as more Senators and Congressmen put themselves on record as being unalterably opposed to the draft of eighteen- and nineteen-year-olds, we had the *Crimson* to thank for giving us a real excuse for having a whing ding that Christmas.

It was too bad that when the stage was so uniquely set, with Wake Island gone and Bataan going fast, there was no whing ding after all. The Norris family had retired to Palm Beach and Chee Wee Gibbons had joined them after New Year's, to fulfill the rendezvous that Lila had given her two years ago in Gentian Cove. George was not invited. He took this as a personal rebuff, the bitterer for the airy way with which Lila was accepting the disaster engulfing us. He returned after the holiday with a stock of grim platitudes about there being a war on, and yet it seemed the girls had had a good time for themselves in Palm Beach. They called us from the railway station in Providence on the day they went back to Miss Eustis', and I spoke for a minute with Chee Wee.

"You poor boys," Chee Wee said. "What are you going to do?"

"That depends," I told her. "General Hershey and the Congressmen can't make up their minds."

"Why aren't you in the Reserves?" she said. "Harry Tilton is staying on at Yale and he's going to be a Naval officer."

"We're going to leave it to General Hershey," I said. "Whatever the general says."

"You should have seen Palm Beach. Do you realize the Germans are torpedoing tankers off the beach practically?"

"I hope you were careful when you went swimming."

I heard her give a curious laugh that started on a high pitch and descended a whole octave to end in a sort of wheeze. It was, apparently, the laugh of a worldly woman.

"Where did you learn to laugh with your windpipe?" I asked.

"I just happen to laugh that way. You don't need to make personal remarks."

"You're all grown up," I said.

"That's right. I'm all grown up."

"And it all happened at Palm Beach?"

"It is much more serious than you think, Gussy. There was this Coast Guard officer who rode us all over in his jeep. Have you ever ridden in a jeep?"

"It must be quite an experience," I said.

"Oh, poor thing! You have to make a joke out of it, don't you?"

"It's not a joke to me," I said.

"Are you boys working hard? I'm glad I'm not a boy."

Chee Wee's voice was tender and forgiving, as though she was sure that at any minute we would gladly lay down our lives in her defense.

"But what are you going to do?" she asked again. "Liles and I worried about you. Don't do anything stupid and please take care of George."

"Everyone tells me to take care of George," I said. "He takes pretty good care of himself."

I would not speak to Chee Wee Gibbons again until the war was over. I would not think of her very often in the next four years. Yet when I did, it was with the feeling that we were running some sort of a race and that already she had outstripped me.

Chapter Sixteen

In February we became sophomores. The one pursuit I took seriously was the piano.

One evening I was invited to a dinner party in Boston where a corpulent gentleman in evening clothes, a bachelor uncle of the young lady we had gathered to honor, played endlessly for the young. He was not professional. He played as much for his own enjoyment as for the audience. Being elderly, he chose his songs for their nostalgia and played them with a low hum or whistle while his eyelids drooped like a man's in prayer. I admired his deft touch, the lingering stubby fingers, and the humor and the verve he achieved with imperceptible effort. More keenly I admired the hushed attention and respect he enjoyed. It was, I gathered, a rare privilege to hear him. He played only selections of his liking, tunes, chiefly, of his college days. He played "Kiss Me Again" with reverence but recoiled from Mo Beach's suggestion of "Tangerine" with an expression of displeasure that delighted everyone. His niece filled and refilled the Scotch and soda on which he drew between songs. Tanker Terhune popped up and down to relight his cigar. Everyone begged and begged him not to stop.

I had not the privilege of hearing that gentleman again, nor could I remember his name, and yet I made a fierce resolve to emulate him. I left the party profoundly impressed and thereafter, at the faintest urging, I played any piano anywhere at any time. I was conscious of critical reception from no friend but Cuppy Vale.

Vale had grown away from us since we had come to Cambridge. He had held himself aloof during the turbulent freshman year in Wigglesworth, and now that he was a sophomore he shared a room with Pansy Peters well off the beaten track. Dunster House was a fitting abode for Vale. It faced the Charles River and stood on the remote perimeter of the undergraduate dormitories. On the other hand, George Marsh, Fuzzy Eaton, and I now lived in the old corner of Adams House that gave on to Mt. Auburn Street and Claverly Hall, a few moments' walk to the subway and the taxi stand on Mass Avenue.

I found Vale alone in his room on a bitter afternoon in March; there was no reason for my visit beyond curiosity and a glowing urge to be friends with everyone. I came to him in good spirits, and yet he did not look up when I called. He was alone in his underwear, poring over a book. His bony elbows rested on the desk and his hands, pressed against the gaunt hollows of his cheeks, supported his head. He was reading with the intense poker face with which he absorbed everything from Aristotle to P. G. Wodehouse, and he allowed his long fingers to stray across the button of his chin in search of one of the ever-present pimples there. I approached him stealthily from behind and leaned and flicked the back of his ear with my forefinger. He cupped a hand over the ear and blandly went on with his reading. I sat down hard on top of the desk and commenced to whistle and drum my fingers.

"O.K., Rollo," he said, not looking up. "We all know you're with us."

He knew that he could best retaliate by using one of the annoying soubriquets that he had imported from Emmanuel. And he knew how to employ that faint suggestion of superiority whenever he wanted me to feel foolish.

"You're a charming sight," I replied. "You're really fragrant this afternoon."

Cuppy Vale was the only friend I had who was on the Dean's List, and the only one who bothered to wear an undershirt.

Vale brought a quart of beer from the wooden icebox in the bedroom. We drank from a pair of plastic cups that gave a strong toothpaste flavor to the drink. I thought that he looked pretty silly in his underwear. He was well over six feet two, nearly as tall as Danny Guile, and skinnier.

"You're a real odd ball," I said. "You're a damn nonconformist, aren't you?"

He poured us another beer and patted the top of my head condescendingly before he sprawled into the swivel chair by his desk. "Little man," he said, "I've about given up on you. I used to think you were a pretty smart cooky. . . . You on probation yet?"

236

"No." To find myself automatically taking the defensive made being there all the more exasperating.

"How did you make out in Fine Arts?"

"B-plus," I said belligerently.

"That's nice. Did George Marsh get B-plus?"

"How should I know?"

"Why don't you get Fuzzy into Fine Arts? That sounds right up his alley."

"Maybe you should wait for me to make the Dean's List," I said. "Then we could have two swelled heads between us."

"Don't scold me," Cuppy Vale said. "You've got to understand. I'm not in the swim. I'm a Goddamn nonconformist, an odd ball. I'm the crew manager type. Look at me. I wear an undershirt and I haven't got a tattoo or a sport coat from Eddy Shawn, and I've never been to the Raemore-Playmore, and I haven't had a load on since I can't remember when. You see I'm out of touch. So don't pick on me. I'm in lousy shape."

He took a pipe and a pouch of tobacco from one of the desk drawers and lit the pipe, pulling slowly and carefully to make sure it had an even burn. It was like him to be the only one of us who smoked a pipe without worrying about being called Joe College. In a bookcase by the desk his textbooks were lying neatly side by side with brown-paper covers to protect them from the dust and a circle cut out on the back of each one to show its title. A pencil sharpener was attached to the bookcase and a pile of freshly sharpened pencils lay nicely within reach of his chair. There was even a desk lamp from the Coop, from which he had not bothered to remove the embarrassing Veritas emblem of Harvard. It was a far cry from our room in Adams, where nobody knew where anything was and where Fuzzy Eaton might be out on Mass Avenue selling your textbooks back to the dealer for party money. It made me unhappy and unsure of myself to look at this room, especially since Cuppy Vale was a good friend of mine.

"The two and a half musketeers," he was saying slowly. "I don't know why it burns me up to see you making a chump of yourself."

"What did you say?"

"Two and a half musketeers."

I felt myself blushing.

"I forget who it was that said it," he said vaguely. "It seemed

237

pretty stupid to me. Marsh, Eaton, and Taylor. The two and a half musketeers."

"Who said that?"

"What's the difference? If you want to play the piano, if you want to be one of the boys, that's your business."

He had said this mildly without any smugness or bitterness. I saw him smiling through a haze of tobacco smoke.

"Is this going to be another pep talk?" I said.

"Don't look so confused." He laughed again. "What's it to me what you do?" Vale said. "But I'm damned if I know how you swing it."

"Swing what?"

"The life you're leading. Is it all on the cuff?"

That was how I came to tell him too much. He was accusing me too much. I told him of Mr. Jennings and the Legatees' Trust who remained in control of the dwindling reserves left by my parents. Mr. Jennings had been forced to break one of the cardinal rules of the Legatees' Trust and to spend from my principal. I was to forward him all college bills and receive from him sixty dollars each month to clothe and entertain myself, and pay all minor medical expenses. With so short a rope, I wanted Vale to know, I could scarcely hang myself. Mr. Jennings, however, had set aside an amount toward dues and initiation fees of the Hasty Pudding and whatever final club I might have the good fortune of being elected to. The Legatees' Trust people liked to call this sort of thing an "excusable extravagance." I thought it a handsome gesture on Mr. Jennings' part and related it to Vale with an enthusiasm to which he failed to respond.

"Why tell me about it? It's none of my business," he said.

"So you won't think I'm blowing money around."

"I think it's pretty embarrassing."

"What's embarrassing?"

"That club stuff," Vale said. "To coin a phrase, it makes me want to blow my lunch. Have you been blowing many lunches lately?"

Jokes about drunkenness and regurgitation were very much in vogue. Vale had memorized them all, with a glum detachment.

"You're always coining phrases. You're so Goddamn smart," I said.

He laughed. "Why do you try so hard? Why take everything to heart?"

238

It was all very well for Cuppy Vale to take this point of view. One of the most important acts in the life of C.U.P. Vale, Sr., before he contrived to kill himself, had been to enter the name of his son and namesake into the records of his college club. Thus my friend had a legacy, a father legacy, which was the most binding kind, in the same eminently desirable club to which three generations of Marshes had belonged. Most likely Vale could afford this apathy. I could not. In my circle, where the club question was hardly a subject for open discussion, one dared not be so bland. Whoever you were, this was the most personal, most delicate of matters.

In ordinary times one became a sophomore in September and was eligible for election to a final club during the fall, when touch football gave the opportunity to display one's desirability as an athlete and well-balanced fellow. But these were not ordinary times. We had become sophomores in February instead of September, and there was no assurance that we would be in Cambridge very much longer. The clubs had had to act fast. The traditional selection of sophomores had been bolluxed as a consequence into a round-the-year, round-the-clock scramble. It began for us shortly before the April Hour Exams and took priority over all else in life for the next six weeks in which we were caught up in it. And it was called the "punching season."

The session began with the Hasty Pudding elections and the choosing of the Dickey, and ended when one formally accepted his election to a final club. The Hasty Pudding had long been the butt of jokes because of its relatively all-inclusive membership. The Dickey, on the other hand, with its colorful initiation rites, represented honest distinction. For it was composed each year of the first fifty of the hundreds of names elected to membership in the Hasty Pudding. Your Dickey listing told how greatly you were in demand. Our list was led by the redoubtable Hank Barthelmess, captain of freshman football. George Marsh was number two man and the remaining forty-eight names included Beach, Tremaine, Eaton, Vale, just about everyone, everyone but bashful Danny Guile, and myself.

I accepted the outcome with equanimity and ignored the consoling attitudes of my friends. Aunt Connie wrote a note of encouragement, recalling that my Uncle Torbert had not made the Dickey in his day. My aunt did not want me to think that I had failed in any

239

way. And my uncle had said to tell me that it was a small failure, one which he considered himself the stronger for having suffered when he was my impressionable age. The Dickey was just a preliminary; the final club was the only one that counted. And in this regard my uncle was of course prepared to use his influence. Aunt Connie wrote that while the club to which my uncle belonged was not one of the best known at Harvard, it was respectable. My Uncle Torbert was as proud of the gold hedgehog which hung from his watch chain as of anything he owned. My aunt knew what a pleasure I would give him if I could prove my right to the same token.

Unfortunately, I hadn't the faintest wish to wear a gold hedgehog on my watch chain. My uncle's club, like everything my uncle was associated with, lacked authenticity. I had privately decided on that club of which George's uncle, Marcus Marsh, had once served as graduate president. That club, or none at all. This proved to be a naïve decision, made before I learned how much more there was to the punching season than the simple act of selection.

It was played off in rounds like a huge tournament. Fuzzy and I went with George Marsh, through the early rounds, accepting invitations to punches, cocktail parties, dinners, and Sunday outings in Dedham and Brookline. Through these adventures in forced joviality we learned about the clubs, and, for their part, the clubs learned about us. So the process of separating the wheat from the chaff; the marathon of invitations and the gradual elimination of undesirables; the assessment of that intangible commodity that was known as "club material." In time the flow of vellum invitations slowed to a trickle for some, ceased altogether for others, and for the few it cascaded with a mounting fury up to the hectic eve of the elections.

George Marsh was among the few. Four clubs pursued him, each confident he was theirs. He spent whole afternoons and evenings avoiding commitments and being polite to the emissaries sent out to trail him. He went from party to party in a desperate effort not to offend. If such a thing had been permitted, he would gladly have joined all four.

Indeed George's indecision carried on dangerously long after others had made up their minds. The graduate presidents of two clubs telephoned from their offices in New York and Boston and asked to speak with him privately. A last-minute outing was planned around him in Framingham. He was trotted in and out of the same

Boston hotel for intimate dinners on three consecutive nights. The vice president of one club offered to procure for him, and an attempt was made by a zealous faction of another to kidnap him to an estate on the North Shore, there to anesthetize him with alcohol and hold him incommunicado until the elections were over.

Toby Tappan, undergraduate president of the club of George's forefathers, refused to believe that a Marsh could consider any but the traditional choice. On the final day, on the last afternoon before the clubs held their elections, he checked our room in Adams House with the regularity of a night watchman in a bank vault. Meanwhile competing delegations drifted in and out of the rooms like pilgrims through a shrine. Oblivious of Tappan, they pleaded and cajoled in shifts. Fuzzy Eaton and I lost count of the campaigners during the eight anxious hours that were wasted in persuading Caesar to cross the Rubicon, but at nine o'clock that night Toby Tappan was still there.

Fuzzy's position and mine were dangerously insecure. The night before, a delegation had taken Fuzzy to the Copley Plaza, and this morning a soberer Fuzzy, arguing that he bore no responsibility for commitments made while drinking, had retracted the pledge he had given them. That very morning I had summarily dismissed a delegation who had invited my pledge to the club my Uncle Torbert Case, '08, had chosen before me. Fuzzy and I had burned our bridges behind us; and our eyes were on Toby Tappan. He had been friendly toward us throughout the day, and yet he had seemed curiously evasive. We sat on the window seat feigning indifference, while Toby Tappan bore down on George Marsh.

"I hate to be a prima donna," George was saying. "I just honest to God don't know. Maybe I should put it off."

Tappan was sitting on the arm of George's chair, leaning forward in a beseeching manner that ill became one who rowed bow oar on the varsity. "If you don't come now, it will be too late. Don't forget there's a war on. I won't be here. Barthelmess won't be here, or Terhune. And neither will you for that matter."

"I could wait," George Marsh said feebly. "I could wait until after the war."

I watched Toby Tappan move to the mantelpiece where his drink was. It had been a pretty alcoholic afternoon for Toby. Properly speaking, Toby was in winter training. The calluses and skin hardener on his hands gave evidence of hours spent pulling an empty blade against the chill dead water of the practice tank. Yet in the urgency of this moment, the loss of George Marsh must be looming a crueler defeat to Toby than a loss to the Yale eight in June. He gulped the contents of his glass and stood by the fireplace and fingered the ends of his necktie upon which the rampant lions of the club stood in white upon a deep red background.

"I'd appreciate a word alone with George," Toby Tappan said in the spuriously British vernacular he adopted when he meant to be extremely polite. "Would you fellows mind terribly?"

All afternoon and all evening Fuzzy and I had been absenting ourselves for the benefit of delegates who would appreciate a word alone with George. This proved the briefest word of all, however.

Suddenly the door opened, and Tappan left us hurriedly. George Marsh asked Fuzzy if he wouldn't mind staying outside a while longer. Now it was George who wanted a word alone with me.

He stood awkwardly, rubbing his hand across his cheek. As George Marsh fumbled for some way to begin, I felt the recurrence of sullen martyrdom.

"You sure packed Tappan off," I told him. I was pleased to discover myself so chipper on the threshold of disaster.

"He's not coming back," George said. "I told him not to bother me until morning."

The telephone rang and I answered it; an anxious voice wanting a word alone with George Marsh.

"Tell them I'm out somewhere," he said.

After I had hung up I took the receiver back off the hook and let it rest on the window seat. The phone had been ringing at steady intervals, most of the day.

"Has anyone asked you to wait?" George said at last.

"I wasn't going to wear a gold hedgehog on my watch chain," I said. "So I told them no, thank you very much."

He grinned, and it was needlessly courteous of him to laugh. "Maybe you had better think it over," he said. "You can always call them up if you change your mind."

And now, when there was no doubt of what he was trying to tell me, when he saw that I understood, he bit his lip and shook his head wretchedly.

"Was it one blackball or a whole slew of them?" I asked him suddenly. "I'll always be curious to know."

George Marsh moved by the bookcase and there preoccupied himself with a row of empty beer quarts. He said at last, "That sort of thing is kept confidential."

"You might as well get it off your chest," I said, and just for a moment I felt sorrier for him than for myself. "You might as well let me have the whole story."

"No story," George said, "but it looks as though you won't be wearing any lions on your necktie, Sport-o." This was not a new word, but George had never used it before. Toby Tappan used it, and his roommate Dinky Putnam.

"I realize this may warp my whole life, but I promise not to slit my wrists," I said.

"It wasn't anything important," George said. "It wasn't because you come from East Northrup or anything like that. After all, look at Cuppy Vale. He comes from Canandaigua."

I laughed aloud. There was no reason why I shouldn't laugh my head off at any time and at anything I wanted.

"He was taken in on the first ballot," George went on. "I don't blame you for being burnt up, Sport-o."

"It serves that Vale right. Think of the razzing I can give him now."

"There were only two or three," George began.

"Blackballs?"

"Guys who didn't know you too well."

"I thought they all knew me. Why did they keep inviting me back if they didn't know me? What a waste of booze."

"Maybe there were just these two or three who didn't know you as well as the others did," George said.

"Look at Vale," I said. "He never said hello to anybody in *any* damn club. Let's not be so formal. After all, what's a blackball? What difference is it going to make in twenty years?"

George sat on the window seat, crossing his legs in front of him, and I wondered if ever George Marsh didn't tend to overdo things. I wondered if his Argyll socks weren't too bright or if there weren't too much mahogany stain on his shoes, and if he weren't just a little too damned eligible to be true.

"We may as well face it," I said. "I'm just not club material."

He must not have appreciated my tone. He was looking at me perfectly seriously.

"Some are. Some aren't," I said deliberately. "That's how it goes."

George Marsh rose from the window seat and began to pace the room, and the hand went back to rubbing the cheek.

"Tappan did say something about maybe appearing a little too eager. Of course that's a perfectly natural mistake."

"Eager! What am I supposed to do? I can't very well act like Vale, you know."

"You understand," George Marsh said, "I'm not blaming you. Maybe I should have said something to you a couple of weeks ago. You didn't have to give the big hello to *everybody*. Let them come to you. All that glad-hand stuff." He shook his head. "Do you remember that last punch in Lowell House? The one I had to leave early?"

"When I played the piano?"

It was a long pause, long enough for me to absorb the idea. "That was a very important punch," he said.

"They *asked* me to play! As a matter of fact Tappan asked me."

"I knew it." He checked his pacing once more and this time endeavored to measure my reactions. "I know it's strictly baloney. Even Tappan doesn't believe you were actually whistling."

"I may have," I said contritely. "I sometimes whistle when I play."

"But after I'd gone," he said, "you didn't *sing*?"

"Yes. Yes, I may have."

"But not a big *production*! You didn't take over the whole party?"

"I can't remember what I did exactly. They all seemed to be enjoying themselves."

He looked at me as he walked, quick alternating glances of incredulity and despair. He spoke like a baffled parent. "What was that tune you kept playing?"

" 'Buckle Down Winsocki.' "

"No," he said. "I don't believe you. It was a very important punch."

"And 'Praise the Lord and Pass the Ammunition.' What's the sense of playing tunes like that if you don't sing them?"

"Oh, no," he murmured. "No. No."

"Well I thought that was what they wanted. I tried to make an impression. What in hell do they want for a nickel?"

"I know," George said. "They want you to try but they don't want you to try too hard. It's perfectly ridiculous."

His voice died gradually away. He shuffled through a stack of records by the bookcase, and so said nothing more. I poured myself some of Tappan's sour mash into a glass and offered some to him. We retreated to the opposite sides of the room and drank, undisturbed for an hour or more. Even Fuzzy's return was not an occasion for merriment. There was no stimulation in the bourbon, no comfort in our idleness. Sometime past eleven, we were brought out of ourselves by a pounding on the door. Toby Tappan flung it open and strode in. He was followed this time by two friends with rampant lions on their neckties and grim aspects on their faces. George Marsh, dressed in striped pajamas, looked at them sullenly from the threshold of his bedroom, and his hand began to rub his cheek.

"Put some pants on," Tappan told George abruptly. "We've got drinking to do."

Toby Tappan was holding a quart of champagne and brandishing it for all to see. At this signal his retinue, who had lingered behind their president, advanced to the mantel and with unconscious ceremony set out a silver ice bucket and glasses.

With a sound uncomfortably like a sigh, George Marsh sidled to the window seat and sat, resignedly examining his bare toes and ankles beneath the cuffs of his pajama pants.

Tappan spoke to him in a tempered voice, firm yet also confiding. He said, "We have to know by midnight. The election has been called for one o'clock. This is an emergency."

They formed a tight quadrant about George Marsh and hedged him into his seat. He accepted a glass from Tappan and held it out apathetically as another poured the cold champagne.

"What we really need," Tappan said engagingly, "what we should really have is a napkin and a hamper filled with watercress sandwiches."

On the sofa across the room Fuzzy Eaton gave a short but distinctly audible yawn. He was dressed for bed, in his undershorts, and had been dozing with a French grammar over his eyes to shield them from the ceiling light. He watched the arrivals sleepily, lightly

245

drumming the flats of his hands upon his bare, swollen abdomen, and yawned again.

"Eaton," Toby Tappan said in his British voice. "If you aren't the most useless bugger I ever saw."

Fuzzy, who could take bouquets from Toby Tappan or leave them alone, continued to beat his stomach. Tappan pranced over to the sofa and slapped the naked belly. Fuzzy retaliated by kicking hard at Tappan with his bare feet; not everyone was privileged to kick Toby Tappan, even in fun.

"Where is the napkin?" Fuzzy demanded. "Where are the watercress sandwiches? You mean you're not going to give him the old watercress-sandwich treatment?"

"I'll watercress you," Toby Tappan said happily. With a decisive pull at the ankles he flung Fuzzy roaring to the floor.

"Not one lousy sandwich! Phonies!"

Fuzzy lay on his back, red-faced, tattooed, bellowing:

> Toby Tappan's a friend of mine.
> For a nickel or a dime,
> He will do it any time.

They held his legs and sought to pinion his shoulders, and he contrived another defamatory jingle at the expense of the club itself.

"Queers! Jerks! Phonies!"

I remained alone on the edge of the window seat, just where I had sat all that afternoon. Dumbly, I looked on at the spectacle, for Fuzzy had now declared himself and had come into his own, proving what an addition he was to any group, proving once and for all that he was club material.

They had taken ice from the wine bucket and while two held him the other applied it to Fuzzy's bare skin. Soon the floor was strewn with melting ice and Fuzzy was sitting on the sofa, his knees drawn under his soaked undershorts.

"It just so happens I'm studying. There's an Hour Exam tomorrow and you guys are a great big help."

There followed the inevitable laughter at the suggestion that Eaton had been studying. The champagne was passed round once more. At length Toby Tappan set down his glass and looked meaningfully at George Marsh. I excused myself and went to bed.

I lay there and listened to the voices on the other side of the door. They were not always as distinct as Tappan's, but his was raised above the rest in pleading. It seemed curious that the voice which answered most often was not Fuzzy's but George Marsh's. A stubborn, repetitious mumbling, lost in the pouring and clinking sounds of bottle upon glass. I found that I was very tired. I did not know how long I slept, but it was not long. I woke with the light shining in my eyes to see Fuzzy Eaton standing over me in his damp shorts, wearing a radiant grin.

"Let me sleep," I said sulkily.

"Nothing wrong with you, except you haven't been drinking enough lately." With that he pressed a ball of crushed ice against the back of my neck, and when I sprang up in a rage, I saw that he was holding an opaque drink in his hand.

"Let me alone," I said. "That's not your booze."

He sat down on the bed and pressed the glass under my chin. "With the compliments of Toby Tappan," he said. "At-a-boy, Gubber. Drink up."

I pushed his arm away and lay back on the pillow and let Fuzzy have a string of oaths, drawing on every stylized epithet that came to mind. He looked at me drowsily and scratched under his arm.

"You Goddamn chimpanzee," I said. "Let me alone."

"Sticks and stones can break my bones, Gubber." He took a bold swallow from the drink which made him shiver from head to toes as it went down. "You sure have a funny way of showing you're grateful."

"Grateful for what?"

"The least you can do," Fuzzy said, "is to thank George. Seriously, Gubber."

It was always a surprise to hear Fuzzy Eaton say something in earnest, but there was no mistaking when he did. He forgot the posturing of the moment and sometimes even forgot his accent. He reverted to his essential self and spoke as he might have spoken to his mother, as a direct, high-principled boy from Chestnut Hill.

"He's really a friend. He's really a hell of a nice guy. A hell of a nice guy, Gubber."

There was not time to discover what Fuzzy meant, for Toby Tappan was beside the bed. The afternoon's drinking appeared to have caught up with him at last. He was in his shirt sleeves and his tie was off, his collar unbuttoned; he had spilled a drink on his dark flannel trousers. "Taylor," Toby Tappan said. "You're to be congratulated."

It was unlike Tappan to allow drunkenness to reflect on his appearance and confusing that he should be congratulating me as though I had just bested him on the squash courts.

"Thanks," I said. "I don't get it."

"Drink up," Fuzzy said.

I took the glass from him and obeyed. It was not easy after having been asleep.

"Good man," Tappan said. "I knew you were a good man." He came closer and shook my hand.

"Old Goph did himself proud," Fuzzy was saying. "You really should have heard him, Gubber."

"You're to be congratulated," Toby Tappan said again and with drunken formality he shook my hand the second time.

"All for one, one for all," Fuzzy said. "That's us, Gubber. The Goph really put it to them."

I was sitting on the edge of my bed and watching Tappan closely. I hoped that I was behaving properly and that I was saying the proper things. "Thanks, Toby."

"It's been a rotten day, hasn't it?" Toby Tappan said. "Messy sort of thing, you know."

"Oh, I know," I said.

"You know I've always thought you were a good man. If you're half the man Marsh says you are, I'm awfully glad it's turned out the way it has."

I got out of bed and escorted Tappan out through the living room. He nodded toward the closed door of George Marsh's bedroom. "There's a good man," he said. "There's the sort of friend to have."

"Do you mind if I speak frankly?" I said. "Does it really mean that much to get him in?"

"Naturally," Tappan said. "Naturally we didn't want to lose him."

"It's a sort of package deal," I said. "Log rolling. I thought that wasn't ethical."

"Don't be a fool," Toby Tappan said. "Eaton's coming in and you're coming in. It's all turned out wonderfully."

There was a point beyond which Toby Tappan could unbend no further. There were some things that were not discussed. Some

248

things were unnecessary, embarrassing for everyone, and in the worst taste, and too frank.

His two companions were waiting in the hall, and they also shook my hand most heartily. Congratulations. Wasn't it swell news? Tappan picked up the empty wine bucket and led them down the stairs. I listened to their heavy nail-studded heels on the wooden floor and to the creaking of the entry door as they went out into the night.

Back inside our room I found that Fuzzy had called it a day. A blast of cold air swept in from his bedroom where with the door and window open wide he slumbered like an infant beneath one torn sheet and a patchwork comforter. He was snoring and the window shade was snapping in the breeze. Another bottle of sour mash stood half empty on a wooden table, its top lost among the litter of old magazines and newspapers. Fuzzy Eaton's French book lay with its leaves creased in the position it had fallen hours before. It could have been any night in the week. The temperature, the sounds, and the debris were the same, and beneath my bare feet the old flooring was cold and dirty as always. There was no clue to what had been said and done here while I had slept, no indication of the consequences. A new distress was knifing upward from the pit of my stomach and I felt perversely lonely, cold, and ashamed.

I went into George Marsh's bedroom and snapped on the light. He sat up right away.

"I want to talk to you."

"We could talk in the morning," George Marsh said.

"There's something I want you to do," I said. "Don't do me any more good turns."

"I knew you'd blow up." He folded his arms about his knees and studied me. "It's all over now," he said.

"I'm just telling you don't do me any more good turns."

"I thought you wanted to wear lions on your necktie."

"Not that much I don't."

He reached to the bureau and took some matches and a pack of cigarettes off it without leaving the bed. I noticed an ashtray on the floor with three or four butts in it and that was curious. I had never known him to smoke in bed. He took a cigarette and flipped the package at me. "I wish you'd be reasonable about it, Sport-o. What

249

do you think friends are for? Fuzzy and I would have been some swell guys to leave you in the lurch."

"You know what they call us?" I asked him. "The two and a half musketeers. Maybe that doesn't bother you."

"That's lousy. That's a damn lousy thing to say."

"It's like playing the piano," I said. "It's one of those unfortunate things."

"Why do you always listen to Vale?" George said. "He gives you an inferiority complex."

"I should have told them to go to hell. It would have been worth it seeing Tappan's face."

"Do you want to make a fool of me?" he said, alarmed. "You'll have to promise me that you won't do that."

And I could not have made a fool of him. No one, not even Cuppy Vale, ever discussed the matter after that. Two weeks afterward, after the initiations were over, Toby Tappan showed us around the clubhouse. In the billiard room there was an upright piano, quite like the one Mo Beach owned. Ever afterward, I was particularly careful not to go near it, not even to enter the billiard room.

Chapter Seventeen

The day of our initiation dinner, a Friday, Fuzzy Eaton was summoned to the Dean's Office and expelled. That evening as we dressed he let the news drop casually, and, knowing Fuzzy's academic record as we did, it was no surprise to us. We lined our stomachs with olive oil, a precaution against getting too drunk too early, and set out for the evening without giving the matter a second thought. We lost Fuzzy in our revels and did not see him until Sunday night when he came back still clad in his tuxedo and with a lewd rolling of the eyes recounted an amatory adventure of his weekend. On Monday he disappeared anew and was not seen again until Thursday at suppertime when he acted supremely pleased with himself. On questioning him we discovered that Fuzzy had outwitted the Dean's Office, and that he had got the jump on us. Fuzzy Eaton, late of the class of 1945, who claimed to see only shooting stars before his eyes and boasted that his blood ran a pale amber from martinis, had passed his physical for the Army Air Corps. Walter Baxter Eaton, Air Cadet.

And Hank Barthelmess had enlisted in the Marines. Together among the first to go, he and Fuzzy rented a ballroom in the Hotel Commander and threw their own farewell party. It was the beginning of the big farewells. The year-end examinations began in May. If there was any purpose to life, it was to escape them. Day by day, though it meant wasting a term's tuition, our ranks were thinned by those who had hit upon the way to bow out honorably. Guilt and academic failure were absolved by the Deans, who granted an automatic leave of absence to a volunteer, who would gladly rub the slate clean in the interests of patriotism. Anyone who answered his country's call was automatically kissed by nobility; he was entitled to a certain amount of superciliousness for having foiled both

General Hershey and the Dean's Office at the same time. Hour Exams and passing grades became a dim ludicrous memory.

During May Air Cadet Eaton was writing to us from Maxwell Field, Alabama. His letters contained obscene language and vile condemnations of the military life. He damned himself for missing the send-off parties in Cambridge and made pitiful allusions to the leave promised him for that far-off day when he would win his wings. The letters were circulated widely, for everyone was anxious for even the seamiest news of Fuzzy Eaton in the wild blue yonder.

George Marsh had made up his mind long before he heard from Fuzzy. He failed even to show up for his April Hour Exams, and thus left himself but one choice. First the Naval, then the Army Air Corps rejected him for faulty vision. Though he consulted an oculist, took corrective exercises and memorized eye charts, though his Uncle Mark attempted to secure a waiver for his eyes from Washington, he still did not qualify. At the end of April he cut a day's classes to go to the recruiting headquarters of the First Service Command in Boston and enlist directly in the Army. Given a two weeks' enlistment furlough, he left to break the news to his uncle and his mother in New York and to Lila Norris in Providence, where she had managed an afternoon's permission from Miss Eustis'. Later he was to speak worshipfully of Lila, who had said that now he was going, we couldn't help but win the war. She tried so hard to make it a cheerful afternoon. They took a long drive by the seashore and she had kissed him constantly. She had given way to tears just once, when he had dropped her off by the gate of the school.

George had been gone exactly three days when my aunt and uncle drove to Cambridge. They would not waste gas coupons; I knew there was a purpose to the visit. I knew by his silence and her nervous conversation that they were waiting for me to talk. She drove the venerable Chrysler along the banks of the Charles so my uncle might watch the crews practicing. At his suggestion we went into Boston for lunch at the Parker House. He ordered tripe for everyone, though tripe disagreed with Aunt Connie. Uncle Torbert saw no reason why we should not enjoy some dry sherry. "It's lunchtime and the sun is over the yardarm, as they say, fellow." In all the years he had been active in the law and had lunched downstairs in the men's grill, he had ordered sherry and tripe. It was a nostalgic occasion. I was older and they were older and there was a waiter, older still, who remembered my uncle and who said, "The tripe is nice today, Mr. Case." We might have been up for the day going to Mr. Jennings' office about clothing me for another year at the Academy. "Isn't it like old times?" Aunt Connie said. It was such a gay lunch for her. I couldn't bring myself to tell her that I had enlisted in the Army until Uncle Torbert had paid the check.

My aunt dabbed at her mouth with her napkin and looked despondently first at me and then at my uncle. She got no answer. I could not reach across the table to touch her with my hand. She folded her napkin into a tidy square and shook her head slowly. It never hurt to be friendly, yet when the waiter came to collect his tip she forgot to smile at him as she would have ordinarily. Ordinarily, one cigarette after a meal was enough, yet my uncle was lighting her a second. Then my uncle was saying something, and I was saying something, but she heard neither of us.

When she did speak it was more to herself than to us who so wanted to hear her. "We were having such a gay lunch."

"It was the best thing to do, Aunt. They'd draft me anyway."

"Your father always did the impulsive thing." She bowed her head and twisted the wedding ring about on her thin finger. "You didn't discuss it with your uncle."

"Con," my uncle said, "it's an accomplished fact. There's nothing we can do, Con. Every young man wants to go to war."

My aunt tucked a hairpin into place in the bun on back of her head. She was wearing one of the floppy hats that I did not think became her. Her eyes were too soft and her mouth too strong to be lost beneath a black, straw brim.

"Are you going because the Marsh boy is going, Gus?"

"This is the time to go," I said. "Everyone's going now."

"That's quite natural," my uncle said. "It's best to go with friends."

"Torbert," my aunt said, "I knew it." She beat softly on the tablecloth with her small fist. "Didn't I tell you so?"

I thought how weary she looked, though that was better than seeing her angry. Perhaps in the car on their way back to East Northrup she might light into him, or burst into tears. She must do that sometimes, though I had certainly never seen her.

"Why didn't you talk to him? You know that Sellers boy never spoke to his mother. And Walter Eaton. I used to know his mother. Poor Emily. She was in my Sewing Circle."

My uncle had no answer, but as proof that he was rising to the occasion, he ordered up a round of brandies. "Your aunt's a stubborn woman," he said, and merrily raised his glass to mine. "I'm proud, Gus. Your aunt's proud too."

She had been quiet during the bringing of the brandies, but she had held her eyes on me. Her face had taken on a terrible martyrdom. "You're only going because George Marsh is going," she said.

"That's not true, Aunt."

"You never think for yourself. Dearie, I don't mean to scold."

"I made up my mind myself."

"We won't discuss it, dearie. It was such a gay lunch."

"Here's to the Field Artillery," Uncle Torbert said. "I had quite a few friends in the Field Artillery."

"Torbert, how long do you think the war will last?"

"There's no telling," my uncle said and gestured manorially with his brandy glass. "This war was inevitable, Con. War is always inevitable. It's a psychological necessity for mankind."

"Oh, Torbert!"

"My dear, it's a dreadful thing. It's not a woman's thing. However, I do believe that a man's life is not complete until he's been to war. I saw quite a bit of the last war with the American Field Service."

"Your father was in the Navy, Gus," Aunt Connie said reminiscently. "But only for a little while."

"Of course the Field Artillery is first rate," my uncle said. "But as it was, we got to France six months ahead of the A.E.F." He set down his glass and looked at me triumphantly.

"I think your father was a little thinner than you," my aunt said. "Dearie, you are so young."

"Of course you'll get a commission," my uncle said.

"I'm a private," I said. "I don't know how I'll end up."

"I should think you would want to get a commission," my uncle said.

"Dearie," my aunt said, "you're not even nineteen years old."

I tried to explain how by volunteering for the Army my R.O.T.C. training would put me automatically in the Field Artillery. I must convince her how serious I was, how carefully I had thought this thing out. She nodded and made faint cooing sounds to show that

254

she understood, but when I was through she said, "Dearie, why didn't you talk it over with your uncle?"

In the end by laughing and teasing her I thought I had made her understand. She gathered up her shawl and her gloves and I held her coat for her. "Nothing I say makes any difference to you now," she said when we were in the car. I promised to spend a few days at East Northrup before I left, but for all purposes we had already said good-by. They dropped me off at the Park Street subway entrance and Aunt Connie even tried to put her heart into an apology for having spoiled our lunch. I had started on a little speech of comfort, but then my uncle, suddenly anxious to get home because he had things to attend to, complained loudly about the traffic.

George Marsh and I found that by no very great coincidence our orders to Fort Devens read for the same day. Hearing this, Mo Beach organized one last party on the spur of the moment. He planned it as the stink to end all stinks and it would have turned out that way, had not the novelty of these occasions begun to wane. I was at first disgruntled to discover that fickle interests were already shifting from the race to the colors. Intelligence was filtering through that it was going to be a long war. There were rumors about the immunity of the Reserves, the inefficiency of draft boards. Now that most of us were leaving, the remainder seemed to be in no hurry to go. The distinction between hero and sucker was narrowing daily. Cuppy Vale must have sensed my annoyance, for he came to Mo Beach's party in an almost apologetic frame of mind.

Vale was not a one for parties, nor good-bys. He came to Mo Beach's party only because he was a friend of George Marsh's and of mine. We had just the chance to speak rapidly and unsatisfactorily through the crowd.

"The way I see it," he said in a somber voice hard to hear above the noise, "it's not going to be any joke. Guys can try to make gags, but I hate it. I hate the whole idea of it. My mother didn't raise her boy to be a soldier."

"I don't blame you," I answered him. "I'd as soon stay around myself, if you really want to know."

We were interrupted there by a chubby girl from Wellesley in

255

whom Mo Beach had been investigating reputed nymphomaniacal tendencies.

"I don't love you," the girl said to me, "but I feel I must kiss you. I've just kissed George Marsh."

A wave of hair blocked off a part of her face and she was a little drunk on Hammertoe's punch.

"Let's go, gang!" Mo Beach was milling, aimlessly, in the background and clapping his hands. "Let's go, gang!"

"Go on, kiss him," Vale said and smacked my back. "He likes to be kissed."

The girl's fingers clasped the back of my neck and she drew my face down toward hers.

"You're sweet," she said and curtsied. "I wanted you to know who I was in case you and George would like someone to come to the station and see you off."

This suggestion seemed extraordinarily funny to Vale, and he was egging her on when Mo Beach jostled between us with a leer. "I have other arrangements for you," Mo said, and nudged us, and tugged his girl away.

"That's what I like to see," Cuppy Vale said. "Do you suppose Veronica Lake will be on hand to give me the big soul-kiss good-by?"

He was loosening up, it seemed he was no longer my critic.

"You homely bastard," I told him. "Don't flatter yourself."

"I hate to see you go. I'm going to miss you. Damned if I'm not," Vale said, and after a moment of reflection, "I won't be far behind. I have a rendezvous with General Hershey. Should be coming up in about two months."

"With that rugged physique you should still make 4-F."

"Hell," Vale said. "I'm putting in for the ski troops. I can't ski worth a damn, but so what?"

"That's no soft touch."

"Camp Hale, Colorado?" he said. "Pando, way up there in the Rockies? Passes to Denver? Saturday night at the Broadmoor Hotel? This war is all deserts and jungles. You name me a better deal."

There was more noise in the room and we were being jostled. Someone was singing "Lady of Spain, I Adore You" à la Lawrence Tibbett. In a minute it would be impossible to talk.

256

"Well," Vale said. "Keep 'em rolling. Keep 'em flying. Keep democracy from dying. Let those be my parting words to you."

When he saw I was laughing he frowned and a dark look of remembering came over his face. "No, that's not so funny. I wonder if we were ever as funny as we thought we were," he said. "We always thought we were so damn smart."

"Always leave them laughing," I said, hoping to head off the mood.

Unexpectedly, he was shaking my hand. "I was rough on you this year. I wanted to say no hard feelings. From one country boy to another."

"Take care of yourself," I said, raising my voice, for he was being pushed away.

"You poor country bastard," I heard him call, "take care of yourself."

I answered something that did not carry over the noise and he grinned as though he had heard, craning his skinny neck, and awkwardly sidled away.

I had letters from Camp Hale, where he was two weeks in the hospital with a bronchitis they called the Pando hack. From U.S.O. clubs and a hotel in Denver; much later from a staging area. Mrs. Vale forwarded me his A.P.O. number enclosed with a short note of encouragement and a pamphlet containing a serviceman's prayer the director of her parish in Canandaigua had read on Easter Sunday. When the Tenth Mountain Division went in at last it was not to a desert or a jungle but to the Apennines. When he wrote me from somewhere in Italy he seemed his snide old self. He said that the Army life had tamed him down; he hadn't really tied one on since that last party of Mo Beach's.

Chapter Eighteen

I spent almost four years futilely telling myself that the Army was a bad dream. It was no dream, though. In all that time there was no ruder awakening than that which lay in store at Fort Devens in Ayer, Massachusetts.

In other brighter days when George Marsh had passed through Ayer he might have realized vaguely that Fort Devens was there. Yet, to George Marsh, Ayer was not a military site. Nearby and still so far away, in such a different corner of the world, lies the manicured campus of Groton School. As an Emmanueler George had ridden past the railroad station and through the streets of Ayer in a bus on his way to an annual athletic event that would little have interested the Fort Devens personnel. He used to make the trip in May. Groton was one of the last games of the baseball schedule and it had been a team to beat. There was nothing new to George about a trip to Ayer, especially in the springtime, and nothing new about the nervousness in his stomach that accompanied that trip. Again in Ayer in May of 1942 he complained of a nervousness in his stomach, though its cause was not the same. He was not riding with his teammates in a chartered bus but under the grimy tarpaulin of an Army six-by-six, one of a bedraggled convoy that had formed at the railroad station and in which everyone was a stranger.

George Marsh and I took the trip together. We sat side by side on the hard slats of the truck. George was difficult to recognize. He had not shaved that morning and by four in the afternoon, when a bored noncom piled us into the six-by-six, the stubble on his cheeks and chin was darkly visible. To further the deception, he had chosen a soiled cotton sweater, old creaseless flannels, and a pair of curled crepe-soled shoes. When he had played touch football on the lawns of Brookline, when he had ridden out a gale at the helm of the *Excalibur*, or shot skeet on the east meadow at Marshmain, he had never looked this unkempt. Today he had achieved at once the antithesis of his Uncle Mark and the denial of Eddy Shawn. Neither of those arbiters of gentility would have recognized his pupil as he slouched and rolled with the pitch of the vehicle, wearily remarking the twenty wan faces about him. On his lap rested a square canvas bag of khaki, the kind of bag that soldiers squatted on in the aisles of day coaches. If he was not every inch a soldier, he was every inch a draftee, though a bit too meticulously so. No one would have guessed that buried in that khaki bag, among the toilet articles and the changes of socks and underwear, there was a portable picture frame in Mark Cross leather and a small photograph of Lila Norris especially posed and prepared for this great adventure. No one in that truckload of abject patriots would have suspected that in a money belt about this one waist were a hundred dollars in cash and uncounted more in traveler's checks. Once the truck stopped with a lurch that banged me against him. I grinned and winked at him. He did not wink back, of course. That was not in the plan.

I had offended him by failing to comply with the plan. I had seen no reason to enter the service of my country incognito or to camouflage my accent, because my accent was quite different from George's. George had been alarmed. When he was arguing with me, George had said, "Do you remember *Captains Courageous?* Remember Harvey Cheyne? The boy who fell off the ocean liner? Well, I don't want to be another Harvey Cheyne. I don't want to be a rich feep. I don't want you to make me look like one."

He did his best. He kept his identity scrupulously to himself. One read in the papers of a movie star or a ball player being inducted and of the difficulties he encountered when recognized by his brothers in arms. I doubted that any celebrity was as assiduously democratic as George Marsh. Though his name registered nothing, though he looked like a thousand others who were processed daily in reception centers all over the land, he could never quite believe it. I know that he hated to wear his dog tags that bore the address of his Uncle Mark's house on Fifth Avenue.

He arrived at Devens on a Tuesday; by Saturday his processing was done. His intelligence had been tested, his aptitudes assessed. He had seen the lurid Medical Corps films, had heard a chaplain's talk on continence. In his first shortarm inspection a doctor had pronounced him a clean-living boy and encouraged him to stay that way. He had been bled, vaccinated, immunized. His arm ached and for a day he believed he was coming down with grippe. Unused to the latrine and the publicity there attendant to all bodily functions, he was also constipated.

And yet by Saturday morning, as we slogged through the mud in our stiff green fatigues and as the hard leather of our shoes bit into our blisters, George had discovered a hazy *esprit de corps*. He seemed even pleased to join his companions in giving the bird to the civilian increments arriving that afternoon. I began to hope it would not be so bad for him after all. That same afternoon, however, I found it was too soon to hope.

Try as he might to hide from it, some bit of the past had had to catch up with him. There was a mail call toward three o'clock, followed by the unhoped-for blessing of a half hour's break in the barracks. He had got a letter from his mother, a long letter from Lila, and a postcard which Lila and Chee Wee had combined to send. It was the photograph of the interior of a New York night club that they three had often visited. Those girls had written on the back to the effect that they were missing him and wishing he were there at the time of the writing. (Soon I would be receiving similar mementos. Bubbly messages of cheer from the home front written in the early morning hours and mailed, compliments of the management. They were to turn up like particles of a prenatal existence.) When I finished reading this postcard I made a remark which caused George to frown—and say to me, fractiously, that he thought it was pretty darn nice of the girls.

He proceeded to read me excerpts from the letter Lila had written, while we squatted on the floor beside our cots. She begged him to call her at Miss Eustis' some afternoon. She wanted so badly to talk with him once more. Lila and Chee Wee had come down to see what could be done about entering Bassett Meadows and they had had a long weekend in New York. They had loved the college and they had loved Dean Brink. They had taken some cinchy tests, and filled out forms, and answered questions about how they saw themselves twenty years from now, and had interpreted ink blots, and had done finger paintings. If they didn't get into Bassett Meadows now they would quietly die, or join the

Waves, or something. So George could see what a lot there was to talk about. He was still in New England and so near. He must call her up soon. He must promise.

This news and the Saturday lull had a cheering effect. George had not been so loquacious since we had come to Devens. But it was a short moment, for suddenly I saw his face freeze into a polite half-smile and his voice dropped.

"It's a small world," George Marsh said pleasantly. "What do you know?"

The intruder, who stepped between us now and sat squarely on George Marsh's bed, was Ned Sellers. He leaned back and dug his elbows into the pillow and rumpled the sheet. That morning George had skipped breakfast in order to fuss with that sheet so that it would be turned down the regulation number of inches and its crease would bisect the U.S. on the blanket.

"Holy Moses," George Marsh said. "I wish you wouldn't do that."

"You can make it over," Ned Sellers said. "Practice makes perfect, I always say."

George stood over the bed, baffled yet smiling.

"Ned," I said. "You remember George Marsh."

"How could I forget?" Ned said, and nodded.

George took a step closer to him. "How have you been, Ned?" Ned Sellers acknowledged him with a grunt.

"Buddy, oh buddy," Ned said to me at length, playfully. "That's some haircut. Damn if you're not the saddest-looking sack I ever did see. Don't you like the Army?"

"I found a home in the Army."

Ned was convulsed. It had never taken much to make Ned laugh. I wondered how long since I had seen him. Three years? Four years? And however much longer since Ned and I had worked his father's gas pumps, or set off cherry bombs under tin cans on the Fourth of July?

"My mother told me you was here and I should look you up," Ned Sellers said. "She heard from your aunt. How is Mrs. Case?"

"Fine."

"How's your uncle? Dad said he don't come to Town Meetings any more."

"He's a busy man," I said and smiled.

"Yeah, busy," Ned Sellers laughed. "They don't come no busier."

261

"He's always doing something. Writing, or something."

"Yeah," Ned said. "Writin'."

"Good to see you, Ned. How's it go?"

"No complaints," he said. "I'll bet you're homesick."

"Kind of," I said.

"Hell, man, you're going to love the Army."

I laughed along with him. It was strange how I felt at home with Ned in the barracks.

George Marsh, meantime, had been standing by. "Whereabouts are you stationed, Ned?"

"Two hundred and —nth M.P.'s," Ned told him curtly.

"Right here on the post?"

"Where the hell do you think I'd be stationed?" Ned said and turned back toward me. "Look at you," he said. "If your aunt could see you now."

"How are they treating you, Ned?" George said.

Ned raised himself on one elbow and glared. "How the hell do you think they're treating me?"

"I just wanted to know what it's like," George said.

"You'll find out what it's like."

George looked surprised. He withdrew to a wall and began to reread his mail.

Ned Sellers sprawled on the ruined cot and laughed quietly at the ceiling. "Sooner or later the Army gets them," he said.

"He's all right," I said. "Why don't you leave him alone?"

"You betcha," Ned said. "I forgot he was your big buddy."

Ned was no broader or heavier than he had been when he'd played tackle for Northrup High. He had the same freckles on his face and his red hair, in a G.I. clip, revealed an albinic stretch of skin on the back of his neck. He was dressed for a pass. There was a high shine on his PX shoes. His o.d. pants were freshly creased and the buttons on his blouse had been worked over with a blitz cloth. He wore glistening white Pfc. stripes and the First Service Command was on his left shoulder and his Marksman's Medal hung on his chest. Ned had been in the Army for more than a year, had gone right in after high school.

"Lookit," Ned was saying, and patting the pocket of his blouse, "I got a batch of passes here. All you do is sign an officer's name. It don't matter what name, they never check. I'll get you through

262

the gate and we can take off for East Northrup. Be there in two hours, just riding on the thumb."

"You know your way around, don't you?" I said.

"I operate," he conceded. As he lay on the bed he twirled a brass M.P. whistle on a chain.

"Thanks for the offer," I said to him. "I guess I'll stick around until I'm through processing anyhow."

"When you're done processing, you expect to sit around on your dead ass?" Ned said, faintly amused. "Hell, man, you got another think coming."

The small canvas bag in which George Marsh kept his most precious possessions lay just under the head of the bed. George came over from the window and picked it up and opened it to put Lila's letter inside. "Excuse me," George said. He had brushed the bag against the top of Ned Sellers' hair.

"What you got in there?" Ned demanded, rising.

"Just my stuff."

"What kind of stuff?"

"The stuff I want to keep. You know."

"You can't keep it there," Ned said. "You can't keep any old non-regulation crap lying around. Where do you think you're at—the Waldorf-Astoria?"

George laughed, very politely.

"What's funny?" Ned Sellers wanted to know. "You've got another think coming, my friend. You can't keep but what's issued to you."

"There's no room in my barracks bag." George took on the same look of alarm he had had when a corporal had told him about bouncing the nickel off his bed.

"I'm just telling you," Ned Sellers said. "It's not going to be my ass."

Then George left us to go to the latrine. I asked Ned, "Why don't you leave him be?"

"Sure," Ned said. "Sure. . . . You want to go to the PX and have a beer?"

"Let's wait for him."

Ned Sellers made a face. "I remember him."

"Why don't you forget about it?" I said.

Ned stood up and straightened his blouse, pulling the skirt down

263

in back. He looked very tidy, sharp. "I hate a kid like that," he said. "You coming for a beer or aren't you?"

"Why do you hate him?"

"He's a snot, that's why. I'm telling you you keep him out of my way. This man's Army isn't big enough for me and a kid like that."

So I did not go with Ned. I remained in the barracks, loyally.

The very next afternoon, Sunday, the day before I shipped out of Devens, I witnessed a scene more painful. When she had done processing us, and was appalled to learn that we had free time on our hands, the Army set us to doing her housekeeping. For sixteen hours on Sunday we pulled K.P. in one of the gigantic mess halls which fed day and night to the station complement and the ever replenishing herds of inductees. At four in the morning we reported to the kitchen of Staff Sergeant Homer Doyle. We were not to bother Sergeant Doyle's cooks; we were not to talk; we were not to smoke. If we were fair with Sergeant Doyle, Sergeant Doyle would be fair with us. Past ten o'clock there was a quiet spell when a momentary idler began to sing "There'll Be Bluebirds Over the White Cliffs of Dover." Sergeant Doyle blew his whistle and demanded to know what there was to sing about. He'd give us something to sing about.

An hour later the K.P.'s began to take their lunch in shifts, and there was time for a smoke. But the first real lull came about mid-afternoon. The mess hall was almost empty then and the K.P. pushers gave the men on the sinks a twenty-minute break. When the break was over, D.R.O. allowed those of us on table-scrubbing detail twenty minutes. We weren't back at work more than a quarter of an hour before the whistle blew again and Sergeant Doyle called everyone back into the kitchen.

He allowed the K.P.'s to arrive from all sides of the mess hall before beginning to speak. Sergeant Doyle had just returned from the Service Club; he was leaning against the meat locker, working open the blouse buttons over his paunch with his right hand and letting his left sleeve full of hash marks dangle. His jaws rose and fell upon a cud of gum. His lips were drawn and his eyes fixed on a lone fatigue-clad figure. The cooks and D.R.O.'s and K.P. pushers moved in behind to see the show. The K.P.'s crowded eagerly against each other. There was an almost holiday atmosphere in the sweltering kitchen.

"I want you to see what we drew today." Sergeant Doyle had a low, rasping style, nothing in the grand manner. The corporal in charge of our squad room did a more spectacular chewing out. "Today," Sergeant Doyle said, "we drew a college man."

He shifted his bulk against the meat locker. "When I say a twenty-minute break, I don't mean no hour and a half. I don't mean twenty-one minutes. I don't mean twenty minutes and one second. Turn around here when I'm talking to you."

Private George Warwick Marsh III turned and faced his tormentor.

"You have to know how to count in college? You have to know how to tell time?"

"Yes."

"What college?"

"Harvard."

Sergeant Doyle extracted another stick of gum from his shirt pocket, unwrapped and bent it, snapped it into his mouth and chawed thoughtfully.

"Dear, dear," Sergeant Doyle said. "My, my." He folded his arms across his chest and gave a mirthless wink to a cook who stood near him.

"Hahvahd," the cook said, and began to sing:

> Defenseless the team falls backwards,
> In the fury of the blahst.
> We'll fight for the name of Hahvahd
> Till the last white line is pahst.

Some of the K.P.'s snickered and others grinned foolishly at what they did not quite understand.

An immense heap of knives and forks and spoons lay to dry on a white mattress cover at Private Marsh's feet.

Sergeant Doyle reached down for a spoon and rubbed his thumb in its hollow. "This what you call clean?" He wiped his thumb disgustedly on George's fatigue jacket, while his jaws worked noisily on the gum.

"Officer from the Inspector General comes around, you want me to tell him this is clean silver?"

"I'm sorry," George Marsh said, as if he had muffed set point in a tournament and Sergeant Doyle was his partner.

Private Marsh turned back to the sink and fumbled with the faucets, and Sergeant Doyle pushed him away. A perforated can hung from the spigot; in it was a bar of G.I. soap. Sergeant Doyle seized the stick of wood from Marsh's hands and whipped a batter of suds. The hot tap water splashed through the can and slowly the sink filled with a frothy solution that Sergeant Doyle had been making for sixteen years. "College man," Sergeant Doyle said. "Can't make soapy water."

The sergeant was saying something further to George, something which must have been drastic, in a tense low voice. It seemed desperately important that I hear it. The adjacent sink was empty and I needed to refill my scrub bucket, but by the time I had edged my way out of the mass of K.P.'s Sergeant Doyle had done with him. The sergeant was smirking maliciously, buttoning his blouse. He checked his buttons and his soiled pre-Pearl Harbor ribbon, and Private Marsh was hunched over the sink, flailing soapsuds as though his life depended on it.

"I'll be back," I heard Sergeant Doyle say. "Don't think I won't. I sure would hate to see a college man leave Devens without he didn't know what soapy water was."

The show was ending and a whistle blew and the K.P.'s were dispersing back to work.

There was just enough time to speak to George Marsh. "What's he going to do to you?" I said.

"Permanent K.P.," George said wretchedly. "I have to report back tomorrow morning. I have to report back every single Goddamned morning at four o'clock."

"You sure screwed it up this time."

"I had to make a phone call."

"You're not serious?"

"I got that letter yesterday," he said. "You knew I was going to call her."

"But why call her now?"

"I thought I could do it in twenty minutes. The circuits were busy. I didn't know I'd have to wait in line."

"You could have called tonight."

"I promised I'd call this afternoon and she was waiting."

The Mess Sergeant had left, and it was up to the Pfc.'s and Acting Jacks, all the vicious jackals of the kitchen, to assert themselves. A whistle blew. A cook yelled for coffee water and the K.P. pushers reminded the men on the sinks that they weren't there for their health. The Dining Room Orderly wanted to know what I thought I was doing with the scrub bucket. I was glad to leave, because his eyes were red and rimmed with tears, and I could have looked no longer on the countenance of Private Marsh.

At three-thirty on Monday morning the naked Mazda bulbs went on in the squad room. A clerk held a clip board and a sheaf of newly cut stencils and struggled to pronounce the names that were on the day's shipping order. Shaking off my stiffness and grogginess, I listened only for my name, and it came. Fall out with equipment on the company street at 600 hours. I was out of bed, dressing, and looking for George Marsh.

His bed was already fretted over and wrinkleless. The fire guard was to have wakened George early, so as to leave time to wash and dress before he reported back to the sinks. There was no sign of him in the squad room below or in the latrine where the earliest risers were cueing up by the washbasins. I looked outside the barrack steps where the night light shone coldly in the darkness and there was a yard bird propped against the barrack wall a few feet from the latrine window. The floppy brim of the fatigue hat was pulled down on the forehead to deflect the unrelenting spring drizzle. The new unwaterproofed shoes had settled into the mud. Curiously, I heard a muted baritone voice that long ago on a Sunday afternoon had risen from the choir loft in the singing of the *Nunc Dimittis*, a moment before Dr. Kew stepped to the lectern to read the lesson. I walked across the mud to where he stood—Harvey Cheyne in herringbone twill. Under the cap's brim I could just see the shadowed eyes, the pale lips as they attempted a smile.

"Sport-o."

"Things are picking up," I said, brightly. "Very merry. Bursting into song all by your lonesome."

"I'm really merry," George Marsh said and he coughed. "I'm about as merry as a ghost."

"Ghost? You're the cream of the nation's youth. Did you hear the shipping order?"

"I'm not on the shipping order," he said dismally. "I've had it."

The lights had gone on just now in the next barracks across the company street. In a minute they would start waking up over there. If the men were new, if it were their first or second morning, there would be more to beginning the day than the simple act of rolling out and dressing robotlike. It took a few days to become a robot.

"They lost my records," George Marsh said. "I'm going to a casual company."

"How could they lose them?" I said.

"We're cattle," George said. "Just so many head of cattle." He hunched himself off the barrack wall and stood like a punchy fighter, his arms dangling. Their sleeves were stiff from newness and from the soap and sweat of yesterday at the sinks. "I feel dead," George said.

We must both have been thinking of the casual companies. Those purgatories for men whose service records had been lost in the infinite bureaucracy of Personnel. The forgotten men of the reception center, neither soldiers nor civilians, whose names appeared only on duty rosters. They lived under a quarantine in a distant part of the post, in tarpaper barracks. And spent their days as permanent latrine orderlies, laborers, K.P.'s. There was no counting the sadistic sixteen-hour stretches that lay ahead of him now in Sergeant Doyle's kitchen.

"They can lose your records forever," George said. "It doesn't matter a damn to them."

Someone opened the latrine window and let out the sounds of the cursing and mumbling of the men washing inside. George Marsh coughed again and sniffled. The barrack stoves had been left to burn for the past cold nights, making the air heavy with soft coal, permeating the moisture with that smell which puts an Army post among earth's most desolate places in the hours before dawn.

"God, I'm sorry," I said.

He sneezed and wiped at his nose with a strange khaki handkerchief the Army had issued him. "I've got this damn cold. This lousy taste in my mouth. . . . Sport-o, I'll see you in the funny papers."

"I'll look for you at Bragg," I said. "We'll both end up down there. At the Field Artillery Replacement Training Center—it's in the bag at Bragg."

268

George didn't attempt to smile. "How do we know what we're going to do? We're just so much livestock," he said. "I'm telling you I can't take this. I'm going to get to O.C.S. if it kills me."

As he made ready to leave, he pulled at the money belt under his fatigues and centered it about him. We said good-by and he was walking off and I was returning to the barracks when something prompted us each to look back. I waved and at first he appeared not to have noticed me. I was about to turn my back and then he was calling something, repeating it over and over, something that sounded like "luck, luck, luck, good luck," but the words were not distinct enough to answer. I turned on the barrack steps for a last look and saw him standing in the same place but now both his arms were outstretched and he was shaking his fists upward, viciously, into the dark.

Chapter Nineteen

In 1945 I spent the second week of April on furlough at the Enlisted Men's Rest and Recreation Center in Nice. Returning, I found my outfit a few kilometers east of Heidelberg, deep in Seventh Army's sector. The talk was that three men in our Regimental S-2 had been fined for fraternizing, that Heidelberg was, or soon would be, off limits as perusal to everyone except service and supply troops, and that wouldn't matter a damn anyhow because as soon as this war ended we were going soon to C.B.I. and not by way of the States either, by way of Persia.

A packet of delayed mail awaited me, plus a fruitcake Aunt Connie had sent last January. For no plausible reason my aunt had forwarded an invitation to the December Maiden's Ball, a pertinacious enterprise that had been sponsored by a French millinery house in the Hotel Pierre. It had taken place, I noted the date, three days after the Ardennes breakthrough. On the list of the Junior Committee I observed the names of Miss Lila Norris and of Seaman Second Class Howard Tighe Tilton, Jr., who, not yet having completed his Naval training at Yale, was evidently still within commuting distance of the Pierre. In addition to this were two of the letters that Aunt Connie customarily wrote on Sunday afternoons, a letter of hazy Chesterfieldian precepts from my Uncle Torbert Case, a tattered copy of *Archivi Emmanuelenses*, and one of those effervescent postcards from Chee Wee Gibbons. The last letter in the packet was a V-mail from 1st Lt. Geo. W. March III. George had knocked about some since I heard from him last. He was writing from a base hospital in the vicinity of Paris where some mortar fragments had just been removed from his hip, extremely successfully he might add, as he would be reporting back to duty within a week.

"Now I have some pretty tough news that has just come to me.

You probably knew that Cuppy Vale got to Italy in February with the Tenth Mountain. I have to tell you he was killed in March. The way I learned about it was that I wanted his address and I happened to write to his mother. . . ."

Vale had been wounded on patrol, the third he had been on that week, and Vale had volunteered. They had been out five hours and were starting home when a grenade exploded by Vale's head. The men had tried to carry him down a mountain but they were no more than halfway when he died in the snow. According to the letter Mrs. Vale had received from the Company Commander, some of the men had cried when they brought in the litter.

Reading this, I fancied I heard, in sounds of celestial laughter, the voice of my self-conscious friend, proven valiant beyond the call of duty and a trifle wary of being written about as a hero in the style of an Ernie Pyle dispatch. Charles Upman Pratt Vale, Jr., was defunct. A corpse in the snow, one of thousands, but his most certainly had been the coldest. I had never seen anybody get so cold in winter. He had used to stand on the steps of Emerson Hall in January and wait for his ten o'clock Philosophy class, a shivering spindle in a muffler. Even his hugest pimples became white and his nose ran preposterously. The wash of memory took me further back, to Emmanuel. Old Stables was always cold and we had kept hidden away in our cubicle there a contraband translation of the *Iliad,* to help us do our Greek assignments for Mr. Frapp. My mind caught on a line: "The mildest manners, and the gentlest heart. . . . In death a hero, as in life a friend." I hoped he would forgive me for embarrassing him, but it would be an appropriate line to include in the letter I must write to Mrs. Vale.

Days passed furiously and every one brought forth its dead men. Marshal Zhukov rammed his way into Berlin and the Reich crumbled like so much cheese under General Patton and after it all stopped you read in the *Stars and Stripes* how at home people were running wild, from New York to San Francisco. And meanwhile George was writing me obituary notices—Mo Beach had died on a hospital ship off Iwo Jima; Dinky Putnam had drowned in the North Atlantic; Fuzzy Eaton was reported K.I.A. after a run over Regensburg. I abandoned reasons and justifications for why they should have died. Maybe they had died for a better world, maybe they had died that we might live, and all that mawkishness

271

and hogwash which set the outraged dead to spinning in their graves. The fact was they had died, while we had not, and that was as much as I understood. No doubt George Marsh understood better. At least he carried on about it in an indefatigable manner; to my way of thinking he was being pretty pompous.

His attitude was the more galling for his sudden espousal of the dead, and of Cuppy Vale in particular. George Marsh had been apprehensive, even distrustful of Vale when he was alive; I could count on the fingers of one hand the number of times I had seen them relaxed and talking with one another. However, now that Vale was dead, George was extolling him to the skies, engineering the most unfortunate sort of deification. No one, George wrote, who had been lucky enough to know him would ever forget C. U. P. Vale, Jr., an odd ball maybe, but one of the great men, one of the really great men. We all owed him something. As I went on receiving these letters, my indignation mounted. He had been dickering with Graves Registration to see what could be done for Mrs. Vale about returning the body for burial in Canandaigua. And if he could swing a few days' leave in M.T.O. and bring his Leica along, he wanted to take some shots of Cuppy's Italian grave and send them to Mrs. Vale. Summer came, and George was soliciting contributions for a booklet he would like to have printed privately some day, in memory of our departed classmates. It appeared that he held the monopoly on grief, was our one-man Memorial Committee. I decided to have it out with him in person.

The opportunity came at the end of June, on a hot dry day when there was nothing doing, when the new S-2, the softest touch in Regimental Headquarters, lent me his jeep and signed my trip ticket. He was a major and had come to us when we settled above Stuttgart just as the war was ending, from Paris, replete with two pair of paratroop boots. You could wangle anything from him if you happened to be one of his N.C.O.'s; he had gotten me my promotion to Tech Sergeant.

Battery C of the Third Battalion of the ——th Artillery was at the end of a dusty road along which tiers of obsolete road markers pointed the way to the command posts, the supply and ammo dumps of other outfits that had paused in the area during the spring sweep to the Elbe. The CP was in a wood and stucco building that had been some German's country home. Its roof was intact but the high stone wall that sheltered it from the road had been sorely battered by shell or mortar fire, and what had been the lawn was now caked and rutted from the passage of great vehicles through mud. Beyond, to the east, lay a field and in it a PW cage of simple wiring. About the top of it ran some strands of barbed wire, fastened to square-cut timbers that would have been scrounged from a Construction Battalion. It would be a temporary cage, since there were no guard towers. A tank was drawn up at either end of the quadrangle and on either side was a machine-gun emplacement. I drove through an opening in the wall, into the yard before the house. Two weapons carriers and a command car were parked there and two G.I.'s sat in the shade of a half track and were listening to its radio. It was mid-day—time for *Luncheon in Muncheon* over the Armed Forces Network. I cut the jeep motor in time to catch the last strains of a peppy recording of "Ac-cen-tuate the Positive," a song AFN was pushing that week. I remembered it from the *Midnight in Munich* program.

On the wall of the house was a bulletin board and a freshly painted sign in red and white that read Orderly Room. A side door was marked Supply and on it was nailed a poster advertising the week's USO shows. One figure in the shade of the half track was finishing his beer ration. Two empties lay beside him in the dust and he drank from a third olive-drab can. C Battery had set up housekeeping, they would be staying here for a while, and long after the temporary cage emptied its last into the compounds near Frankfort, they would still be drawing PX rations. For this was a green division, an impostor among the veterans that had traveled from Normandy and the Alpes Maritimes, and it would be one of the last divisions to leave. On the sleeves of their Eisenhower jackets most of C Battery, not yet a year from home, would wear but one Hershey bar, and, on their E.T.O. ribbons, at the most two battle stars. If the Army stuck to its point system, C Battery would be around quite a while. I watched them do their waiting, sitting in the field by the gun emplacements, propped against their bedrolls, helmet liners pulled over their eyes to visor the sun. And in that indifferently guarded arena, crouched or sleeping on their field equipment, were some of the sweltering survivors of the Wehrmacht, for whom there were no battle stars, no Hershey bars, no point system. Soon they would be dismembering their uniforms, even the belt buckles that had "Gott Mit Uns" stamped upon them.

"You from Ordnance, Mac?" It was the beer drinker speaking.

I turned slowly to expose my new chevrons, to let the rank pull itself.

"There was a guy last Monday looked a lot like you, came to fix the ice-cream freezer. You from Ordnance, Sarge?"

I shook my head to make plain that I was not from Ordnance.

"I thought maybe you came to fix the generator. It's kaput again. We ain't got electricity for the Frigidaire. Can't run the movie projector. Alles kaput."

"I'm looking for Lieutenant Marsh," I said.

"Lieutenant Marsh?" He looked me up and down. "You better try the Orderly Room."

In the library of the house, the Battery Commander's large desk fronted a high, emptied bookshelf and from the ceiling directly above it hung a grotesque chandelier of cut, colored glass. Two more desks of diminishing sizes, for the First Sergeant and clerk, were off to a side, and sharp to my right as I entered the Battery communications were installed—a single switchboard, unattended. The player organ was built into a section of the wall. A soldier was pumping the foot pedal and operating the hand levers to control the volume as it was indicated to him by the undulating blue lines on the roll that were visible through a glass case. The organist was experimenting with "Lili Marlene." He sang softly to himself a verse of one of the numberless G.I. parodies of that song:

> Fraulein is pregnant?
> Bitte schön?
> Nicht verstehen,
> Auf Wiedersehen . . . Lili Marlene. . . .

Dark muslin curtains covered nearly all of two windows and the room had the pungent odor of a German house that came partly from the thick, porous carpeting in hot weather.

It was lunch hour. The only presence in the Battery's nerve center was the organist. "Das war ein prima Song, nicht wahr?" he said.

"Prima," I said, purposely gruff. I disliked and was embarrassed by pidgin German, though I had used it frequently enough.

"I'm looking for Lieutenant Marsh," I said.

"Bitte?"

"Lieutenant Marsh."

"Oh, der Leutnant?" he said. He was a T/5 and pretty young. He walked over to his desk and patted the In and Out baskets with an air of authority. "What did you want to see the Lieutenant about?"

"He's a friend of mine."

"I didn't know the Lieutenant fraternized with enlisted men," he said.

The clerk was wearing a division patch on the shoulder of his field jacket. It was a division that had gone green into the line in December and had waited, overextended, in what was presumed to be a quiet sector north of Epinal for a week until Von Runstedt let go at its flank. George Marsh had not been with the division then, but his original battalion had been attached to lend it artillery support. They had been overrun and had lost an unconscionable number of men as prisoners and George had stayed on with the new division to make up for the shortage of officers. George had been with this battery, then, since before the Rhine crossings.

"I knew him when he was an enlisted man," I said.

The clerk brushed some dust from his typewriter. "That must have been quite some time ago," he said finally, being very careful.

There was a sound in the doorway. The First Sergeant came in carrying his mess kit, which was still wet from the hot rinse water. The handle was open with the top half of the kit and the knife, fork, spoon, and canteen cup hanging on its handle and clattering as he shook it to dry. He went to his desk without speaking, fished a piece of steel wool out of it, and sat there polishing the bottom of his canteen cup. A sullen, thick-set man, and he looked as though he had tended bar or driven a bus.

"Top?" the clerk said. "Top?"

"Yow?"

"Man asking after Lieutenant Marsh."

The First Sergeant, who had been waiting for this introduction, dropped the mess kit on the desk and turned on me. "That your vee-hicle outside?"

"You mean the jeep?" I said.

275

"What kind of outfit you from?" the First Sergeant asked. "You leave your vee-hicle any place you damn please."

"I was going to look up Lieutenant Marsh," I told him. "I haven't seen him in quite a while."

"He ain't here," the First Sergeant said. "He's on leave."

"In Italy?" I said. "You mean about that Graves Registration business?"

He crossed to the organ bench and sat and pumped one of the pedals, hitting one of the low notes of "Lili Marlene."

"Say, Top," the clerk said.

"Thought I told you not to play this thing," the Top Kick said. "You got the pumper stuck."

"Say, this is a friend of Lieutenant Marsh."

The First Sergeant permitted himself an actual glimmer of interest. "Your name Taylor?" he said.

He strolled over to the big desk of the Battery Commander, which was uncluttered but for a piece of blotting paper and a small leather picture frame. "He'll be sorry to miss you, Taylor."

"Would you tell him to look me up," I said, "if he gets the chance?"

"I don't know about that," the First Sergeant said and slapped the desk. "He's going to be one busy man. Lieutenant Marsh has been put in for Captain."

"Our new B.C., no less," the clerk said. "The orders came through last night. Only twenty-two years old. This is worse than the God-damn Air Corps."

"That'll be enough of that old stuff," the First Sergeant said.

"Captain Marsh," I said. "Well, what do you know?" and I laughed.

The First Sergeant was sitting at the Battery Commander's desk, and when the clerk snickered just then, the First Sergeant's eyes snapped on him in anger. "He's a good officer," the First Sergeant said. "Or maybe you wasn't with us around Christmas?"

"I ain't saying he ain't a good officer," the clerk was saying. Sure, he would be the first man to admit that Lieutenant Marsh earned the Silver Star he'd gotten last December. There had been just two Silver Stars in the Battery, only the other guy hadn't been around to have it pinned on his chest. And then the Frenchmen had already given Lieutenant Marsh some kind of medal. "Too bad there's no point system for officers. That Lieutenant Marsh got himself a real fruit salad, isn't that right?"

"He don't need the fruit salad," the First Sergeant said.

"Only you can't figure him out," the clerk said. "You say it yourself."

"What do I want to figure him out? I'd as leave him run this Battery any time."

"Yeah, but Gaynor that was here. You could talk to that Gaynor. But this guy, you can't tell if he's a Looey or the Goddamn King of England."

"What are you?" the First Sergeant asked him slowly. "The Adjutant General?"

The clerk bent his head and fiddled with his typewriter ribbon and the First Sergeant looked at him contemptuously. "Next time we need a new CO, I'll be sure and get your approval."

The First Sergeant beckoned me over to the desk. He was holding the picture in the red leather frame. The old Mark Cross frame, big as life on the desk of the future Battery Commander.

"You recognize the girl friend?" the First Sergeant asked.

The clerk darted from his chair. "Man! Will you look at that! Eine kleine mädchen. Ein Stuck Schokolade!"

"Sit down," the First Sergeant told him. "You stick to your chocolate bars."

Lila Norris was smiling into the camera in a light summer dress, under the porch awning of her family's home in Far Hills.

"I been a year with the son of a bitch," the First Sergeant said. "I never saw him look at one woman twice."

"He's the faithful type," the clerk said. "Say, has he ever got money, though?"

The First Sergeant put the picture back in position on the corner of the desk, leaned back in the chair, and surveyed it ruminatingly.

"Say?" the clerk was asking me. "Say, did you know that friend of his got hisself knocked off in Italy?"

"The man that was with the Tenth Mountain?" I said.

"Talk about paper work," the clerk said. "Division. Army. Army *Group*. Just to get a lousy seventy-two hours in the Mediterranean Theater. And Graves Registration! Maybe they never heard of a dead man before."

"Maybe you'd be a dead man, if he wasn't with this Battery," the

277

First Sergeant said. "No. He's all right. He's gonna make out." The sergeant was picking his teeth with a broken match. He blew out a splinter that lighted on the desk, and quickly brushed it off with his thick fingers. "He's gonna make an O.K. Battery Commander."

I did not ever see Lieutenant nor, eventually, Captain Marsh. When next we met, all the war, like his six years at Emmanuel, was one glorious achievement against which he could draw for self-congratulation, when life took a turn for the worse, in a world of ruptured ducks, of bright promises, and Fords in our future.

Chapter Twenty

"Don't you honestly think," Ava Norris had just said, "that you're a big enough boy now to call me Ava?"

She fixed her most maternal smile and passed me a Gibson cocktail. There on the bar table was a cut-glass carafe, a bottle of hearts of onion, and a bowl of ice cubes, intransigent and indestructible, like props on a stage set. They've been waiting there all through the war, I thought implausibly, standing sturdy and staunch like Mr. Field's little toy dog, though they aren't covered with dust. Ava Norris believed in keeping the home fires burning at Sutton Place and she believed in keeping everything spick-and-span.

She had been saying that George Marsh and I were her war heroes. Her husband Hadley was not a well man. He had tried, hard, to offer himself to the Navy, the Army, the OSS, the War Production Board, but he simply was not well enough. How glad she was to be welcoming home someone who had actually been in the thick of it.

Her hair was the identical shade of henna that I remembered. It was pressed into waves against her head by an invisible hair net. Her indeterminate age was preserved nicely indeterminate by deft, not immodest applications of make-up. She wore an elaborately casual costume, a sort of fuchsia-colored kimono, you might guess, but it had a skirt, or what seemed to be a skirt until she moved her legs and you saw it was in reality a pair of pajamas.

"Darling," she said. "You're welcome to spend the night. Chee Wee and Liles are here for the weekend."

"Thank you. I wish I could do it," I said, "but I must get back to East Northrup. My uncle's not well."

"I'm so dreadfully sorry to hear that," Ava Norris said, and plopped a heart of onion into her cocktail.

"I don't think it's anything very serious," I said. "I'm afraid it's George's uncle who is the really sick man."

"The poor old duck," Ava Norris said. "We're all getting feeble, us older generation. We take our strength from watching you young grow up. I wish you'd stay and see the girls. Can't you wait and go home tomorrow?"

"I don't think I ought to, but thank you, Ava."

She smiled at me. It was an historic moment, the first I'd called her Ava. "You dog," Ava Norris said. "When you come to New York, why don't you let us know beforehand?"

A maid came in, carrying a tray of canapés.

"You remember Mr. Taylor, Hannah? Mr. Taylor is just back from the wars."

"And Mr. Marsh?" Hannah asked as we shook hands. "I hope he is well."

"He's fine, Hannah. He should be home very soon."

"Mr. Taylor was abroad longer than Mr. Marsh, Hannah," Ava Norris said. "They can't all rush back at once."

"Oh yes'm," said Hannah.

"I'm trying to persuade Mr. Taylor to spend the night," Ava Norris said. "I think we could fit him in to Miss Mathilde's room. You'd best turn down the bed anyway. I think he can be persuaded."

"Oh yes'm," Hannah repeated and swiftly left the room.

"I don't want to dispossess Mathilde," I said.

"Idiot, Mathilde is at Miss Eustis'. Time marches on, Duck. Lila graduates from Bassett Meadows in June."

She was pulling shut the rich, creamish draperies that had passed as blackout curtains in the Norris living room during the war. I could hear outside the lonely whistles of the tugs and barges plying the East River. If I were ever to live in New York, I could like to be by the river where the transience and the loneliness of its sounds would keep reminding me that I did not belong here and that I never would.

"Didn't you hear me, Gus? I said Lila was graduating from Bassett Meadows in June."

"Does she like Bassett?" I asked.

My feeling about Bassett Meadows was no doubt unfair, as it was colored by recollections of the Bassett girls I had known.

Bassett was situated in Connecticut, off the Merritt Parkway, at a point equidistant between New York and New Haven, and I had heard more than one Bassett girl give this as her reason for attending. Others, of a heavier bent, said Bassett was the best women's progressive college in America. Undoubtedly it could have been the most expensive college in America, as it had no endowment.

An elementary purpose of its program was to shock girls into an awareness of the world about them. Yet lumber magnate fathers who could not be bothered to read the college circulars, who were under the impression that Bassett Meadows was a finishing school, found it difficult to gauge the emotional turmoil of a debutante who had suddenly learned the simple lessons of equality. That, say, Daddy's colored chauffeur possessed the same number of white corpuscles and was entitled by the Bill of Rights to the same privileges as Daddy himself, struck more as a thunderbolt than as a homely fact of life. Such truisms, though not upsetting to a chauffeur, and quite possibly not to Daddy, were embraced by an impressionable freshman with evangelistic ardor. Then when the proselyte went home she took on an aloofness and chilly scorn, and condescended to answer her parents' questions with a distinctly smug inner glow, as though, in her Brooks Brothers shirt and blue jeans, she were stout Cortez, silent upon a peak in Darien. Thus it was that Daddy poured more and more money which the Republican National Committee could have used into the Bassett Meadows' experiment, chiefly to finance the psychiatric treatment that was available on the campus. For extremer cases, of course, there were the soundproof, tearproof offices of the very busy psychoanalysts in New York.

"Ava?" I said. "What does she do at Bassett?"

"Medieval Concepts in Twentieth Century Thought. Origins of the Dance. Vision and Abstraction. Oh, I'm sure they work hard. Except Liles spends too much time in New Haven."

"I take it that Harry Tilton is still on deck up there at New Haven?" I said.

"And don't try to be cynical about Harry. His turn will come, Duck. The war's all over and you boys are coming home and Harry will have to leave for sea duty."

"That's not what I meant," I said.

"You mean you don't approve of Lila seeing Harry? Harry is a friend of George's."

"Sure he is, Ava. We're all friends."

"What are you going to make of yourself, darling, now that you've become a man?"

She was smiling at me over a brimming Gibson cocktail.

"Oh, you're ever so manly," she said "There's no doubt about it."

It was not ten years since she had prophesied on the verandah at Gentian Cove. It was only November of 1945, but I had come a long way. But I wasn't consulting any oracles just now. Also, a distressing kind of sexuality was intruding upon us.

"Don't look so uncomfortable, Gus."

"I've got to finish college," I said. "I want to go to Law School."

"That's commendable—following in the footsteps of your Uncle Torbert Case."

"You don't need to put it that way," I said. "I had lunch today with Mr. Seidel."

"Bert Seidel?"

"I came all the way down from East Northrup to see him."

"I'm glad Bert takes an interest in you."

"He was pretty tough. He said George and I would have to get a hump on."

"That sounds like Bert Seidel," Ava Norris said. "I have the greatest respect for Bert. I'd say that was a fine piece of advice, and I hope you act on it. . . . I'll be so very interested to see what you do, and what George does—"

"Yes," I started to say, "George has some plans—"

"And what Liles does and what Chee Wee does. . . ."

Her face brightened, for she wanted to talk about the girls. First it was Chee Wee. That willful waif had spent six years as a sort of adopted daughter of the family, and now Ava Norris had her future well mapped. An alert child, with a flair for fashion, and a touch of what Ava Norris called "style," had a better than average chance in this town. Ava was willing to risk a summer job on the child at *Blythe*, beginning this June.

Would that she had that much confidence in her own child; there was something unsettled about Lila. There seemed no end to her enthusiasms and that was just the trouble. This was a delightful trait in the young, but Lila was going to be twenty-one very soon.

Ava had tried in a thousand ways to guide her daughter. During the summers, she had set her to doing Red Cross work, canteen work, to being a nurse's aide. Lila worked hard, got herself completely exhausted physically, and still she gave no indication of what she was looking for. Right now she wanted to be a model, because her allowance was evidently not enough to pay for all the clothes she wanted. She wasn't hard to look at, Lord knew, and she was thin, and had good bones. Any smart fashion editor would grab for her, and Lila knew it. She could pick up thirty to fifty dollars for a few hours' work, but it was such a purposeless existence for a girl. At Miss Eustis' Lila had been interested in dramatics, and at Bassett Meadows last year she had been in the Theater Workshop's production of *Antigone*. Lila had no serious inclination toward the stage—and her father would have fits if she had—but that was the one even remotely constructive tendency she had. Ava Norris intended to see that she stuck to it. Next winter she would see that Lila settled down and went to classes at the American Academy of Dramatic Art, and damn well liked it.

"I don't know what you're worrying about," I said. "Isn't George planning to take her off your hands?"

Ava Norris set her glass down on the table, angrily.

"Your one trouble," she said, "is your flair for the obvious."

"But it's a known fact," I said. "It's inevitable, Ava."

I answered her so pleasantly, with so little perceivable impertinence that she forgave me, with one of her perfect thirty-second smiles.

"I'd have you know that we're ambitious for our little girl. We're not going to settle for the inevitable. George is a fine boy and a very eligible boy and we love him dearly. But we're not going to bulldoze Lila into anything. We're going to have no calamities in this family. We mean to exhaust all the possibilities, as it were."

We laughed a little stiffly. An honest laugh was not easy with Ava Norris.

"You've got style, Gus. I've always said so. You're going to get along." She leaned forward slightly in her chair. "Let's be completely frank, Duck. Admit you think Liles is attractive."

"I certainly do admit it," I said. "I haven't seen her in a long time."

"Four years," Ava Norris said. "She's improved. She's unsettled,

283

but you should see her. A great deal can happen in four years and she has improved, tremendously."

"George is a lucky boy," I said.

There followed the sound of Ava Norris' titter. She meant it as a relaxing, flirtatious sound, but to me it was like the squeaking of a broken chalk against a blackboard.

"That's right, darling. Be loyal to George. He would be to you."

"That's right," I said.

"Don't look so grim, darling. . . . I don't know why I'm letting my hair down like this with you. You go away to war, a clever but a very confused little boy, and, bingo, you're an adult."

To enter the Norris apartment, one did not ring a bell but an electric chime which emitted soothing tones that I took to be the four opening notes of the "Londonderry Air." They sounded now, twice over, rapidly. I heard the door opening and a commotion in the hallway. There was a man's voice and Chee Wee's affected laughter and presently Lila Norris was talking: "I'm sorry, Hannah. I've lost my keys *again!*"

"Just stay where you are, darling," Ava Norris was telling me. "And try not to look so callow. What do you think we've been waiting for this past hour?"

She was going to the hall, I knew, to warn her daughter that I was there, to tell her to change her dress. But there was no time, Lila had burst through the open door.

"Mummy, could we have ten dollars? We've got to put Harry on the train for New Haven and we thought we'd have supper at Grand Central in the Oyster Bar. Please?"

"You've been gone all day," her mother answered. "I thought you were going to study this weekend."

"Mummy, I am going to study this weekend." A little crease of disappointment formed about Lila's mouth. She advanced toward her mother, passing the sofa; it was exactly like her to be blind to everything but the cause at hand. "But we've got to put Harry on the train," Lila said.

I was on my feet, but Ava Norris was standing there between us, more a referee than a chaperone. "I'd rather you stayed here and helped entertain our guest," she said. "See if you can persuade him to spend the night."

Lila turned her face to me. I saw the play of her features as one emotion rose to supplant the other.

"Hi, Liles."

"Gussy."

I was only faintly aware of Ava Norris' being there at all, smiling at us, maternally.

"You look thin," Lila said. "Gussy, please stay for the weekend."

"I can't. I promised I'd go back to East Northrup."

"I do want to see you. You've got to wait till Monday."

"I can't."

"You've got to, Gussy."

"Well," I said. "All right."

"Now," Ava Norris said. "Aren't you glad Liles was here to beg you?"

I found that I was immobilized and embarrassed. I realized that my shoes weren't shined and were curled at the toes, that there was a spot on my red necktie, and that the jacket which Eddy Shawn had made for me in sophomore year hung in loose folds about my waist and buttocks. My hands were caught inextricably in my trouser pockets.

"He does look dreadful," Ava Norris said, "but he hasn't been readjusted. Tomorrow we'll have to find him some white shirts somewhere."

Lila was laughing. "I wish someone had told me. Oh, Gussy, you're so sloppy. It's wonderful to see you. . . . Chee Wee, Chee, look who's here. Look what the cat dragged in."

Before I could turn my head, Chee Wee Gibbons was upon me and I was in her fond, lipstick-proof embrace.

"The mature veteran," Chee Wee said. "Don't criticize him. He's probably embittered."

"Chee Wee's been reading all the magazines," Lila said.

"That's it." Chee Wee counted up the points on her fingers: "Don't force him to talk about his war experiences. Don't let him feel that he's being coddled. Above all, don't feel sorry for him. Isn't it a riot? The stuff they print?"

My hand fell about Chee Wee's waist and I laughed to oblige her. Bassett Meadows had brought no great visible change to Chee Wee and yet she gave the impression of having become accustomed to herself at last. The plaid slacks and the cashmere sweater in

285

which she was returning from an autumn's day in the country were appropriate to a Bassett girl. And the copious bracelets and the leather fob with the brass sunburst which hung from her belt were distinctly Chee Wee. She wore them with an assurance that had at one time been lacking. But now her pale, plump face and gray-green eyes looked right at you and said: "If you don't like what I am, bat shingles to you. I like what I am." I noticed that a streak of peroxide ran from her temple and over her head, bisecting the black hair. This was something new.

"Gussy," Lila said. "Aren't you going to kiss *me?*"

She was smiling plaintively. As the summer months had passed, and it was autumn, her hair was at its deepest coloring. The low ends that hung about her throat and over the neck of the yellow sweater were an auburn shade. The November air of the country had brightened her cheeks and she wore a short tweed skirt, open at the side and held together, it seemed, entirely by a belt that was studded with foreign coins. The sisterliness that the girls had cherished at Miss Eustis' had been destroyed by their young womanhood. Chee Wee was dark and full-bosomed. She seemed to depend on spangles to offset a Mediterranean suggestion of grossness. Lila was nothing like her, and her face was thin, with a kind of exquisite impertinence, and her eyes at this moment were the craziest blue.

"Honestly, Gussy. Are you just going to let me stand here?"

I stepped toward her, thinking how lithe and compact she was. It was not good for me to stand close, where her perfume, sent off by the moist warmth of her body, evaporated and hung piquantly in the air. Still, I would have kissed her directly under her mother's eye.

"Oh, kiss me once. Oh, kiss me twice. Oh, kiss me once again," a man's voice sang out. "It's been a long, long time."

Harry Tilton had come in, to stand directly behind her, all dressed up in his Navy suit.

"Hi, Harry," I said, and he hurried up to shake my hand.

"Good to see you. Welcome home. Well done."

"How's the boy?" I said.

"Any Purple Hearts, Champ?"

"I got a clasp for my Good Conduct Ribbon," I said. "Good to see you, Harry."

He grinned with those fine white teeth and shook his head like a sport. Mr. Vitalis. How handsome and combed he was, and how faithfully he adhered to Naval regulations. He wore proudly on his chest the American Theater Ribbon and the Victory Ribbon. He was a good sailor and, of course, these were a part of the required uniform.

Chapter Twenty-one

When George Marsh returned to college at the start of the spring term in 1946 and roomed with us, he spoke to Fuzzy Eaton and myself of his intention to settle down. "Times have changed, Sport-o. Things are going to be very, very different from here on in. I can tell you that." George reiterated his conviction in a variety of phrases, all of them containing the recently acquired colloquialism, "I can tell you that." He had a bellyful of the complacencies of the prewar. "I came back to accomplish something. I wasted enough time already. I can tell you that," he would say, that first month back in college. Traces of an old esteem were creeping back. Fuzzy and I began to envision the renascence of the head proctor who had harangued us so splendidly, and, beyond that, a shade of the Captain Marsh who, at the age of twenty-two, had commanded a battery of Field Artillery.

Yet somehow we were skeptical. Fuzzy Eaton was particularly, and something he said stuck in my mind. It was so unlike Fuzzy to think twice about anything, or at least to put the thought into words.

"He's talking like the old Boy Scout again," I remember Fuzzy's saying. "How long do you bet it will last?"

"I hope it lasts," I remember saying.

"I wouldn't lay money on it, Gubber. The Goph is a prince, a prince among men. But I don't know. He has to be football captain or he has to have bars on his shoulders so he can tell a bunch of G.I. dopes not to get clapped up. It's always got to be school or the Army, somewhere where they go by rules. That's what makes a man of him, those damn rules."

"You mean they prop him up?" I must have said. "Like corsets?"

It shall be said for George Marsh that for quite a time he did adhere to his firm resolves. He knowingly enrolled in courses

288

which the generally reliable Crimson Confidential Guide to the undergraduate held to be the most exhausting in the curriculum. He spent five nights a week in the Adams House Library, struggling with his scholastic burden. He received B-plus for a report on Emerson and the Transcendentalists, and, for an ambitious essay on Jean Jacques Rousseau as a precursor of nineteenth-century romanticism, straight A. He began to speak determinedly of going out for Honors.

His extra-curricular activities were as vigorous and as worthy. He returned to Weld Boathouse to practice rowing in the tanks. In early March, he was number three on the Adams House Squash Ladder. Except to buy some shirts and a suit of badly needed dinner clothes, he gave a wide berth to Eddy Shawn. He wanted a new car, but refused to pay the under-the-table surcharge demanded by his Uncle Mark's dealer at Great Neck. To reduce telephone expenses, he was content to communicate with Lila through the mails, and as often he wrote to his uncle, who, like my own uncle, had lately been bedridden. He attended a banquet for the Sons of Emmanuel at the Harvard Club on Commonwealth Avenue and accepted, bashfully, an invitation from Dr. Kew to address the school on his war experiences. He joined the Cambridge chapter of the American Veterans Committee and voiced persuasive arguments on a range of issues from civil rights to universal military training.

When it came time to elect a new slate of officers for the club, George was a logical nominee for president. Indeed, George had already ably demonstrated his qualifications. In the war years the club had been administered by a board of undergraduates who belonged to the Naval Reserve Officer Training Corps. They had had, it is needless to say, no more opportunity to leave Cambridge than Harry Tilton had had to leave New Haven. Hence their derogatory nickname, the Mt. Auburn Street Navy. But this, George Marsh would point out to us patiently, was in no way their fault. The Navy had handpicked them for extensive, valuable training, and they had done their job. Sadly enough, to those who had just returned from far-flung parts, the Mt. Auburn Street Navy, a collection of wan, unremembered faces and midshipmen's uniforms, was not an object of sympathy.

The most antagonistic of the lot was Fuzzy Eaton. The details of his heroism were known only to Fuzzy's intimates and to the Dean's Office, which had been so impressed by the exploits of Lieutenant Walter Baxter Eaton that it had reinstated him as a second-term freshman. But those who were meeting Fuzzy for the first time were understandably skeptical of the tales of his having parachuted from a burning plane and of his extraordinary escape from a prison camp. In four months of civilian life, Fuzzy had fattened to a point where only his mother would have recognized him as the firm-jawed airman in a flying helmet whose picture appeared in the "Alumni at War" section of *Archivi Emmanuelenses*. His hair remained in a close crop and weekend skiing jaunts and alcohol had restored to his face its familiar redness. A great many strangers had written Fuzzy off as a feckless inebriate. A sequence of calamities had brought about his banishment from the Ritz Bar in Boston, and when he took to breaking furniture in the club and mouthing loud insults at the Naval Reservists, a motion was submitted that Fuzzy Eaton be suspended from membership. Disaster was in the offing, threatening to destroy club unity.

It was a time for leadership, and we found our leader in George Marsh. He hastened Fuzzy off to New York for a weekend, and on their return a contrite Fuzzy apologized to each offended member and the motion for his suspension was forthwith withdrawn. The club had not witnessed diplomacy of this caliber since the days before the war when Toby Tappan had wielded the president's gavel. George's name was formally proposed at the annual election of undergraduate officers.

That day, when he was most assured of triumph, there occurred an incident which unraveled the first thread in the scanty fabric of George Marsh's undergraduate career.

It arose from a vote, taken directly before the balloting for officers was to begin, on the appropriation of funds for the purchase of a new war tablet. The old tablet which listed the brothers of the rampant lion who had given their lives in every war since the club's founding occupied the west wall of the billiard room. It was large enough to accommodate the fifteen or twenty names of brothers fallen since 1940, and the erection of the new tablet which George Marsh proposed involved architectural problems quite beyond our means. The proposal was voted down.

George requested recognition from the chair, rose, and reproached the meeting in severe tones. It was unbelievable to George that we could have forgotten so soon. It was a hell of a note to George, that we were willing to squeeze these names onto the bottom of the plaque just to save a few dollars. It seemed a pretty crummy way of showing loyalty. He begged us to think it over for a minute. Think of Mo Beach, of Cuppy Vale. And so we did think it over and the proposal was put again to vote, and was of course defeated. From the rear of the meeting room came a snickering, not unlike the snickering of the K.P.'s in Sergeant Doyle's kitchen.

When George Marsh lost his temper, the effect was of shock, a bolt from the blue. His friends had seen him sulking and sullen when things went against him. He had shown hurt, irritation, defensiveness; but fury—never. The brothers of the rampant lion, on the verge of naming him their leader, listened aghast to his ultimatum:

"You think it's funny? *Funny?* Okay, so screw it. And screw you, every damn one of you!"

They could only clutch their chair arms as he stamped from the room. Many never laid eyes on him again. His appearances in the club house were subsequently very few.

I never knew precisely at what point George Marsh began not to care any more, but one by one I watched him shed his firm resolves. The war tablet episode had been damaging. And, try as he had at rowing, he had failed to make even the Jayvee boat. His courses grew harder and harder; he was disillusioned by his grades. That April he was spending only three nights out of seven in Cambridge.

He returned from one trip to New York with a brand-new Pontiac car which he said he had gotten on a trade-in for the one he'd owned before the war. As spring came on, he took to going down to Eddy Shawn's for fittings on a new wardrobe which Eddy had convinced him was a sensible investment. George failed to appear at two of his Hour Exams, because he was having a fitting at Eddy Shawn's. Some afternoons Eddy turned over the shop for the afternoon to his father-in-law, and he and George hopped in the Pontiac and were off to Suffolk Downs. The weather grew warmer, the grass greener, the breezes balmier, off the Charles. The Red

Sox and the Braves were back in town. George hardly ever went to class.

On a May evening he took Fuzzy and me in to Locke Ober's, fed us drinks and a lobster dinner, cigars and brandy, and told us his decision. College was not for him. He couldn't see waiting around until he was twenty-five, twenty-six years old, just so he could say he was a Harvard graduate. There were more important things in life. Life was beginning at last. He had to hand it to us, to Fuzzy and me, for having the will power to stick it through here. For himself, he had gotten all he would ever get out of college and it was time, he told us rather condescendingly, to get out and face the world.

Right now he was off to Europe for a little trip. It would be his only chance to see Europe properly, for in the fall he was going to find himself a job. Not any old job; one that led somewhere. He'd been doing a lot of thinking about a job that would prove something. And, he was sure it would be no surprise to us if he let us in on the secret that he and Lila were definitely going to be engaged, as soon as they could convince Mrs. Norris that they were serious and as soon as he'd got settled on his job. Oh, and he'd got himself an apartment in New York. On Seventy-first Street. He was moving in Manuelo, who had looked after his old man. Manuelo had been a long time out of work. George would be able to keep him a little while at least, while it was still a bachelor apartment. Fuzzy and I could stay there any time. There would always be an extra sack.

In the morning we helped him load his clothes into the back seat of the Pontiac. He took the top down and made his last Cambridge to New York run in the sunshine, and we inherited his furniture.

If I had thought during that summer that George Marsh had taken leave of his senses, my very first visit convinced me to the contrary. I arrived on a Friday evening in the autumn of 1946, to find him dressing to go out to dinner. He looked extremely well, and his spirits were, if anything, higher than they had been that surprising evening in Locke Ober's.

"Been working hard?" he asked cheerfully.

"Pretty hard," I said.

"That's the boy. When do you finish up?"

"June," I said. "I went to summer school this summer."

"I certainly got to hand it to you. I can tell you that. . . . So, what do you think of the place?"

"Quite a layout," I said.

Chee Wee Gibbons had taken care that the apartment look "masculine." The walls were painted in hardy greens and grays. The carpets, the curtains, the furniture covering blended with white stripes and virile textures into an atmosphere which bore no coincidental resemblance to a feature in a recent issue of *Blythe,* "Keep His Rooms Right for HIM." And Lila had herself chosen the heavy mahoganies and upholstery. George had added importations from the house his father had built on Fishers Island. These were the canes, the silver cups and the trophies, the portrait of Andy Marsh which hung in the dining room. They lent an intensity to the place, an air that was imitative of the main hall at Marshmain, of old Marcus Marsh's house on Fifth Avenue.

Still more symptomatic of the owner's trend of mind were the paraphernalia I found in the small study that adjoined George's bedroom. A small daybed by the window was covered with a Nazi battle flag, its huge swastika enclosed in a circle of white on a flaming red background resting plumb in the center of the bed, without a wrinkle, where Manuelo had carefully tucked it. On a wall at the head of the bed hung the collection: the dress hat to an S.S. officer's uniform, and the elaborate, ivory-handled dagger of an officer in the Kriegsmarine, a Storm Trooper's helmet, two bayonets crossed, and two Luger pistols. Over the desk George had placed a framed cover of *Yank,* the magazine by and for the enlisted men, Strasbourg edition, dated August 19, 1945. It was Howard Brodie's sketch of a weary infantryman with huge bony hands letting go his rifle, and it symbolized the end of the war.

"That's my favorite," George said reverently. "Poor dogface son of a bitch."

"But why? Why all the stuff?"

"Why not?" he said, flaring. "It's my apartment, I guess."

I didn't appreciate then what these memories meant to him. I didn't know that a certain newsreel showed a shot of a soldier yanking the lanyard of a 105 who, George swore, was a man of his who had been killed, and I didn't know that whenever a new war movie came to town, George was one of the first to see it. From *A Walk in the Sun* and *The Capture of San Pietro* he saw them all. He read every war novel, every general's memoirs. In time his friends would have to understand this about George.

Quickly, I inquired about his Uncle Mark.

"He's in pretty bad shape. Arteriosclerosis of the brain," George said.

"I'd like to see him," I said.

"He wouldn't know you, Sport-o. He hardly knows me from Adam, poor old gent."

"You must miss him," I said. "This must be lonely at times."

"I've got Manuelo. Hell, I'm not lonely. Hell, I'm getting married."

"When will that be?"

"Three months. Six months. What does it matter? It's all set and definite. I've got a damn fine job, if I do say so."

Bert Seidel had helped him find the job. He had been at it nearly a month now, in a training program at J. P. Morgan and Co. There was no training like it; it could lead to all sorts of things. He had started as a runner, and spent the first weeks finding his way around the financial district with a brief case. He had seen most of Wall Street; already he had made three trips to the New York Stock Exchange. There was no salary to speak of, but there had never been the problem of salary. He was pleased and Bert Seidel and Lila and, which was most important, Ava Norris was pleased. All that he could ask of security and self-respect. God was in His Heaven.

"Mix yourself a drink, Sport-o. And come in here and talk."

I sat on his bed while he finished dressing and he whistled snatches from a tune called "Spring Will Be a Little Late This Year." He was preparing to celebrate his first month of gainful employment by taking Lila to dinner, then to see *Call Me Mister*. His shoulders looked broad and powerful, not prodigious or obtrusive, beneath the midnight blue of the dinner jacket that Eddy Shawn's head tailor had cut for him. He was erect and clean-shaven. There was a fine conviction in his deep brown eyes and in the set of his chin. He had nothing Hollywood about him, nor the hair-tonic flashiness of Harry Tilton. And tonight he was the confident, never-to-be-denied male, and you believed in him.

"And how's Fuzzy making out?" he said casually.

"About the same."

"Tell him I miss him. Tell him to stay sober." George smiled the accepted, automatic smile provoked by the mere mention of Fuzzy's name.

"How's everything at old Cambridge?" he said. "Just as screwed up as ever?"

"That depends," I answered. "I try to keep my nose to the grindstone."

"I like the feeling that I'm going somewhere," he said. "And it's about time I was." They expected him to work at night in the training program. He had to be on call for whatever department was shorthanded. All the last week he had worked until after ten o'clock.

"They really keep you at it," I said.

"I eat it up." He was straightening his tie before the mirror, fixing it into the neat bow that Lila required.

"I have to hand it to you, Sport-o. You're really going to graduate this June?"

"I really am."

I was annoyed to find myself half laughing at him. He had never understood that it was no labor of Hercules to get your work done. Work was a fierce challenge to him, requiring every last gram of enthusiasm, because he had done so little.

"Seidel hopes you'll go to Columbia Law," George said. "Bert has his eye on you. I can tell you that."

"Don't think I don't appreciate it," I said.

"I slip in the good word for you all the time," he said. "You're going great guns. I really have to hand it to you."

"I'm a mature veteran," I said.

"Don't you have the feeling that we're on our way at last? That we're all going somewhere?"

"We're all mature veterans," I said.

"You think I'm crazy but you watch us. You just watch our dust."

He was so delirious and so cocksure. You wouldn't believe that, before spring came round again, George Marsh and the House of Morgan would have reached a parting of the ways.

295

Chapter Twenty-two

My Uncle Torbert Case had trouble with his heart. Aunt Connie said it was a condition brought on by the strain of the war. I would never dream, Aunt Connie said, what he had gone through while I was away, how touching and severe his worry had been. He had had his first attack in 1945 while I was in Germany—she hadn't the heart to mention it in her letters. In February, 1947, on St. Valentine's Day, he had his second. I left Cambridge for East Northrup instantly, telling Fuzzy Eaton that there was no way of knowing how long I might be gone. When Aunt Connie met me at the Trailways bus depot in Northrup Center that evening she tried to tell me that I should go immediately back to Cambridge and get on with my work. When she said this and I saw her, standing on a mound of snow by the old Chrysler with her overshoes on and the squirrel muff that had belonged to her bride's trousseau, I thought certainly she was mad. I could not imagine anyone so old and innocent living alone in a cold house with a demanding invalid. I announced that I would stay on in the house. "No!" she said; during the First War she had taken a nursing course, and there were doctors and a good hospital in Worcester. I saw that she meant every word of it, by the serene look of her face and her smiling. It was as if she had been waiting for this time when there would no longer be a limit to what she could do for my uncle. There was no longer the flimsy pretense of his pride to prevent her from doing absolutely everything.

How she bore him, I would never know. He interrupted her, contradicted her advice, scolded when she misplaced her glasses, and swore torrentially if the soup was cold. Aunt Connie had a bevy of excuses for his behavior. "Dearie, there are things that you've never known about your uncle. He's been under strain for years, only of course he would never show it." She did delight in her burden, all the more for her determination that he would get well. Uncle Torbert was determined that he would not. Out of his illness he manufactured a last redoubt for his ego. It was essential to the equilibrium of their lives that he be in some way dominant, and it did not matter now if no one took him seriously, so long as Aunt Connie would only pretend to. This she did faithfully.

"Kiss me, fellow," he said one afternoon that spring as I was leaving the house. "The doctor has come and gone, but I have never had respect for doctors. I doubt that you will see me after this. So do make it brief. I've never enjoyed the prolonged farewell." This was the most patent hypocrisy but he mustered so much conviction into it that I actually kissed that hoary forehead, below the part of his yellowing hair. When I came home the next weekend, I found him sitting on the porch, and he wanted to know if he had ever shown me his article on Otto Kreuger.

Uncle Torbert's great pleasure, as he was convalescing from his second attack, was to reminisce. Aunt Connie said the most helpful thing I could do would be to keep him company, and so I did during the warm summer afternoons. I heard how Uncle Torbert had sat in his sister's lap at B. F. Keith's family vaudeville in Boston and had watched Sarah Bernhardt do the last act of *Phèdre*. I learned that a building called Beck Hall had stood near Bow Street and that it was the first Harvard dormitory with respectable plumbing, and that Uncle Torbert had lived there at considerable expense to his father. I was offered cigars from a cannister that Professor Kittredge had used. ("Ah, there were giants on the earth in those days, fellow.") I heard dissertations on the rewards of poverty and erudition, on humility as the true source of pride. I might have been a boy again in shorts and sneakers, listening as in the old days on that porch in summer, wondering what Ned Sellers was up to, yawning when his head was turned.

At times Aunt Connie could not bear to listen to him. She could not bear to hear him talk about his will. I was usually alone on the porch when he made those extravagant statements:

"Fellow, I want you to know that I've made arrangements for you and your aunt to be looked after. You will both be comfortable, and your aunt shall have all she so well deserves."

Uncle Torbert was reclining in the front yard one August afternoon when he observed that a strand of the Dutchman's pipe had slipped its trellis on the porch. He called for a stepladder and some twine, and I brought them, for the doctor permitted mild physical activity as an aid to his morale. He was on the top step, tying the first knot, and there his heart beat its last. He gasped and fell with a curious lightness to the grass before I could reach him.

The estate he had alluded to so often was revealed to consist of six hundred dollars, a portrait of his grandfather, some candlesticks and a pair of candle snuffers, a silk fire screen that had belonged to his mother, some fishing tackle, and the gold watch and chain he had always promised me. Aunt Connie and I agreed that the money should be put toward something in his memory. That winter she took the matter up with Mr. Jennings of the Legatees' Trust, and as a result of those meetings, my uncle's fortune, supplemented by a donation of Aunt Connie's, makes possible the Torbert Case Memorial Prize for Expository Prose, which is presented each Awards Day at Emmanuel.

On the evening of the day we buried Uncle Torbert, when the last guest had left the house, Aunt Connie took out her handkerchief and asked if I wouldn't sit with her for a few minutes in the living room.

"Dearie, it was the loveliest funeral. It went just as he would have liked it. I felt all the time that he was directing it himself."

"It was a fine funeral," I told her. "Everyone said what a wonderful job you did."

Everyone had said so. The cousins and the maiden aunt from Albany and Uncle John Case whom we hadn't seen in fourteen years, the Kews and the faculty couples who had interrupted their summer holiday to come to the ceremony, and the villagers. Bishop Wash had read the service in the Academy chapel, specially opened for the day, and he had ridden behind the casket to the cemetery.

There had been but one embarrassing hitch, for which the American Legion Post was responsible, but Aunt Connie had surely not noticed it. The Legionnaires had planned to march with the casket and fire a salute with rifles at the grave, but at the last moment the Post Commander recalled that Uncle Torbert, who had driven an ambulance for the American Field Service in the First War, was not technically a veteran, and therefore not entitled to the regular formalities of the Post. Fortunately Dr. Kew, a friend of the Post Commander, took the liberty of paying him a personal call. Thus, while the Legionnaires made no formal observance, they did appear en masse in blue suits and caps and carnations to attend the service at the Academy chapel. Uncle John and Uncle Torbert's surviving law partners were honorary pallbearers, and the Massachusetts Historical Society sent a spray of roses. Mr. Eaves, who had taught me to play the piano, played a Bach Fugue on the organ. The Academy ensign flew at half mast. Mr. Wendel Sellers, not to be accused of carrying old antipathies beyond the grave, came with his wife to the graveyard and stood through the interment service, hat in hand, shifting from one foot to the other. Ned Sellers, with the Worcester girl he had married after he had got his job with the telephone company, stood just behind his father. Afterward, for anyone who cared to drop by Elm Street, there had been a chicken salad, fruit punch, sauterne, and devil's food cake.

"I was proud of you," Aunt Connie said. "I know Uncle Torbert would have been proud."

She was sniffling, tucking and untucking the handkerchief in and out of the sleeve of her dress.

"Aunt," I said, "why don't we drive out to Albany for a week or so? You've wanted to go up there for years."

"Dearie, who could drive me? I don't like to drive any more and you have to move to New York."

"I think I'll stay here this winter, Aunt."

"And what about law school?"

"There are all sorts of law schools near Boston."

"There's really only Harvard Law School and you say your marks weren't high enough for that. I wish you'd tried harder when you first went to college."

"It was the war, Aunt. Nobody tried."

"I hope it will be all right in New York, when you stay with the Marsh boy."

"I told you, Aunt. I'm going to stay here with you."

"No." Her eyes became dry and stern just then.

"It's lonely here. You can't stay all by yourself."

"And why can't I? I can take care of a house. I'm sixty-four years old."

I thought of the four-poster bed upstairs where she had been

299

the last four nights. When I passed down the hall on my way to my bedroom, for the first time in my life I had missed the monstrous snoring.

"You don't understand," she was saying. "This is my house."

She had taken her handkerchief out of her sleeve. The banjo clock over the mantel ticked nearly a minute before she spoke again, her voice small and dry.

"What is the name of that college?"

"Columbia," I said.

"I'm trying to remember what your uncle said—Columbia is a fine law school, provided you don't want to work for a Boston firm. I know I can't say these things the way your uncle could. I wish your uncle had had time to tell you—about principle."

"He did, Aunt. He told me all the time."

"What does Mr. Marsh do, dearie?"

"He's ill, Aunt. He's a very old gentleman."

"I don't mean Marcus Marsh."

"George?" I said. "He's looking for a job. He's getting married very soon."

"I keep thinking about the Marsh boy," my aunt said, wearily. "I wonder if there weren't some things that Uncle Torbert might have forgotten to tell you. Promise me that you'll always behave with people, if they don't have the principles he had, just the way he would want you to."

"I promise," I said, and once again I leaned over and kissed her forehead gently.

Chapter Twenty-three

Sooner or later, everyone heard what had gone wrong at the House of Morgan. George Marsh was only too glad to discuss it if asked, but he was seldom asked.

So, bristling with good intentions, Chee Wee Gibbons took up the explanation for him and gave it that much broader circulation. George had failed, if you wanted to call it that, because he had been ambitious. It wasn't that George hadn't liked the firm, but he hadn't liked those eager, diploma-waving kids he worked with. They hadn't seemed to care if they stayed in the training program forever, and they weren't as mature as George. If George cared to stay around for about five years, they might begin to take notice of him at Morgan. It was all right for some boys to sit around and wait for the breaks. George believed in making his own breaks, and that, Chee Wee told the world, was the reason he had quit.

One person who did not subscribe to this view was Ava Norris. The day she heard the news, she telephoned Bert Seidel to ask if there wasn't some way of persuading George to stick through the training program, at least. George's attitude about finding another job seemed to her, frankly, rather cavalier. Bert Seidel courteously heard Ava Norris out, and then he explained to her that he was not the boy's father and he was in no position to dictate to George. Ava Norris, accustomed to settling things quickly over the telephone, hung up on him fast.

George did not have much fun that summer, which he spent making a careful check of the smaller firms. He stayed at his uncle's house at Great Neck, as it was so hot in New York, and yet at least two times a week he commuted into the city to keep the interview appointments Bert Seidel had set up for him.

I moved into the apartment on Seventy-first Street on the first of September, in time to find that the Norrises had invited George and me to Far Hills for the Labor Day weekend. I noticed, even then, how George was doing his best to avoid Ava Norris, and he did so quite successfully until the last day.

We spent that Monday afternoon by the swimming pool. Hadley and Ava Norris were seated at a white umbrella table, playing gin rummy. The table, like all Ava Norris' lawn furniture, was burnished and sun-bleached to an antiseptic chalky finish that somehow never came off on your clothes. The umbrella, like the beach chairs, was striped and lent the lawn a gay, Parisian note. Ava Norris' pajamas were bright and cool. The pool and the greenery surrounding resembled a Hollywood set, but for the balding Hadley Norris who, with his tight duck pants and goldenrod allergy, didn't seem to belong there at all. The suntan equipment—the towels, sun reflectors, lotion bottles—were strewn by the diving board, where Chee Wee Gibbons had usurped Lila's patch of grass and was draining from the fading rays of summer as though she would never see a sun again. Mathilde Norris lay beside her sister's friend, relishing the last of her long vacation.

George Marsh and Lila emerged from the pool. They were drying themselves in the sun while George read to her from the list of potential employers that Bert Seidel's secretary had listed for him in a small loose-leaf notebook. Lila stretched beside him, allowing her wet hair to fall over the grass. Perhaps she was thinking of how beautifully they had swum together. They had been perfecting a tandem crawl in which she locked her legs about his waist, and, propelled by his kicking, they swept the pool from end to end, quite conscious of the precision of their brown arms striking the smooth blue water.

"Now there's a real little firm," George Marsh was telling her. "All young fellows, and they know where they're going. I'm going to hit them up on Wednesday."

Lila said, "What a priceless name. Tuck, Fiddle, and Pinch. You've got to work for them."

Hadley Norris was at that interlude between games when his wife shuffled the deck and marked up the score. "What was his name?" he called to George.

"Tuck, Fiddler, and Pinchley," George said. "Howard Pinchley. It's down here on my list."

"That Howard Pinchley's son?"

"All right, Hadley," Ava Norris said. "Here's your chance."

"All right, Mother," Hadley Norris said and picked up his hand.

"Manship and Boggs," George read on.

"It won't do," Lila said. "Boggs—ugh."

"Bache and Company."

"If that's Jerry Boggs," Hadley Norris called, "I'd advise you to stay away from him."

George continued reading the names.

"How about Merrill Lynch?" Hadley Norris said.

"Merrill Lynch, Pierce, Fenner and Bean. I've got it right here on top of the page."

"You haven't drawn," Ava Norris said to her husband. "Do you want to play cards or don't you?"

"Sweetie, why don't you pick the firm with the longest string of names?" Lila said.

She assumed a sitting posture, undid the halter of her bathing suit, and rolled over on her stomach so the sun would strike her back.

"You tie that up again," her mother said. "You're not at Bassett Meadows."

Lila rolled on her side, presenting her back to George. He reached for the dangling ends of the halter and tied them.

Ava Norris laid down her hand and glared across the pool. "Chee Wee! Mathilde! You too. You know the pool regulations."

Chee Wee got to her knees and sheepishly did up the back of her bathing suit. Mathilde followed suit though she did so defiantly. At sixteen years of age, Mathilde was endeavoring to make of herself a carbon copy of her sister, but her hair was too dark and she was too thin. Sorely aware of this, she was the more sensitive for catching blame for transgressions that were Lila's.

"They want an even tan. That's all it was, Ava." George Marsh was smiling and conciliatory.

"If you don't mind, I'll continue to discipline my children," Ava Norris said.

"I'm sorry, Ava."

"Your turn, Mother," Hadley Norris said quickly. "Pay attention now, before I walk off with the grocery money."

Ava Norris fingered through her hand. It fairly crackled as she chose her discards. Lila shrugged. George winked at her, and went back to the little notebook. All was quiet until George found a particularly amusing name and Lila giggled.

Ava Norris threw down her cards. "Why don't you forget it?" she said to George. "Can't you find something else to amuse yourself with?"

"I don't know what you mean, Ava. I'm sorry if we disturbed your game."

"Don't apologize. You're always sorry."

Lila sat up suddenly. "Mummy!"

For an instant Hadley Norris' and George's eyes met desperately, and, having shared some sad wisdom, parted. Their heads turned slowly away.

"George, why don't you stop pretending?" Ava Norris stood up and stepped toward him. "You don't want a job. You'd do us all a great favor by saying so."

George stood up bravely and said, "That's not fair, Ava. You don't want me to take just any job?"

"Mercy no," Ava Norris said. "Your Uncle Mark can buy you a seat on the Stock Exchange."

"Mummy," her daughter cried. "I won't let you talk to him that way. It's cruel and it isn't true at all."

"Isn't it?"

"Mummy!"

Lila's temper flared and died, like a summer storm. It ended in an effusive reconciliation, and admissions of guilt from George, and romantic promises for the future. Ava Norris seemed appeased, and reaffirmed her fondness for George by allowing him to kiss her cheek.

Lila ran over the grass, her hair waving crazily, and flung herself upon her mother. "I'm sorry, Mummy. I was so upset."

"It's all right," Ava Norris said, "now, now." But a moment later she had pushed Lila away. "You're sopping, Duck. You've put a damp spot on my pajamas."

The sun was setting behind the oak trees on the driveway, and it was chilly by the pool. If the girls expected cocktails in the house, they would have to change their dresses. Ava Norris recommended one last dip and we all complied but George. I thought it curious that he did not, but when I climbed out of the water I saw two figures retreating upward over the green curve of the terrace and toward the house. Hadley Norris' hand lay on George's shoulder.

And by the end of the month George Marsh had a job in the securities analysis department of Norris, Brion, and Heath. Even though he was in semiretirement, Hadley Norris prided himself on carrying his weight as a partner. Hadley Norris believed that as long as it remained a family business, a little nepotism was all to the good.

Ava Norris demanded that the engagement period be extended at least six months. Beyond that, she spoke no more about the future. George and Lila agreed readily enough. It would be better to wait until George was fully broken in at Norris, Brion.

In general, it was a placid winter. George went at his new work with gratifying vigor. Right up until Christmas he rose when the alarm rang at seven-thirty, and he walked across the hall to rout me out of my bed. Manuelo's breakfasts were hearty and nutritious, and served under Andy Marsh's portrait at eight o'clock sharp. We would meet again in the evening and have a drink before supper. Often he would go out then, to dine with his Uncle Mark or with the Norrises, or to take Lila to the theater or to a prize fight. This would leave me the apartment to study in. I did a lot of studying that winter, while George Marsh was in the securities analysis department. "I've got to hand it to you," George told me constantly. "Keep up the good work, Sport-o, you'll be a Supreme Court Justice one of these days."

It was not all work, however. As I grew accustomed to the apartment, I began to take its luxuries for granted. George had the baby grand piano moved in from the house at Fishers Island. I took up practicing again. "Footsteps on the Ceiling," "We're Just a Kiss Apart." "There's an Awful Lot of Coffee in Brazil." Soon I was playing whenever George threw a party, and Manuelo served drinks from a tablecloth spread over the mahogany surface of the piano. I would leave my shoes in the kitchen for Manuelo to shine before breakfast. Manuelo cooked my meals, made my bed, and sent my suits to the cleaners every Monday. All of this seemed natural and right at the time, but I felt foolish when the first of the month came round and I wrote out my skimpy check to George Marsh. It was as if he knew better than I what I could afford. I had three years of law school to accomplish. Between the G.I. Bill and the Legatees' Trust, it was a question of which would hold out the longer. When I saw my uncashed checks piling up month after month on George Marsh's bureau, I told myself not to make an issue, that he would be insulted. But at the same time I cursed him silently; it was the simplest way of foisting off some of my self-resentment.

After Christmas George was promoted from the securities analysis department and given a five-dollar raise. The extent of George Marsh's promotion was to remove him from the direct supervision of an office chief and to place him under the absentee control of Hadley Norris. He became, in effect, Hadley Norris' lieutenant. George was installed in an office of his own with a third line connected directly with the apartment at Sutton Place. George was seldom beyond his mentor's reach. While it had its privileges, the new position carried its share of special responsibilities. As Hadley Norris did not visit the office more than twice in any week, he required a form of communication with his partners. Now and then George had lunch with Hadley Norris at the Squash and Quoit, where Mr. Norris was Chairman of the Special Events Committee. George admitted that it was quite a change from the securities analysis department, but he stressed the responsibility involved. For one thing, he had to carry a lot of information about in his head. And he was constantly nervous lest the Old Man order more than the customary two cocktails before lunch.

Now I began to see less of George, who no longer went to work before ten in the morning. The atmosphere of the apartment no longer invited concentration. So I spent most evenings with my law books in Kent Hall on 116th Street. I didn't wish to seem unappreciative, though, when I came home at night. I would help serve the drinks on Manuelo's night off. Whenever I could I did my part, and sometimes when I was tired and doing my damnedest to play requests on the piano, or explaining to people why it was wiser not to remark on the war souvenirs they found hanging in the study, an old disillusionment would return. I would go to my bed and lie there in anger, unable to sleep for the noise. It would take a long while, lying there very still in the dark.

I remembered the faces. The young marrieds. The beaux Chee Wee brought in. Ted Botts, whom she had met at a fashion show.

306

Gabriel Paster, who wrote the gossip notes for *Blythe*. Harry Tilton's girls—and Doris Slater whom he brought only on quiet evenings and who was the only one who came from Hartford or anywhere like Hartford. The Cable Stitch Sweater Set from Greenwich. The Jet Set from Southampton. The undergraduate entourage that Fuzzy Eaton imported from Cambridge for George to evaluate as club material. The coddled, embattled little phalanx of beauties, twenty-five years and under, who gave stern counsel that marriage was a serious business, and who should have known how serious, because they were, every one, in the process of divorce.

I remembered the conversations. What a racket the New Look was. Henry Wallace, and Thomas E. Dewey, and the inevitable Republican landslide. J. Parnell Thomas and the Hollywood Reds. The marriages, always of parties not with us that week, that were headed straight for the rocks. Who was indubitably sleeping with whom. The Collyer brothers. *The Naked and the Dead.* Moscow Mules. And the great gag: "Crying on the outside, laughing on the inside."

Through it all I did the best I knew. I made an effort over the girls whom no one else appeared to notice. Pretending not to notice how Harry Tilton had cornered Lila on the arm of an easy chair, I would listen to Harry's new girl, Doris Slater, tell about her receptionist's job at the advertising agency and how she had met Harry there, and what a fascinating life we all were leading in New York.

Lila Norris was apt to be with us at any time of the day. She might walk in on me of a Sunday morning while I was shaving, or burst into my bedroom while I was still asleep, but we were seeing less of Chee. She had begun a gradual breaking away from Lila, though this was not the result of a disaffection between the girls. It came from Chee Wee's regenerating desire for more. Chee Wee had been pulling down ninety dollars a week at *Blythe* by the time she left, with Ava Norris' blessing, to do free-lance fashion photography. Thanks to a small loan from her father and to assiduous budgeting, she had acquired a modest stock of equipment at bargain prices, and had enough to spare to redecorate her apartment in the Fifties east of Third Avenue. And Chee Wee rented a studio in the same building with Telemachus. Telemachus was

307

the man in the field and if he thought that much of Chee Wee, that proved she was getting somewhere.

Though we looked on him as the focal point of all our activities, George Marsh complained every so often that he was lonely. He missed the family ties. He saw little of Bert Seidel since he'd got the job at Norris, Brion, and it was depressing to sit alone with his old Uncle Mark, who could no longer finish a sentence without being prompted. And George saw little of his silver-haired mother. He had hoped Baby would finally give up the idea of marriage, and yet she had married again, this time to a rootin'-tootin' Princeton grad named Ellison. Zip Ellison. Zip worked in one of the small, live-wire agencies, and George said he was everything the name implied. Zip had been at the apartment just twice with Baby, in a double-breasted chalk-striped suit. He was a runty bow-tie type, and he made remarks about Coach Caldwell and the Princeton team, and remarks about the unsuccessful Harvard teams that got really boring. And each time, as he was leaving the apartment, Zip had cased all the pictures and furniture and asked, in a loud voice, if any of them didn't belong to Baby. Personally, George had no use for anyone like that. Still, Baby said she loved him and that she was happy. George didn't mind, but it did leave him lonely once in a while.

It must have been the aspect of George Marsh pining amid the glories of the spring that softened the heart of Ava Norris. For at last she consented that the engagement be announced. The notice appeared beneath a photograph of Lila's face in the *Times* and the *Herald Tribune* society sections and in the afternoon papers as well. A small cocktail party was given by the Norrises, with a few old friends and Baby and Zip Ellison in attendance. It was understood that it would be a long engagement, but the step had been taken. It did much to ease the loneliness, but George needed something more.

One morning, he surprised me by showing up for breakfast, fully dressed and smiling.

"Sport-o, I wanted to ask you first. Harry Tilton wants to move in with us."

"Whatever you say," I answered. "This is your apartment."

"It will cut expenses, having one other guy."

"Yeah," I said.

"He works hard at the agency, damn hard. Assistant to an account executive. You'd like Harry, if you gave him half the chance. Harry's a not half-bad guy. I can tell you that."

George Marsh had an extra bed sent up from the storage warehouse and Harry Tilton became my roommate. He asked considerately if I would mind sharing my closet with him. He had too much stuff to fit in one closet and he noticed that I didn't have as much stuff. I told him I didn't mind in the least. Harry said I could feel free to borrow any of his neckties any time. We always kept on cordial terms.

Life picked up at Seventy-first Street after Harry moved in, and I found myself spending Saturdays in the New York Public Library. Almost two years later, looking back on this interlude, George Marsh would call it the best time he'd ever had. Yet George had been the one to call an end to it.

The end came without warning, at the dinner table on an evening early in June. George had left work early to spend that afternoon with Lila; so she knew before we did. She said not a word during dinner. She sat and picked at her food and looked back and forth from Harry Tilton's face to mine, furtively, as though our reactions might yet save the day.

George Marsh began at his cheerful best. "Laddies, I've got news for you. I'm shoving off. I'm going to try my luck in Texas."

As one, Harry and I laid down our forks and stared. We were waiting for him to draw the carpet out from under us, but instead he said: "You guys are going to stay right here. I'm counting on you to keep the home fires burning." He laughed and looked around for us to laugh.

I said, "Old Man Norris is going to be tickled pink to hear that."

"If you want to know the truth, he couldn't have taken it better. He understood completely. And he's going to write some letters for me. He knows someone on the board of the Texas Company. . . . I'll tell you what the trouble was—"

The trouble was, George had not been satisfied. He'd had a deal at Norris, Brion and he appreciated that he had. The trouble was, he'd had all kinds of guilt feelings about being the boss's lackey. They had been nice to him in the office, but he was always imagining what they said behind his back. No, he had to go where he could make his own way and Texas was just the place for that. Nobody played favorites in Texas. He knew a few guys who had gone there fresh out of college to work on the oil rigs. They all had terrific jobs by now and a couple were drilling on their own. George was going to be entirely on his own; it was an idea that had been on his mind for a long time.

Harry Tilton was the first to offer his opinion. He did so with a fine measure of sincerity. "That took some gumption, boy."

"This pushes the wedding up a bit," I said.

I looked at Lila. I was puzzled to see that she was not listening, she was lost in an intricate design on the tablecloth. "Gussy," she said. "Stop *looking* at me!"

"Just as soon as I get settled and get a job," George was saying, "I'm going to look around for a house. Soon as I find a house, I'm flying right back here and I'm going to get married. You wouldn't think Lila Norris would wind up in Midland, Texas—but she's going to."

We three smiled and went on looking at Lila.

"How about Ava?" I asked. "She's going to have a hemorrhage."

"You see," George said, "you see, we aren't going to tell Ava right away. The Old Man is going to say the office has transferred me temporarily."

"Temporarily to what?" I asked.

"To a survey—of conditions. Some kind of survey. How should I know what?"

"I was just asking," I said.

After dinner we had some drinks to celebrate. Lila sat quietly in an armchair. She had taken nothing to drink, not so much as her usual crème de menthe.

"George," she said, "I don't see why you keep this apartment. It won't be doing you any good in Texas."

"I want some sort of home to come back to. Where do you want me to go for vacations?"

"*Vacations?*"

"Sweetie, what do you want me to do over Christmas and New Year's?"

"I thought you were going to work in Texas," Lila said. "George, stop *looking* at me!"

"How do you like that?" George asked us, with a brief laugh.

310

"Put a sparkler on their finger, and they've got a ring in your nose. Ask them to marry you and, brother, you've had it."

Lila examined the highly visible diamonds set in her engagement ring. She was polishing the stones, rubbing them across the folds of her skirt.

"Sweetie," George said. "I was only kidding. I'm sorry if it was a dumb joke."

"Will you stop saying you're sorry?" Lila said. "You're sorry about everything lately."

"I was apologizing—"

"Please! Don't keep apologizing."

George studied her a moment, then turned his attention back to Harry and me, and tried to take up where he had left off. "I don't suppose you guys will be around this summer. We'll have to close the apartment up for three months."

"I'll be here this summer," I said. "I have to go to summer school."

"Again?" George said. "In all the heat? Gee, Sport-o, I've got to hand it to you."

"It'll be hot in Texas."

"I forgot about that," he said, and laughed.

"How hot *is* it in Texas?" Lila asked.

George went to her chair and patted her on the head. Her little explosions never failed to delight him.

"I'm going to put her in your hands," he said, addressing Harry Tilton and myself. "You can look out for Liles. It's one favor you can do for me."

Chapter Twenty-four

On the fifth of July George Marsh headed bravely westward in a new Buick. We were not to lay eyes on him for a good long time.

Perhaps thirty-six hours later the telephone rang at Seventy-first Street, and Harry Tilton ran for it.

"It's for you, Lover," he said.

"If it's Chee Wee," I said, "I'm studying."

"It's Liles. She's all alone and lonely."

"Why don't you do something about it, Champ?"

"I tell you how it is," Harry said. "I'd like to give the kid a break, but how? I've got young Doris to worry about, and I'm carrying a heavy schedule this summer. It's a crime."

"What does she want?" I said.

"Why don't you find out?"

There was a rather widely taken impression that I became irate when my studying was interrupted. Lila sounded tense and contrite over the phone.

"Gussy? I know you're revoltingly busy but you look pale. You'd better come out to Far Hills this weekend and sit in the sun. It will be very proper. Pappy's not there and Chee Wee is bringing out someone for Mummy to look over. He does something with marionettes."

"Listen, Liles, do you think it's a good idea?"

"I don't want to talk about marionettes all weekend. I'd rather talk to you. Gussy, don't make a face. You can bring out your books and study your head off for all I care."

I did not do an impressive amount of studying in all the month of July, and I was spending too much money. The model agency had cautioned Lila to stay thin. She said she was terribly busy all day and tired at night; she generally had fruit juice and a cream

312

cheese and chopped olive sandwich for supper. Since we both had time on our hands at the end of the day, we agreed to spend a cheap evening together now and then. Our plan was to do them Dutch. Yet Lila seldom retained more than a dollar's change in her purse at the end of the day. (Lila cashed a ten-dollar check every morning, but what with lunch and cab fare and cigarettes and magazines, "it was a marvel" she had anything left by evening.) As a guarantee of economy the first several evenings, I picked her up after supper. Even so, our frugal intentions were swept aside. We went to a Broadway movie, and to a night club to hear a boy monologist who had studied at dramatic school with Lila, and to Palisades Park and back in a taxicab. Lila kept promising that the next time she would make it up to me.

She eventually did so by inviting me to her new apartment on a hot night. It was much pleasanter to stay there with all but one window closed against the heat of the street, and to sit in the breeze of the floor-based air circulator she had snitched from Sutton Place. Lila had bought some peanuts, some limes, some tonic water, and some Dixie Belle gin, and it was to be her party.

She had a bedroom, a bath and a sitting room on Madison Avenue—much nicer than living with the family, she said. Lila had not begun to decorate the place; in its present state, there was not much in the apartment but two lamps, a wicker chair, a flat, armless chair, and a pine-wood magazine table that she had bought at Finland House. No curtains, no rugs, no victrola, but Lila swore that we would be comfortable. It was cool with the air circulator, probably the coolest spot in town.

By about eleven we had done an amount of talking about George Marsh and the Texas Company, and we had several gin and tonics inside us. I found among her magazines a copy of an old term report from Bassett Meadows and in a spirit of facetiousness and whimsy I began to read aloud from it. Lila sat beside me on the sofa, weak with laughter. She protested occasionally by attempting to snatch the paper from my hands.

I teased her and she was tremendously amused; the spherical tears tumbled from her cheeks. She was wearing a lavender linen dress that was bare about the shoulders, and she had removed her earrings.

"Don't they give grades at Bassett? I mean letter grades?"

313

"Gussy! Not at a progressive school. Those are comments from my teachers. You give that back to me."

"What's this? Who is M.G.H.?"

"That's Michael Hoenig. He taught me Vision and Abstraction. And he happens to be quite a well-known poet, but that wouldn't mean anything to you."

"Vision and Abstraction—" I fended her off with my arm. "Let me read—"

"Give it back!"

Defeated, she fell limply inside my arm, and her head lay on my shoulder.

"'Now that Lila's health picture has improved,'" I read, "'we are confident that she will make more significant contributions to class discussions. It is a pity that Lila was unable to attend all her classes during the first part of the course when we were analyzing root influences of modern poetry.'—I didn't know you'd had a bad health picture, old girl."

"Daddy wanted me to go south with him. So I got sick. Flu or something. Virus X."

Lila was like a compact package beside me, trembling with laughter. "You think you're pretty funny. Give it back to me."

"'Unfortunately, Lila seems reluctant to volunteer her observations. When directly called upon, however, her ideas are well expressed, direct, and illuminating. Her last two papers reflect a sound grasp of the dynamics of the verse form, as well as an unusual imaginative stimulus.'"

Lila had at last succeeded in clutching the paper, tearing a corner off it. "Funny man," she said.

"I'm impressed, Liles. I should think you'd be proud."

"You charlatan. You're just sneering at something you don't understand. You think you're pretty funny—well, I have news for you."

I turned my head to answer her but, when I saw her face on my shoulder, no word came. Then a lifting of her head, and either she was giving me her mouth or she was taking mine. Our bodies and our arms moved, a little clumsily at first. I pushed her away.

"Gussy," I heard her whisper. "Oh, God, Gussy."

"That's all. That's absolutely all," I said. "Don't worry about it."

"Gussy, I'm not worried. I never dared think it but I must have wanted this so long. I want you to kiss me again, now."

"That's all, Liles. That's all there's going to be."

"I'm not ashamed." She was half talking. "I want you to. I know you want to. So you may as well kiss me again, Gussy."

Next morning, Harry Tilton and I received postcards from George Marsh. He had decided to settle in Midland, Texas, and prospects for a job looked pretty swell.

Chapter Twenty-five

In the Indian summer of that September our troubles began.
For a while we would meet in the Weylin Bar in the evenings:
"I guess we've one of those things on our hands."
"I guess so," I would answer her.
"It didn't take much time, did it?"
"Once it started, it didn't take a minute."
"Gussy, why couldn't it have happened before? Think of all the
trouble we'd have saved ourselves."
About here she would smile at me.
"I used to laugh at you smiling. I used to say you thought you
could get away with anything. You thought you could move moun-
tains, just by wrinkling your nose like that."
"I don't want to get away with anything," Lila would say.
She would take my hand carefully, under the table, and clasp
it to her.
"It could have happened so long ago if we hadn't been afraid.
If you hadn't been so strange. How long ago was it you talked
with Mummy on the porch?"
"Eight years. Almost nine years."
"Then we went swimming and you wouldn't kiss me. Darling,
why couldn't we have done something about it then?"
"I wish I knew what we were going to do about it now."
"Gussy, do you think we're going to roast in hell?"
"I don't know."
"I don't care, and I'm so happy I'll do whatever you say. You're
the man. I look up to you."
"We're going to be calm about it. You can't ever tell, it may
blow over."
"Do you really think so? I'm sorry to disappoint you, darling,
but I'm not calm at all."

While it was going on, I never stopped to think how quickly we consummated our treachery. Yet, lest we both forget the consequences, I did hold on to a sort of objectivity against Lila's efforts to romanticize. I would tell her that we had no excuses and that we would not look for any. I would try to make her see the black and white of things, that we did not belong in a storybook, that however innocent our feelings might be, our actions were deliberate. Lila nodded that she understood and she stared at me soberly when I tried to tell her this. There was always the danger of tiring her with words and of losing her attention. When this happened, she became kittenish and teasing. "Oh, let's be dramatic!" she would cry with glee, and she would kiss my mouth to stop my answering back.

While it was going on, I never considered how Lila had captivated me. Her helplessness and energy worked like power magnets. The more I teased her, the harder she drew me. Like George, I longed to protect her. She let me believe that I alone in the world was responsible for her and that she was incontestably mine.

No one had played so tellingly upon my vanity.

"I love you when you're looking well. I wish you'd buy a seersucker suit."

"They wrinkle, Liles."

"Darling, nylon seersucker, like George and Harry have. You'd be divine in one of those suits with narrow, steel blue stripes."

Then we were in Brooks Brothers before I could catch my breath and I was opening a charge account, using George Marsh's name as a reference.

"We're the best-looking couple on Madison Avenue," Lila said. "Do you know I was crossing the street this morning? And this truck driver just yelled at me, 'I could move mountains for you, Baby.' Just yelled it out. I could have kissed him."

I was not suspicious of her beauty, since it was but an extension of myself. Her vanity became my own. I took an egoistic pride in Lila. I was happy when she kissed my cheek impulsively in the street or when she placed her arm about my waist, under my coat, when we were walking. On the great occasions when we could afford the restaurants where she and George had gone, I enjoyed the obsequiousness of the waiters and captains who scurried to pull her chair.

I admired her awareness of herself, her dread of seeming mousy, her demand that heads turn when she entered the room. Herein lay her utter assurance. I admired the exhibitionism which enabled her to walk radiantly naked about her apartment. I rejoiced that this was my creature, my very own.

I had not known sexual jealousy before. A toy dog rested on the pillow of her bed. She tried to hide it when I came. I soon noticed that it had a significance about which she was sensitive. It was a black poodle with a bell and a red ribbon about its neck. At first, she evaded my questions, and so I pressed her. When she was at Miss Eustis', the dog had been a birthday present from George Marsh.

"It's my silly old dog, darling. I've had it for years. George always wanted to see him and so I kept him on my bed. You know how easy it is to hurt George's feelings. I can put him away, if you insist."

"Then George was here too? You didn't tell me that."

"Yes, he was here once or twice, but he never stayed with me."

"He stayed with you in your family's apartment?"

"You're wildly jealous, aren't you?"

"Did he?"

"You know George. You know he wanted me to be pure for him, Gussy."

"What about you? Did you want to be pure? You may as well tell me the truth, Liles. You weren't any virgin when you came to me."

"Darling, George never even asked to stay with me."

"I wish you'd tell me the truth."

"Don't be unreasonable, darling. There's nothing I can do about the past."

"You can throw out that damn bed toy."

"Oh, I love you when you're surly. Let's fight!" As usual she kissed me. With some pride, I watched her putting the dog in the closet.

"It is dumb, darling. To behave like that. It is dumb, when you say I still must wear my engagement ring."

"You'll wear it until you see George."

"Then can't I keep my dog until I see him?"

"No!"

318

"I love you, Gussy. You make no sense at all."

I knew she must be lying to me, though I couldn't tell how. I had no illusions about her chastity, and yet she had given her word of honor about George Marsh and I believed her. It might seem preposterous to a stranger that a man could have been in love with a girl like Lila Norris for twelve years, could be engaged to marry her, and still ask her to remain pure. Yet it made sense to anyone who knew George Marsh.

And Lila was quite right. She could do nothing about the past. It would help, she said, if I allowed her to speak freely about herself and George. It was nothing to feel ashamed of; she refused to be made to feel guilty. So I encouraged her, masochistically, since her talk ticked off an unjustifiable, inner fury against them both. I was convinced in my jealousy that I would find further outrage. On this impulse I questioned her about Harry Tilton:

"That was in the war. Harry was the only boy around. It wasn't anything, Gussy."

"Not anything? He never tried?"

"Of course he tried."

"You were pretty young, Liles."

"Darling, you don't have to believe it but it's true. I don't care what Harry says. You're right about him. He's a real stinker."

"So Harry didn't have any conscience either? He was at New Haven and George was lying on his back in a field hospital."

"Gussy, you don't know what a dreadful boy he can be. I feel sorry for Doris Slater."

"Conscience. I don't know who the hell I am to talk about conscience."

"I've told you, darling. I've told you and told you. This is different. You love me. I love you. We can't help that."

Our greatest labor was security. Harry Tilton was the obvious threat. When the summer was over, he had stopped commuting from his mother's house in Connecticut and had moved back into the apartment permanently. Because of her habit of exchanging cheery nothings with Manuelo, I forbade Lila to visit Seventy-first Street alone. For old times' sake, ostensibly, she would come with Chee Wee now and then. Or if, on a Saturday night, Harry Tilton had a girl to dinner I might telephone her casually, always at the last minute, in case she had nothing else to do. When Hadley

319

Norris turned over four World's Series tickets to Lila, we invited Harry to share them. He brought Doris Slater along and kept up a running commentary on the fine points of baseball, and soothed the pangs of her Hartford conscience, for she had skipped off from the office to be with Harry. I was careful to keep up with my work, as Harry would have noticed the first slackening. Week nights I rarely returned to the apartment until after he had gone to bed. I took drastic precautions with lipstick and perfume traces and undressed silently in the study behind a closed door.

I was quite confident about Harry, and yet there had been a night in early December when he spoke to me as I entered the dark bedroom.

"Where've you been?" I heard him say. "What you been up to, hot pants?"

"I thought you were asleep," I said.

He switched on the lamp, reached for his cigarettes on the bed table, and lit one.

"I'm an insomniac. Haven't you heard?"

"O.K.," I said. "Starting tomorrow night I won't bother to tiptoe."

"Where are you going tomorrow night?"

"I'll give you the whole schedule of my day," I said. "I'll tack it up in the can where you can see it in case you're worried about me."

I got into bed and closed my eyes. Harry switched off the light and continued smoking in the dark. "Make hay while the sun shines," I heard him say distinctly, and then he pretended to laugh quietly to himself.

I stayed awake a long while and tried to plan what I would say to him. There was that one sure way of calling his bluff, if I had to.

At breakfast, though, Harry was quiet. He was reading George's copy of the *Daily News* and had reached Danton Walker's column. I waited. The only remark he made was that I ought to borrow his sunlamp. Staying out all hours was making me look fairly seedy, Harry said.

Of course, no secret was ever kept from Chee Wee Gibbons. Chee Wee had known immediately and she had been waiting for this to happen. In the beginning, Chee Wee was almost shy with me, but when Lila brought me to her apartment, Chee Wee lost her inhibitions. The occasion was a Pyramid Club party.

Chee Wee was not unnerved, though I was, by the macabre influx gathered there to present Chee Wee with their dollars and to taste the claret punch which she had prepared. Chee Wee was, in her own words, having a high old time. She was gay and confiding, she was meeting some extraordinary new people that I would want to look at, if I had any curiosity at all. There was a television director, and a girl who collected amusing news breaks for the "How's That Again? Department" of *The New Yorker*, and even two elevator men from the Graybar Building. Chee Wee had netted two hundred and sixty-three dollars so far, which would more than pay for the improvements she had planned for her studio. And I must meet Telemachus, the photographer, her idol. Telemachus was in her pyramid.

"That's very nice," I said.

"Don't high-hat me, Gus Taylor. I know all about you—I knew it was going to happen, and I'm all on your side. Did you ever see the movie, *Meyerling?*"

"This is no movie," I said. "I wish you girls would get that out of your heads."

"But I know it isn't, Gussy, but wouldn't it be nice if it were? What are you going to do?"

"We'll do the right thing, whatever it is."

"I mean *you*, Gussy. What are you going to do? Have you told George? He's coming back for Christmas."

"Lila is going to tell him," I answered. "When the time is ripe."

"She's going to write him a letter?"

"She won't know her own mind until she sees George. I want her to see him when he comes back for Christmas."

"And you want her to tell him then?"

"If she's absolutely sure of herself," I said. "I want her to tell him then."

"I'm warning you, Gussy. She'll never be able to. Lila couldn't bear to hurt George. She loves him, but she's not *in* love with him—don't make that face, Gussy. She does *love* him. She adores him."

"Kindly soft-pedal the clichés," I said.

"I wish you'd listen to me, Gussy. It isn't going to work. You can't expect Liles to do a thing like that."

321

"Baby doll," I said, "why don't you let me worry about it, Baby Doll?"

"This isn't funny," Chee Wee said. "Don't try to make it funny. Don't you have any more plan than that?"

"I'm damn well going to move out of George's apartment in a hurry," I said.

"That isn't enough, Gussy. Gussy, you won't prove anything if you move out without telling him the reason why. You've got to have some plan."

"Please let me worry about it," I said. "When George comes back for Christmas, we'll settle the whole thing."

Then George Marsh wrote to Lila that things were beginning to open up in Texas, and he didn't think it was a good idea to come home for Christmas, so why couldn't she visit him down there? Lila answered him rather curtly that she was tied up herself, with dramatics school, and couldn't afford the plane fare besides. Thereafter Lila permanently altered the tone of her correspondence; you would have thought that George would begin to smell a rat. Yet his own letters, and Lila was showing me every one, became frantically apologetic, repetitious, overexplanatory. He wasn't quite settled yet, but he would be soon, as soon as he'd found the right spot. According to one letter, he and a friend of his were thinking of doing a little speculating. According to the next letter, he and an entirely different friend were thinking of switching from oil to natural gas. He wasn't quite set yet, and he knew he was keeping her waiting a long time, but he knew Lila would agree with him that it wasn't right to get married until he was set, absolutely.

When I wrote George that I was leaving the apartment and asked him how much money I owed, I hoped he would suspect something, and that it would bring him back to New York. But I succeeded only in dismaying him: "Honest to God," he wrote, "I don't know what's eating you. You don't owe me a nickel. If you want to be a loner, I'm not stopping you. But I think you're nuts.—Don't you think there's such a thing as carrying this independent routine too far?"

Ava Norris, who was uncommonly anxious to please, found me an apartment I could afford, a railroad flat at the foot of East End Avenue. My lease began the second of January, 1949.

My last term at law school would begin in September, but there

322

was no summer school in 1949. So I became a volunteer worker for the Legal Aid Society. Each day in the main office at Park Place, I learned about hardship cases, desertion cases, evictions, bankruptcy. It was not always a cheering job but it was experience, and Bert Seidel, who had suggested that I take it, said there was nothing like experience. My consolation was that I didn't work at night.

Lila and I might meet for dinner in one of the cheap restaurants on the far west side that she had discovered for me to take her to. We would ride home on the Fiftieth Street crosstown bus, which was an adventure for Lila. I was sure, seeing her laughing and tossing the reddish, sun-bleached mass of hair among the tired and perspiring faces, that she was the most beautiful girl in New York, and my feelings of vanity returned.

We played a game. We were to pick a car, the best and very handsomest car on Fiftieth Street, the one we would like best to be our own. We required ourselves to choose before the bus crossed Seventh Avenue, and to remain faithful to our choice all the way across to Madison, where we left the bus. If, after Seventh Avenue, either of us saw a car he liked better, he was honor bound to admit it and a point was scored against him. Lila loved this game because she lost consistently. She might pick five or six cars before we reached Madison. There was always a shinier, a handsomer car.

Lila was good about laughing and keeping our spirits up. Although, more and more often this summer, I was finding it hard to be cheerful.

Lila would remonstrate.

"You're worse than George! I honestly don't think *he* would carry on the way you do, about something we neither of us can help."

"We can do something any time we want. One way or the other we're going to do it, Liles. Or call the whole thing quits."

"Maybe you can, Gussy. . . . I can't."

"What have you been telling him in your letters?"

"I've told him I can't bear the thought of living in Texas. That's a beginning, at least."

"That's nothing he doesn't know already, poor sap."

"We'll work something out, darling. Don't be dramatic. Don't tell me we're living a lie."

"I'm having a hell of a time, Liles."

323

"Darling, I really believe you're more worried about George than you are about us. I'd like to know why. . . . I know what you think of George."

"What do I think of him?"

"Well, that he's dear, and you'd cut off your right arm for him—but I know you're disappointed. I know you don't like him the way you used to. It's got something to do with respect."

"Did I tell you that?"

"You don't have to tell me . . . and I know you probably want to shoot yourself. That's crazy too. I wanted *you,* don't forget. It's just as much my fault. It's probably all my fault because I'm a girl. Always blame the girl— You darling Gussy, I can always make you laugh."

Thus we made our way evasively, through labyrinths of uncertainty for almost another year. And we were still hard at it in November, hard at it, and having gotten nowhere, right to the day Lila called my apartment at seven in the morning.

"Can you come over for breakfast?"

"I have a class at nine o'clock."

"Can I come up there and talk while you get dressed?"

"No," I said. "I'd never get dressed."

"Darling, I promise I wouldn't bother you if it wasn't the most terrible thing in the world."

"Can you hold on till lunch?"

"Yes, Gussy."

"I'll meet you at the Sandwich Shop," I said. "Have you got that written down? It's on Broadway and 115th, on the west side, by the subway. I'll try to save you a seat, but you be there by five minutes past twelve."

"Can we talk?"

"A little."

"Do you love me, Gussy?"

"Yes," I said. "I love you."

The Sandwich Shop, the lunchroom with curving counters and high, revolving stools. By a quarter past twelve it was jammed with Columbia boys and Barnard girls and law students who went there for a fast meal between classes. Lots of them people George and Lila might have known. Having just come from the classroom, their faces shone and they wore nondescript raincoats, and there lay the danger. You couldn't tell who might be hanging over your shoulder, reaching for a menu, while you talked.

Lila arrived, wearing a red wool coat and a pair of white bunny mittens, looking very young and frightened, like a girl who had just run away from Miss Eustis'. When she saw me, she tried to smile. I tried to raise my hand confidently and beckon her to the seat I had been saving.

"Gussy, it's been so dreadful. I didn't have enough for the taxi. I owed him twenty cents."

"It's all right. Everything's going to be all right."

I pushed my plate toward her, with a half of a grilled cheese sandwich.

"I couldn't eat a bite."

"That's all right."

"George is coming back tonight and he wants me to meet him at the airport. I only got the telegram this morning." Lila avoided my eyes and she spoke directly to the lunch counter, forcing the words so that they tumbled out two or three at a time in tight bursts. "Darling, what are we going to do?"

"The airport?" I said vaguely.

"La Guardia Field. . . . Darling, aren't you frightened too?"

"It could be much worse," I said. "I thought you were having quintuplets."

This gave us, at least, the chance to smile.

"If I only were, I'd know what to do about a baby. I'd tell Mummy and I wouldn't be ashamed at all. . . . He's all through with Texas and he wants to come back and settle down. He wants us to get married right away. It's not just a visit, Gussy. George is coming home for good."

"That's fine," I said quickly, not to show a moment's hesitation. "You meet him at the airport."

"Yes," she said, very quietly and dubiously.

"This is your show, Liles. If you don't think you can do it, I'll talk to George myself."

"Let me. It's got to be me."

"Try to keep your voice down," I said softly. "Don't say anything and listen to me."

Lila was to meet him at La Guardia. She was to meet him and spend as much time with him as she needed. She could call me on the telephone, but she was not to see me until everything was settled. She should take her time and she should tell the truth to George as soon as she had the opportunity. This was the last and only chance, and when it was over, Lila should call me up and I would go to George Marsh.

"Gussy, what will I tell Pappy?"

"Try to keep your voice down," I said. "There are only about five hundred people looking at us."

"It will kill my Pappy."

"It won't," I said. "I promise you."

"Can't I even see you once, Gussy? Can't I even come to the apartment?"

"I told you, not until it's all over with."

"Say you love me, Gussy. Tell me it's going to be all right."

I hailed a cab at 113th Street and gave her a dollar to cover her fare and put her in the cab and waved her off.

A week, two weeks afterward—I forced myself not to count the days—my telephone woke me at night.

"Sport-o, where have you been holing up? I've been trying to get you all day. I've got news, real big news."

"Hello, George."

"Why the formality?"

"I guess I'm sleepy," I said.

"Are you browned off over something?"

"Why should I be browned off?"

"No reason. . . . Lila didn't want me to call you. I don't see why."

"Where's Lila now?"

"She was tired. I just took her home. I wish I could figure her out . . . but, hell, she had to wait so long and this has been a rough week. Lots of plans, lots of details. Why don't you call a guy up sometime?"

"I'm in the middle of exams," I said. "I was going to get in touch with you when they were out of the way."

"Will they be out of the way by February fourteenth? You set to be an usher in my wedding?"

"The fourteenth," I said. "Things happen fast."

"It's been two years. I don't call that fast—what in hell is eating

326

you, Sport-o? There's going to be a big bachelor dinner, many drinks."

"Is this definite?" I said.

"The invitations are going out next week. How definite can you get?"

Lila's voice was faint and distant in my receiver; and it was harsh, like an antique gramophone. "I can't talk now. I don't want to see anyone now."

"You're going to see me. You're going to see me tomorrow," I said.

"Oh, darling. Why weren't you there? Why didn't you help me?"

Chee Wee Gibbons had seen Lila through it all. She had not engineered anything; Chee Wee had simply stood by, as any friend would, and tried to make it as easy as possible for Lila to make up her own mind. Now Lila had made up her mind, and was wrung dry by the decision and Chee Wee did not intend to let me go on being cruel.

Nor was it my intention to be cruel. I doubted that it was as abominable of me as Chee Wee implied, to insist on seeing Lila. The rendezvous took place in Chee Wee's apartment, for that seemed the discreetest spot, and it lasted, almost to the minute, one and one quarter hours of fruitless talk. "I don't know what's right," Lila said in that scratchy, tired voice, "or what's wrong. But he was so definite and he needs me in ways you never did. I'm going to marry him, Gussy. Please don't make it any harder than it is. I feel dead." When we were about half done, Chee Wee mixed us high, dark drinks, the last of her Christmas bourbon, and considerately retired behind the bamboo screen to the pullman kitchenette.

At the end I was sitting, my head in my hands, on the red leather pouf in the center of Chee Wee's one room, and I had given up. Lila was on the studio couch, her legs tucked behind her. Her face was strained and pale, and during our long pauses she gnawed the polish on her fingernails. The molasses of ultimate despair had claimed us, had oozed even in back of the bamboo screen where Chee Wee bustled about, rattling a week's unwashed breakfast dishes.

"We passed Seventh Avenue a long way back, and we've reached Madison," I said, "and it's time to get off the bus."

"Don't be cryptic," Lila said. "Or are you trying to make me laugh? We always could laugh, Gussy."

"And you've changed your mind three times about your favorite car. We should have remembered that game."

"I don't blame you if you want to be horrid," Lila said.

Chee Wee emerged from the kitchenette, protective, sisterly, aggressive.

"You'd better go, Gussy. It's cruel to drag this on."

"Does Lila want me to go?"

"You're not the only one who's suffered. You don't know how this has been for Liles."

"Last year you told me you were all on my side," I said.

"You know what I told you last year, Gussy. Can't you see, she couldn't have done anything else? You were no help to her. You left her all alone to be with George. It's just as much your fault."

"Thanks," I said. "Thanks for the kind words."

"Yes, it was your fault. You didn't want to be the one to hurt George. You wanted Liles to do it for you. . . . Well, you can't have your lollipop *and* your ice cream, Gussy. You can't go on being a little boy forever."

"Coming from you," I said, "that's an extraordinary statement."

"I know it hurts dreadfully, Gussy. You'll have to admit, though, it was a damn foolish and romantic thing, and it was completely unrealistic. You don't realize what it did to Liles. A girl has to have some security. She can't live on daydreams forever, Gussy."

"Darling!" Lila cried. "I can't bear it! Can't you cry? Can't you ever cry?"

"I could try it," I said, "if you think it would help. I'm perfectly willing to try."

"I've cried and cried," Lila said. "I don't think there's another tear in me."

"Oh, can't you leave her alone, Gussy," Chee Wee said.

"I'll always love you, Gussy. You don't stop loving someone."

"You've got to go now," Chee Wee said. "You really have."

I stood up, buttoning my collar and straightening my necktie. I remembered to thank Chee Wee for the bourbon. "It will be much better this way," Chee Wee said. "I don't care who it is, a person

328

must go through life doing what is right for them. This is right for Liles and it's the only way she'll ever be happy."

Her eyes were a vitreous blue green and firm, as they generally became when Chee Wee had done expressing a Great Truth.

My overcoat was on the studio couch beside Lila. As I reached for it, she held my arm.

"When will we see you?" she said. "It's ridiculous that we can't be friends."

"There's no reason why you shouldn't be friends," Chee Wee said. Chee Wee was standing by the door, holding it open for me.

"Listen to me, Liles," I said. "Tell George I'll look him up over the weekend. I have some things to talk to him about."

Lila squeezed my arm very hard. "Gussy, there's nothing to tell! Gussy, you gave me your word of honor!"

"You want to be a good wife, don't you?"

"Gussy, there are some things that I can't tell him, and you know it. Do you want me to hurt him too?"

"O.K.," I said. "If that's how you want it, Liles."

Lila helped me into my coat and walked after me two or three steps to the hall. "You're going to be in the wedding, aren't you?"

"Sure," I said. "What could be cozier?"

"Don't be foolish, Gus," Chee Wee said indignantly. "George would never forgive you if you weren't in his wedding. You've got to be willing to pretend. You're a friend of George's, and if you ask me, you're getting off pretty easy."

"You mean he has enough to forgive me for as it is?"

"I didn't say that," Chee Wee said. "Good-by, Gussy."

Lila joined her at the head of the stairs as I went down.

"Good-by, Gussy! Good-by!"

Because I thought her voice sounded plaintive, I looked back up the stairwell. She and Chee Wee were clasping each other's waists and were waving down at me. They were wishing me well, no hard feelings, and no harm done. I might have been leaving for a week's vacation in Bermuda. So it was I learned, once and for all, that one's private passions are not necessarily interesting to others.

Chapter Twenty-six

Swain, Seidel, and Lawler was not an old firm, or a large one. It had occupied its offices on the seventeenth floor of a building on Pine Street only since 1935. The partnership had been formed as recently as the first year of Bert Seidel's marriage to Baby Marsh, a year when a seedling in the forest of corporation law had had to battle for survival. The Driv-Urself car in which Bert had driven Baby to visit her son at Emmanuel Academy had been indicative of the hand-to-mouth existence of the firm. In 1950, however, Bert Seidel could well afford any automobile he liked. Though this is not to say that he was a grasping or immodest man.

Since the decline of old Mr. Marsh, Bert Seidel's had been the only true adult concern given George. Guided by the orthodox moralities of his upbringing, Bert Seidel was opposed to divorce. He had, however, been unhappily exposed to it by Baby Marsh, both professionally, when as a younger man in search of clients he had been retained for the action against Andy, and personally, when Baby had instituted her own action against him. Yet there was a humaneness about Bert, and he had continued as a sympathetic administrator of Baby's lot even after the divorce. And he had proven a genuine fondness for George. Nor is this to call him a sentimentalist.

In the law he had enjoyed a distinguished, though not phenomenal, career. As a youth he had started at the District Attorney's office of the city of Newark. From there he had begun his rise. He had been in and out of the service of the city, state, and federal governments. He had been appointed to commissions by Fiorello La Guardia and Al Smith and his name lent prestige to reports of fact-finding committees emanating from Washington. In the war, his name had cropped up in news stories as having visited the overseas theaters as a "consultant." In the more competitive sphere of private law, Bert Seidel had the reputation of having put the Messrs. Swain and Lawler on the map. Bert Seidel was not above arguing a case in court, no matter how unpleasant the details, if he believed a just principle was involved. Though the firm preferred to avoid the stigma of divorce cases, and handled only those few that came up in the families of long-standing clients, Bert Seidel could be prevailed upon to manage these. As Ava Norris said, he was a good man to know. I was lucky, for, as a young lawyer knows, the firm that will take him on fresh out of school is not easy to come by.

I was mightily conscious of all this, as I stood before his desk, and waited to shake his hand. I waited like a schoolboy hopeful of parental approval, and not quite sure that he deserves it. Bert Seidel rose, flicking ash from his sleeve, buttoning the bottom button of his double-breasted coat; a big, cigar-smoking man with a solid handshake. He moved deliberately but meticulously, and he addressed the young in the gruff, benevolent manner of some beloved football coach.

"Sit down, Gus. Let's thrash this thing out."

He motioned me to a black chair, from a hole in the arm of which were bursting horsehairs and cotton. This was an immense, bare room, and it was not to be judged by appearances, not by the yellowing walls or the high ceiling of stained and peeling plaster. The air was stale from the steady incineration of Havana tobaccos. Pigeons roosted on the heavy stone ledges of the two windows which might never have been opened, and on the far wall hung a framed lithograph of an august gentleman with a beard whom I took to be Charles Evans Hughes. Bert Seidel had been thrashing things out in this big office for fifteen years and he had not had time to refurbish it. By contrast, the reception room, where Mrs. O'Mara tended the switchboard behind an enclosure of clouded glass, resembled the lobby of a smart hotel, and it revealed to the visitor no insight to the toil and austerity that had paid for those furnishings, that paid Mrs. O'Mara's salary, and that would, I desperately hoped, pay mine.

"In words of a syllable, please—what makes you want a job?"

"I've finished college and I've finished law school, sir, and I have to have a job. That's all."

The evanescence of a smile played about Bert Seidel's lips and

331

eyes. Whether that was sarcasm or enjoyment, I could not guess.

"Tell me about law school," Bert Seidel said. "Did you work hard up there?"

"I tried to," I said. "But I can't pretend I made the Law Review."

"And you haven't taken the Bar exams."

"I expect to take them in the spring."

"And now you want a job. George told you you could hit us up any time."

"That's not true."

"This is an employment agency for Emmanuel boys. Is that what you're thinking?"

He was begining to smile, but only beginning. I wasn't sure.

"I'm not going to give you a lot of talk, Mr. Seidel. You told me to look you up when I was ready to go to work."

"You seem unhappy," Bert Seidel said, amused. "Did I say there was no job?"

He shoved his chair away from the desk and spun it in a neat quarter circle and checked himself with his wrist. "I'm being rough with you, Gus. I don't know what you've been thinking. This isn't the Piping Rock Club. This isn't Emmanuel Academy."

"I realize it isn't," I said.

"If you're going to work for me, you remember that. You know, when George fanned out at Harvard I got him started in the training program at J. P. Morgan and Co.? They weren't going to make him a vice-president right away, but it was a nice job. And George fanned out of that one. Then he got himself taken on by Lila's father, and then he went to Texas to make himself an oil baron. And he fanned out of that—you see what I'm getting at?"

"It's pretty clear," I said.

"You live in that apartment. You're one of the crowd."

I felt myself blushing, smarting under his stare. "We'd better get something straight, sir. I'm not one of the crowd. I haven't seen the inside of that apartment for a year."

Bert Seidel had picked up a letter opener and was tapping it restlessly against the butt of his hand, listening, weighing my words quite placidly.

"So!" he said suddenly. "You finally climbed off the merry-go-round."

He left his chair and walked to one of the windows and gazed down the seventeen floors to Pine Street.

"You finally climbed off the merry-go-round," he repeated, as his thoughts coalesced. "I didn't think you had it in you."

He swung about on his heels, and began to pace the end of the room. "You and I don't belong there, and that's God's truth. I remember the day we took that drive in East Northrup and you showed me your house. I knew all about you, Gus, right then. When I was married to George's mother, I was a fish out of water, just like you. All I had to do was take one look at you when you were a kid, going to school with George Marsh." Bert Seidel hesitated, apparently censoring his thoughts. Slowly, and, it seemed to me, wearily, he moved back to his desk and sat. "It's none of my business what you do. I'm only telling you that if you want to work here, you're going to shake loose and get acquainted with the world. You stay away from the bright lights and the pretty music, Gus. If you expect to last down here with us."

He reached beneath the desk. A buzzer sounded in the outer office, and his secretary came promptly to the door, with pencils and a shorthand pad.

"Get me Mr. Stacy." He cracked his fingers, trying to remember the name. "The skinny fellah who works in the bull pen. Never goes out to lunch."

"Mr. Macy, sir?"

"Macy. I never can remember the name."

He was quiet a moment after the girl had gone.

"I just want to thank you for giving me a chance," I said.

"That's all that it is. We'll keep you busy for three months and then we'll see what you've made of your chance. If you get in trouble, don't come running to me."

"I understand that," I said.

"Did George tell you I'm going to be his best man?" he asked me quietly. "I'd like to know what you think about this wedding?"

"If you don't mind, I'd rather not answer that, Mr. Seidel."

He reached into a drawer and extracted a cigar. He was handling it thoughtfully when our conversation ended.

"You wanted to see me, Mr. Seidel?"

A figure stood in the doorway, in an uncomfortable, rigid pose. A pair of steel-rimmed glasses and a pen and pencil set jutted from the pocket of his salt-and-pepper suit. He was pale and he squinted. I was reminded of a molting bird, and a little of Uriah Heep.

"I'm Macy, sir." The voice was low and somewhat petulant.

"I'm sorry, Macy," Bert Seidel said. "I can't ever seem to get names to stick."

"Just think of the department store, sir. 'Does Macy's tell Gimbel's?'"

"Oh, very good. I'll have to remember that. . . . Now, Macy, we have a new lamb in the fold."

Macy and I walked down the corridor, through the reception room, past the partners' offices, past Mrs. O'Mara and the switchboard, past the library, the files, the typing pool and into the hall-like room that was known as the "bull pen." There were no windows, but a fluorescent lamp hung from the ceiling over two desks which faced each other.

"There's only this telephone," Macy said. "I can put it on your desk, if you think you'll be using it. The last guy that had your desk used it too much. That was one of his troubles. The phone is supposed to be for business only and Mrs. O'Mara is a caution on the switchboard."

On my desk were an inkwell, a pencil sharpener, and a flexible reading lamp with a tarnished brass stem. I sat down and blew the dust off my desk.

"You can put your galoshes and stuff in this corner," Macy said, "and you might use the black coat hangers. That way we won't be getting them mixed up."

I tried the desk drawers and found them stuck on one side.

"A guy who sat there went off with the key," Macy said.

"Have there been so many guys?" I asked.

"There can be quite a turnover. You wait till spring. They'll be in after your job and mine when the schools graduate."

"Is that so?" I said. "Then we're pretty lucky."

"Mind if I ask how old you are?"

"Twenty-seven," I said.

"Married?"

"No. Are you married?"

He was not. You hardly got married on forty-two hundred a year, and a third of that was going to his mother and sisters in Pennsylvania. It was a depressing thing to say but he was thirty-one years old and his career had been interrupted by the war. People in the office found it hard to believe that Macy had been in the Engineers, but he had, in the Combat Engineers.

There was a conspicuous worthiness about Macy, an aura of industry, all unrewarded, that he appeared to exude from his pores.

"Don't let me discourage you," Macy said. He gave me a tolerant, not entirely trusting look. "When I came here I was eager too."

Macy donned his steel-rimmed glasses and lost himself in a volume that lay open on his desk, but when I burst a drawer open with a loud rattling of its contents, he glared at me peevishly. Then and thus the pattern was fixed. The burden of proof was squarely upon me. To prove my word to Bert Seidel. To prove to Macy that I had not, no more than he, come to the bull pen a sinecured dilettante. Monday morning at half-past eight I reported at Swain, Seidel, and Lawler, where my first duty was to obtain a Social Security card.

Meantime, Ava Norris and Miss Ballou were arranging a wedding. George and Lila were making plans for a honeymoon. They were going off on the *Excalibur,* they were telling their friends. Off on a long, long cruise through the Caribbean, and perhaps through the Canal to Peru and Chile. They had dreamed of doing it for years, they were telling their friends, and they were going to take courses together in celestial navigation at the Hayden Planetarium. To me, learning the ropes in the bull pen, spending hours alone with only Macy, it seemed they had gone long ago. Seventy-first Street was as far away as Peru, and I was safe, I would say to myself, safe and sound at last.

Chapter Twenty-seven

The best I can say for George Marsh's ushers' dinner was that it happened on Saturday night. No one had to work the next day; no one had to go to school. It happened on the evening of February 7, 1950, and that was exactly one week before the wedding day.

Because he believed strongly in the presence of an older man or two at these occasions, Hadley Norris had assumed the position of co-host, and insisted on sharing expenses. George had respectfully acquiesced to the recommendations of his future father-in-law, remembering previous dinners that had been given in the downstairs banquet room of the Squash and Quoit.

Hadley Norris had in mind a boisterous dinner, but not an uproarious one. He expected the boys to get pleasantly tight. He anticipated that there would be a certain amount of broken crockery, and that some inexpensive glasses would be smashed into the artificial fireplace that was rolled into the room on casters when it came time to toast the bride. All this was tradition at the Squash and Quoit. But Hadley Norris would not tolerate the pilfering of silverware, the indiscriminate bashing of the club's trophies, the destruction of the woodwork, or any other of those costly embarrassments that friends of his had suffered while doing their best by their sons and sons-in-law.

Above all Hadley Norris expected that the boys would show respect for their elders. As best man, Bert Seidel should certainly be shown respect. And the same was true of Mr. Ellison. To judge from the little he had seen of George's current stepfather, Hadley Norris would say that Zip Ellison seemed a lively enough fellow, and not likely to annoy others. Hadley Norris would be on hand himself, naturally, and he had taken the liberty of inviting his brother, Trumbull Norris. Trumbull was a bachelor and a great hand for breaking the ice.

The younger players in this drama of obligatory merriment had been cast entirely by the groom. Each was an old hand at the ushers' dinner. Twenty strong, they came out of loyalty to George, to do for him what he had done for many of them when they too had hovered on the brink of matrimony. The unwed remainder also came out of loyalty, for they shared an interior sympathy for the groom, and this sentiment, fleeting though it was, was for the early moments at least stronger than the selfish curiosity to observe the behavior of a friend in crisis.

It would have been difficult indeed to refuse outright to be an usher for George Marsh, and this alone explained my presence in the Squash and Quoit Club this February evening; my New England conscience would, otherwise, have excluded me. Only Johnny Groats, with whom George had shared a room in Texas, had a legitimate excuse. And Johnny had sent a regretful telegram explaining that at almost any moment he was to become a father. But Johnny would be flying east for the wedding, and if the doctor gave permission, he would be bringing Lucy along.

I did not know Groats, but every other name was familiar. Toby Tappan, recently married, and employed by the Manufacturers Trust. Lou Tremaine, father of two, a salesman for the Equitable Life Assurance Society of the United States. Danny Guile, too shy to wed, a medical student at Tufts. Fuzzy Eaton, a college graduate at last and in spite of himself, temporarily an employee of the Coca-Cola Bottling Company of Cambridge, but toying with brighter prospects for the future, of which the most satisfying was that of assisting a man who ran a Dog Obedience School in Dedham, Massachusetts. Harry Tilton, of course, and Neddy Nepham, who had almost roomed with George at Emmanuel. Hank Barthelmess, Pansy Peters, forsaking wives and office jobs in Boston for this evening's revel. And Barney Blake and Spooky Dodge, with whom George had conceived the outlines of a promising import-export business while at a Hallowe'en party in Greenwich, Connecticut. Six or seven more.

They arrived in dinner clothes and soft white shirts with button-down collars, of varying degrees of freshness determined by the distances they had traveled. Several of the sweller dressers, notably Tilton and Tappan, wore white carnations. Fuzzy Eaton, on the other hand, had on a dinner jacket which perhaps had been a

337

proper fit when he bought it, for the First Classmen's Dance at Emmanuel, but which was a fit no longer, and was mercilessly wrinkled as well. And Fuzzy, given to dressing in a hurry, had not thought to change his yellow Argyll socks. Yet it took more than the provocative aspects of Eaton to relieve the tension at the start. Put a maturing male on the carpet and try inducing him to forget the uncertain, unaccustomed bride he has abandoned for the night, and try persuading him to revert to the ass he played so well just a few short years ago. It is a bitter struggle, and is rarely won without the aid of alcohol.

I was not surprised, though some were, to be greeted outside the downstairs banquet room by an overbearingly genial Hadley Norris. He stood at the door and shook hands, quick to put a stranger at his ease.

"Hadley Norris." His handclasp was affable yet reserved. This was not Rotary. "I think it's splendid that you could come."

"Lou Tremaine, sir."

"Jeff Tremaine's boy?"

I was among the first to arrive. In back of Hadley Norris were two tables, decked out in white linen and laden with bottles, ice-banked platters of oysters on the half shell, canapés, and glassware. A waiter in the club uniform stood by to mix the cocktail you wanted. George Marsh was alone in a corner, checking the cigarettes and matches on a table there. He held a glass and a small silver shaker snugly in one hand.

"How many of those have you put away?" I asked him, pleasantly.

George Marsh was grinning as he grabbed my arm above the elbow and dug his thumb under the biceps where it hurt. You were never certain what he meant by this, whether it was purely friendly or a form of anger. He seldom took advantage of his strength, except when he was drinking.

"It's my own private stock, Sport-o. Something to go on until the guys arrive."

He wore his magnificent tuxedo and his face was fresh and cleanly shaven. Yet I thought he looked drawn, tense, and he was grinning too hard.

"It'll all be over in a few hours," I said, consolingly.

"Don't you fret. Why isn't there a glass in your hand?" He handed me a glass and poured from the small shaker he carried.

"Why should I want it to be over in a few hours? This is my big night."

The room was filling up. As the ushers passed by Hadley Norris they were buttonholed by a taller and more portly man who, I was to discover, was Trumbull Norris. Once by him, the young men made for the drinks and started to greet George Marsh, but seeing him in conference with me, they held their ground and talked in uneasy twos and threes. There was the jagged atmosphere of the unlaunched party, of murmurs and abrupt laughter, and the still trepidation of those not quite sure they can face up to the occasion.

"You'd better shake a few hands," I said to George.

"I'll have one quickie," he said. "I hate this damn straining, don't you? I hate throwing a party."

"You've got something on your mind. You might as well tell me."

We had seen each other here and there since he'd come back from Texas, but this was as close as we had come to being alone. I knew that if I couldn't talk with him now, there would be no other chance.

"This is a hell of a time to talk about that," George said.

"You and Lila had a crise," I said flatly.

"You and I ought to have had a talk about Liles. We never did."

"I wanted to have a talk," I said.

George rotated the shaker in his big hand, his lips muttering something he dared not say, and then, so quickly and cruelly that I gasped, he gripped my arm above the elbow. For a moment he applied his thumb menacingly against my nerve and muscle, and he said, "Confidentially, I should have kicked your teeth in."

I was able to hold quite still and ignore the pain. "Confidentially, why didn't you?" I was able to say to him. "You had every right."

"No, Sport-o. What for?" The pressure was off as suddenly as it had come, and in place of my arm George was squeezing the cocktail shaker. Already he was ashamed of his hostile emotion. We were all old friends here, gathered for the one big night. Loyalty. When all else failed there was Loyalty, which was everlasting, and substantial, and always made sense.

"What for?" he said. "It wasn't your fault. It was damn hard on you."

"That's a generous way of looking at it," I said.

I watched him drain off the last of his shaker into his glass.

339

From across the room someone was calling for the Goph. Everyone wanted to see the Goph.

"You fool," he was telling me, "I don't see why all the drama. I don't see why you had to walk out on me. It was a perfectly natural thing to happen."

"Perfectly natural?" I said, startled. "For Christ's sake, maybe we *ought* to have a little talk."

"Liles told me everything, Sport-o. So why don't we just forget it."

"She didn't tell you everything. You know perfectly well."

"Look." He was endeavoring to sound bored by the whole dreary subject. "Don't you think I know Lila? Do you think for one minute that she can kid me? It was written all over her face when I got back from Texas. I didn't have to ask a thing."

"You didn't ask for details. You just took her at her word."

"Why brew up another crise? This is a hell of a time to say it, but we've had enough crises already. I have to watch every little thing I say. I don't want to go begging for trouble."

When he turned to face the waiting throng, I saw his shoulders stiffen and the dark circles and the lines on his cheeks were still deeper under the glow of the light bulbs.

George Marsh walked among his ushers, making sure they had fresh drinks, introducing them to each other. As the liquor flowed, total strangers paired off incongruously. Toby Tappan, the former bow oar of the Crimson eight, listened sedately as Zip Ellison, Princeton '27, opined that rowing was the most overrated sport in the world. Fuzzy Eaton, plumper and redder-faced this evening than at any time in our memory, harangued Bert Seidel with an account of having been picked up for speeding on the outskirts of New Haven. Trumbull Norris talked with Harry Tilton, and because this was a great occasion, Hadley Norris had a drink with me. I could not remember the last time he had condescended so. Hadley Norris had not drunk a drop since August, but tonight was a celebration. The party was warming up, Hadley Norris observed. As the saying went, a good time would be had by all.

At last a waiter opened the double doors of the banquet room. Twenty-five studded leather chairs were drawn up around the long table, and before each place the groom had laid a small box in white wrapping. A large box lay at the end of the table where George was to sit. At every second place was a fifth of Scotch or

340

of bourbon. At one end of the table Bert Seidel, the best man, took his seat with the father of the bride on his right. Opposite his brother and on Bert Seidel's left sat Trumbull Norris, with Zip Ellison at his side. At George Marsh's end, Harry Tilton took his place in the seat of honor, for Harry was to be our toastmaster. I sat on George's left and between us and the adult end the mob settled themselves in two careless rows. An upright piano stood by the fireplace and the room was stripped of all breakable ornaments, saving the irremovable woodwork and dark paneling which the club management was forced to entrust to the Fates the remainder of the evening. There were water and wine glasses at each place, and two expendable flowered centerpieces. Printed menus promised a feast of consommé, larded sirloin steak, string beans, potatoes Lyonnaise, and *cerises Jubilées*.

The presents were opened and dutifully acknowledged. For the ushers, gold money clips bearing the wedding date, and the initials of both owner and groom. For George, a silver cocktail shaker bearing the date, his initials, and those of his bride engraved against a firmament of signatures. The latter was a tribute to Toby Tappan's sense of protocol. For Toby, of all us twenty, had been the lone volunteer to select a gift for the groom. Contributions were fifteen dollars a man, and even as the meal began Toby was still discreetly dunning. The cocktail shaker was passed from hand to hand in formal inspection, and if Hank Barthelmess dented its side while rescuing it from beneath Pansy Peters' chair, its souvenir value was that much enhanced.

"Damn nice present," George remarked to no one in particular. His uneasiness was receding now with the champagne, just as it had before with the cocktails, but he remained the quiet figure among us.

"A damn nice bunch of guys," he was saying later and smiling vacantly down the table where the waiters were passing the vegetables.

"You're not drunk enough," Harry said. "Chug a lug."

"I'm drunk as a goat," George said.

Harry asked if it wasn't time to begin the toasts. All the glasses had been newly filled and two waiters had wheeled in the artificial fireplace. It stood well out from the wall on the side of the table that was opposite the real fireplace; thus there would be no excuse for glass broken against the valuable woodwork. Harry reminded George of the amenities which required the groom to offer the opening toast to his bride.

"Does it have to be a gag?" George wanted to know. "I never can think of anything funny when I have to."

Harry slapped his friend playfully. "Just this one toast and I promise you won't have to do a damn thing more. And you don't have to be so funny."

George rose and stepped smartly behind his chair while Harry called for silence by ringing his water glass with a fork.

One after the other, the heads turned toward our end. George was supporting himself on his chair and pressing his lips intently in a fine oratorical pose. I was reminded, briefly, of our head proctor at Emmanuel who had also posed this way in his football sweater, allowing the school to quiet down before he led them in a long cheer for Mrs. Kew. Our head proctor, however, had not been glassy-eyed, and he had held no wine glass in his hand.

"I don't have too many words about me tonight."

The glad faces that had been anticipating a joke lapsed with this into various attitudes of patience.

"But I've been doing a lot of thinking. I've been thinking about what a hell of a bunch of guys you all are—"

Hadley Norris sprang to his feet, glass upraised.

"Hear! Hear!"

Several chairs were drawn back noisily, but George signaled that this was not a cue for an ovation.

"And I don't have to say how much it means to have you here. I just want to say that I consider myself the luckiest bum on earth."

Hadley Norris did not rise to this. He remained seated, his mouth partially open. The others sensed, too, this was to be a moving tribute, something that would have to be coped with, though they weren't sure how.

"And there's a bigger reason that makes me the luckiest bum. That reason is that a week from tonight, when none of you bastards will be around—"

Some laughter here, for this was an allusion to the wedding night and could not be let by unacknowledged.

"A week from tonight I'll be married to—to the—the—the most tremendous girl in the world!"

342

Applause. Loud, but not thunderous.

"One thing more. At school, I used to play a little football—"

A mixed reaction here. Groans and laughter. It was hard to interpret the modesty of one who had been the only twice-elected captain of football in the history of Emmanuel Academy.

"But what I want to tell you about is a time I remember after we beat Middlesex—"

A jeer from Barney Blake, who had gone to Middlesex.

"There was an old gentleman, an old alumnus, who came right up to me in the shower room. He said that that would be one of the two happiest days of my life. I've never forgotten what that gentleman said. He was certainly right about that being the first happiest day, and now I just want to say that I know next Saturday will be the second happiest day of my life."

"To the second happiest day!" cried Hadley Norris. "Hear! Hear!"

Laughter from those who had feared at the start that Mr. Norris might be a bit on the pompous side.

"I'll admit it's not the most *brilliant* toast in the world," George Marsh was concluding, "but that's what I've been thinking. I'd like to ask you all to please stand and please drink a toast to Lila, who has agreed to be my wife."

He raised the glass to his lips and drank, dribbling a bit of the champagne. He turned to the artificial fireplace, wiping his chin with the back of one hand, and flung the glass. It struck the painted bricks and shattered. Then glass after empty glass hurtled in the direction of the wooden device. Some fell short of the mark and bounced unbroken on the carpet. Danny Guile did a pitcher's wind-up and cleared the wood completely, and struck the pantry door. The last glass to shatter, which nearly caught a waiter stooping with a dustpan and broom, belonged to Mr. Trumbull Norris. It fell a minute behind the rest, and then only after Zip Ellison's urging, for Trumbull Norris had been dozing and was not aware that the bridegroom had given his toast.

We had scarcely sat down, when Hadley Norris rose once more, unannounced.

"What's got into the old blade? He's supposed to wait till he's called on," Harry Tilton said.

"Now, Goddamn it! I call for quiet! Stand up down there. On

343

your feet, Goddamn it!" Slowly the voices died. Slowly the mob surrendered to this veteran strategist of the stag dinner.

"I want all hands to drink to the man who has just given the most sincere and the finest toast it's ever been my honor to hear. I want you all to join me in welcoming a new son into our family. I know you all realize what sort of a girl he's getting in my Liles. I don't remember who the poet was who said marriages were made in heaven. I don't even know if that's true, but it has always seemed to me that a lot of work goes into marriage. But I don't have to be a poet to tell you that my Liles was made in heaven, or to tell you how damn proud it makes me to be giving her to this splendid boy—"

"Oh," I heard Harry Tilton mutter. "Oh, Mother, kiss me."

"I don't have to tell you that I love him like a son, and that I loved his father like a brother. You all know George—a boy whose childhood life may not have been too happy in some respects, a boy whose bravery and decency all of us have admired as long as it has been our honor to know him, an outstandingly fine and splendid boy who served his country with honor. He would have plenty to boast about if he were the boasting kind. I don't remember the name of the poet who said that gentlemen are born, not made, but I'm not here tonight to recite poetry. I'm not ashamed of the tears in my eyes. I'm proud. Gentlemen, I ask you all to stand and drink to George."

Harry Tilton had no easy time restoring ebullience to the gathering. The toast just ended called for a respectful interlude. And the heart of the silence was at the adult end of the table, where Hadley Norris slumped in his chair and Bert Seidel, with priestly calm, was pouring him a glass of water.

George Marsh had been hanging his head. "What do you think I'd better do about the old man?" he asked me.

"Bert Seidel will take care of him," I said.

"The trouble is he doesn't like Bert. He think's Bert's an opportunist Fair Dealer. I wish I hadn't seated them together."

"Don't worry about it," I said.

"I don't know what's coming off, Sport-o. I'm drunk as a goat, but I feel lousy."

"Want to take a walk around the block?"

"I couldn't crap out on my own party," he said and tossed off another glass. He would be game, of course, game as a gopher.

Harry Tilton was on and off his feet, calling for toasts from everyone with an ingenious fillip that brought attention to some foible or comic misadventure of the speaker. Thus I was sent to the piano to accompany Toby Tappan as he sang in his purest British accent an old standby that had seen him through many a dinner, a chantey about an outhouse adrift on the deep. Thus, someone told the joke about the Siamese twins in love with the traveling salesman, and someone the joke about the flea in the whore house, and someone the joke about two Eskimos in an igloo who became confused by a seal. And thus, Hank Barthelmess got off his limericks and Danny Guile recited a poem that had come to him that afternoon during his train ride from Philadelphia.

Harry Tilton called for us to chug a lug the toasts. "We have to chug a lug highballs?" Pansy Peters inquired and Harry told him yes, what else? At last Mr. Trumbull Norris rose and made a speech of welcome to another male member in the family, which, he noted, had been run by women just about long enough. His speech, unfortunately, was steadily interrupted by catcalls and cries of "Hey, old Dun and Bradstreet!"

Zip Ellison, in a wine-colored cummerbund, rose and made, with many smiles, a statement to the effect that he was just another of us boys for the evening and that we should go right on with the party and not mind him. And it was then that Fuzzy Eaton caught him full in the face with a substantial portion of *cerises Jubilées*.

As if by a prearrangement, the air was thick with flying fruit and rolls and butter patties, catapulted from spoons and napkins. Plates crashed into the artificial fireplace and a leftover of larded tenderloin marred the portrait of an elderly man in a hunting habit in whose honor the banquet room had been donated. Spooky Dodge asked a waiter if there weren't some ice cream so we could have an ice-cream fight. Harry Tilton banged helplessly against an empty bottle in an attempt to restore the peace.

And George Marsh sat through it all with a listless grin.

"You think they're having a good time?" he said.

The question was being answered before our eyes by Fuzzy, who had discovered the siphon bottles on the sideboard and was just now spraying a row of enemies that sat across the table from him. By a misfire that was perhaps calculated Fuzzy succeeded in vaporizing the jowls and vest of Mr. Trumbull Norris, and instantly the culprit received his just deserts. Hank Barthelmess, suddenly a champion of the oppressed and elderly, seized a flower bowl from the center of the table and upturned it on the offender. Fuzzy sat limply and submitted to the saturation by water and gladiolas with burbles of delight. In the moment's hush that followed, Harry Tilton seized his chance.

"All right! All right now! There's one man we haven't heard from and we're going to hear from him now. Gentlemen, I give you the best man, Mr. Bert Seidel!"

"Yow!" whooped Fuzzy Eaton. "The legal eagle!" He sprang up, waving a gladiola stem to lead the applause.

At this stage, a man of less commanding presence would have been an easy mark for Fuzzy. When Bert Seidel rose, not a plate fell and not an ice cube tinkled.

"Yow—wow!"

Fuzzy Eaton clapped his hands and raked the table with an appealing, puzzled glance, for he could not fathom why suddenly he had been robbed of our support.

Bert Seidel looked calmly at his wrist watch, cleared his throat and began:

"We certainly had quite a time for ourselves this evening and I've enjoyed meeting all you fellahs. I look forward to seeing you all next week at the wedding and I can promise that then I'll be able to leave a whole evening open, a whole weekend if necessary, because it isn't every day that a fellah you've watched grow up gets married on you. George has been a friend of mine since he was eleven years old. I want to say that I agree a hundred per cent with all the fine things Mr. Norris has said about him. I wish I didn't have to run along right now because this has been a great party. I just want to say I'm honored to be your best man, and, George, here's to you and here's all the luck. Tell Lila for me that she's a lucky girl."

The speaker waved and would have left us then, had not Hadley Norris leaped up shouting. He was clutching Bert Seidel by the lapel of his dinner jacket.

"I beg your pardon. I beg your pardon! I'd like an apology for what you said about my daughter."

We watched, fascinated, and in the quiet we could hear Bert Seidel's faint snort of surprise. "I don't believe I said anything, Mr. Norris, that would have given offense."

"I beg your pardon! I beg—" Hadley Norris' voice was stifled in phlegm and he was forced to clear his throat loudly. "I beg your pardon, but I'm not accustomed to being called a liar!"

"No one said you were a liar," Bert Seidel said. He forced Hadley Norris' arm away.

The older man stepped closer, speechless in his fury, and thrust his chin forward.

"I think you're making a great mistake," Bert Seidel said.

"Don't patronize me!" Hadley Norris landed a lurching blow on the chest of Bert Seidel and charged like a bantam, if unstable, bull.

His adversary took a quick step and plucked the limp hand of Hadley Norris from himself distastefully, as though it were a piece of decayed animal matter. He swung on his heel and walked for the door. Left off balance, Hadley Norris toppled to the carpet.

At my right, George Marsh fell back in his chair with a sharp moan.

A circle had formed about our fallen host before I reached him. Trumbull Norris and Lou Tremaine were lifting him off the floor and grunting with the effort.

"No brandy," Mr. Trumbull Norris was saying. "For heaven's sake, no brandy."

"Now take it easy," Lou Tremaine was saying. "Take it easy, Mr. Norris."

"Send that man back here!" Hadley Norris cleared another sheet of mucus from his throat. "I'm not going to let him insult my daughter."

"Nobody insulted your daughter," his brother said. "Hadley, now for God's sake."

"Hadley, I'm going to take you home."

"I can't go home."

"All right, Hadley, you can spend the night at my place," his brother said. "Honest to God, Hadley."

347

When things got quiet, I noticed that George Marsh had left his seat. Harry Tilton was sitting alone, fixing himself a highball from one of the bottles.

"He'll be back," Harry said. "Why don't you scramble off a few tunes?"

"I'm sick of tunes."

"What the hell kind of an usher are you? We've got to get this party back on its feet, boy."

Nearly half of our number had gone, although plenty of liquor was left in the bottles, and some of them were unopened. Fuzzy Eaton had curled up on the carpet with his head under the table and was sleeping his deep sleep which was the next thing to unconsciousness. Toby Tappan was moving about the table and trying to collect the money still owed him for the cocktail shaker. Others talked and smoked cigars, and others, who had no wives to return to, consulted address books, then filed out in pairs to make their clandestine arrangements over the telephone. No one asked after Hadley Norris or after old Dun and Bradstreet Norris, or after George Marsh. By half-past ten, Harry Tilton was prepared to admit that the party was dead.

"We'd better check the Goph," he said to me. "I think he's in the can."

The lavatory light reflected antiseptically from the white tiling and starkly from the mirrors that stood over the row of wash basins. Paper towels were strewn on the floor and a dinner jacket hung over one of the toilet stalls. The sound of a running tap drew us to George Marsh. He was sitting on a trash basket that bulged with more paper towels, and leaning over the end basin where the water ran over his head.

I took him by the shirt and shook.

"Let's go home."

His eyes were red and his head and neck were dripping, and for the first time that evening he didn't try to smile.

"Can't crap out now, Sport-o."

"The party's over."

"It can't be over. Didn't say good-by."

"That's all right. You'll see us next week."

Harry Tilton had taken down the dinner jacket and was wiping off the vomit. We helped George into his coat, but he insisted on combing his hair and tying his tie by himself. It mattered a great deal how he looked when he left the Club.

Harry and I each took an arm and guided him through the door and down the hall.

"D'you think they had a pretty good time?" he asked.

As we stopped at the coat room and helped him on with his overcoat, two old members, old enough to be friends of his Uncle Mark, stared at us.

We found a cab on the avenue. Harry Tilton climbed in first and helped George, but when I tried to close the door George jammed it open with his foot.

"You want a ride, Sport-o?"

"I'm going way up. I'll take the bus, thanks."

"Say, forgot my cocktail shaker . . . awful nice you guys to give it to me."

"I'll get it," I said. "I'll see that it gets over to you tomorrow." Harry Tilton was trying to get him to close the door.

"One other thing," George said.

"Yes?"

"This 's a hell of a time t' say it."

Harry was saying something inside the cab, and he was pulling at George's leg.

"I wanted to ask if everything was O.K. with you, Sport-o. Don't know what it was I was going to say—maybe you should've talked to me. Maybe you should've talked to Liles, I don't know."

"For Christ's sweet sake," Harry Tilton whined. "Come on, George. Come *on!*"

Chapter Twenty-eight

I badly wanted to forget this night's experience, and the best way was to go to bed and sleep, sleep the weekend through if need be. I should have known that the chances of doing this were negligible when you had a telephone by your bed, and in particular a telephone like mine that was incapable of ringing except when I was asleep.

The phone rang on and on in the dark, then cut off while the caller redialed, then came back on insistently. I groped beside the bed.

"Try me tomorrow," I said to the mouthpiece. "Sometime in the afternoon," and I started to put the receiver down on the table, intending to leave it off its hook.

"Gussy? I had to wake you. I had to talk."

"This is a hell of a time to talk," I said.

"I'm at the family's, and there's no one here. Gussy, what happened? What happened to Pappy?"

"Everything's O.K.," I said. "He's spending the night at your Uncle Trumbull's."

"Where is George? He promised he'd call as soon as he got home."

"He'll call you tomorrow," I said. "We're all trying to get some sleep."

"I can't sleep."

"Why don't you wake your mother up?"

"Mummy's in California and she won't be home till Monday. I told you there's no one here. I have to talk to you. You've got to come here right away."

"Do you remember what happened the last time you had to see me right away? We met in the Sandwich Shop."

"That was so long ago, Gussy."

350

"It was in November," I said.

"I don't care, Gussy. You've got to come."

"Are you frightened?" I said.

"No," she said. "As a matter of fact, I'm not frightened at all."

Through force of habit I gave the driver the address of Lila's old apartment on Madison Avenue, and we were almost at the door before I remembered that of course she no longer lived there. And I remembered that George had told me why.

Ava Norris had decided that Lila should take some responsibility for her own wedding. Ava wanted Lila to attend to the presents as they arrived, to see that the flowers and liquor were ordered, the musicians hired, transportation arranged, the bridesmaids' dresses chosen. This was not going to be the typical wedding for which the mother of the bride did all the work. Personally, Ava Norris would have preferred a simple wedding, but since Lila had wanted an enormous one she was jolly well going to help with the arrangements. The ceremony was to be performed at the main altar of St. Bartholomew's, and not in the chapel, as Ava Norris would have preferred. The reception would not be held in the Colony Club, for that was a world Ava Norris had never made, but on a glossier scale at the Park Lane Hotel. So Lila had given up her apartment and gone home to live out her last maiden weeks with her family.

Tony, the night elevator man at Sutton Place, was waiting at the door. "Yes, sir?" he said belligerently.

"Miss Norris is expecting me," I said.

"Miss Norris?"

Tony was not an argumentative type, but he was an old friend of George Marsh, and for more than a month he had been delivering wedding presents at the Norris' apartment. Quite understandably, Tony was disturbed by this unconventional rendezvous in the after-midnight hours.

When we reached the ninth floor, Tony stepped out of the elevator ahead of me and rang the bell of the apartment.

"Are you expecting visitors, Miss Norris?"

Lila peered at us around the door. "It's all right, Tony."

"Shall I hold the car?"

"Mr. Taylor will ring when he's ready to leave, Tony. It won't be necessary to wait for him."

351

Lila closed the door and took my hand and led me past the hall mirrors into the sitting room where the wedding presents were on display. A light shone over the sofa and another over the card table where her wedding present book lay open beside a pinkish clutter of note paper.

"Mummy has been making me write thank-you notes," Lila said. "Oh, I knew you'd come."

She held both my hands and squeezed them, smiling, wrinkling her nose. Pallor and strain showed on her face. Her eyes were puffy and the tiny cat's paws in their corners were red and inflamed. Yet she had taken the trouble to look well. Her lipstick was fresh and her deep red hair had been brushed and was gathered behind her head tidily in a tortoise-shell barrette. She was wearing white shantung pajamas that had the flowery monogram over the left breast pocket, and a tight string of pearls and earrings, and a red sash about her waist, and on her feet were a pair of white woolly slippers.

"Aren't the maids home?" I said. "Where's Hannah?"

"I told you there was nobody. I've been sitting here, with all these damned presents."

I drew away from her and stood by a long table on which china plates and breakfast sets were on display.

"Gussy?" she said impatiently. "Were they disgusting?"

"Who?" I said. I was examining the array of Ronson lighters and checking for duplicates among the Steuben glass, wondering how in one lifetime two people would be able to use so many things.

"Pappy and George," she said. "You know damned well who."

"You don't understand about ushers' dinners."

"They're exactly the same. They're like father and son, aren't they? And I'm like Mummy. I would do to George exactly what Mummy did to my father."

"That's your pipe dream, Liles. I don't know why you unload it on me. I'm not Dr. Freud."

"Because you understand me. You're the only person I can talk to. . . . I'm tired of all this Bassett Meadows conversation about being neurotic. Why does everyone go around telling you how neurotic you are? People don't go around telling other people how syphilitic they are."

The silverware was on another table by itself—two open cases

352

showing their velvet lining, large Georgian spoons, vegetable dishes, silent butlers, a tea service. It was as if I were in a show room at Black, Starr and Gorham.

I was touching a brass-surfaced ice bucket which was in the shape of an apple, with a metal stem serving as a handle for the top.

"Isn't that hideous?" Lila said. "Eddy Shawn sent it. George always wanted me to meet Eddy."

She had drawn her legs up on the sofa and was hugging them against her chest.

"I haven't been nice to George lately," she said. "Did he tell you anything about it?"

"I imagine it's bound to be hectic before a wedding like this one."

"Everything presses in on me when I have to be alone," Lila said. "I know it was selfish to call you, but I knew you'd come. Look at all those damn presents, Gussy."

"Sometimes," I said, "you remind me of your mother."

"You thought I was going to fling myself in your arms, didn't you?"

"It's just a little late for that," I said.

"That wasn't what I had in mind, and I'm tired of flinging myself in people's arms. . . . I've made up my mind what I'm going to do, Gussy, and I had to tell you first."

She was resting her chin on her knees over which her pajamas were drawn tight. Her head was tilted toward me, and her eyes shone wildly.

"I know just what I'm doing . . . and I'm not going to marry George."

I thought just then of the old snapshot that George had shown me at Emmanuel, the photo of Lila in a tennis dress wearing a ribbon in her hair and holding a racquet in her hand. She had had a fierceness that had not seemed real in a skinny fourteen-year-old.

"Nobody is going to like this very much, and I'm going to be called a lot of names. You can call me whatever you want to, Gussy." She was speaking from a made-up mind—no vagueness, and no vacillation. "I'm not afraid of facing Mummy and Pappy. Because I know there's nothing else to do but this, and I know I'm right."

353

"Just don't expect them to believe you right away. One doesn't change like that—overnight."

"I expect them to let me prove it. I'll get my friends back again, Gussy. And this is a lot better than what I've been doing to George. I was just like my mother, and she's the last person in the world I want to be like. . . . I made him miserable."

"You should have seen him tonight," I said.

"I'll go on punishing him if he lets me, and he always has let me. . . . I don't care about the others, not even Chee Wee. But do *you* blame me, Gussy?"

"Who am I to be blaming you?"

"Nobody knows what it was to be with him! Maybe he *is* as weak as Mummy thinks and maybe it *was* up to me to help him, but I couldn't, and I know I never could. I couldn't bear to be alone with him. Do you realize? I couldn't let him touch me, and I nagged and picked."

"What are you going to do exactly?"

"The first thing, tell George. I'll go over in the morning as soon as he's awake. And he'll be apologetic about his hangover. That will be the most awful part, so I'm going to do it first. Then Pappy, when he gets back, if he's well enough to hear me, and on Monday morning, Mummy—"

"Nobody's going to help you," I said.

"I don't expect help," Lila said, quite angrily. "I told you I'm tired of flinging myself in people's arms."

It was hard, when I looked back at the past, to believe her. Yet I had to grant her her due. She did not demand that I believe her, only that she be allowed to demonstrate the proof, if it took her through hell and back.

"I'll tell the family and when that's over," she said, "I'll handle the rest of it too."

Calling friends, calling the newspapers, sending telegrams, returning wedding presents, canceling this, canceling that, and all of it the most dreadful ignominy for a girl. Afterward she would go away, and stay out of sight until she deserved to come back.

"You know what they say after a girl leaves town," she said. "You know those jokes about how she is having her appendix taken out? I don't care what people think."

"You're a brave girl," I said. "I didn't think you had it in you."

354

"I had no other choice. I don't call that brave." She was managing to relax a little. She let go her knees and laid her head against the back of the sofa, taking in the tables with their menacing display with a sort of smile. "I lied about the thank-you notes. I haven't written one in days. As soon as I couldn't bear to write another word, I knew I was sure."

"It will be hard," I said. "I guarantee you."

"Gussy?" she said idly, as though by afterthought. "Do you think we were ever in love, you and I?"

"There was a time when I was under that impression."

"You think you're well out of it?"

"I'm going to stay out of it, too."

She tilted her head and gave a rather brittle laugh, I thought not of bitterness but because I had embarrassed her.

"I don't blame you. I don't expect anything—so please don't pretend that you're surly."

"I'm not surly."

"Do you remember when we walked on the beach? I told you I knew you were someone I could count on?"

"I remember," I said. "I told you not to leap to conclusions."

She paused for a moment and looked me up and down. "You were very tired tonight and you wanted to sleep, but you came here."

There she had me, and there was nothing to say to that.

"Have you gotten over it so quickly, Gussy?"

"Let's not start that, Liles."

"Frankly I think about you all the time. That is I think I do, but how could I expect you to believe me?"

"This is a lot of talk. It's no use, Liles."

"It's more than talk. I looked up to you, Gussy. You were different from everybody. If you ever had—"

Her last words hung in the air, shattered by Ava Norris' electric door chime. The four opening notes of the "Londonderry Air."

"It's Tony making a delivery," Lila said. "I don't think I can face another wedding present."

"At two o'clock on Sunday morning who's going to send a wedding present?"

"It's a mistake. The people across the hall have guests that always ring our bell."

355

We each had risen up, she from the sofa, and I from the chair, and we were standing close to each other in the center of the room. For the moment the chiming ceased and it did appear to have been a mistake.

"Darling, if you ever had asserted yourself," Lila said in the sudden quiet. "I know I wasn't capable of very much, and I don't care if you believe me."

I had forgot how delicately she could move, and how fresh she smelled, and now the gentle promise of her eyes.

"You're not a fairy princess waving your magic wand," I said, "presto-changeo."

"It isn't presto-changeo, Gussy, but don't take my word for it. I've been a prime little bitch, but I'm going to get what's coming to me. Perhaps I've begun to grow up."

"One way or another you may turn into a big girl," I said, and I must have been smiling too.

"It doesn't mean anything, Gussy, but I think I'd like you to kiss me, if you want to."

Either then or just after the sound of the door chimes burst angrily upon us. Lila and I jumped apart like a pair of naughty children. I followed her to the hall and stood by her before one of the tall mirrors where she brushed her hair into place with a loose movement of her fingers.

"You'd better go in the kitchen," Lila whispered.

"I'm going to stay right here."

The sound again. Oh, Dan-ny boy.

Lila squared her shoulders and went brazenly to the door.

"Honestly, Tony. You might give me half a second."

"I beg pardon, Miss Norris. This gentleman said it was important."

"Harry! You might have telephoned."

It was Mr. Vitalis all right. Mr. Ipana Vitalis. His camel's hair coat was unbuttoned, exposing the front of his dinner jacket. He closed the door behind him and nuzzled deferentially on Lila's neck below her hair.

"Hello, Harry," I said.

He puffed his cigarette once and blew smoke through his nostrils in the manner of an adolescent smitten by Humphrey Bogart.

356

"I'm glad you had time to stick in your shirt tails," he said.

"Anything we can do for you, Harry?"

"I got to thinking about that cocktail shaker and I called you up, but no answer. I called you again and no answer. I recalled what George said when we were putting him into the cab. I got to putting two and two together, lover boy."

Lila was clutching the lapels of his polo coat. "Harry, if you're any friend of George's, you'll get out of here right now."

He was looking over her and squarely at me.

"Make hay while the sun shines, boy. I thought you knocked this off a long time ago. I thought you were that smart."

"Harry," Lila said. "Think before you start accusing others. People in glass houses, Harry."

"If you want to get personal about old times, there's a thing or two you made me promise. The old zipped lip. I like to keep my promises, doll."

"You can tell what you damn well please," Lila said, pushing him toward the door. "There's not going to be any wedding, Harry. So you go right ahead and tell George all the lies you can think of, because I'm going to see him in the morning."

"You're quite a little personality. You've got a great sense of timing . . . me, I would have just stuck a knife in George's back. I've got to admit this is subtle." He grinned at me. "Orchids to you, lover boy. This is one for the books."

Now Lila rushed toward me. "Don't listen to him, Gussy. Don't *you* make a fuss."

"I guess I'll skedaddle," Harry Tilton said. "I thought I might be finding a damsel in distress, but no. So long, lover. Sorry to have busted up your pajama party."

I heard Lila's cry and felt her fingers digging into my back. My fist struck on Harry Tilton's chest, jarring my arm all the way up to its socket. I had to struggle with her in order to hit him again, but this time my knuckles scraped against his teeth.

"Don't make it worse!" Lila was crying. "Don't be a fool, Gussy!"

Harry Tilton leaned against the wall, wiping at his lip with the sleeve of his polo coat. His nose was ever so slightly off center because I had broken it once, I remembered now, on the hockey rink.

"You try that again, and I'll call the building superintendent."

357

"Go on and call him," I said. "He'll be a lot of help to you."

As he left, I noticed that there was a fine bloody cut on Harry Tilton's mouth, and it looked as though it would leave a fine scar.

Lila closed the door behind him and ran to me.

"I'm so sick of the whole bunch of them! After all the years I've spent with them, I can't stand a single one. You're the only one that amounts to anything, Gussy. I wish you could take me away."

Chapter Twenty-nine

At dusk on the following Monday, I paid my visit to the editorial offices of *Blythe* in the Mannix Publications Building on lower Park Avenue. The summons had come on the telephone, just as I was leaving work. Whatever I had to do, Ava Norris had said, could wait. This was an emergency.

It was after six when I stepped out onto the eighth floor and found the corridors deserted, the receptionist's desk empty. The night watchman who operated the service elevator treated me with the suspicion that I brought out in building staffs everywhere. He did not quite believe that I could have an appointment with Mrs. Norris, and so he led me to her outer office where I identified myself to a middle-aged woman in a florid print dress.

"Mr. Taylor," she said. "We're in a fine little hassle now, aren't we? We've been expecting you, Mr. Taylor." She sat behind the cumbersome office typewriter where she had been finishing off Ava Norris' late correspondence which was piped to her through a tiny plastic earpiece attached to a dictating machine.

"A V must think the world of you," she said. "She hasn't called for anyone else all day."

With a handful of the tried and true, Miss Ballou—or "Miss Bally" as she was known to the Norris family—shared in an after-hours sorosis whose privilege it was to call the boss "A V." She was an older woman than her boss, and had indeed been earning fifteen dollars a week in the stenographic pool at Mannix Publications for nearly two years before Ava discovered her. Together they had suffered, each on her echelon, through the thorny paths and mantraps of office competition until they had reached the eighth floor. Miss Bally, coming from an old Ohio town, reminded Ava of her own Midwestern origin, and lest the year go by without this humble

359

truth's being impressed upon the Norris household, Miss Bally was a regular guest for Thanksgiving lunch at Sutton Place.

"It's been quite a hassle," Miss Ballou said. "A V didn't get in until eleven this morning and we cancelled everything for the day. Just after lunch the papers started calling. She's been shut in with the telephone all afternoon. It looks like you're the man of the hour, if you know what I mean."

I nodded; I would rather not have known what she meant.

"You can go right in," Miss Ballou said.

It was not at all what I had supposed I would find at the pulse of *Blythe*. Never having recovered from what *Blythe's* interior decorating staff had wrought with the interior of the Norris' apartment, I was prepared for a still richer concentration of mirrors and Haitian art and polished, photogenic fixtures. The room from which Ava Norris directed the taste of her readers, however, was a rather different proposition.

The walls were paneled in light pine and upon one of them hung a series of simple black frames. They contained old patterns and illustrations taken from *Godey's Lady's Book* and samples of the work of Charles Dana Gibson. Ladies in bustles, ladies in long bathing costumes waving from the steps of portable bath houses, ladies with parasols, with bloomers—a humorous and yet nostalgic pageant of fashion in a benighted era when there had been no *Blythe*.

"Does it amuse you?" Ava Norris asked. "I like to spring it on people blind."

"You must have had quite a time fixing it up," I said.

"This is the only room where I can concentrate," Ava Norris said.

She sat behind the desk and I took the sofa. I looked carefully at her face, which, in the light of a wine-colored glass lamp with jingling prisms, looked drawn.

"You and I did some thinking today," she said flatly.

Suddenly she extended an arm toward where my hand lay on the mahogany arm of the sofa and patted me. Not being a lapdog, I withdrew the hand.

"Don't look dumbfounded, Duck," she said. "It will all come out in the wash. What's done's done. What you and I want to talk about is the future."

The future? I looked to her face again inquiringly, and saw it had softened in a disturbing way.

"You poor kids," Ava Norris said in her matronly tone. "What you must be going through."

It was dark out of doors by this time. I heard a rustling and a sliding of drawers in the outer office, as Miss Ballou tidied up and prepared to leave. I was totally alone with Ava Norris in that dim light. The realization came on me softly and not without a kind of eeriness. I had the feeling of acting in a dream where all speech and movement were distorted and grotesque as the deep cherry shade of this carpet and the blown glass paperweights and other antiquarian oddments with which Ava Norris decorated her lair. I was being lulled, narcotized into saying all manner of things that would be twisted, if I did not watch out, and used against me.

"You're in love, aren't you?" Ava Norris was asking. "Or aren't you?"

Ava Norris waited and I waited with her, for she must have known well that I would not answer. She was free to draw her own conclusions, and she did so cheerfully. "Of course, you're on the spot, and you're being careful. There are many things to think about at a time like this."

"George," I said, "for one."

"George has got to learn to take life as it comes."

"In other words, you want us to forget about George? He's not our responsibility."

A year, six months ago, I could sooner have flown to the moon than talk back to Ava Norris. And she, arranging herself on that incongruous Queen Anne chair, was extremely surprised.

"I've had my theory about George," she began to answer, even hesitantly at the start. "You know what my premonitions were. . . . I'm sorry to say that every one of them is confirmed—according to schedule."

"Some people believe I did this to George," I said. "Tilton, for instance, and his friends."

"Harry Tilton can go straight to hell."

"I'm not sure he isn't right," I said.

"But it's plain as the nose on your face. What do *you* suppose was wrong with George?"

"I don't know which came first. He was so different from anyone I knew. He used to talk about his mother, and his father—he always loved his father."

"And his money—" she started to say.

"It wasn't so much the money. It was the world, I suppose. I mean he couldn't get out of his world into any other. Dr. Kew used to tell us about the world beyond—"

"How he loved that school."

"He's not weak," I said. "What about the things that eat away at him? It takes something to stand up and keep going."

"Keep going downhill," she said nastily. "He did well at school and in the Army because he saw what was expected of him. But when he was older and he didn't know what was expected of him," the tapering manicured fingers drummed upon the desk, "pfft—the floundering began. I saw it. I knew what was going to happen, and what did I do about it? I relied on you. You see I'm a selfish woman, darling. I was worried about my little girl."

"And that's why we're here?" I said.

"Let me tell you the scheme," she said. "We're packing Liles off on the plane tomorrow evening—"

The scheme was entirely of Ava Norris' devising, though by using the plural pronoun she implied that her husband Hadley had had a hand in it too. It called for a flight to California, and a long stay there, of six months minimum, at the home of Lila's cousins in La Jolla. There she would have time to get a grip on herself. Avoid as much of the scandal and waste of motion as possible, was the idea. Lila might not be happy right away, but they would set her to doing things. There was a good summer theater in La Jolla.

"We all bore a responsibility for this," Ava Norris said, "and this is how we are meeting it, Gus. I think I have the right to ask what you intend to do."

Ava Norris' fingers were busy with an engagement calendar, riffling through the pages in an impatient all-or-nothing fashion, as though she were behind in a gin rummy game. "In October, September at the earliest, Lila will be home. That gives you plenty of time, but just the same I think we are entitled to know your feelings as of now."

"I don't know what to tell you, Ava. I don't know what I think now."

"You're hedging, Duck. You're playing a game."

"It's no game. I don't know, that's all. Is there such a rush?"

"But you must have some predisposition?" she said, leaning

362

forward so that her hennaed hair was almost brushing my cheek. "It isn't as if you and Liles were strangers," she said, fairly purring. "And I know how Liles feels about you."

"Liles is an unpredictable girl," I said. "That's putting it mildly."

"I do believe she knows what she's doing, and she knows that she knows. Even that's a great step when you think of the past."

"I don't want to think of the past," I said. "That's the trouble."

"I'm proud of her, for the first time really rather terribly proud."

"Yes," I said, considering. "I must say I admired her the other night."

"She said you were wonderful. Calm, strong, deliberate. That's what she needs, darling—someone who wears trousers. I'm glad to see you've learned that much about women, and you've learned that this is a man's world."

"Ava, I can't tell you what I don't know about now. Leave us alone. Can't you let us work it out for ourselves?"

Ava Norris raised her head imperiously. "I hear you're getting along so nicely with Bert Seidel. One day you'll be a Junior Partner."

"Or a real Supreme Court Justice."

"You're being fresh, darling. The point is you're established. You're starting to earn an income. That's something I know about, and care about."

"I can't support a wife."

"Is it so perfectly extraordinary that my husband and I might arrange something?"

"I don't want those arrangements," I said.

"You're being belligerent."

"We may as well have this understood, Ava. If you want to manage Lila's life, or Mathilde's or Chee Wee's, maybe you can do it. But you're not going to manage mine. I'm resigning from the puppet show."

I was glaring across the desk at her, scarcely recording my own words in the jubilant rush of my temper. I was primarily aware that I had committed myself to a touchy piece of parlor heroics. To a position from which there was no retreat. I saw the manicured fingers close over the appointment calendar, lift, and slam it to the surface of the desk. A pair of glass paperweights trembled. The prisms jingled at the base of the lamp. A hostile silence followed, and this was broken, faintly, by the dry sound of her breathing.

"I suggest you think it over," Ava Norris said quietly, "before you burn your bridges behind you."

"I don't have to think it over," I said.

"Aren't you being perhaps impetuous? Have you thought where you'd be if it hadn't been for George? If it hadn't been for Lila, or for me? You think that over carefully before you leap." Her expression changed now into a wan and pacificatory smile. "I apologize for my temper. Will you come for dinner soon, now that we've cleared the air?"

"Please don't ask me, Ava. The air hasn't cleared that much."

"Are you perfectly certain? Do you realize what my husband and I could do for you? What connections will you have? I shouldn't say that George is likely to do very much for you now."

"I'll do things for myself."

"How pompous we are!" she said flirtatiously. "Well, there'll be plenty of time to work this out."

"You don't believe I meant that," I said. "I'm going to look out for myself, and I don't want to be taken in hand."

"Pompous," she said. "You're not walking out on me, not when I've been counting on you for ten years, my dear young man."

"I mean it, Ava."

She smiled again and tried to pat my hand again. "But I don't believe you for a minute."

When I left, she accompanied me as far as the elevator. She was quiet and sullen, as though for one time she was unsure of herself.

"Good night, Ava," I said, "that's quite an office you have."

"Poor thing. What are you going to do?"

"I'll be all right," I said.

"We'll be waiting for your call, Miss Bally and I."

She lifted her hand half-heartedly, then let it drop and kept watching me while I moved to the back of the car and buttoned up my raincoat, and the elevator doors slid together and shut out that impenetrable face.

Chapter Thirty

Lower Park Avenue was unfamiliar ground. As I walked north-ward to Grand Central a cold rain that had been threatening all day began to fall. It splashed rudely against the sidewalk and onto the pools of melting snow and the sodden bits of refuse in the gutters. It seemed a harsh and alien world; I was furiously homesick.

I had a sandwich and a milkshake for supper at Liggett's on the Forty-second Street side of Grand Central, and then descended to the subway and rode to the Sixty-eighth Street exit at Hunter College and Lexington. Up on the street once more, the hard rain continued to cleanse the city night. I walked in it quietly, per-mitting my reflexes to guide me through that familiar neighborhood, where George had purchased flowers for Lila, past the Bachelor's Friend Laundry and Dry Cleaners, and past the Gotham Wine & Spirits that had made deliveries to us faithfully six nights a week until midnight, all of them closed and waiting cheerlessly for morning. My mind was blank, easing deeply into a vacuum, for now all the decisions were made; everything I did henceforth would be by predirection. So I had no choice but I must go to George Marsh, and offer, for what it was worth, some token of commiseration.

Harry Tilton was on hand to greet me, with a flesh-colored band of adhesive beneath his lip.

"Slugger," he said with a dishonest grin. "I knew you'd show up sooner or later."

"The mouth hurt?" I asked.

"Not so's you'd notice. I should have decked you, but I didn't have the heart."

Harry's indirect apology came as I had anticipated. Bygones very easily became bygones with Harry once he had lost a showdown.

"Is George home?" I asked.

365

"Where else? I carted him home Saturday night. He hasn't been out since."

"Did Lila see him yesterday?"

"But naturally."

Wait, I thought. There was one last score to settle with Harry Tilton. "Did you talk to George before Lila did? Did you see him when you came back the other night?" I asked.

Harry's eyes darted sideways, dropped to the carpet. "Talk to him? He was out like a light."

"You seemed to have something on your mind," I said stepping toward him, "about Lila and me. What were you going to say, Harry?"

"You and Liles?" Harry Tilton's back was against the wall. He leaned there in a not quite convincing attitude of laissez-faire.

"What's there to tell, lover?"

"I'm asking you," I said.

There was a guilty, begging look about him which, rather than stay my threatening, invited it.

"What's this talk from you about me and Lila?" I said, taking one step closer.

"You don't deny it?" he said faintly. "It's not exactly news that something's going on."

"Exactly what is going on?"

"Don't get me wrong," Harry said. "Don't put words in my mouth. I didn't say you were shacking up or anything."

"You're sure you didn't say that?"

He shrugged. "You have to admit it looks fairly queer. When George was in Texas, Saturday night . . . and now the wedding's off. Just put two and two together, from George's point of view. I'd say it was a funny way of being buddies. . . . Hell, I'm not blaming you. I had that hankering myself. I'm being very honest with you."

"You'd better be honest," I said. "You tried your licks while you were in the Navy, and don't think that's news either."

Harry produced a pocket comb and drew it several times hastily through the shiny black locks on the back of his head.

"Next time you feel like talking to George," I said, "you just remember that."

I stabbed a finger at Harry's chest, on the white shirt below the striped bow tie. "I have an idea—we'll go in there and tell him, both of us. That way he'll get it all straight. Straight from the horse's mouth."

"That's childish," he said, recoiling. "What would it prove? Maybe you believe in kicking a guy when he's down."

"All right," I said, "I called your bluff, and I'm ready to call it again any time. Now I want to see George."

"He wants to see you," Harry answered, and grinned. He looked so relieved. "Hey, don't put that wet coat on the *sofa!*"

I found George Marsh in the study. He was reading on the cot, his stockinged feet on the white center of the Nazi flag, and there was a glass in his hand.

"It's about time," he said shyly. "I thought you'd skipped town."

"That's what I should have done," I said.

He laughed, unnecessarily loudly, as though he hadn't heard a joke in weeks, and he got up from the cot. He was wearing a cashmere sweater and flannel pants and no shoes. George looked worse than at the ushers' dinner, and his smile was painful to watch. He cleared his throat.

"I've got a piss-whistler of a cold. Manuelo's been fixing me toddies. Can you use a toddy, Sport-o?"

He bounded on stockinged feet into the hall, taking his glass with him, and called to Manuelo in the kitchen.

Left to myself, I made a last inspection of his sanctuary. I followed the glint of the reading lamp against the souvenirs: the storm trooper's helmet, the weapons, the staggering infantryman on the cover of *Yank*. Above the cot the ornaments had been rearranged to make space for new additions: the commission he had earned at Fort Sill, the Diploma in Merit from Emmanuel, a photograph of the triumphant eleven: *E–27; M–O, G. Marsh, Capt.* Gopher Marsh, in shoulder pads, with the proud E on his chest, stood in the center of his backfield, exactly bisecting the white goal posts, stood behind his seven crouching linemen. Untired, unself-conscious faces, reminding me of a Housman sonnet.

I didn't hear his return; shoeless, he could move silently on the carpet. I didn't know how long he'd been beside me, a hot toddy glass in either hand.

"We never throw things away," he said. "It's an old family trait. Did I ever show you the organ alcove at Uncle Mark's?"

367

He passed me a glass and we each took an end of the cot. He started to speak and a racking cough prevented him. He blew his nose and swore quietly, then his hand, retreating from the Kleenex box, touched the book he had been reading.

"You read *The Young Lions*, Sport-o? Great book. Great war story."

"Thought you wanted to see me," I said sternly.

"Oh, sure, sure."

He raised his glass and indicated that I raise mine. "Here's to our mutual friend, Sport-o. She's a done gone and left us. Let's you and me get drunk, stay drunk all week if we want to."

"If there's anything you want to know, anything I can tell you—"

"What's there to tell?"

"You have the right to know the truth."

"Why do I have to know the truth? Hell, I don't want details. It's bad enough knowing what I do know. . . . I don't want to know what you did, or how many times, or where you did it. I'm telling you I can't stand to know. Let's drop it, forget the whole thing."

"But Lila did tell you?" I said.

"I wouldn't let her. Why should I? It wasn't her fault, and it wasn't yours. You were just a symptom of hers, Sport-o. It could have happened to anybody."

He shook his head hopelessly, and turned his shadowed face to the light. He had no temper to challenge, only this instinct to retreat, and that was why he had kept to his sanctuary since Saturday, surrounded by the bric-a-brac of the past.

He had consumed almost half of the hot drink. Each of us sipped industriously in the silence.

"Aren't you going to get mad?" I asked him. "You do feel something?"

"You mean am I jealous? Sure. I could have knocked your teeth in, but what's the use? I'm no good at that."

"It's not too late to get mad," I said. "You'd feel better. Try hating somebody."

"I don't hate anybody, Sport-o. I'm no good at it."

"You're so Goddamn noble," I said. "You make me sick."

"Why?" He looked at me, vaguely offended. "I like to keep my friends." He turned back, shyly, to face the light. "You can move back any time," he said quietly.

"Are you actually asking me to move back now?"

"Damned right I am."

"I don't believe you. One or the other of us is crazy."

"Honest to God, I don't understand anything. I might as well be talking to a stranger."

"That's it," I said. "I always have been a stranger."

"I don't see. I don't see anything."

George Marsh rolled the now empty glass back and forth between his palms, but he made no attempt to move. He sat on the edge of the cot, broad shoulders hunched, quiet but for the bronchitic breathing. There was the sound of a dialing telephone in the hall, and Harry Tilton laughing and talking softly to a girl.

"Explain it to me," George said. "Something happened. You tell me what it was."

"Once upon a time you lent me thirteen dollars for a football that you said I had to have. It all started right there."

"Funny, I don't remember."

"I've been taking things from you ever since, and not only me—"

"I don't want a lecture," he said, once more holding up his hand. "I've heard it all and you know what I think."

"What do you think?"

"We're all friends. I don't see why everyone can't be friends," he said desperately. "What else do you remember? It was so damned long ago."

"All kinds of things. Do you remember Dismal Gregore?"

George was deep in his own thoughts. "Damn," he said. "I think I'll go back and give the old place the once-over. Damn, I was there six years." He was glancing about the walls of the room. "And here we are, you and I, like this. I don't understand."

"Things have a way of changing. You expect them to go on forever."

"You talk like Cuppy Vale. . . . Vale never liked me, did he?"

"Of course he liked you."

"I liked him," George said petulantly. "Goddamn it, why didn't he like me? I don't think you even like me. Honest to God, I don't. What's the matter, are we so different?"

"Yes," I said, "but that doesn't mean I don't like you."

"Yeah, I suppose that's why you ran out."

"I can't play in your league. That's why."

"Is this going to be a little talk about economic advantages?" George said. "You know what I care about money."

"You know what I mean," I said firmly. "I never did fit your scheme. It was so much oil and so much water."

"You didn't use to think so," George said.

"No."

"Then what's it all about? Why did you run out? Are you so superior to everybody?"

"Why do you think Lila ran out?" I said.

He had set down the glass and was holding it between his stockinged feet and glaring at it. His fingers, their tendons bulging, dug like talons into his thighs. He looked like the soldier on the *Yank* cover.

"You think I'm a mess—a dim bulb."

"Don't be an ass."

"Don't lie to me," he was muttering. "Don't ever lie. . . ."

He let go his thighs. Even his wrists hung loose as he glared at the floor. I waited for him to tear at his hair or beat his chest or lash out wildly at space, anything. Instead his broad shoulders drooped lower, his jaw slacked, as though the last sinew of pride had been severed. I wanted to seize and shake him.

The cravings, denied. The happy old dependencies, vanished. Leadership, duty, obedience, the corset stays of his life, all sprung. And love? Gone too. Even such a burning, giddy love, gone, gone.

Grab your bootstraps, man.

He only coughed, a mild, sobbing cough this time.

Suddenly I had no desire to watch him, and no faith in the power of consolation. I had looked too close and I recoiled. And, as with a soldier who had seen the man next him die, my immediate instinct was joy that it had been he and not I.

"I don't believe you any more," George was saying hollowly. "I don't even understand you. I'll have to get to know you all over again. It may take some time. What I want to know is—Sport-o, where do we go from here on in?"

"Let's shake hands," I said.

"Let's do that."

He rose from the cot and shook hands, very stiffly and formally.

370

"I'm sorry," George said, "I feel putrid tonight, putrid. Shall we get Manuelo to fix some more toddies?"

When we went into the living room, there was Harry Tilton pretending to read *Adrift in a Boneyard* by Robert Lewis Smith.

"That was Doris on the phone," he said to George. "She's going to be with us for supper."

"Fine," George said.

"And I took the liberty of asking Manuelo to cook us up a steak."

"Fine."

"We're running fairly low on gin," Harry said.

"Right you are. I'll call for some."

"Oh, I can call," Harry said.

George grinned at him fondly and nodded and he managed to grin at me as well. "There should be plenty of steak," he said to me. "You might as well stay for some."

"I've had supper, thanks."

"Stay for another toddy."

"No thanks."

"Don't forget. You still got that cocktail shaker of mine."

"I won't forget."

He was walking after me to the front door and when we were outside the apartment, he rang the elevator bell.

"What are you going to do with yourself now?" he asked. "Hibernate?"

I laughed. "What are you going to do?"

"Don't you fret," George said.

"What about the export business you talked about?"

"That," he said. "I guess I can find something better if I take my time. That's the important thing, take your time. As soon as I'm over this cold, I'm thinking of a little spear fishing in the Bahamas. You know I've never seen Nassau."

"Have a good time," I said.

We waited, stupidly, in the hallway, and it must have seemed to him, as it did to me, that the automatic elevator would never come.

George Marsh telephoned several times as spring was coming on. Once, to ask if I couldn't take off an afternoon to go with him to opening day at Belmont, and naturally I couldn't do it. And once

371

he was going to a dance with Chee Wee Gibbons at Greenwich and Chee Wee wanted an extra man, because she didn't trust his driving when he wasn't sober. But I had to work late that evening and couldn't go to Greenwich. Finally, he was insistent to get back the cocktail shaker his ushers had given him. He wanted to keep it in the study, kind of gag, he said. But I never found the time to stop off at Seventy-first Street. So, for a dollar, I had the office boy wrap up the shaker and mail it parcel post.

My place was in the bull pen, trying to please Bert Seidel. I did all the dull and dirty jobs that Macy had done before me, and by night I went to school to study for the bar examination that came in June. Late in May, I got the wedding invitation:

Mr. and Mrs. Marion Barton Slater

request the honor of your presence

at the marriage of their daughter

Doris

to

Mr. Howard Tighe Tilton, Junior

Friday, the sixteenth of June, nineteen hundred and fifty

at four o'clock

Church of St. James

New York City

R.S.V.P.
    Bluebonnet Farm
    Hartford, Connecticut

It came as a complete surprise to me, but Chee Wee Gibbons had been anticipating it for months. Evidently she had just got her

372

invitation too, for that same day she telephoned me to my chagrin and Macy's disapproval at the office.

"Gussy, where on earth have you been hiding?"

"I'm hibernating. My nose is to the grindstone."

"Rat. You might have called me. Have you heard the news?"

"Is it legitimate? Why should he want to marry Doris? Is she that rich?"

"Gussy darling, you're rather unsophisticated. Don't you know that handsome men choose plain wives?"

"Why don't they do it in Hartford at the home of the bride?"

"Really, Gussy. Can you imagine poor Harry getting married at Hartford?"

"Look, I'll call you sometime. I can't talk now."

"No, you don't brush me off, Gus Taylor. You're going to that wedding and you're going with me. The reception is at the Water Club. I understand it's going to be the most lavish city wedding of the spring, and I'm desperate for an acceptable escort."

"What makes me acceptable?"

"That's it. The same old Taylor. Insist on being difficult. Where have you been keeping yourself?"

BOOK III

The Chimney Sweepers

Chapter One

Lila Norris, being constitutionally incapable of following a plan precisely, found it impossible to return to New York in September, as agreed. She gave all manner of excuses for her delay, and I accepted them with equanimity. When she did return, at the very end of October, I was thankful for the extra weeks of procrastination. Regarding each other, we had not yet made up our minds. Many another decision had been made for us that summer, however, by Joseph Stalin and Harry Truman and by the panicky wardens of military manpower, none of whom had troubled to consult us.

Lila was looking beautiful with a durable California tan. She was composed, penitent, and wistful, and she swept back into the city on a surge of good cheer that buoyed us all just after General MacArthur had recaptured an essential port in an Oriental land that Chee Wee Gibbons and others made quite a show of having always thought to be a part of Egypt. Our spirits were rising, moreover, because of the rumors that Reservists were wanted no longer, that no more would be called, that those gone already would soon be released. Such devoted brides as Doris Slater Tilton, whose husbands had seemed the most vulnerable to recall, were unboundedly relieved and often festive. Doris had planned the cocktail party to which I promised to take Lila on Wednesday afternoon as a joint housewarming and celebration. Oddly enough, this party had not been planned by Harry, as Doris made plain by her novel invitation cards. On the front of mine, a crowing rooster appeared in crimson beneath the words, "Come for Cocktails, BUT—" and I had turned the leaf to be confronted by a baby girl in a sunbonnet whose finger was pressed against bowed lips, enjoining me to: "Shhhh, it's a surprise!" Underneath, in a rectangular

377

girls'-school hand Doris had written: "Say, stranger, we haven't seen you in ages!"

In October I was feeling less gregarious even than I had felt at the Water Club in June, and the necessity for perpetuating my camaraderie with Harry was that much more obscure to me. But since Lila and I must face Harry sometime, the cleanest, most logical way to do it would be to visit his new apartment in Peter Cooper Village together. Lila had said it would be a simple matter to lay aside old grudges, and I was sure that she was right. For the newness of seeing one another again was wearing off, leaving a queer and undiscussed pressure distressing to both of us. Therefore, when the day came the prospect changed to one of perverse relief. It was preferable to be going with Lila to a party instead of being alone with her.

I was in a placid frame of mind that autumn morning, for two reasons. For one, my companion Macy's spirits were soaring. As of the last twenty-four hours his servitude at Swain, Seidel, and Lawler had been terminated with a communication from the Department of Defense. In sixty days' time Macy was to report to the Commanding General, Yokohama Military District, for assignment. He was to leave us on Friday and spend his last weeks at home in Pennsylvania. It was hard to envisage my birdlike companion in G.I. glasses and steel helmet once more, participating in the advance to the Yalu, yet he was unrestrainably eager to go. His boyish jubilation had taken the office by storm from the partners to Mrs. O'Mara.

The other reason for my good spirits was the afternoon off granted me by Bert Seidel. I had not made a habit of requesting free afternoons, but today was an exception, for Aunt Connie was in town on her way home from her annual visit to Albany and I was to have lunch with her.

We met at a quarter past twelve, the Elm Street dinner hour, at Longchamps at Madison Avenue and Seventy-ninth Street. My aunt had chosen this restaurant, which was some ten blocks from the genteel little hotel where she stayed when visiting New York, because Uncle Torbert had always taken her there. She and Uncle Torbert had lunched in this tinseled emporium on their last spree in Manhattan; and the name of Longchamps was indelibly stricken upon her mind as a synonym for gaiety and sophistication.

I found her seated on a banquette of simulated leather, waving at me across a room of vacant, plastic-topped tables as happily as if we were in one of the Parisian cafés to which my uncle, during a lifetime of promising, had never taken her. She was a small figure in widow's black, wearing a new hat and a veil. A sentimental medley of Andre Kostelanetz was being piped rather distastefully from a wall, through the courtesy of Muzak.

"Hello, Aunt."

She had been sipping sherry. I kissed her on the cheek, upon the veil. "I hope I'm not late," I said.

"Dearie," she said, "I wanted to make sure we'd have a nice table. They wouldn't take a reservation over the telephone, not even after twelve o'clock."

"Not many people eat at twelve o'clock in these parts, Aunt, unless they're having breakfast."

"Gus, you've gotten so sophisticated, I hardly know you any more," she said, and I sat opposite her and smiled back across the little table.

"It's not as if the place were jam packed," I said.

"Don't tease me, dearie, I know you know all about New York."

She tucked a hairpin into her hair just under her hat. Her hair, which she had done in Worcester for the Albany visit, was a nearly pure white. It was clean and chaste in contrast to the futuristic gold, reddish design of the walls.

A drink was waiting at my place, an amber concoction of gin and too much Vermouth with a wizened dwarf of an onion nestling on its bottom.

"They told me it was a genuine Gibson cocktail," Aunt Connie said. "I thought I'd prove that I can be just as grand as your New York friends. Don't you want your cocktail?"

"It looks delicious," I said.

"Dearie, who was the lady who always gave you Gibson cocktails?"

"She doesn't give me cocktails any more."

"I thought she was very grand."

"She wasn't so grand," I said.

Aunt Connie sighed. "I'm so glad your uncle and I never had to live in New York."

"It's not as bad as that, Aunt. Mrs. Norris and I didn't end up on

379

very good terms. I haven't seen her since a wedding I went to in June."

"I wish your uncle and I could have done more for you, dearie."

"You did everything for me. All summer I've been thinking about how much you did."

I knew she was listening, but I couldn't see her face, for that was hidden behind the huge cardboard folds of a menu.

"Aunt, what's that you have there?"

I reached to the banquette before she could snatch the object away. It was a magazine. The November issue of *Blythe*. On the cover was a photograph in autumnal colors of a slender girl, her hands thrust deep in the pockets of a billowing tweed coat, her underfed face looking over one shoulder with an expression of stifled agony at two male models dressed as athletes who were occupying themselves with a football.

"What are you laughing at?" Aunt Connie said.

"I thought you only read the *Atlantic Monthly*."

"You never tell me about your life. I have to find out as best I can."

"That's not my life, Aunt. I promise you."

Still, there was a haze of doubt in her eyes. "I had such a nice visit with your cousin Nella in Albany," she said. "Cousin Nella has always been interested in you. She has friends in New York."

"And they've been telling her things?" I said. "And Cousin Nella's gotten you all at sixes and sevens."

"I'm not at sixes and sevens, dearie. She did have a newspaper clipping. I must say I didn't like it. Your uncle always said that the only respectable place for one's name to appear in print was on the obituary page."

"Uncle Torbert never saw a gossip columnist," I answered. "I used to know one very slightly, his name was Gabriel Paster. It got to the newspapers through him."

"I'm glad your uncle never saw that clipping. He was so interested in your friends."

"I had a set of friends, Aunt, and I promise you they all tried to be respectable. Cousin Nella would say they were vulgar, but I don't believe they were. I wish you'd explain that to Cousin Nella."

"Dearie, you hardly ever mention your girl. I hear she's terribly grand and glamorous." My aunt looked at me suspiciously.

"There wasn't any scandal," I said, positively, "and there isn't going to be."

"Gus, you'll tell me if you're going to get married?"

"I promise there's nothing to tell," I said.

"You're in a position to get married. You have such a good job and you've had your first promotion."

"I should have told you about Lila, Aunt. She's a luxury product. You don't marry a girl like that on a hundred dollars a week."

"Your uncle was making much less than that when I married him. It doesn't matter what she is, dearie, as long as she's a nice girl."

"She is a nice girl."

"I hope you'll let me meet her," she said.

"I don't think you'd have much to talk about, Aunt. You wouldn't like her family."

"It doesn't matter what I think. You're the one who must consider her family. You've been attentive to their daughter for a long while. What do you suppose they think, dearie?"

"I don't care what they think."

"You've got to make up your mind," she said gently.

"I know it, Aunt. I know it."

I ordered for her, since she was baffled by the complexities of the Longchamps menu. She requested a second glass of sweet sherry and sipped from it recklessly through the meal, and all the while the Muzak oozed luncheon music through the wall. We talked of this and that, about plays and New York prices, and about the variety of people you met in New York. And we talked about the war. I explained what it meant to be in the reserves.

"You won't do anything foolish this time? You were in the Army long enough."

"Aunt," I said, "if they want me they'll have to come and get me."

"It isn't fair," she muttered angrily. "The Bolsheviks. The Bolsheviks . . ."

"I remember Uncle Torbert telling me about the little Princesses being stabbed to death in their nightgowns. That was the first time I ever heard of Bolsheviks."

"Your uncle was a perceptive man. I often thought he should have entered the Government. He foresaw events. He greatly admired William Howard Taft. . . . Everything's changed too fast, the world's changed too fast. I'm glad that I don't live in New York."

She shook her head and said something more so softly, too softly to be heard through the luncheon music.

We had coffee after lunch. Aunt Connie asked if she mightn't have a finger bowl and when that was brought, she announced that she would like a cigarette. She smoked, pinching the cigarette between her thumb and forefinger as though if she relaxed for an instant, it might drop and burn her skirt. She watched the arrival of patrons who were filling the nearby tables. Some of them caught her gaze and stared back, and she smiled at them vaguely.

"Who do you suppose they are?" she said. "They seem so bored."

The check came. My aunt fussed with the snap of her purse and gave me a peremptory frown; this was to be her party.

"You promised to show me your apartment," she said.

Aunt Connie had seen neither of my dwelling places in Manhattan. Until quite recently my second, on East End Avenue, had not been fit for inspection. In the spring and for a great part of the summer, it had been a desultory shambles, visited only by friends as undiscriminating as Fuzzy Eaton. But after my raise, I acquired a new rug and some badly needed furniture, and a Hoover vacuum cleaner. I had the windows washed periodically, and Mrs. Rowe came two times a week to clean.

It was with a sense of achievement that I escorted my aunt slowly up the flights of narrow stairs and sat her in the easy chair on which I owed but two more payments to Bloomingdale's. Aunt Connie was pleased. She accepted a glass of ginger ale as another woman might of vintage wine and when she'd recoverd her breath from the climb, she thought she would like another cigarette.

I opened the window slightly. It was a warm day for October and my aunt was not accustomed to the fumes of tobacco. Outside, through the leafless trees the city had planted in Carl Schurz Park and around Gracie Mansion, we watched the tugs coursing toward the harbor and bucking the swift tides by Randall's Island. Here and there a stray gull which had penetrated this far into the city careened and plummeted over the murky water. If there was a power to this view, if its force lay in the solitude of the viewer, I was sure my aunt sensed it also. We were the same flesh and blood, the more purely so for this moment together in an outpost.

Chapter Two

Lila waited for me in the vestibule at Sutton Place. She was smiling rather more enthusiastically than was called for, as I was a good fifteen minutes late.

"I'm sorry," I said.

"Don't be silly."

"It was a nice afternoon. I was taking a walk in Carl Schurz Park."

"That's mean. Here I was all alone for two hours. . . . Did you miss me?"

"I was lost in thought," I said. "I lost all sense of time. There were all sorts of children playing in the park, with roller skates and dachshunds."

"Oh, you go to hell."

Lile smiled even more and her nose wrinkled, of course, like a little girl's.

"The family's dressing for dinner. They're going out, and I love you too much to let you run into them down here."

Out on the street I found a taxi headed downtown on First Avenue. Howard Tighe Tilton, Jr., and his bride lived in a modern, middle-income group housing development called Peter Cooper Village, but I hadn't found them in the phone book. Luckily Lila had the address handy on a piece of her mother's blue memo paper. She was perched on the seat, reading off a Twentieth Street address to the driver even before I closed the door of the cab. This attended to, she tucked it neatly into her purse, snapped the catch, and moved in such a way that the top of her head was leant upon my shoulder. I shifted my head to look at her and her lips confronted me, partly open.

"I have some Kleenex," she said presently, but there was disappointment in her voice. I didn't know why it was these semipublic displays of affection embarrassed me.

Lila wiped my mouth and cheek. Then she was consulting the mirror in her compact under the passing lights of the street lamps, and I was looking beyond her out of the window.

"A penny," she said, and squeezed my hand. "Gussy, what's the matter? What *is* it?"

"Not a thing," I said. "I was lost in thought."

I was looking at a sign posted on the seat of the cab:

SIT BACK AND RELAX

WATCH OUT FOR SHORT STOPS

"You never tell me what you're thinking. You're so far off that I can't get near you. It makes me frightened."

"I'm sorry," I said.

"Don't say that. You make me think of George."

"If you must know," I said, "I was thinking about my aunt."

"Oh, when can I meet Aunt Connie? When will you take me to East Northrup? You promised."

"Yes."

"I can wash dishes and I can cook a roast chicken. Damn it, I learned to do a lot of things in California!"

"I believe you," I said. "There's no call to scream."

I was smiling at her, though, from instinct; I was discovering that you could tell her nearly anything with a smile and she became meek.

"I do love you, Gussy, when you handle me like that," Lila said. "I only need to be handled."

It was hard to be stern, to "handle" her, while her perfume enveloped the back of the cab—as she very well knew—and when she was this penitent and biddable.

"Are you still mad at Mummy?" she said. "Don't you think it's quite silly to carry things on and on?"

"Let's not discuss it."

"My mother admired you too much. That was her mistake. She was fatuous."

The cab had turned up to First Avenue and was pushing downtown slowly through the rush-hour traffic, proceeding with much shifting of gears in the vicinity of Beekman Place.

386

Lila was saying there would have to be some reconciliation between me and her mother. Obviously, if we were to have any peace at all.

We were going through the Forties on First Avenue, going by the torn-down houses and the excavations and the rising UN building where a grinning Harry Truman, an old hand at laying corner-stones, had laid one just last fall. I rolled down my window and looked out in the chill dusk at the cranes and hydraulic equipment and the sawhorses marked off by burning pots.

"Will you look?" Lila said. "All those ideas and work and money, as if they never read a newspaper. They just go blissfully on, as if nothing had happened. I wish I was that idealistic, Gussy."

"You used to be," I said. "You had all sorts of ideals at Bassett Meadows."

"You know what Pappy said when the Rockefellers gave that land? He said it bore out everything he'd said about their being dangerously left-wing."

"And don't think he doesn't believe it," I said.

"And he wants General MacArthur for President."

"Your father should run for President. He'd have a wonderful time."

I could tell from her silence that I'd hurt her, so I placed a hand on her shoulder. "Cheer up," I said.

"I wish I weren't a coward, Gussy. At night I think I hear an airplane and I think how little time it would take me to jump under the bed, but what good would a bed do? I'd much rather have my bed with you, a great big bed, and be in it, not under it."

"Because you're scared?"

"I rely on you. I'm not a coward with you."

A moment later she said, "Harry Tilton may be called back in the Navy. At any minute."

"I won't lose sleep over that," I said.

"And Fuzzy Eaton was called."

"He volunteered."

"Is George in the Reserves? I can't remember."

"They can't get him very well, as long as he stays in Europe."

"And you? Will you be called?"

"We don't need to think about it now," I said.

So Lila squeezed my hand, hoping to elicit something. Her hand,

387

very small and cold, tightened and at last relaxed its pressure, as though she had conceded me a point. Once more the top of her head alighted on my shoulder, barely perceptible this time, like a delicate bird.

"Oh, what is going to happen?" she said aloud.

I was thinking of George Marsh standing in fatigues over the sink in Sergeant Doyle's kitchen. He was constipated and his cold was just beginning. He looked haggard, bereft, and tears welled in his eyes, the second time I'd seen him cry. I was thinking of the next morning, when my name appeared on the shipping list. George stood outside the barracks in the rain, in the rain and dark, singing and talking numbly, like a ghost. And I was remembering Cuppy Vale, our imperturbable martyr. . . . Now? I thought. So soon? Well, we'd had four years—no, five.

The driver made a determined stop at Twenty-first Street and the outer edges of Peter Cooper Village, slapped the flag down on his meter, and declared he would go no further. "I'm not goin' in there and drive around them circles, Mac. I got things better to do 'n take you on some goose-chase," the driver said, and I paid him with a smile, and tipped him well. Lila and I got out and stood on the sidewalk, looking up at that gigantic enclosure of monstrous brick and brazen windowpanes. I thought of the works of Mr. Kafka and Mr. Aldous Huxley.

"Why do you let him talk to you like that?" Lila was saying. "He's required by law to take you to the doorstep.

"You're awfully lenient with people," she said. "Why, even George would have done *something*."

These quiet words of hers brought sensations of annoyance and entrapment. I was annoyed by Lila's caviling, and her turn of mood. Lila was anticipating, most astutely, that we would become lost in this architectural jungle where the Tiltons made their home with hundreds upon hundreds of qualified newlyweds. She knew that I could not find our way alone, and that she might be called upon to help me. And so the timeless drama of male-female, of aggressiveness-passivity was about to be re-enacted. The drama was trying on Lila, choosing as she did to rely on me through thick and thin, to count on me for everything down to and including the most exasperating trivia. It seemed to me, in this initial moment of reaction, too much that I should be asked to be a

388

shelter from atomic blast, reassurance against the pathos of her father's mind, buttress against her mother, and walking, talking ground plan simultaneously.

"That scowl," she said. "I believe you could actually bite me."

"What was that Goddamned number?" I asked.

Inside, Lila waited while I searched the directory of tenants for the Tiltons' apartment. I went over to her and we both waited for the automatic elevator to descend, just staring at each other in the angry incandescent light.

"Darling," she said at last. "What's happened? This isn't how we were meant to be."

"It's my fault. This place drives me crazy."

"Darling, I didn't mean to be bossy. You should slap me down when I try."

"I know. You like to be handled."

"I can't stand it like this. I love you, Gussy. I really do."

She bobbed up smiling bravely and kissed me on the cheek. "You don't have to stay a moment longer than you want to."

"I'll have to leave around seven," I answered. "I've got to get downtown to work."

The elevator arrived and opened up its doors to us. Lila pressed a plastic button which caused us to rise slowly to the accompaniment of a dull electrical whine. Watching her smiling, I also wished desperately for a better communication between us. There were certain emotional miracles I could not achieve for her any longer. She would have liked things to be crystal clear, and they weren't.

"But you told me you had the afternoon off," Lila was saying, reproachfully.

"But I have to make up the work tonight," I said.

"But *why?*"

"Bert Seidel goes into court on Tuesday, Liles. He's trying to break the will of a rich old dead lady named Monaghan, and there's a lot of work to be done." I found myself offering a number of pat excuses. I told her about Macy leaving, about the piles of my own work to be cleared up before I took over his job.

"You spent all last Saturday cleaning up your work, and all Sunday afternoon."

"I'm an old drudge," I said.

"I think it's wonderful that you can work as hard as you do,"

Lila said, flatly. "I worry too much, Gussy. . . . I've had fearful dreams."

All summer she had been having bad dreams. Some had hung over her like shadows for days at a time. She found herself crying and frightened, for no reason. That was discouraging, because she'd believed she was all over that little-girl business. "At least I know what's wrong with me," she liked to say in a hopeful, touching voice. "At least I'll admit it. And that's half the battle, isn't it, Gussy? You can't improve, you can't grow up, if you don't see your faults. That's *true*, isn't it?" She had been so pleased and independent in February, all through probably the worst time in her life, for having at last done something on her own. It was discouraging to find it was not a permanent feeling, but she knew it would be a long time before she could make it permanent. So many things kept coming up, all conspiring to make the process slower and more difficult.

The car stopped itself on the eleventh floor and slid open its doors. Lila stepped out and I followed in her musky wake, admiring the reddish neatness of her hair. She took my arm and with her head brushing against my shoulder we proceeded down the hall with an almost matrimonial stateliness. We turned to the left in search of Apartment D. Smack on the wall before us, attached by bits of scotch tape, was a sheet of paper upon which appeared in lipstick the bold device: F. SCOTT TILTON'S DONKEY ROAST. A volley of lipstick arrows pointed down the hall where a door stood partly ajar. There was a great deal of noise, echoes of song and laughter.

"I thought it was going to be a surprise party."

"No one ever kept a secret from Harry," Lila said lightly.

"You can say that again."

"You won't mind if Harry asks questions about you and me?" she said. "Gussy, don't get sore. People can't help being curious. Everybody I lunch with is asking me. Chee Wee asks every day."

"I wish they'd leave us alone," I said.

I felt her hand on my arm. She had stopped walking and was trying to hold me back.

"Look at me," Lila said. "Look in my eyes. You'll be a good boy and be friendly, you swear?"

390

"For your sake I'll be friends with everybody," I said. "I'll do my damnedest."

Bursts of accordion music and hearty song were coming from the Tiltons' apartment.

"Jesus," I said. "Don't tell me that's the Chanticleers."

"It's only a small party," I heard her say. "Gussy, look in my eyes."

She had let her hair grow long in defiance of the prevailing vogue. It hung in a soft wave just above the shoulders of her woolen dress which matched it and gave it the color of autumn leaves. Her face smiling, her incredibly sweet scent, her lithe arms and breasts and legs had never seemed as attainable. I smiled, to prove I was not going to be difficult, and fingered the ends of her hair, then the small warm nape of her neck, affectionately, as I had used to. She was endeavoring to smile back, though all I saw was a sad tremor of doubt about her lips and her eyes far from shining.

"Bug?" she said. "Something's wrong."

"Everything has to change. Nothing's the same from one day to the next."

"Don't philosophize," Lila said. "Don't mumble things."

"Will you promise me there aren't any Chanticleers inside that door? Do you give me your word of honor?" I asked.

"Look at me, Gussy. Why aren't we sure? After everything that happened."

She was looking up, anxiously, and for that expression alone, I thought, she was easily the most desirable creature in the world. It was easy to forget the recent weeks, the dreadful minutes we had spent outside just now.

"You know I love you," I said.

"It doesn't make sense. I wanted everything to be changed."

The party sounds were coming louder from the apartment; someone had opened the door wide. We spun round in embarrassment and saw Chee Wee Gibbons standing there in a shoulderless, full-skirted dress, its purplish sheen accentuated by an array of scatter pins in shapes of bottleflies and beetles. She tossed her head to one side in a mocking gesture that suggested she knew our purest secret, and lit a cigarette with her new butane lighter.

391

"All right, you two," Chee Wee called. "I've got my eye on you. You're late."

Lila took my arm again and led me over the threshold.

I heard Harry Tilton: "Hey, lovey dovies, if I'da knowed you was comin', I'da baked a cake. Glad to *see* yez!"

Now he was scrupulously shaking Lila's hand. An old married man, he was above the brash neck-nuzzling greetings of the past.

And before I could move, Chee Wee had an arm about my waist and was saying into my ear: "Liles looks *delicious!* I'm so excited for you both, my baby."

And now Lila had me by the hand, guiding me into the living room toward a swarm of people and a fat, bald man playing "Good Night, Irene" on an accordion.

"Just be with me," Lila was saying. "Just let's be ourselves."

We were not together long. Her hand broke from mine and she looked back with a half smile. Someone pushed between us bearing drinks and three or four steps further on I lost her completely—to an unnecessarily suave boy who greeted her like a crazed Adonis. He wore a Stork Club tie, compliments of Sherman Billingsley. "Liles," I heard myself muttering. "Please," but I had been too late, too undetermined.

The party had been in progress some time, as was evidenced by conditions in the dining-living-room area. Two ashtrays and a dish of peanuts had been spilled on Doris' steel gray carpet; also, only a moment ago, an unsteady lieutenant, j.g., had turned too suddenly, and upset a vase of autumn flowers. The carpet had been scuffed, some chairs and lamps buffeted from their proper positions. Even now from where I stood I saw Doris Tilton darting about, tidying here and there, emptying cigarette butts into a silent butler.

With everyone having such a good time, you couldn't hope to have the room look as it had before this friendly invasion, and yet its original appearance was easy to imagine.

If you had come early enough, she might have taken you, shyly, on tour. And you would have admired the oyster white walls of the bedroom, the chintz-covered headboard of the low flat bed in which Harry and Doris may have attained the full rapture of marriage, largely by accident, after ten apprehensive days of honeymoon, and the snapshots of the honeymoon itself, the Tiltons in Bermuda, wearing shorts, holding bicycles, the publicity photo of Doris and Harry dining at the Little Club at the time of their engagement, the pictures of the wedding day—Doris tossing her bouquet, Harry clowning with the Chanticleers on the terrace of the Water Club—each fled moment recorded and enlarged on film, reasonably framed in red tape, and hung for posterity above Doris' pristine dressing table. Now a quick peek at the kitchen, with its burnished Hammacher Schlemmer copperware, and now the small, shipshape bathroom, and there above the tub the picture of the little French boy in a straw hat, bent back relieving himself into a pastoral stream and the whimsical caption: *Ne buvez jamais d'eau*. And back to the living-dining-room area to admire the sheet mirror which lent depth to the room, and the Van Gogh reproduction which lent it individuality, the scantily filled book shelves and their mirrored boxes of drooping philodendron. The oyster white walls again, and the wall pots of ivy, the racks of inconsequential Lowestoft and Dresden, to notice the Steuben glass dolphins parading across the dining table, beneath the oil portrait that Doris had done of her cocker spaniel her junior year at Bennington, only a year before he died. Be sure to see the cabinet-model television-phonograph-radio. ("That suitcase-type arrangement on the top is the wire recorder that Harry bought me for our third month-anniversary.") See it, believe it, right down to the last flap-winged coffee table, each receptacle stocked with cigarettes or nuts, each Ronson table lighter primed and ready. . . . The place was pretty scuffed up now. What I needed was a drink.

Cokes, Dubonnet, Bellows Partner's Choice, and even Gilbey's gin were available at the portable twin-shelved bar I had seen by the kitchen door. A kind of stag line had formed there, and I moved toward it, but my way was blocked by the accordion player. I saw the white silk shawl was tied about his waist in the form of a cummerbund and damn if he didn't have on a red fez, black tassel and all.

"Tune?" he said, and I attempted to dodge aside.

"Name me a tune," he said.

"Hell," I said. "I don't care."

"I know three thousand tunes."

"'Avalon.'"

"Now there's a tune."

Then I encountered some faces and I was shaking hands. I confused a Murray Tait with one Jarvis Polk, who had been one of Harry's friends on the Yale rugby team and might even have been a Chanticleer, for all I knew. I bumped into a petulant girl in a poodle cut who was dipping a piece of cauliflower into some Russian dressing.

I shoved in toward the kitchen door and reached it as the last notes of "Avalon" choked and died in the accordion. I came upon the Tiltons bustling between the sink and the portable bar, hands full of rinsed-out glasses. I was careful to keep out of their way and not disturb them. This was a rare phenomenon, a view of them alone in their native habitat.

Harry was looking nearly unkempt, and Doris almost plump, but marriage had wrought greater miracles than that to the Tiltons:

She had been handling wet glasses, was drying her hands on a checked red gingham apron. "Darling, we're out of ice."

He had just set down two highball, four old-fashioned, and three martini glasses, so meticulously. (The martini glasses, which were the fragilest of wedding presents, were decorated with hand-painted troutflies and could probably be used for orange juice in the mornings.) "But I ordered a gallon of cubes, sweetie pie."

"Sweetie, they're about gone."

"Did we invite the Andrewses from across the hall?"

"Sweetie, you said not to."

"Damn, we can't ask them for cubes. Goddamn it to hell. . . . . Sweetie, I wasn't swearing at you."

Eyes cast down on the linoleum, a timid, puppylike sound of grief.

"Aw, sweetie pie."

A rush, a cheek kiss, an almost broken sherry glass, and now, the just reward of perseverance, the discovery of a completely untouched icetray which Doris, searching frantically, had overlooked.

Harry started for the door again, taking an uncut head of cheese wrapped in red cellophane, upon a blond wood breadboard.

"Sweetie?" his wife said.

"Sweetie?"

"It's sticky. Nobody is circulating."

"Baby, listen. Listen to that noise."

"You didn't ask Enos to play 'The Most Beautiful Girl in the World.'"

"I'll ask him. I promise, angel baby."

Meek, unspectacular Doris, no Conover girl, no Quiz Kid either, yet nonetheless imperatrix of her home. Then this was why Harry had selected her, without realizing it, from dozens of others not so supremely endowed with the savage weapons of frailty, who did not know how to practice the tyranny of tears. I looked again at Harry holding the cheese on the blond wood breadboard and knew that this was the reason.

Doris had seen me. She was waiting, unsure of how to acknowledge me.

"Hello, Doris," I said first. "It's swell to see you again."

I was holding Doris' hand, a moist, boneless-seeming end of flesh. She withdrew it and wiped it on her apron.

"I must look a fright," she said. "Oh dear."

"You look darned well," I said enthusiastically. "Marriage agrees with you. I can see that."

"Thank you, sir!" She gathered up her gingham apron and curtsied.

"She's gained twelve pounds," Harry put in ardently. "On her own cooking."

Doris was saying, "We ought to see more of you, Gus. You must come for a meal some night."

"You and Liles come together," Harry said.

"Yes," Doris said. "Liles looks so lovely."

Mercifully, the doorbell rang and Doris rustled off to receive the new arrivals. Harry looked after her proudly, even fondly.

"You got to feed 'em compliments and all that stuff," Harry said. "It makes a girl sure of herself, you know."

I nodded and smiled, but I could think of nothing to say.

"Matrimony," Harry said. "It's a great old institution. And what about yourself, boy? When are *you* taking the plunge?"

"I don't know what you're talking about," I said.

Harry clapped my shoulder. "Still the same old sourball."

At the portable bar he served me up a generous glass of Bellows and soda, and he was kind enough to light me a cigarette too. We stood there in the kitchen door and made elaborate efforts to be palsy, jocose. Harry was trying so and I was trying so, and it was telling on each of us.

"They shouldn't take family men," Harry was saying. "Let them take the kids first."

"They're really breathing down your neck?" I asked. It was a sadistic thing to wish anyone back into the Navy and I was doing it.

"I had six months sea duty. I admit it wasn't rough compared to some guys, but I was in. I tell you, I'll write letters, pull strings, anything. I'm not proud. I'm a *married* man."

"It shouldn't happen to you," I said. "You of all people."

I watched him frown, watched his lips press together, his deeply wronged look.

"Aren't you being fairly childish?" Harry said. "I don't hold anything against you."

"I don't hold anything against you," I said.

"Can't we knock this off, then?"

"Sure," I said. "Why can't we?"

"Dee says I gave you a fairly hard time at the wedding."

Dee. He was calling her Dee.

"That was my fault," I said. "I busted into the Serenade."

"I don't hold anything against you," Harry said. "I really don't. Now I don't know who you've been talking to, but—"

"I didn't talk to anybody. I just listened to a couple of your ushers talking on the terrace at the Water Club."

"Let's get it straight," Harry pleaded. "We're on your team, guy. I like you and Dee likes you—a lot."

"I didn't get that impression from those ushers of yours. They were giving out some pretty ugly talk, Harry."

"For your information," Harry said, "there was a lot of talk last winter, in case you disremember. I had to say something. I had to give *some* explanation."

"You gave them an explanation all right."

"Get this right," Harry said. "I'm no blabbermouth."

Enos was torturing the accordion. *Bye bye, baby. Don't forget that you're my baby, when they give you the eye. . . .*

I was staring at Harry, trying to catch his eyes and hold them, because Harry was a liar.

We'd made our last demonstration of palship. We eyed each

other silently. His nose was ever so slightly off center and there was a faint scar beneath his lip, souvenirs.

Harry swallowed and he made a hurt frown. "If you want to nurse a grudge. . . . It seems fairly moronic to me."

"I bear no grudges, Harry. I came here to be friends with everybody."

Harry simply grinned and patted into position some oily hair which must have come loose at the back of his head. He ducked into the kitchen where the lieutenant junior grade had come to look for ice, and so I lost him.

Enos had taken off the fez again, having reached the strenuous group-participation phase of his repertoire. He was playing "Smile, Smile, Smile" and "I've Been Working on the Railroad," accompanied by stray voices. But not the Chanticleers'. Thank merciful God.

One fellow approached the bar and served himself a glass of Dubonnet. Something about him, the fat hips and tight trousers, the fleshiness of the face struck a chord in me.

"Soaker!" I called. "Soaker Means!"

He smiled at me stiffly. "Seen you in a long time," he said.

We shook hands.

"You've put on weight," I said. "You certainly have changed, Soaker."

"Oh, Taylor," he said. "Really," and made a ponderous sort of frown.

I tried to smile; I was ashamed. Alfred Means was irreparably damned, had been so since the age of twelve, since that sad morning of his Sixth Class year when he had arisen from a prostration of homesickness and fear without realizing what he had done in his bed. He went to the washroom and brushed his teeth, unaware that his wet rayon pajama bottoms were drawn tight and transparent over his thighs. It had been his tragedy to choose a basin next to Eaton and Tilton and other yahoos. Thenceforth he was relegated to the limbo of the outcasts, with Boo Hoo Beemer and Frazzle Fern, and we had abused him, I no less cruelly than the rest, and forgot that Alfred was his name.

"You've changed yourself," Soaker Means said.

He stood before me like some bloated sea bird. Confident, reso-

397

lute, aggressive he looked, and it must have been years since anyone had called him Soaker.

"What are you up to?" he asked and so I asked him the same.

"I'm working in Washington," he said, "if you follow me."

"At the Bureau of Weights and Standards?" I said.

That provoked a patronizing, chesty laugh. "I'm afraid I can't be too specific. You know the way it goes, old boy."

Muttering about someone he had been talking to, Alfred Means vanished. Alfred Means, representing the eyes and ears of freedom, representing America's answer to the N.K.V.D.

You kept encountering people like Soaker who had gone to Washington with their brand-new Bachelor of Arts Degrees and a loose desire to Get Into Some Interesting Work, and had settled like schooners in a fog bank into the socially desirable, low-salaried, storybook vastness of the Sensitive Services. Though they were adjured to violent secrecies, meticulously instructed in deception and petty disguise, off the job they were as subtle, as inscrutable as any Irishman on St. Patrick's Day. A Sensitive Service man had instructions to adopt the name of a more prosaic government agency and to use it, cannily, as his camouflage. While he complied with this instruction faithfully, it was often difficult to resist the awesome réclame of officialdom, the sense of patriotic service which entitled one to such things as code names and celluloid building passes. Being dedicated body and soul to the grim and devious causes of the Sensitive Services, it was impossible to underact his role. The perils and cataclysmic intrigues with which they dealt, the maps and documents and files over which they pored daily, all had their effect on this tender zealot. And he and his companions acted out laborious masquerades, almost as though they had never heard of E. Phillips Oppenheim. They told you they worked for the Departments of State, Defense, Navy, or the Bureaus of Weights and Standards, of Fisheries, but you weren't expected to believe them. They would, in fact, have been quite hurt if you had. Their very reticence proclaimed what honor forbade them to say, that they knew more about trends than Lippmann, greater doom than the Alsop brothers, hotter poop than Krock.

Enos was playing the "Whiffenpoof Song" and as he paused between bars I heard a man's plaintive voice singing loudly and quite off key. It seemed to originate from a vacant part of the wall.

> Hah's ah pooah litul lambs that have lost their way,
> Hah-baah, baah, baah. . . .

The cherub.

His face was red, burned by the winds of autumn, and, not surprisingly, he was rather drunk. The cherub looked thinner; his hair which was clipped all round about a quarter inch from the scalp looked like turkey pinfeathers. He was propped against the wall, yet he held his trunk rigidly, his chest out proudly, as though he were in uniform. The uniform was optional on off-duty hours and so he had selected an odd chocolate brown and double-breasted suit borrowed from a companion in the Bachelors Officers Quarters. I had seen Fuzzy several times since August when he had been assigned to Mitchell Field, but I had yet to see him in the new Air Force uniform. He said it was corny, made you look like a Greyhound bus driver.

> Hah-genulmen songsters, out on a spree.
> Hah-baah, baah, baah. . . .

He kept time, waving a half-empty glass.

"What say, Gubber? You want to form a small song group?"

"Captain Eaton," I said, "is about to make a spectacle of himself."

"Wipe that smirk off your face, when you're addressing a field grade officer. Put away that glass."

"You were *promoted?*"

"Yes indeedy."

"It can't be," I said. "What is to become of our nation's defenses?"

"Put that glass away, young fella. Major Walter B. Eaton, United States Air Force, Commanding."

"No! Say it isn't so."

"You want I should let you touch my oak leaves?" he said. "I'll let you in on a little secret, Gubber. I'm a comer, a supersonic wonder. Buck general or bust—hey-yay!"

"Don't be a disgrace to your rank," I said. "Control yourself."

"And I'll tell you something, Gubber. Talk about Curtis Le May. Talk about old Hoyt Vandenberg." He assumed the position of the soldier at attention and saluted me two snappy highballs.

399

"You talk big," I said, "for a reservist."

"Little do you know, lad, what a comer I am. I'm all signed over. Put in for permanent rank. Yes suh, old General Vandenberg."

"You quit the dog obedience school?"

"Go 'way," he said. "I don't see why a college graduate and a superb physical specimen like myself has to fraternize with you enlisted men."

The cherub was so very happy, burbling. He was in like Flynn, fat. So far he had been an instructor but they were sending him somewhere soon. Soon he'd be barreling along in the big hairy-ass B-50's, leaving his very own vapor trail in the sky. The supersonic wonder. Move over, Curtis Le May.

I thought, you impenitent hero. You rootin' tootin' Mickey Rooney you. Can you never go back now to Chestnut Hill? Talk Grotonese? Or marry, settle down, be a Chestnut Hill boy? Send your children to Miss Windsor's and to Dexter School, go to every Alumni Day at Emmanuel, work off the Sunday A.M. hangover playing fast shinny with the college boys in the high board rink at the Country Club, Brookline? Last year you spent your days teaching obedience to dogs and evenings seeing something of one Prudence Mapes in Brookline or piling up your old man's car on the Worcester Turnpike. But you wanted wings and now you've got the Goddamn things, and you wanted them in 1942 as badly, when they canned you from college. They marked you KIA like Vale, but you fooled them and came back and with a fistful of oak-leaf clusters. Do you remember Vale, I wonder? Vale and Mo Beach and the outraged dead? I wonder what you think about or if your mind stirs at all when you are aloft, beaming like a ten-year-old and spewing vapor trails all over the wild blue yonder. Pig Alley to Mig Alley, with time out for chuckles. Major Walter B. Eaton, fiendish cherub. Bombs away.

"Do you hear from Gopher?"

"I get postcards," Fuzzy said. "I got one after he'd seen some grotto in Capri. He wrote he'd got blotto in the grotto. Yuk yuk. . . . Yes, and I got a wacky chain letter the other day."

"You mean the luck of Khufu?" I said. "I've been carrying it around in my pocket."

I made him talk about George and about all sorts of other things. It was too bad about this evening. I had to get back to work and Fuzzy wasn't drunk enough, he said, only somewhat uncertain. Which was lucky, because he had to be back at the base by 0 eight hundred.

We were doing fine until the very last, when he had to say, perfectly innocently: "What's this about you marrying up with Lila? I admit she's a sweet dolly and horny. But look what she did to the Goph. Buddy, she could murder you."

Chee Wee, when I talked with her, was somewhat less direct. She descended on me from a cluster of people to demand a cigaboo. Chee Wee was aflame with gossip, vagrant thoughts, and lofty purposes. She had read *The Far Side of Paradise*, and found it outstanding and terrific, and this summer she had discovered Colette. Speaking of this summer, why had I been so difficult, avoiding her, avoiding everyone? Why? And when Ava Norris asked me to New Jersey had it been necessary to be quite so ridiculous and rude? Had I no idea what I was doing to Liles?

"You don't have to look so baleful and withdrawn," Chee Wee said when she came to an end. "I love you, even with that dreadful Bahs-ton accent."

"You make me very nervous, dear heart."

"You can be so cute when you want. You remember how lovely you were at the wedding? We had that lovely soul scrape together."

"That was different. We needed each other there."

"You're boring," Chee Wee said. "I adore you and admire you, but you are boring. This reformed-character routine. It's so holier than thou."

"You're absolutely right," I said. "Aren't I just about the worst?"

She smiled defiantly. "I'm a phony but I'm a happy phony. You're an ex-phony and look at you. You even *look* like a monk. . . . Gussy darling, we're supposed to be friends."

"Ever since I got here," I told her, "I've been trying my level best to be friends with everybody. Just like the old days."

"You're a darling, but you're narrow-minded and stubborn. A reverse type snob. An antisnob snob." I put my hands in my pockets and glared at the floor. I was not in a fettle for parrying quips with Chee Wee.

"Did you read that book on snobs?" Chee Wee said. "It's sensational."

And I lost her too, off among the voices and the gay young people.

Whatever was I? A monk, an old man, a misanthrope? I walked among them, halfheartedly wishing that Lila, who was in the entryway laughing herself teary-eyed at something said by Jarvis Polk, and I might have a drink together. I talked some more or, better, listened to one of the couples from the floor below who had played tennis the past summer with the Tiltons at Manursing. She predicted that Doris would be a top-flight player if she went on taking lessons from Harry and he predicted that cotton futures would fall away off again at the end of the so-called police action. I talked to somebody and to somebody else, but there was too much noise. Right there I stopped feeling comfortable. I stood beside a very recent divorcée named Swiftie McGraw, hoping that I was smiling. I seemed to be looking at everyone through one of those one-way windows and I thought that if I kept smiling, kept up a gay façade, no one could see back through at me. Soon Enos was playing "Dixie" and the Goddamnedest loud group-participation songs. The voices and the laughter swelled like fury and everyone shouted the louder just for the sheer joy of being heard. Swiftie McGraw moved her lips and eyes as if to say something. I answered by whispering at her through the din the first thought which came to mind. Which was: "Life is real and life is earnest, Swiftie kid, and the grave is not the goal. Aren't we a gallant, sweet bunch of kids?" One of the Steuben glass dolphins fell from the table and shattered into a great number of pieces on the floor and Harry Tilton rushed over with a dustpan and broom before Doris got wind of the calamity. Enos stopped for a breather and the sound burst into silence. Yet only briefly, for somebody was playing with the wire recorder. It began with the squealing gibberish of the spool being played back through the amplifier, that followed by Harry's voice imitating Danny Kaye imitating Maurice Chevalier imitating the English language, and that followed by Chee Wee Gibbons' voice singing, "Oh violate me in the violet time. . . ." And then like an electric current the high shocking laughter of Lila Norris. . . . My watch said seven forty-three and it was time to go. I had to go, had to.

I crept off unnoticed and pushed into the closet in the entryway where my coat should have been but wasn't. Lila was holding my

coat and hers against her belly. She was doubled over in the aftermath of laughter. Her face was flushed and her eyes watery, leaving minute overflows in the crowsfeet below her eyebrows.

She straightened up and drew a deep breath, attempting to control her giggling. "Darling, you don't know how funny! Chee Wee
used to sing those songs at Miss Eustis'. Darling, if you could have
seen Colton Cutter's face!"

"I'm leaving," I said. "I'll buy you dinner if you want to come."

She backed away, teasingly, and put the coats behind her. "It's
too soon," she said. "I was going to hide the coats."

"Liles, I have to leave. Remember?"

"We just got here, darling. Aren't you having a fun time?"

"I'm having a fit of nerves."

"Oh Gussy, you aren't."

"Severe claustrophobia," I said. "Please let me have my coat."

She danced backward to the doorway, holding the coats behind
her.

"Don't be cute," I said.

"Oh let's fight!" Lila wrinkled her nose, made a bow of her lips,
and skipping forward, placed them on the point of my chin. The
coats dropped to the floor.

"You're lipsticky."

"You're loaded."

"Slightly. Harry made me drink three marts."

"Do you want to eat or don't you?" I said, and retrieved our overcoats.

Her smile faded. "I don't know."

"I'm sorry I have to work tonight, but I told you."

"Darling," she said softly. "What's the matter now? Did I make
you mad?"

"Couldn't we get away from this noise?" I said.

I took her by the waist and led her into the hall and around the
corner where the situation was quieter.

"I'll go with you," she said. "Kiss me."

"I don't want to make you go if you don't want to."

"I was having fun, Gussy. They're all old friends I haven't seen
for ages. You don't know how dismal I was, serving out my sentence at La Jolla."

"I thought you were sick of the whole bunch. You wanted me to take you away from them."

"I know." She nodded sadly. "I know I did."

"Okay then."

"I'll go with you, Gussy. Kiss me first."

"I'm not going to make you go. It's your decision, Liles. If you want to come, I'd love to have you."

"Darling, I don't know what I want. You shouldn't ask me. You should tell me what to do and I'd do it."

"And how long could we go on like that?"

"Gussy, kiss me now. I don't want to think."

I moved away from her and put my hands on her shoulders. "We might as well be on the bus playing the bus game. Pick a car and stick to your choice until we reach Madison Avenue. You never could stick to your choice." I was looking hard into her eyes.

"Don't draw parallels," Lila said. "This is only a party."

"Whichever you pick now, Liles, you'll be stuck with. If you pick me, it will be one of those hell or high-water propositions."

"Don't talk like that. Darling, don't *scare* me."

"Put on your coat then and come with me."

"Without saying good-by? That's rude."

"Nobody will be the wiser."

"Don't you want to keep *any* friends? You can't be happy if you use everybody and then desert them."

"This isn't desertion," I said. "This is escape."

"Tell me what to do, Gussy. You're my private Rock of Gibraltar."

"I want you to decide for yourself," I said. I moved away from her and down the hall to the elevator door, but when I reached it and looked back I saw she hadn't taken a step.

She had to raise her voice to carry above the shouts from the apartment and she sounded cross. "Tell me what you want. I don't understand you. Just tell me."

"The question is, what do *you* want?"

She hesitated, turning her head to me and back toward the party noises. I could tell about her expression. Bafflement growing into fright growing into anger; it must have been like that in the dreams she had.

I started back to her, scarcely aware that my arms were stretched out to her beneath the overcoats.

404

"Come on," I said, "if you want to," and I said it very gently.

"Why must you behave this way? You know my love, how much I have to give. There's such a lot bottled up in me and you can handle me. You know how to unbottle me."

"I'm going to eat," I said.

An invisible line was drawn through a linoleum floor in Peter Cooper Village and no force outside of her would bring her across it.

"Oh Gussy."

There came a mean clacking of heels and platform soles upon the hard linoleum, and Chee Wee's laugh progressing from falsetto to wheeze. "What is this, you two? An elopement? You come back, both of you. Harry's thought of the most sensational game with the wire recorder."

"Chee—" The furrows vanished from Lila's brow; her face went smooth. She looked at Chee Wee as she might at a delivering angel.

"I was telling him good night," Lila said. "He's going back to that office of his."

"I'll take this back," Chee Wee said. "Just to make sure you don't elope." She lifted Lila's overcoat from my arm and left us discreetly, clacked off around the corner, and we heard the apartment door shut.

"Good night, Liles."

"We could meet you later," she said. "Chee Wee and Colton Cutter were thinking of a cheap evening. We could meet you at P. J. Clarke's at about ten thirty."

"I guess not," I said.

"I could meet you at the apartment. I could let myself in if you let me have the key."

"No," I said. "I don't think so."

"Well, when can I see you?"

"I'll call you," I said. "I'll buy you dinner some other night and we'll have our long talk."

"Darling, did I make you mad?"

"I promise I'm not mad at anybody."

"I always thought we would be so good together," Lila said faintly. "This is so sad."

"I don't know if it is or not," I said.

She was trying to smile, perhaps she was trying to say something

405

more for just a moment before we turned our backs and walked off in different directions. The last I heard was the blast of party noise when she opened the door down the hall.

To eat supper in a drugstore alone should have been no trick by now, much less in one of the super chain stores where the gaudiness was sufficient to distract you. On a night in February after I had closed the elevator door on Ava Norris I ate my supper at Liggett's, and tonight it was Liggett's, an immense desolate emporium where toiletries and hardware were featured in the Rockbottom October Price Slash. A few paper pennants were still visible, drooping from their string riggings, above the glassware shelves and the cosmetics counter, which bore the dilatory tidings of September's Colossal One Cent Sale. But you wouldn't have noticed them among the engulfing bargains of October unless you were a stickler or unless you were playing supercilious mental games with yourself, for purposes of morale. I sat on a stool at the end of the lunch counter, bathed in the cold drugstore light, and studied the week's delights as advertised on the fountain mirror. A trio of Spanish galleons, in green, crimson, and lavender inks, sailing on a paper background in the direction of a colorful sundae—presumably the Niña, the Pinta and the Santa Maria, for this was the Christopher Columbus Parfait. A photo of Mary Margaret McBride and her WJZ microphone, presumably about to deliver a paean in behalf of Master Yogurt. MIKE the counterman and MARIE who attended the grill and the Snowcrop dispenser were recognizable by block-letter badges, which, unlike Good Humor men, they wore with no discernible pride. I tried to think of Mike and Marie and of what time they came on duty, and where they would go when the store closed at ten o'clock. When Marie gave me my order, my coffee and my Kingburger, I was still trying to lose myself. Now Mike, showing the strain of his eight-hour day, was sneaking a cigarette and listening to a miniature radio turned on low but vibrating on the high notes—"Call for Philip Maah-reees."

I'm tired, so damn tired and numb.

Once I told her she was a brave girl, and she was. It was a good thing, too, to be brave when you were fighting her kind of battle. She couldn't come with me. She couldn't cross the line, but of course it's harder for her, it's so hard to leave what you belong to. It would be desertion for her, and for me it's escape. In a month, a year, I could be coldblooded. I could say she was helpless, a gorgeous ninny, but I would have to say she had done all she could, even if that wasn't very much. The leopard won't change his spots. You can't help what you are.

I thought about escape. The word had a glad ring, though not an exhilarating one. It was too late to be exhilarated. This victory had cost a lot, and it was only mine. At this very moment somewhere in Italy George Marsh might be toasting me. Poor loyal George Marsh, whom I had bled dry, blotto in some grotto.

I remembered the two envelopes with the lurid Italian postage stamps that I had been carrying in my pocket ever since I had got them. The chain letter had come first. While I waited for my coffee to cool, I took it out and read it over:

The Luck of Khufu Has Been Sent to You

The mighty Egyptian ruler, who was also known as King Cheops and built the renowned pyramid at Giza Egypt has been dead more than five thousand years. However, it is said that before he died he presented one of his trusted attendants, a high priest, with a Secret Token which would bring great power and luck. Thus the great chain began thousands of years ago.

How the chain has continued to the present day and has brought luck to all who kept it faithfully is of course not known exactly. Members of the chain are known to have taken part in the famous "gold rush" of 1849 in the USA. An American businessman received the luck of Khufu and the next day he did some business that earned him over ten million dollars. Colonel Blessington-Tynge, the famous English explorer, broke the chain just before he left on a dangerous expedition in Tibet in 1921 and he has not been seen or heard from to this day.

The luck of Khufu has come to you. Make two exact copies of this letter. Leave off the name on top of the list and add to it the names of two persons you know. Mail each of them a copy of the letter.
Above all, DO NOT BREAK THE CHAIN.

There followed twenty names in two sloppily typed columns. His name was third from the bottom and below it was Fuzzy's and below that mine.

And then I took out the second envelope and reread the longer letter that was inside:

I really hear you're going great. I hope you believe me when I tell you I am glad to hear it. I'm sorry if I was stupid last June or if I said

407

anything that made you sore. You know how it was. I didn't mean it. And as for Liles, I don't think we have to bring that up again, but you can tell her that I still think she's the most tremendous gal and give her all my love. You may have heard that I bought some property near Waterbury, Conn., with the intention of trying to farm a little. Well, I don't know about a farm, but I am glad to have a place to come back to. I have a lot of ideas about things, and a couple of damn good schemes, but I'm taking my time. I think it's a good idea to bat around a little before you settle down, because when you do it's for always. Once I get back, though, you watch my dust. . . .

I wouldn't throw the letter away. I meant to keep it until I could answer it properly, but he had been writing on hotel stationery, from hotels in Dublin and Oslo and Naples, and so I hadn't the faintest idea what his address was.

At twenty minutes to nine, the only lighted chamber at Swain, Seidel, and Lawler was the bull pen. Its only occupant was little Harold Macy—and he did not look to be working hard. His desk was littered with file cards and correspondence folders and rubber bands. Its drawers were pulled open. As I entered, Macy was stuffing letters from home and the dog-eared law bulletins with which he had gamely striven to keep abreast of the profession into the imitation leather brief case his mother gave him for his thirty-first birthday. Macy's steel-rimmed glasses lay rakishly on top of his head and he was whistling "Goody, Goody," piercingly, through his front teeth. He greeted me with a broad smile.

"What brings you back? I call this pretty eager."

"I have a lot of work to do," I said.

"Who are you trying to impress? You won't do anything tonight, and you know it."

"Mace, you sure have changed."

"This is my last night in this rat trap," Macy said. "I've reverted to type."

I turned on my desk lamp and sat down. Confronting me was a pile of correspondence and memoranda that Mr. Seidel's secretary had left there.

"It's a shame you and I never got to know each other," Macy was saying. He maintained his broad smile, and he had removed his glasses and was twirling them on his finger. "I'm a bookworm, a researcher," Macy was saying. "But I yearn for the violent life."

"You'll get that all right," I told him. "If that's what you want, Hal."

"Yuh," he said. "There's my meat. Rebuild Inchon. Resurrect the power plants by the Yalu. The old Corps of Engineers."

I laughed at him, as he had wished me to, and then he was whistling through his teeth once more. I picked up the top page from the pile before me and fell to interpreting Mrs. Monaghan's estate, a morass of facts and imponderable clauses. I got to the end of paragraph one, and I was too tired. My mind was clogged with the flotsam of the day, and of the years, the almost exactly fourteen years.

I took one of the envelopes from my pocket and read over the Luck of Khufu. I would not be the one to break the chain, not I. On the back of the envelope I wrote out the name and Sutton address of Hadley Norris, a man who could use some luck. And for a second name I wrote out Macy's; Macy's luck would be coming to him care of postmaster, San Francisco.

"Do you *realize?*" Macy said suddenly. "This is my last night in this rat trap?" He was laughing aloud, the first time I had ever heard him.

I must have been smiling back at Macy. I was thankful for his being there. His quaint rebellion had been resuscitating as a dash of cold water against my face.

"You're a funny guy," Macy said. "It's a damn shame we never got friendly. Mrs. O'Mara says you're an orphan. I didn't know you were."

Macy fastened his brief case. He started to put on the purplish double-breasted overcoat he wore in winter.

"You're not going to get anything done tonight," he said.

"I've had a big day," I said. "I feel as though I'd climbed out of purgatory, and I'm waiting on the edge for my breath to come back, if you know what I mean."

Macy merely picked up his brief case and plumped it on my desk.

"Let's get out of here," he said. "We might have a beer."

"I'll buy the beers. I'll tell you the story of my life," I said.